SOMETHING ABOUT THE AUTHOR®

Something about
the Author *was named
an "Outstanding
Reference Source,"
the highest honor given
by the American
Library Association
Reference and Adult
Services Division.*

ISSN 0276-816X

SOMETHING ABOUT THE AUTHOR®

**Facts and Pictures about Authors
and Illustrators of Books for Young People**

volume 244

GALE
CENGAGE Learning®

Detroit • New York • San Francisco • New Haven, Conn • Waterville, Maine • London

Something about the Author, Volume 244

Project Editor: Lisa Kumar

Permissions: Robyn Young

Imaging and Multimedia: John Watkins, Robyn Young

Composition and Electronic Capture: Amy Darga

Manufacturing: Rhonda Dover

Product Manager: Mary Onorato

© 2013 Gale, Cengage Learning

For product information and technology assistance, contact us at **Gale Customer Support, 1-800-877-4253.**
For permission to use material from this text or product, submit all requests online at **www.cengage.com/permissions.**
Further permissions questions can be emailed to **permissionrequest@cengage.com**

Since this page cannot legibly accommodate all copyright notices, the acknowledgments constitute an extension of the copyright notice.

While every effort has been made to ensure the reliability of the information presented in this publication, Gale, a part of Cengage Learning, does not guarantee the accuracy of the data contained herein. Gale accepts no payment for listing; and inclusion in the publication of any organization, agency, institution, publication, service, or individual does not imply endorsement of the editors or publisher. Errors brought to the attention of the publisher and verified to the satisfaction of the publisher will be corrected in future editions.

EDITORIAL DATA PRIVACY POLICY: Does this publication contain information about you as an individual? If so, for more information about our editorial data privacy policies, please see our Privacy Statement at www.gale.cengage.com.

Gale, Cengage Learning
27500 Drake Rd.
Farmington Hills, MI, 48331-3535

LIBRARY OF CONGRESS CATALOG CARD NUMBER 62-52046

ISBN-13: 978-1-4144-8100-5
ISBN-10: 1-4144-8100-4

ISSN 0276-816X

This title is also available as an e-book.
ISBN-13: 978-1-4144-8246-0
ISBN-10: 1-4144-8246-9
Contact your Gale, Cengage Learning sales representative for ordering information.

Printed in Mexico
1 2 3 4 5 6 7 16 15 14 13 12

Contents

Authors in Forthcoming Volumes

Below are some of the authors and illustrators that will be featured in upcoming volumes of *SATA*. These include new entries on the swiftly rising stars of the field, as well as completely revised and updated entries (indicated with *) on some of the most notable and best-loved creators of books for children.

*Mary Amato ▮ In addition to working as a nonfiction writer, puppeteer, and choreographer, Amato has made her mark as a children's book writer with quirky stories like *The Word Eater, The Naked Mole-Rat Letters, Edgar Allan's Official Crime Investigation Notebook,* and the popular "Riot Brothers" adventures. Turning to younger readers, she has also produced the picture book *The Chicken of the Family,* while teens are the focus of her novel *Guitar Notes,* which uses emails, text messages, and song lyrics to capture the evolving relationship between two music-loving teens.

Paul Budnitz ▮ The ultra-industrious Budnitz is best known as the founder of Kidrobot, which produces cutting-edge art toys and fashion apparel. Believing that diversity is the key to his success, he also exhibits as a photographer, owns a specialty bicycle company, dabbles in iPhone apps, and has produced the children's book *The Hole in the Middle,* featuring illustrations by graphic artist Aya Kakeda.

Heather Cocks ▮ Teaming up with Jessica Morgan to create the celebrity Web log *Go Fug Yourself,* the California-based Cocks left a career in reality television to write full time. Their success as bloggers has allowed the women to expand their fan base to teens via the novels *Spoiled* and *Messy,* which capture the same snarky dialogue and Southern California attitude that made *Go Fug Yourself* so popular.

*Keith Graves ▮ Raised in Louisiana but now living in Texas, Graves shares his quirky humor and love of monster movies with fans in picture books such as *Frank Was a Monster Who Wanted to Dance, Pet Boy, The Unexpectedly Bad Hair of Barcelona Smith,* and *Chicken Big.* His macabre humor is also at play in the middle-grade novel *The Orphan of Awkward Falls,* as well as in the illustrations he has contributed to stories by a roster of other authors that includes J. Patrick Lewis, Sandy Asher, and Margie Palatini.

*Jean Marzollo ▮ Marzollo has worked in many different genres, producing rhythmic picture books for children, easy readers and chapter books for elementary-grade students, nonfiction for middle graders, novels for young adults, and practical nonfiction for grown ups. Among the versatile author's best-known books are the "I Spy" picture-riddle books, created in collaboration with photographer Walter Wick, and her entertaining "39 Kids" reader series.

*Andrea Davis Pinkney ▮ A member of the talented Pinkney family that includes father-and-son artists Jerry and Brian Pinkney, Andrea Pinkney celebrates the heritage of African Americans through her work as both a book editor and a writer of fiction and nonfiction for young people. Her lyrical, well-researched books include the novels *Silent Thunder* and *Bird in a Box* as well as the picture books *Bill Pickett: Rodeo Ridin' Cowboy* and *Sit-In: How Four Friends Stood up by Sitting Down.*

Dave Roman ▮ The former comics editor for *Nickelodeon* magazine, Roman is married to Raina Telgemeier, a popular graphic novelist. The author of *Astronaut Academy: Zero Gravity,* an award-winning, self-illustrated Web comic-turned-graphic novel, Roman's own work also includes *Teen Boat!,* a zany collaboration with artist John Green about an adolescent who has the ability to metamorphose into a small yacht.

Laura Shaefer ▮ A fertile imagination and the ability to spot opportunity have allowed Schaefer to combine her interests in history and writing. One of her first book projects included a historical overview of quirky personal advertisements titled *Man with Farm Seeks Woman with Tractor: The Best and Worst Personal Ads of All Time.* She eventually entered into a serendipitous match with YA literature when she produced *The Teashop Girls,* her first novel for teen girls. In addition to her book publications, she is the founder/publisher of "Planet Explorers," a selection of kid-friendly travel guides.

*Chris Van Allsburg ▮ A two-time Caldecott Medal-winner, Van Allsburg draws readers into a meticulously crafted, magical, and sometimes even surreal world through his many illustrated picture books, each which showcases his versatility as an artist. In addition to *Jumanji* and its sequel *Zathura,* his stories include *Two Bad Ants, Bad Day at Riverbend,* and *Queen of the Falls.* His award-winning picture book *The Polar Express* has become a modern Christmas classic, and its engaging story has been adapted for video and as a popular motion picture starring Tom Hanks.

M.L. Welsh ▮ British-born novelist Welsh developed the basic plot of her YA debut *Mistress of the Storm* six years before the evocative story became a published book. The first novel in her "Verity Gallant" mystery series, *Mistress of the Storm* transports readers to the Isle of Wight, an island three miles off the southern coast of England, where a preteen girl is given a magic book that provides the key to the region's many mysteries.

Introduction

Something about the Author (*SATA*) is an ongoing reference series that examines the lives and works of authors and illustrators of books for children. *SATA* includes not only well-known writers and artists but also less prominent individuals whose works are just coming to be recognized. This series is often the only readily available information source on emerging authors and illustrators. You'll find *SATA* informative and entertaining, whether you are a student, a librarian, an English teacher, a parent, or simply an adult who enjoys children's literature.

What's Inside *SATA*

SATA provides detailed information about authors and illustrators who span the full time range of children's literature, from early figures like John Newbery and L. Frank Baum to contemporary figures like Judy Blume and Richard Peck. Authors in the series represent primarily English-speaking countries, particularly the United States, Canada, and the United Kingdom. Also included, however, are authors from around the world whose works are available in English translation. The writings represented in *SATA* include those created intentionally for children and young adults as well as those written for a general audience and known to interest younger readers. These writings cover the entire spectrum of children's literature, including picture books, humor, folk and fairy tales, animal stories, mystery and adventure, science fiction and fantasy, historical fiction, poetry and nonsense verse, drama, biography, and nonfiction. Obituaries are also included in many volumes of *SATA* and are intended not only as death notices but also as concise overviews of people's lives and work. Additionally, each edition features newly revised and updated entries for a selection of *SATA* listees who remain of interest to today's readers and who have been active enough to require extensive revisions of their earlier biographies.

Autobiography Feature

Beginning with Volume 103, many volumes of *SATA* feature one or more specially commissioned autobiographical essays. These unique essays, averaging about ten thousand words in length and illustrated with an abundance of personal photos, present an entertaining and informative first-person perspective on the lives and careers of prominent authors and illustrators profiled in *SATA*.

Two Convenient Indexes

In response to suggestions from librarians, *SATA* indexes no longer appear in every volume but are included in alternate (odd-numbered) volumes of the series, beginning with Volume 57.

SATA continues to include two indexes that cumulate with each alternate volume: the Illustrations Index, arranged by the name of the illustrator, gives the number of the volume and page where the illustrator's work appears in the current volume as well as all preceding volumes in the series; the Author Index gives the number of the volume in which a person's biographical sketch, autobiographical essay, or obituary appears in the current volume as well as all preceding volumes in the series.

These indexes also include references to authors and illustrators who appear in *Gale's Yesterday's Authors of Books for Children, Children's Literature Review,* and *Something about the Author Autobiography Series.*

Easy-to-Use Entry Format

Whether you're already familiar with the *SATA* series or just getting acquainted, you will want to be aware of the kind of information that an entry provides. In every *SATA* entry the editors attempt to give as complete a picture of the person's life and work as possible. A typical entry in *SATA* includes the following clearly labeled information sections:

PERSONAL: date and place of birth and death, parents' names and occupations, name of spouse, date of marriage, names of children, educational institutions attended, degrees received, religious and political affiliations, hobbies and other interests.

ADDRESSES: complete home, office, electronic mail, and agent addresses, whenever available.

CAREER: name of employer, position, and dates for each career post; art exhibitions; military service; memberships and offices held in professional and civic organizations.

MEMBER: professional, civic, and other association memberships and any official posts held.

AWARDS, HONORS: literary and professional awards received.

WRITINGS: title-by-title chronological bibliography of books written and/or illustrated, listed by genre when known; lists of other notable publications, such as plays, screenplays, and periodical contributions.

ADAPTATIONS: a list of films, television programs, plays, CD-ROMs, recordings, and other media presentations that have been adapted from the author's work.

WORK IN PROGRESS: description of projects in progress.

SIDELIGHTS: a biographical portrait of the author or illustrator's development, either directly from the biographee—and often written specifically for the *SATA* entry—or gathered from diaries, letters, interviews, or other published sources.

BIOGRAPHICAL AND CRITICAL SOURCES: cites sources quoted in "Sidelights" along with references for further reading.

EXTENSIVE ILLUSTRATIONS: photographs, movie stills, book illustrations, and other interesting visual materials supplement the text.

How a *SATA* Entry Is Compiled

SATA editors examine a wide variety of published sources to gather information for an entry. Biographical and bibliographic sources are consulted, as are book reviews, feature articles, published interviews, and material sometimes obtained from the biographee's family, publishers, agent, or other associates. Whenever possible, the author or illustrator is sent a copy of the entry to check for accuracy and completeness.

Entries that have not been verified by the biographees or their representatives are marked with an asterisk (*).

Contact the Editor

We encourage our readers to examine the entire *SATA* series. Please write and tell us if we can make *SATA* even more helpful to you. Give your comments and suggestions to the editor:

Editor
Something about the Author
Gale, Cengage Learning
27500 Drake Rd.
Farmington Hills MI 48331-3535

Toll-free: 800-877-GALE
Fax: 248-699-8070

Something about the Author Product Advisory Board

The editors of *Something about the Author* are dedicated to maintaining a high standard of excellence by publishing comprehensive, accurate, and highly readable entries on a wide array of writers for children and young adults. In addition to the quality of the content, the editors take pride in the graphic design of the series, which is intended to be orderly yet inviting, allowing readers to utilize the pages of *SATA* easily and with efficiency. Despite the longevity of the *SATA* print series, and the success of its format, we are mindful that the vitality of a literary reference product is dependent on its ability to serve its users over time. As literature, and attitudes about literature, constantly evolve, so do the reference needs of students, teachers, scholars, journalists, researchers, and book club members. To be certain that we continue to keep pace with the expectations of our customers, the editors of *SATA* listen carefully to their comments regarding the value, utility, and quality of the series. Librarians, who have firsthand knowledge of the needs of library users, are a valuable resource for us. The *Something about the Author* Product Advisory Board, made up of school, public, and academic librarians, is a forum to promote focused feedback about *SATA* on a regular basis. The nine-member advisory board includes the following individuals, whom the editors wish to thank for sharing their expertise:

something ABOUT the AUThor

ANTLE, Bhagavan "Doc"
(Dr. Bhagavan Antle)

Personal

Male; children: Cody, Tawny Sky. *Education:* M.D. (China).

Addresses

Office—The Institute of Greatly Endangered and Rare Species (T.I.G.E.R.S.), P.O. Box 31210, Myrtle Beach, SC 29588.

Career

Animal trainer, conservationist, educator, and author. Worked as a traveling physician in China and other Asian nations; Integral Health Services (therapy clinic), Buckingham, VA, founder, c. 1980s; The Institute of Greatly Endangered and Rare Species (T.I.G.E.R.S.), and Rare Species Fund (RSF), Myrtle Beach, SC, founder and director. Animal trainer for major motion pictures, including *Ace Ventura: When Nature Calls,* 1995, *Mighty Joe Young,* 1998, and *The Jungle Book 2,* 2003.

Writings

(As Dr. Bhagavan Antle) *Big Cat Studio,* photographs by Barry Bland, Ammonite Press, 2009.

(With Thea Feldman) *Suryia and Roscoe: The True Story of an Unlikely Friendship,* photographs by Barry Bland, Henry Holt (New York, NY), 2011.

(With Thea Feldman) *Suryia Swims! The True Story of How an Orangutan Learned to Swim,* photographs by Barry Bland, Henry Holt (New York, NY), 2012.

Fierce Beauty: Preserving the World of Wild Cats, photographs by Barry Bland and Tim Flach, foreword by Robert Duvall, Insight Editions, 2012.

Sidelights

In *Suryia and Roscoe: The True Story of an Unlikely Friendship* world-renown animal trainer and conservationist Bhagavan "Doc" Antle explores the special bond between an orangutan and a stray dog. Antle, the founder and director of The Institute of Greatly Endangered and Rare Species, a wildlife refuge located in South Carolina, attests that Suryia was patrolling the grounds when Roscoe, a Blue Tick hound that had followed staff members home, bounded from the woods. Although dogs are normally frightened of primates, this pair became instant and inseparable pals.

Cowritten with Thea Feldman and featuring photographs by Barry Bland, *Suryia and Roscoe* features a "smoothly paced" narrative, as Nancy Call remarked in *School Library Journal,* the critic adding of the book that "the engaging animals will appeal to children." *Booklist* critic Andrew Medlar commented that Bland's "photographs of the buddies playing together or just hanging out" help make Antle's story "undeniably awww-induc-

Wildlife advocate Bhagavan "Doc" Antle chronicles the surprising friendship that is captured in Barry Bland's photographs for **Suryia and Roscoe.** (Jacket photography copyright © 2011 by Barry Bland. Reproduced by permission of Henry Holt and Company, LLC.)

ing." "The clean, photo album-like design, high-interest topic, accessible text and captivating images will likely garner *Suryia and Roscoe* legions of new friends," a *Kirkus Reviews* writer concluded in an appraisal of *Suryia and Roscoe.*

In Antle's companion volume, *Suryia Swims! The True Story of How an Orangutan Learned to Swim,* the animal trainer teams up again with Feldman and Bland to offer another tale featuring the seemingly fearless primate. After Suryia takes a bath with his human trainer—an unusual act for an orangutan, most of whom do not like the water—the primate bravely enters a swimming pool, with fascinating results. "Suryia's interactions with his pool pals will bring smiles to the faces of animal lovers young and old," a critic maintained in *Kirkus Reviews.*

Biographical and Critical Sources

PERIODICALS

Booklist, April 15, 2011, Andrew Medlar, review of *Suryia and Roscoe: The True Story of an Unlikely Friendship,* p. 61.
Kirkus Reviews, March 1, 2011, review of *Suryia and Roscoe;* April 15, 2012, review of *Suryia Swims! The True Story of How an Orangutan Learned to Swim.*
School Library Journal, May, 2011, Nancy Call, review of *Suryia and Roscoe,* p. 93.

ONLINE

Bhagavan Antle Home Page, http://www.bhagavanantle. com (August 1, 2012).

Suryia and Roscoe Web site, http://www.suryiaandroscoe. com/ (August 1, 2012).
The Institute of Greatly Endangered and Rare Species Web site, http://www.tigerfriends.com/ (August 1, 2012).*

* * *

ANTLE, Dr. Bhagavan
See ANTLE, Bhagavan "Doc"

* * *

BARBER, Tiki 1975-

Personal

Born Atiim Kiambu Barber, April 7, 1975, in Roanoke, VA; son of James "J.B." and Geraldine (a financial director) Barber; married Ginny Cha (a fashion publicist), 1999 (divorced, 2012); married Traci Lynn Johnson, July 19, 2012; children: (first marriage) A.J., Chason (sons), Ella and Riley (twin daughters). *Education:* University of Virginia, B.A. (management information systems), 1997.

Addresses

Home—New York, NY.

Career

Professional football player and broadcaster. Played college football at University of Virginia; second-round draft pick of New York Giants in National Football League (NFL) entry draft, 1997; running back for New York Giants, 1997-2006. WCBS-TV, sports commentator, 2000; WFAN-AM-FM, fill-in host, c. 2000; Fox News, commentator for *Fox & Friends* (morning show), 2004-06; YES Network, host of *This Week in Football;* Sirius Satellite Radio, cohost of *The Barber Shop,* 2005-06; National Broadcasting Company, correspondent for *Today Show* and analyst on Sunday-night football coverage, 2007-09; Yahoo! Sports, football analyst, beginning 2010.

Awards, Honors

Named National Football League (NFL) Player of the Year, *Sports Illustrated,* 2005; named to NFL All-Pro team, Associated Press, 2005; selected to NFL Pro Bowl, 2005, 2006, 2007; inducted into Virginia High School Hall of Fame, 2006; Christopher Award (with others), 2006, for *Game Day;* inducted into New York Giants' Ring of Honor, 2011.

Writings

FOR CHILDREN

(With brother Ronde Barber and Robert Burleigh) *By My Brother's Side,* illustrated by Barry Root, Simon & Schuster Books for Young Readers (New York, NY), 2004.

(With Ronde Barber and Robert Burleigh) *Game Day,* illustrated by Barry Root, Simon & Schuster Books for Young Readers (New York, NY), 2005.

(With Ronde Barber and Robert Burleigh) *Teammates,* illustrated by Barry Root, Simon & Schuster Books for Young Readers (New York, NY), 2006.

(With Ronde Barber and Paul Mantell) *Kickoff!,* Simon & Schuster Books for Young Readers (New York, NY), 2007.

(With Ronde Barber and Paul Mantell) *Go Long!,* Simon & Schuster Books for Young Readers (New York, NY), 2008.

(With Ronde Barber and Paul Mantell) *Wild Card,* Simon & Schuster Books for Young Readers (New York, NY), 2009.

(With Ronde Barber and Paul Mantell) *Red Zone,* Simon & Schuster Books for Young Readers (New York, NY), 2010.

(With Ronde Barber and Paul Mantell) *Goal Line,* Simon & Schuster Books for Young Readers (New York, NY), 2011.

FOR ADULTS

(With Gil Reavill) *Tiki: My Life in the Game and Beyond* (autobiography), Simon Spotlight Entertainment (New York, NY), 2007.

(With Joe Carini and Scott Hays) *Tiki Barber's Pure Hard Workout: Stop Wasting Time and Start Building Real Strength and Muscle,* Gotham Books (New York, NY), 2008.

Adaptations

Film rights to create a cartoon based on their picture books were optioned by the Barbers.

Sidelights

Tiki Barber, a former National Football League (NFL) star with the New York Giants, teamed up with his identical twin brother Ronde Barber, an All-Pro cornerback with the Tampa Bay Buccaneers, to write *Teammates, Red Zone,* and several other sports books for young readers. The multi-talented Barber brothers, whose off-field activities include radio and television broadcasting, have made literacy a cornerstone of their volunteer efforts. "We work essentially as spokesmen and conduits to get the message of literacy to the public," Ronde Barber told Suzanne Rust in the *Black Issues Book Review.*

Born on April 7, 1975 (Ronde is older by seven minutes), the Barbers excelled at both sports and academics at Cave Spring High School in Roanoke, Virginia. After graduatin, they decided to play football and room together at the University of Virginia, where they earned All-Atlantic Coast Conference honors and graduated from the McIntire School of Commerce. A second-round selection of the Giants in the 1997 NFL draft, Tiki enjoyed a brilliant career, becoming the first player to

rush for 1,800 yards and have 500 yards receiving in a single season; he retired after the 2006 season. Ronde, who was drafted in the third round by the Buccaneers, earned a Super Bowl ring in 2003 and became the first NFL cornerback to register twenty interceptions and twenty quarterback sacks in a career. The Barbers were encouraged to enter the publishing field by editor Paula Wiseman, whose son avidly followed their careers. "It just so happens that the idea fell right into line with the initiatives and ideals that are important to my brother and me," Ronde recalled to Maughan.

Coauthored by Robert Burleigh, *By My Brother's Side* recounts a defining moment from the Barber brothers' childhood that taught them about love and perseverance. The virtually inseparable twins must spend their first summer apart after Tiki suffers a severe leg injury in a bicycle accident. With Ronde's support and encouragement, he makes a full recovery, joining his brother in time for their team's pee-wee football league opener in the fall. According to a *Publishers Weekly* reviewer, the Barbers "give a warm focus to the family foundation they believe is instrumental to their successes and their lives." *By My Brother's Side* "will inspire those peewee football players out there who are recuperating from their own breaks," observed a critic in *Kirkus Reviews.*

Tiki and Ronde Barber's picture-book memoir **Teammates** *is brought to life in Barry Root's energetic paintings.* (Illustration © 2006 by Barry Root. Reprinted by permission of Simon & Schuster Books for Young Readers, an imprint of Simon & Schuster Macmillan.)

Game Day focuses on the Barbers' exploits with the Cave Spring Vikings, their pee-wee team. Tiki, the squad's star halfback, gets most of the credit for his team's success. This leaves Ronde feeling a bit under-appreciated, because his devastating blocks clear the way for his brother's touchdown runs. The boys' coach has noticed Ronde's contributions, however, and devises a trick play that gives Ronde a chance to demonstrate his talents. "What works best here is the feel-good mood," remarked *Booklist* contributor Ilene Cooper, and a *Publishers Weekly* reviewer similarly noted that the narrative "is equal parts sunny reminiscence and inspirational game-day pep talk; the text sails along like a skillfully thrown spiral." Mary Hazelton, writing in *School Library Journal,* described *Game Day* as "an engaging memoir that touches on themes of co-operation and individual differences."

In *Teammates* the brothers develop a novel solution to a vexing problem. After Tiki fumbles the ball during a critical possession, his coach notes the importance of developing good habits during practice. In response, the Barbers start a secret early-morning practice club, "leading to an ending that is believable as well as happy," wrote *Booklist* contributor Carolyn Phelan. "Tiki and Ronde have a warm, supportive relationship, rare in tales featuring siblings," remarked Rachel G. Payne in her review of *Teammates* for *School Library Journal.*

The Barbers have also collaborated with Paul Mantell on a series of chapter books aimed at middle-grade readers. Based on the brothers' experiences in junior high school, *Kickoff!* centers on the new challenges they face the brothers by becoming more independent and by taking separate classes for the first time. The boys also face adjustments on the gridiron for their new team, the Hidden Valley Eagles. Smaller and less experienced than many of their teammates, Tiki and Ronde begin the season as seldom-used backups. When they are finally offered playing time during a crucial game against their heated rival, though, the brothers make the most of the opportunity. "Even as the game races to an expected outcome," a *Publishers Weekly* critic noted, "the swift action delivers genuine tension." According to Cheryl Ashton, reviewing *Kickoff!* in *School Library Journal,* "Football enthusiasts will . . . recognize how the value of team sports is portrayed throughout the book."

The Hidden Valley Eagles receive some unexpected news while preparing to defend their district championship in *Go Long!,* which focuses on Tiki and Ronde's eighth-grade season. When the boys' popular and respected coach announces that he has been offered a new job, Mr. Wheeler, a science teacher at Hidden Valley, is asked to lead the team. This sudden turn of events fractures the team's chemistry and Tiki and Ronde must assume leadership roles to pull the squad back together. Although *School Library Journal* contributor Laura

Cover of Tiki and Ronde Barber's inspiring sports-themed novel **Red Zone,** *featuring artwork by Kadir Nelson.* (Jacket copyright © 2010 by Kadir Nelson. Reproduced by permission of Kadir Nelson.)

Lutz noted that *Go Long!* contains complex football terminology, she predicted that the work will appeal to "avid football fans."

The Eagles' playoff chances hit a roadblock in *Wild Card,* which explores the balance between sports and academics. As the regular season draws to a close, the team learns that one of its star players has received poor grades in biology and math and cannot play again until he improves in the classroom. Rallying their teammates to the cause, Tiki and Ronde devise a clever solution to the problem. The brothers' relationship gives "a realistic edge to this appealing chapter book," Carolyn Phelan maintained in her *Booklist* review of *Wild Card.*

The Barbers continue to draw stories from their sports career in *Red Zone,* and this time an outbreak of chicken pox at Hidden Valley Eagles threatens to derail the football team's chance at winning the state championship. When both Tiki and Ronde fall ill and miss action during the playoff run, their teammates offer comfort and support. Audiences "looking for play-by-play football action will find plenty here," Phelan reported.

Biographical and Critical Sources

BOOKS

Barber, Tiki, with Gil Reavill, *Tiki: My Life in the Game and Beyond* (autobiography), Simon Spotlight Entertainment (New York, NY), 2007.
Contemporary Black Biography, Volume 57, Gale (Detroit, MI), 2007.

PERIODICALS

Black Issues Book Review, September-October, 2004, Suzanne Rust, "He Ain't Heavy," p. 60.
Booklist, September 1, 2004, Todd Morning, review of *By My Brother's Side,* p. 114; September 1, 2005, Ilene Cooper, review of *Game Day,* p. 119; September 1, 2006, Carolyn Phelan, review of *Teammates,* p. 116; September 1, 2007, Carolyn Phelan, review of *Kickoff!,* p. 136; September 1, 2008, Carolyn Phelan, review of *Go Long!,* p. 115; September 15, 2009, Carolyn Phelan, review of *Wild Card,* p. 60; September 1, 2010, Carolyn Phelan, review of *Red Zone,* p. 120.
Bulletin of the Center for Children's Books, January, 2006, Elizabeth Bush, review of *Game Day,* p. 218.
Ebony, December, 2005, review of *Game Day,* p. 30; September, 2008, review of *Go Long!,* p. 55.
Kirkus Reviews, September 15, 2004, review of *By My Brother's Side,* p. 909; September 15, 2005, review of *Game Day,* p. 1020; October 1, 2007, review of *Kickoff!*; July 1, 2010, review of *Red Zone.*
New York Times, August 12, 1997, Bill Pennington, "The Barber Brothers Stay in Touch as Rookie Rivals with the Giants and Bucs"; November 29, 1997, Bill Pennington, "It's Barber vs. Barber When Giants Play Bucs"; January 8, 2007, David Picker, "Barber Leaves His Mark on Giants and Moves on to a New Career," p. D7.
Publishers Weekly, August 30, 2004, Shannon Maughan, "Double Duty," p. 54, and review of *By My Brother's Side,* p. 55; October 3, 2005, review of *Game Day,* p. 70; October 15, 2007, review of *Kickoff!,* p. 61.
Sarasota Herald Tribune, October 29, 2006, Tom Balog, "Barbers' Final Meeting?," p. C3.
School Library Journal, November, 2004, Ann M. Holcomb, review of *By My Brother's Side,* p. 122; January, 2006, Mary Hazelton, review of *Game Day,* p. 116; November, 2006, Rachel G. Payne, review of *Teammates,* p. 117; December, 2007, Cheryl Ashton, review of *Kickoff!,* p. 148; October, 2008, Laura Lutz, review of *Go Long!,* p. 138.
Sports Illustrated, July 23, 2001, John Ed Bradley, "Play Mates," p. 52; December 18, 2006, Karl Taro Greenfield, "Media Giant?"
USA Today, July 6, 2011, Tom Pedulla, "In Comeback, Barber Needs Lift from Game," p. 7C.

ONLINE

ESPN Web site, http://espn.go.com/ (July 20, 2007), "Tiki Barber."

University of Virginia Magazine Online, http://www.uvamagazine.org/ (spring, 2006), Ben Cramer, "The Power of Two."*

* * *

BARROW, Randi

Personal

Married Arthur Barrow (a musician and composer). *Education:* University of California, Los Angeles, degree; Loyola University, J.D., 1987.

Addresses

Home—Los Angeles, CA. *Agent*—Marlene Stringer, The Stringer Literary Agency; stringerlit@comcast.net. *E-mail*—randibar@earthlink.net.

Career

Writer and attorney. Admitted to the Bar of the State of California, 1988; adoption attorney, 1988-2006; instructor in adoption courses for California State Bar.

Awards, Honors

Parents' Choice Award, 2011, and Best Children's Books selection, Bank Street College of Education, and Children's Choice listee, International Reading Association, both 2012, all for *Saving Zasha.*

Writings

Saving Zasha (middle-grade novel), Scholastic Press (New York, NY), 2011.

ADULT NONFICTION

Somebody's Child: Stories from the Private Files of an Adoption Attorney, Perigee (New York, NY), 2002.

Contributor to *Infertility Counseling: A Comprehensive Handbook for Clinicians.*

Adaptations

Saving Zasha was adapted as an audiobook.

Sidelights

In her debut work of fiction, *Saving Zasha,* Randi Barrow recounts the tale of a Russian teenager who dared to shelter a German shepherd in the aftermath of World War II. Barrow was inspired to write the novel after meeting a Russian citizen who recalled the intense animosity Russians felt toward everything German—including dogs—during that era and she followed that meeting with hours of research into Russian history. "I'm excited by learning about historical events and characters, and ways of living I knew nothing about," Barrow remarked to Bonnie O'Brian in a *California Readers* interview. "But the research is a springboard for the imagination. After you've learned all you can you have to create a world and the people who exist in that world, and understand the types of conflicts and adventures that are believable in that context."

In *Saving Zasha* Mikhail, a thirteen-year-old Russian farm boy, discovers a man dying in the forest and agrees to care for Zasha, the man's German shepherd. Mikhail's decision places his family in danger, for many Russians view owning a German breed of canine as a traitorous act. Although he is determined to keep Zasha a secret from his neighbors, Mikhail learns that Katia, his nemesis and the daughter of the local newspaper owner, is equally determined to unveil his secret.

"Mikhail's first-person account will grab readers," Hazel Rochman predicted in her review of *Saving Zasha* for *Booklist,* and a writer in *Kirkus Reviews* described Barrow's debut novel as a "highly engaging and ultimately hopeful animal story with a strong sense of time and place." According to Connie Tyrrell Burns in *School Library Journal,* the work "reflects the dark effects of war on both humans and animals," and a *Publishers Weekly* reviewer wrote that *Saving Zasha* "is quick reading yet weighty, and captures the prejudices and aftereffects of war."

Biographical and Critical Sources

PERIODICALS

Booklist, February 1, 2011, Hazel Rochman, review of *Saving Zasha,* p. 80.
Kirkus Reviews, December 15, 2010, review of *Saving Zasha.*
Publishers Weekly, November 8, 2010, review of *Saving Zasha,* p. 60.
School Library Journal, April, 2011, Connie Tyrrell Burns, review of *Saving Zasha,* p. 167.
Voice of Youth Advocates, April, 2011, Jen McIntosh, review of *Saving Zasha,* p. 51.

ONLINE

California Readers Web site, http://www.californiareaders. org/ (September, 2011), Bonnie O'Brian, "Meet Randi Barrow."
Randi Barrow Home Page, http://randibarrow.com (July 15, 2012).*

*   *   *

BLUMENTHAL, Karen

Personal

Married Scott McCartney; children: two daughters. *Education:* Duke University, A.B. (economics), 1981; South Methodist University, M.B.A., 1990. *Hobbies and other interests:* Baking, needlepoint, watching sports.

Addresses

Home—Dallas, TX. *Agent*—Ken Wright, Writers House, 21 W. 26th St., New York, NY 10010; kwright@ writershouse.com, *E-mail*—karen.blumenthal@wsj.com.

Career

Journalist and author. Dallas Morning News, Dallas, TX, metro and business reporter, 1981-84, business editor, 1992-94; Wall Street Journal, editor and reporter, 1984-96, Dallas bureau chief, 1996-2004, senior editor of *Wall Street Journal Reports,* 2004-06, author of "Getting Going" (personal finance column); freelance writer, beginning 2007. Donald W. Reynolds visiting professor, Texas Christian University, 2012. Board member, Friends of the Dallas Public Library and First Book-Dallas.

Awards, Honors

Robert F. Sibert Award Honor Book selection, American Library Association (ALA), 2003, and Notable Social Studies Trade Book for Young People selection, Children's Book Council/National Council for the Social Studies (CBC/NCSS), both for *Six Days in October;* Best Books for Young Adults designation, Notable Children's Book designation, and Amelia Bloomer Project list, all ALA, CBC/NCSS Notable Social Studies Trade Book for Young People selection, Best Children's Book of the Year selection, Bank Street College of Education, Choices selection, Cooperative Children's Book Council (CCBC), Golden Spur Award honor book designation, Children's Book Award Notable Book designation, International Reading Association, and Jane Addams Children's Book Award, Jane Addams Peace Association, all 2006, all for *Let Me Play;* CCBC Choices selection, and Excellence in Nonfiction Award finalist, ALA, both 2012, both for *Bootleg.*

Writings

NONFICTION FOR CHILDREN

Six Days in October: The Stock Market Crash of 1929, Atheneum Books for Young Readers (New York, NY), 2002.
Let Me Play: The Story of Title IX: The Law That Changed the Future of Girls in America, Atheneum Books for Young Readers (New York, NY), 2005.
Bootleg: Murder, Moonshine, and the Lawless Years of Prohibition, Roaring Brook Press (New York, NY), 2011.
Mr. Sam: How Sam Walton Built Wal-Mart and Became America's Richest Man, Viking (New York, NY), 2011.

Steve Jobs: The Man Who Thought Different, Feiwel & Friends (New York, NY), 2012.

NONFICTION FOR ADULTS

Grande Expectations: A Year in the Life of Starbucks' Stock, Crown Business (New York, NY), 2007.
The Wall Street Journal Guide to Starting Your Financial Life, Three Rivers Press (New York, NY), 2009.
The Wall Street Journal Guide to Starting Fresh: How to Leave Financial Hardships Behind and Take Control of Your Financial Life, Crown Business (New York, NY), 2011.

Sidelights

A respected financial journalist who writes a regular column for the *Wall Street Journal,* Karen Blumenthal is also the author of award-winning nonfiction books for young adults that include *Six Days in October: The Stock Market Crash of 1929* and *Bootleg: Murder, Moonshine, and the Lawless Years of Prohibition.* "I have always loved reading and writing," Blumenthal commented on her home page. "And I feel very lucky to be able to make a living doing just that!"

In *Six Days in October* Blumenthal presents an in-depth look at the devastating stock-market crash in the fall of 1929 that presaged the Great Depression. Illustrated with archival photographs, cartoons, and other documents, the work offers a day-by-day account of the historical developments while also keeping the focus on the human side of the tragedy by profiling such key players as Richard Whitney, an executive at the New York Stock Exchange who attempted to forestall the disaster by purchasing shares of U.S. Steel and other blue-chip companies.

According to a *Kirkus Reviews* writer, *Six Days in October* "is a solid exploration of an event whose importance is undisputed but which is rarely so lucidly explained for anyone, let alone young readers." "Rapid, simply constructed sentences increase the drama and suspense while making difficult concepts easily understood," Gillian Engberg explained in *Booklist.* Discussing the impact of her work with *Publishers Weekly* contributor Ingrid Roper, Blumenthal stated: "I hope readers see that you can make choices not to be too greedy and to be ethical as an investor or as a business player—and that those choices have broader impact for our nation. I think that is the moral tale underlying this story."

Let Me Play: The Story of Title IX: The Law That Changed the Future of Girls in America received a host of honors, including the Jane Addams Children's Book Award. Blumenthal details the long battle over Title IX of the Education Amendments of 1972, a landmark piece of legislation that granted girls and women equal access to educational institutions. *School Library Journal* reviewer Julie Webb described the work as a "fascinating look at the birth, growth, stagnation, and final

emergence of Title IX," and Margaret A. Bush, writing in *Horn Book,* observed that "Blumenthal follows its political support and opposition decade by decade, interweaving the parallel increases in sports participation and accomplishment." "Few books cover the last few decades of American women's history with such clarity and detail," Engberg noted.

In *Bootleg* Blumenthal traces the history of the Eighteenth Amendment to the U.S. Constitution, which outlawed the manufacture, sale, and transport of alcohol. Blumenthal also profiles such colorful figures as Carrie Nation, the hatchet-wielding face of the temperance movement; Morris Sheppard, the loquacious Texas senator who authored the amendment; and Al Capone, the notorious mobster who rose to power during Prohibition. "Extensive historical research gives a comprehensive picture of the era," Barbara Johnston reported in her *Voice of Youth Advocates* review of *Bootleg* and *Horn Book* contributor Jonathan Hunt also praised the volume, calling Blumenthal "one of the more intellectually adventurous authors writing for young adults today."

Blumenthal's *Mr. Sam: How Sam Walton Built Wal-Mart and Became America's Richest Man* chronicles the life of the hard-working entrepreneur who founded the nation's leading retailer. A critic in *Kirkus Reviews* remarked that "Blumenthal succeeds in bringing Walton's driven personality and obsession with winning to life," and Hunt commented that the author "has done a splendid job of not only introducing Sam Walton but making his story relevant and timely."

The brilliant and idiosyncratic cofounder of Apple, Inc., is the focus of *Steve Jobs: The Man Who Thought*

In Mr. Sam *Karen Blumenthal profiles the life of Sam Walton, the man who built the WalMart department-store chain.* (Jacket illustration copyright © 2011 by Eli Reichman/Time & Life Pictures/Getty Images.)

Different. "This is a smart book about a smart subject by a smart writer," Ilene Cooper observed in *Booklist,* and a *Kirkus Reviews* writer noted that Blumenthal's the biography "is thoroughly researched and clear on the subject's foibles as well as his genius."

Biographical and Critical Sources

PERIODICALS

Booklist, November 1, 2002, Gillian Engberg, review of *Six Days in October: The Stock Market Crash of 1929,* p. 483; July, 2005, Gillian Engberg, review of *Let Me Play: The Story of Title IX: The Law That Changed the Future of Girls in America,* p. 1914; April 1, 2007, David Siegfried, review of *Grande Expectations: A Year in the Life of the Starbucks' Stock,* p. 10; April 15, 2011, Ian Chipman, review of *Bootleg: Murder, Moonshine, and the Lawless Years of Prohibition,* p. 52; June 1, 2011, John Peters, review of *Mr. Sam: How Sam Walton Build Wal-Mart and Became America's Richest Man,* p. 78; February 15, 2012, Ilene Cooper, review of *Steve Jobs: The Man Who Thought Different,* p. 46.

Horn Book, January-February, 2003, Peter D. Sieruta, review of *Six Days in October,* p. 94; September-October, 2005, Margaret A. Bush, review of *Let Me Play* p. 597; May-June, 2011, Jonathan Hunt, review of *Bootleg,* p. 116; July-August, 2011, Jonathan Hunt, review of *Mr. Sam,* p. 168; May-June, 2012, Jonathan Hunt, review of *Steve Jobs,* p. 109.

Kirkus Reviews, August 15, 2002, review of *Six Days in October,* p. 1217; June 1, 2011, review of *Mr. Sam;* February 15, 2012, review of *Steve Jobs.*

Publishers Weekly, September 2, 2002, review of *Six Days in October,* p. 77, and Ingrid Roper, "Lessons of the Crash of 1929" (interview with Blumethal), p. 78.

School Library Journal, October, 2002, Carol Fazioli, review of *Six Days in October,* p. 180; July, 2005, Julie Webb, review of *Let Me Play,* p. p. 113; July, 2011, Janet S. Thompson, review of *Mr. Sam,* p. 112.

Voice of Youth Advocates, June, 2011, Barbara Johnston, review of *Bootleg,* p. 198.

What Investment, June, 2007, review of *Grande Expectations,* p. 91.

ONLINE

Karen Blumenthal Home Page, http://www.karenblumenthal.com (August 1, 2012).
Karen Blumenthal Web log, http://karenblumenthal.blogspot.com (August 1, 2012).
Simon & Schuster Web site, http://www.simonandschuster.com/ (August 1, 2012), "Karen Blumenthal."*

* * *

BOND, Michael 1926-

Personal

Born January 13, 1926, in Newbury, Berkshire, England; son of Norman Robert (a civil servant) and Frances

Michael Bond (Photograph courtesy of Michael Bond.)

Mary Bond; married Brenda Mary Johnson, June 29, 1950 (divorced, 1981); married Susan Marfrey Rogers, 1981; children: Karen Mary Jankel, Anthony Thomas Barwell. *Politics: Religion: Hobbies and other interests:*

Addresses

Home—London, England. *Agent*—Holly Tonks, The Agency, 24-32 Pottery Lane, Holland Park, London W11 4LZ, England.

Career

Author of books for children. British Broadcasting Corp. (BBC), Reading, England, engineer's assistant, 1941-43; BBC, Caversham, England, with monitoring service, 1947-54; BBC, London, England, television cameraman, 1954-65; full-time writer, 1965—. *Military service:* Royal Air Force, 1943-44, member of air crew; British Army, Middlesex Regiment, 1944-47.

Awards, Honors

Named to Order of the British Empire, 1997; honorary D.Let., Reading University, 2007; British Animation Award for Best Animated Character of All Time, 2012, for Paddington Bear, 2012.

Writings

JUVENILE

(Editor) *Michael Bond's Book of Bears,* Purnell (London, England), 1971.

The Day the Animals Went on Strike (picture book), illustrated by Jim Hodgson, American Heritage (New York, NY), 1972.

(Editor) *Michael Bond's Book of Mice,* Purnell (London, England), 1972.

(Translator, with Barbara von Johnson) *The Motormalgamation,* Studio Vista (London, England), 1974.

Windmill, illustrated by Tony Cattaneo, Studio Vista (London, England), 1975.

How to Make Flying Things (nonfiction), photographs by Peter Kibble, Studio Vista (London, England), 1975.

Mr. Cram's Magic Bubbles, illustrated by Gioia Fiammenghi, Penguin (London, England), 1975.

Picnic on the River, illustrated by Barry Wilkinson, Collins (London, England), 1980.

J.D. Polson and the Liberty Head Dime, illustrated by Roger Wade Walker, hand lettering by Leslie Lee, Mayflower (New York, NY), 1980.

J.D. Polson and the Dillogate Affair, illustrated by Roger Wade Walker, Hodder & Stoughton (London, England), 1981.

The Caravan Puppets, illustrated by Vanessa Julian-Ottie, Collins (London, England), 1983.

(With Paul Parnes) *Oliver the Greedy Elephant,* illustrated by Jim Hodgson, Methuen (New York, NY), 1985.

A Day by the Sea, illustrated by Ross Design, Young Lions (London, England), 1992.

"PADDINGTON" READER SERIES

A Bear Called Paddington (also see below), illustrated by Peggy Fortnum, Collins (London, England), 1958, Houghton (Boston, MA), 1960.

More about Paddington (also see below), illustrated by Peggy Fortnum, Collins (London, England), 1959, Houghton (Boston, MA), 1962.

Paddington Helps Out, illustrated by Peggy Fortnum, Collins (London, England), 1960, Houghton (Boston, MA), 1961.

Paddington Abroad, illustrated by Peggy Fortnum, Collins (London, England), 1961, Houghton (Boston, MA), 1972.

Paddington at Large, illustrated by Peggy Fortnum, Collins (London, England), 1962, Houghton (Boston, MA), 1963.

Paddington Marches On, illustrated by Peggy Fortnum, Collins (London, England), 1964, Houghton (Boston, MA), 1965.

The Adventures of Paddington (contains *A Bear Called Paddington* and *More about Paddington*), illustrated by Peggy Fortnum, Collins (London, England), 1965.

Paddington at Work, illustrated by Peggy Fortnum, Collins (London, England), 1966, Houghton (Boston, MA), 1967.

Paddington Goes to Town, illustrated by Peggy Fortnum, Houghton (Boston, MA), 1968, illustrated by Nick Lo Bianco, Cademon (New York, NY), 1986.

Paddington Takes the Air, illustrated by Peggy Fortnum, Collins (London, England), 1970, Houghton (Boston, MA), 1971.

Paddington's Blue Peter Story Book, illustrated by Ivor Wood, Collins (London, England), 1973, published as *Paddington Takes to TV,* Houghton (Boston, MA), 1974.

Paddington on Top, illustrated by Peggy Fortnum, Collins (London, England), 1974, Houghton (Boston, MA), 1975.

(With Albert Bradley) *Paddington on Stage* (play; adapted from Bond's *Adventures of Paddington*), illustrated by Peggy Fortnum, Collins (London, England), 1974, Houghton Mifflin (Boston, MA), 1977, acting edition, Samuel French (New York, NY), 1976.

Paddington Takes the Test, illustrated by Peggy Fortnum, Collins (London, England), 1979, Houghton (Boston, MA), 1980.

Paddington: A Disappearing Trick and Other Stories (anthology), Collins (London, England), 1979, selections published as *Paddington's Disappearing Trick,* Young Lions (London, England), 1993.

Paddington for Christmas, Collins (London, England), 1979.

Paddington on Screen: The Second Blue Peter Story Book, illustrated by Barry Macey, Collins (London, England), 1981, Houghton (Boston, MA), 1982.

Paddington's Storybook, illustrated by Peggy Fortnum, Collins (London, England), 1983, Houghton (Boston, MA), 1984.

The Hilarious Adventures of Paddington (contains *A Bear Called Paddington, More about Paddington, Paddington at Large, Paddington at Work,* and *Paddington Helps Out*), Dell (New York, NY), 1986.

(With Russell Ash) *The Life and Times of Paddington Bear,* Pavilion Books (London, England), 1988, Viking (New York, NY), 1989.

Giant Paddington Storybook, W.H. Smith (New York, NY), 1989.

Paddington Breaks the Peace, Young Lions (London, England), 1992.

Paddington Does the Decorating, Young Lions (London, England), 1992.

Paddington: A Classic Collection, illustrated by Peggy Fortnum, hand-colored by Caroline Nuttall-Smith, Collins (London, England), 1998, published as *Paddington Treasury,* Houghton (Boston, MA), 1999.

Paddington at the Carnival, illustrated by R.W. Alley, HarperCollins (London, England), 2002.

Paddington Here and Now, illustrated by R.W. Alley, HarperCollins (New York, NY), 2008.

Paddington: A Treasury, illustrated by R.W. Alley, HarperCollins (London, England), 2010.

Paddington Races Ahead, illustrated by R.W. Alley, HarperCollins (London, England), 2012.

The "Paddington Bear" books have been published in over thirty languages.

"PADDINGTON" PICTURE BOOK SERIES

Paddington Bear, illustrated by Fred Banbery, Collins (London, England), 1972, Random House (New York, NY), 1973, illustrated by John Lobban, HarperCollins (New York, NY), 1992, illustrated by R.W. Alley, HarperCollins (New York, NY), 1998.

Paddington's Garden, illustrated by Fred Banbery, Collins (London, England), 1972, Random House (New York, NY), 1973, illustrated by John Lobban, HarperFestival (New York, NY), 1993.

Paddington at the Circus, illustrated by Fred Banbery, Collins (London, England), 1973, Random House (New York, NY), 1974, illustrated by John Lobban, HarperFestival (New York, NY), 1992.

Paddington Goes Shopping, illustrated by Fred Banbery, Collins (London, England), 1973, published as *Paddington's Lucky Day,* Random House (New York, NY), 1974.

Paddington Goes to School, illustrated by Fred Banbery, Collins (London, England), 1974, illustrated by Nick Lo Bianco, Cademon (New York, NY), 1986.

Paddington at the Tower, illustrated by Fred Banbery, Collins (London, England), 1975, Random House (New York, NY), 1978, reprinted, HarperCollins (London, England), 2011.

Paddington at the Seaside, illustrated by Fred Banbery, Collins (London, England), 1975, Random House (New York, NY), 1978.

Paddington Takes a Bath, illustrated by Barry Wilkinson, Collins (London, England), 1976.

Paddington Goes to the Sales, illustrated by Barry Wilkinson, Collins (London, England), 1976.

Paddington's New Room, illustrated by Barry Wilkinson, Collins (London, England), 1976.

Paddington at the Station, illustrated by Barry Wilkinson, Collins (London, England), 1976.

Paddington Hits Out, illustrated by Barry Wilkinson, Collins (London, England), 1977.

Paddington Does It Himself, illustrated by Barry Wilkinson, Collins (London, England), 1977.

Paddington in the Kitchen, illustrated by Barry Wilkinson, Collins (London, England), 1977.

Paddington Goes Out, illustrated by Barry Wilkinson, Collins (London, England), 1980.

Paddington Weighs In, illustrated by Barry Wilkinson, Collins (London, England), 1980.

Paddington at Home, illustrated by Barry Wilkinson, Collins (London, England), 1980.

Paddington and Aunt Lucy, illustrated by Barry Wilkinson, Collins (London, England), 1980.

Paddington in Touch, illustrated by Barry Wilkinson, Collins (London, England), 1980.

Paddington Has Fun, illustrated by Barry Wilkinson, Collins (London, England), 1982.

Paddington Works Hard, illustrated by Barry Wilkinson, Collins (London, England), 1982.

Paddington on the River, illustrated by Barry Wilkinson, Collins (London, England), 1983.

Paddington at the Zoo, illustrated by David McKee, Collins (London, England), 1984, Putnam (New York, NY), 1985, illustrated by R.W. Alley, Collins (London, England), 1998.

Paddington and the Knickerbocker Rainbow, illustrated by David McKee, Collins (London, England), 1984, Putnam (New York, NY), 1985, published as *Paddington and the Tutti Frutti Rainbow,* illustrated by R.W. Alley, Collins (London, England), 1988.

Paddington's Painting Exhibition, illustrated by David McKee, Collins (London, England), 1985, published as *Paddington's Art Exhibition,* Putnam (New York, NY), 1986, published as *Paddington the Artist,* illustrated by R.W. Alley, Collins (London, England), 1998.

Paddington at the Fair, illustrated by David McKee, Collins (London, England), 1985, Putnam (New York, NY), 1986, illustrated by R.W. Alley, Collins (London, England), 1998.

Paddington at the Palace, illustrated by David McKee, Putnam (New York NY), 1986, illustrated by R.W. Alley, Collins (London, England), 1999.

Paddington Minds the House, illustrated by David McKee, Collins (London, England), 1986, illustrated by R.W. Alley, Collins (London, England), 1999.

Paddington Spring Cleans, illustrated by David McKee, Collins (London, England), 1986, published as *Paddington Cleans Up,* Putnam (New York, NY), 1986.

Paddington's Busy Day, illustrated by David McKee, Collins (London, England), 1987, illustrated by R.W. Alley, Collins (London, England), 1999.

Paddington and the Marmalade Maze, illustrated by David McKee, Collins (London, England), 1987, illustrated by R.W. Alley, Collins (London, England), 1999.

Paddington's Magical Christmas, illustrated by David McKee, Collins (London, England), 1988, illustrated by John Lobban, HarperFestival (New York, NY), 1993.

Something Nasty in the Kitchen, illustrated by Nick Ward, Young Lions (London, England), 1992.

Paddington Meets the Queen, illustrated by John Lobban, HarperFestival (New York, NY), 1993.

Paddington Rides On!, illustrated by John Lobban, HarperFestival (New York, NY), 1993.

Paddington Bear and the Christmas Surprise (board book), illustrated by R.W. Alley, HarperFestival (New York, NY), 1997, published as *Paddington and the Christmas Surprise,* HarperCollins (New York, NY), 2008.

Paddington Bear All Day (board book), illustrated by R.W. Alley, HarperFestival (New York, NY), 1998.

Paddington Bear and the Busy Bee Carnival, illustrated by R.W. Alley, HarperFestival (New York, NY), 1998.

Paddington at the Seashore (board book), illustrated by John Lobban, HarperFestival (New York, NY), 1998.

Paddington Bear Goes to Market (board book), illustrated by R.W. Alley, HarperFestival (New York, NY), 1998.

Paddington up and About, illustrated by R.W. Alley, HarperCollins (New York, NY), 1999.

Paddington Bear at the Circus, illustrated by R.W. Alley, HarperCollins (New York, NY), 2000.

Paddington's Party Tricks, illustrated by R.W. Alley, Collins (London, England), 2000.

Paddington in Hot Water, illustrated by R.W. Alley, Collins (London, England), 2000.

(With Karen Jankel) *Paddington Bear Goes to the Hospital,* illustrated by R.W. Alley, HarperFestival (New York, NY), 2001.

Paddington Bear in the Garden (board book), illustrated by R.W. Alley, HarperFestival (New York, NY), 2002.

Paddington's Grand Tour, illustrated by R.W. Alley, Collins (London, England), 2003.

Paddington: My Book of Marmalade, illustrated by R.W. Alley, HarperCollins (London, England), 2008.

Paddington Rules the Waves, illustrated by R.W. Alley, HarperCollins (London, England), 2008.

Paddington and the Disappearing Sandwich, illustrated by R.W. Alley, HarperCollins (London, England), 2008.

Paddington at the Rainbow's End, illustrated by R.W. Alley, HarperCollins (London, England), 2008.

Paddington King of the Castle, illustrated by R.W. Alley, HarperCollins (London, England), 2008.

Paddington at the Beach, illustrated by R.W. Alley, Harper (New York, NY), 2009.

Paddington Buggy Book (board book), illustrated by R.W. Alley, HarperCollins (New York, NY), 2011.

The Paddington Treasury for the Very Young, illustrated by R.W. Alley, HarperCollins (London, England), 2011.

Paddington Goes for Gold, illustrated by R.W. Alley, HarperCollins (London, England), 2012.

"PADDINGTON" LEARNING AND ACTIVITY BOOKS

The Great Big Paddington Book, illustrated by Ivor Wood, Collins (London, England), 1976, published as *The Great Big Paddington Bear Picture Book,* Collins & World (Cleveland, OH), 1977, reprinted under the latter title, Pan (London, England), 1984.

Paddington's Loose-End Book: An ABC of Things to Do, illustrated by Ivor Wood, Collins (London, England), 1976.

Paddington's Party Book, illustrated by Ivor Wood, Collins (London, England), 1976.

Fun and Games with Paddington, illustrated by Ivor Wood, Collins (London, England), 1977.

Paddington's First Book: An Object Recognition Book with Pictures to Colour, illustrated by Barry Wilkinson, Collins (London, England), 1977.

Paddington's First Word Book: Words to Copy, Pictures to Colour, illustrated by Barry Wilkinson, Collins (London, England), 1977.

Paddington's First Play Book: Things to Make, Games to Play, Pictures to Colour, illustrated by Barry Wilkinson, Collins (London, England), 1977.

Paddington's First Counting Book: Learn the Numbers, Colour the Pictures, illustrated by Barry Wilkinson, Collins (London, England), 1977.

Paddington's Picture Book, Collins (London, England), 1978.

Paddington's Cartoon Book, illustrated by Ivor Wood, Collins (London, England), 1979.

(With daughter, Karen Bond) *Paddington at the Airport,* illustrated by Toni Goffe, Macmillan (New York, NY), 1986.

(With Karen Bond) *Paddington Mails a Letter,* illustrated by Toni Goffe, Macmillan (New York, NY), 1986, published as *Paddington Bear Posts a Letter,* Hutchinson (London, England), 1986.

(With Karen Bond) *Paddington's Clock Book,* illustrated by Toni Goffe, Hutchinson (London, England), 1986.

(With Karen Bond) *Paddington's London,* Hutchinson (London, England), 1986.

(With Karen Bond) *Paddington's First Puzzle Book,* Crocodile (New York, NY), 1987.

(With Karen Bond) *Paddington's Second Puzzle Book,* Crocodile (New York, NY), 1987.

Paddington's Jar of Jokes, Carnival (London, England), 1992.

Paddington Bear: My Scrapbook, illustrated by R.W. Alley, HarperFestival (New York, NY), 1999.

(With Lesley Young) *Paddington's Cookery Book,* illustrated by R.W. Alley, HarperCollins (London, England), 2011.

Paddington's London Treasury, illustrated by R.W. Alley, HarperCollins (London, England), 2011.

Paddington's Guide to London, illustrated by R.W. Alley, HarperCollins (London, England), 2011.

Also author, with Karen Bond, of *Paddington's Wheel Book,* illustrated by Toni Goffe, Macmillan.

"PADDINGTON" POP-UP BOOKS

Paddington's Pop-up Book, Collins (London, England), 1977.

Paddington and the Snowbear, Collins (London, England), 1981.

Paddington at the Launderette, Collins (London, England), 1981.

Paddington's Shopping Adventure, Collins (London, England), 1981.

Paddington's Birthday Treat, Collins (London, England), 1981.

"THURSDAY" READER SERIES

Here Comes Thursday! illustrated by Daphne Rowles, Harrap (London, England), 1966, Lothrop (New York, NY), 1967.

Thursday Rides Again, illustrated by Beryl Sanders, Harrap (London, England), 1968, Lothrop (New York, NY), 1969.

Thursday Ahoy! illustrated by Leslie Wood, Harrap (London, England), 1969, Lothrop (New York, NY), 1970.

Thursday in Paris, illustrated by Leslie Wood, Harrap (London, England), 1971, Penguin (New York, NY), 1974.

"OLGA DA POLGA" READER SERIES

The Tales of Olga da Polga (also see below), illustrated by Hans Helweg, Penguin (London, England), 1971, Macmillan (New York, NY), 1973, 40th anniversary edition, illustrated by Catherine Rayner, Oxford University Press (New York, NY), 2011, published in two volumes as *First Big Olga da Polga Book* and *Second Big Olga da Polga Book,* both Longman (London, England), 1983.

Olga Meets Her Match (also see below), illustrated by Hans Helweg, Longman (London, England), 1973, Hastings House (Fern Park, FL), 1975, reprinted, Oxford University Press (New York, NY), 2001.

Olga Carries On (also see below), illustrated by Hans Helweg, Kestrel (London, England), 1976, Hastings House (Fern Park, FL), 1977, reprinted, Oxford University Press (New York, NY), 2001.

Olga Takes Charge (also see below), illustrated by Hans Helweg, Kestrel (London, England), 1982, Dell (New York, NY), 1983.

The Complete Adventures of Olga da Polga (omnibus volume; contains *The Tales of Olga da Polga, Olga Meets Her Match, Olga Carries On,* and *Olga Takes Charge*), illustrated by Hans Helweg, Delacorte (New York, NY), 1983.

Olga Moves House, illustrated by Hans Helweg, Oxford University Press (New York, NY), 2001.

Olga Follows Her Nose, illustrated by Hans Helweg, Oxford University Press (New York, NY), 2002.

The "Olga da Polga" stories have been translated into ten languages.

"OLGA'S ADVENTURES" SERIES; BASED ON "THE TALES OF OLGA DA POLGA"

Olga Counts Her Blessings, illustrated by Hans Helweg, Puffin (New York, NY), 1975.

Olga Makes a Friend, illustrated by Hans Helweg, Puffin (New York, NY), 1975.

Olga Makes a Wish, illustrated by Hans Helweg, Puffin (New York, NY), 1975.

Olga Makes Her Mark, illustrated by Hans Helweg, Puffin (New York, NY), 1975.

Olga Takes a Bite, illustrated by Hans Helweg, Puffin (New York, NY), 1975.

Olga's New Home, illustrated by Hans Helweg, Puffin (New York, NY), 1975.

Olga's Second House, illustrated by Hans Helweg, Puffin (New York, NY), 1975.

Olga's Special Day, illustrated by Hans Helweg, Puffin (New York, NY), 1975.

"PARSLEY" SERIES

Parsley's Tail, illustrated by Esor, BBC Publications (London, England), 1969.

Parsley's Good Deed, illustrated by Esor, BBC Publications (London, England), 1969.

Parsley's Last Stand, illustrated by Esor, BBC Publications (London, England), 1970.

Parsley's Problem Present, illustrated by Esor, BBC Publications (London, England), 1970.

Parsley's Parade, illustrated by Ivor Wood, Collins (London, England), 1972.

Parsley the Lion, illustrated by Ivor Wood, Collins (London, England), 1972.

Parsley and the Herbs, illustrated by Ivor Wood, Ward, Lock (London, England), 1976.

"MONSIEUR PAMPLEMOUSSE" MYSTERY SERIES

Monsieur Pamplemousse, Hodder & Stoughton (London, England), 1983, Beaufort (New York, NY), 1985.

Monsieur Pamplemousse and the Secret Mission, Hodder & Stoughton (London, England), 1984, Beaufort (New York, NY), 1986.

Monsieur Pamplemousse on the Spot, Hodder & Stoughton (London, England), 1986, Beaufort (New York, NY), 1987.

Monsieur Pamplemousse Takes the Cure, Hodder & Stoughton (London, England), 1987, Random House (New York, NY), 1988.

Monsieur Pamplemousse Aloft, Fawcett (New York, NY), 1989.

Monsieur Pamplemousse Investigates, Fawcett (New York, NY), 1990.

Monsieur Pamplemousse Rests His Case, Headline (London, England), 1991.

Monsieur Pamplemousse Stands Firm, Headline (London, England), 1992.

Monsieur Pamplemousse on Location, Headline (London, England), 1992.

Monsieur Pamplemousse Takes the Train, Headline (London, England), 1993.

Monsieur Pamplemousse Afloat, Allison & Busby (London, England), 1998.

Monsieur Pamplemousse Omnibus, three volumes, Allison & Busby (London, England), 1998–1999.

Monsieur Pamplemousse on Probation, Allison & Busby (London, England), 2000.

Monsieur Pamplemousse on Vacation, Allison & Busby (London, England), 2002.

Monsieur Pamplemousse Hits the Headlines, Allison & Busby (London, England), 2003.

Monsieur Pamplemousse and the Militant Midwives, Allison & Busby (London, England), 2006.

Monsieur Pamplemousse and the French Solution, Allison & Busby (London, England), 2007.

Monsieur Pamplemousse and the Carbon Footprint, Allison & Busby (London, England), 2010.

OTHER

(And photographer) *A Gastronomic Companion* (adult guidebook), Crown (New York, NY), 1987, published as *The Pleasures of Paris,* Pavilion (London, England), 1987.

Bears & Forebears: A Life so Far (autobiography), HarperCollins (New York, NY), 1996.

Author of radio and television plays for adults and children, including *Simon's Good Deed, Napoleon's Day Out,* and *Open House.* Author of *Paddington* (fifty-six-episode animated television series and three half-hour specials), Home Box Office. Author of *Eight Olga Readers,* 1975. Author of *The Herbs* (thirteen-episode puppet series) and *The Adventures of Parsley* (thirty-two-episode puppet series). Contributor of stories to periodicals, including *London Opinion, Strand,* and *Malice Domestic 7.*

Adaptations

The "Paddington Bear" character was adapted for use in concept books, activity books, and other learning materials, as well as being merchandised as a stuffed toy. The "Olga da Polga" books were adapted for film-strip with cassette, ENC Corp, 1977. Other media adaptations include *A Bear Called Paddington* (record or cassette), Caedmon, 1978; *Paddington for Christmas* (record or cassette), Caedmon, 1979; *Paddington: A Disappearing Trick and Other Stories* (record or cassette), Caedmon, 1979; *Paddington Turns Detective* (record or cassette), Caedmon, 1979; *Paddington Bear—Series II* (film series), FilmFair, 1980; *Paddington on Top* (film series; with teacher's guide), Learning Tree, 1984; *Paddington Bear* (cassette), Caedmon, 1985; and *Paddington Bear* (film), Walt Disney Productions, 1985. Books adapted for audiocassette include *Paddington Bear: A Visit to the Dentist, and Something in the Kitchen, Paddington Bear and the Christmas Shopping, Paddington Goes to the Movies, Please Look after This Bear, Paddington Bear: A Birthday Treat and Other Stories, Paddington Goes to School, Paddington Goes to Town,* and *The Complete Adventures of Olga da Polga.*

Sidelights

British author Michael Bond has delighted children all over the world with his stories of Paddington the Bear. Bond began his series with *A Bear Called Paddington* in 1958, and he has continued writing for decades about the bear from Peru who lives with the Brown family. Bond's "Paddington" character has appeared in everything from picture and pop-up books for younger children to activity books and coloring books and has even starred in plays as well as on television. The bear's appeal, according to critics, comes from his ability to get into trouble and come out of it without any major harm being done. Bond has also created such memorable children's characters as the lovable guinea pig Olga da Polga, Thursday the mouse, Parsley the lion, and J.D. Polson the armadillo. In the early 1980s he also began publishing works for adults, producing the long-running "Monsieur Pamplemousse" mysteries.

Born in Newbury, England, Bond grew up surrounded by books and he began to read at an early age. Young Bond enjoyed reading at home more than he liked attending school—his favorite books were *Bulldog Drummond* and *The Swiss Family Robinson*—and he often faked illnesses to avoid attending class. Something of a loner, he also developed an interest in radio sets that would prove advantageous later in his life.

Completing school at age fourteen, Bond went to work in a lawyer's office. Soon afterward, he responded to an advertisement for radio work, and thus began his career at the British Broadcasting Corporation (BBC). One of his colleagues at the BBC supplemented his income by writing short stories and this coworker inspired Bond to attempt something creative. When he submitted a cartoon to *Punch* it was rejected, but the editor's favorable comments encouraged Bond to continue writing.

During World War II Bond served in the Royal Air Force until airsickness forced him to transfer to the British Army. While serving in Egypt he wrote an adult short story and submitted it to *London Opinion*. To his delight, it was accepted. From that time on, he continued to write and submit stories and plays, making occasional sales. On a Christmas Eve shopping strip in 1957 Bond stopped in a London store and discovered the stuffed toy that inspired Paddington. *A Bear Called Paddington,* a beginning reader, was published in 1958 and the rest is history.

Since first appearing on the literary scene, Paddington has "become part of the folklore of childhood," wrote Marcus Crouch in *The Nesbit Tradition: The Children's Novel in England 1945-70.* Despite being represented by a variety of illustrators, the bear is always unkempt and looks well-traveled in his Wellington boots, rumpled hat, and duffel coat. A foreigner from Peru, Paddington exhibits both innocence and a knack for trouble. "The humour of Paddington is largely visual; it is not what he is but what he does and how he does it that is funny," observed Crouch. In the *New York Times Book Review,* Ellen Lewis Buell cited the bear's "endearing combination of bearishness and boyishness" as one reason for his popularity. According to Pico Iyer in the *Village Voice,* "Paddington is a resolute little fellow of strong principles and few prejudices, full of resourcefulness and free of rancor: both the bear next door and something of a role model."

With sequels such as *Paddington Helps Out, Paddington Abroad,* and *Paddington at Work* Bond has continued to broaden to his creation's popularity. Eric Hudson wrote in *Children's Book Review* that "one is immensely impressed by the way each collection of stories comes up so fresh and full of humorous and highly original situations." Bond has also adapted his Paddington readers for younger children, creating a series of picture books that includes *Paddington Bear* and *Paddington at the Circus.* He has also written several "Paddington" activity books, some with the assistance of his daughter, Karen Bond.

In the late 1960s Bond began experimenting with other children's characters, such as Thursday the mouse and Parsley the lion. The latter was a feature of a stop-action animation show on the BBC television network in addition to being the subject of children's books. Bond's most successful children's character, after Paddington, is perhaps Olga da Polga, the guinea pig he began writing about in the early 1970s. Although Olga is restricted to the hutch where her owners keep her, she entertains herself and her animal friends by telling imaginative stories. *Horn Book* contributor Virginia Haviland asserted that in Olga Bond "has drawn another beguiling creature with a distinct personality—a guinea pig whose cleverness equals that of Paddington." Olga is featured in books such as *Tales of Olga da Polga, Olga Meets Her Match,* and *Olga Moves House.*

In the early 1980s Bond branched out into the field of adult mystery books with the "Monsieur Pamplemousse" books. The hero of these, Monsieur Pamplemousse, is a French food inspector who solves mysteries with the aid of his dog, Pommes Frites. For these works Bond draws on his knowledge of France, a country he visits frequently. Sybil Steinberg, writing in *Publishers Weekly,* noted that "Pamplemousse and his faithful hound are an appealing pair and offer an evening of civilized entertainment."

Despite Bond's varied literary output, he will always be remembered for the character of Paddington. "Most critics agree . . . that to think of Michael Bond is to think of Paddington Bear," observed *Dictionary of Literary Biography* contributor Charles E. Matthews. Over the years, Paddington has become something of a cottage industry: he has been reproduced as a stuffed animal and as a float balloon in the Macy's Thanksgiving Day Parade, and his image has even appeared on a British postage stamp. In 2000 a life-sized bronze statue of the bear was unveiled in Paddington Station in London, and the official Paddington Bear Web site debuted in 2003. In 2012 Paddington Bear won the British Animation Award for best animated character of all time.

In 1997 Bond was awarded the Order of the British Empire for services to children's literature. In 2012 he was asked in the London *Evening Standard* why he believed Paddington remains so popular more than fifty years after his creation. "Paddington is very polite in a world where people have become more selfish," Bond responded to interviewer Katie Law. "I think people are envious of Paddington's lifestyle because he does things in his own time."

Biographical and Critical Sources

BOOKS

Children's Literature Review, Volume 1, Gale (Detroit, MI), 1976.
Crouch, Marcus, *The Nesbit Tradition: The Children's Novel in England, 1945-70,* Benn (London, England), 1972.
Dictionary of Literary Biography, Volume 161: *British Children's Writers since 1960,* Gale (Detroit, MI), 1996.
St. James Guide to Children's Writers, 5th edition, St. James Press (Detroit, MI), 1999.

PERIODICALS

Armchair Detective, summer, 1991, review of *Monsieur Pamplemousse Aloft,* p. 348.
Booklist, September 15, 1991, review of *Monsieur Pamplemousse Rests His Case,* p. 123; December 15, 1991, review of *Paddington's Colors,* p. 769; September 15, 1997, Carolyn Phelan, review of *Paddington Bear and the Christmas Surprise,* p. 239; April, 1998, Carolyn Phelan, reviews of *Paddington Bear All Day* and *Paddington Bear Goes to Market,* both p. 1329; May 15, 1998, Carolyn Phelan, review of *Paddington Bear and the Busy Bee Carnival,* pp. 1629-1630; August, 1998, Shelle Rosenfeld, review of *Paddington at Large,* p. 2002; January 1, 1999, Carolyn Phelan, review of *Paddington Bear,* p. 886; April 15, 2002, Carolyn Phelan, review of *Paddington Bear in the Garden,* p. 1405; May 15, 2008, Carolyn Phelan, review of *Paddington Here and Now,* p. 45.
Children's Book Review, February, 1971, Eric Hudson, article about Paddington, p. 16.
Evening Standard (London, England), March 27, 2012, Katie Law, interview with Bond, p. 26.
Horn Book, June, 1973, Virginia Haviland, review of *The Tales of Olga da Polga,* p. 443, September-October, 2008, Sarah Ellis, review of *Paddington Here and Now,* p. 577.
Los Angeles Times Book Review, June 9, 1985, review of *Monsieur Pamplemousse,* p. 11.
New Statesman, June 16, 2008, Alyssa McDonald, review of *Paddington Here and Now,* p. 19.
New Yorker, December 4, 1971, review of *Paddington Takes the Air,* p. 196; December 1, 1975, review of *Paddington on Top,* p. 185.
Publishers Weekly, July 29, 1988, Sybil Steinberg, review of *Monsieur Pamplemousse Takes the Cure,* p. 223; June 23, 1989, review of *Monsieur Pamplemousse Takes the Cure,* p. 56; July 28, 1989, Sybil Steinberg, review of *Monsieur Pamplemousse Aloft,* p. 207; October 12, 1990, Sybil Steinberg, review of *Monsieur Pamplemousse Investigates,* p. 48; September 6, 1991, review of *Monsieur Pamplemousse Rests His Case,* p. 97; November 8, 1999, "Together for the First Time," p. 70.
School Library Journal, August, 2008, Joy Fleishhacker, review of *Paddington Here and Now,* p. 83.

ONLINE

Offical Paddington Bear Web Site, http://www.paddington bear.co.uk (May 2, 2012).

Autobiography Feature

Michael Bond

Michael Bond contributed the following autobiographical essay to *SATA:*

I was born at West Mills in Newbury, England, on January 13, 1926. The event went unreported in the *Times* of London, who were more concerned with matters like the theft of a motor car and its contents, the adverse trade balance (nothing changes!), and something they called "weather probabilities."

I weighed over eleven pounds at birth and my mother used to stand me in bowls of Tidman's Sea Salt to stop me going bandy when I started to walk. It must have done the trick because in an early photograph of me sitting on a cushion I look perfectly normal. When I was a little older I worried for a time about the round object lying between my legs, wondering if some vital part had become detached. If it had, then it was probably lost for ever; Mother was a great tidier-up. But I consulted my best friend and after exchanging notes we decided that all was well.

My father was a civil servant and when I was six months old he was transferred some seventeen miles away to Reading, and that was where I spent my childhood. Life was very tranquil in those prewar days. Television hadn't been invented, so people had to devise their own entertainment. The word "radio" still meant a crystal set to many, and if you went into a room and saw someone wearing headphones you had to be very careful how you closed the door in case the "cat's whisker" became detached.

Practically everything was delivered to the house; freshly baked bread arrived by horse-drawn van, vegetables came on a horse and cart, milk arrived in churns on a hand cart and it was always a high spot of the day to be allowed to take a jug into the street so that a pint could be poured from a copper-and-brass measure. There were no refrigerators, so in the summer it went off very quickly. For the same reason pork was only eaten when there was an *R* in the month. Strawberries arrived in time for Ascot Week and were a great treat. They stayed for Wimbledon, then disappeared again. There was no question of their being available at any other time of the year, but we enjoyed them much more because of that.

Street games came in strict rotation. Hoops made of iron or wood came out as if by magic on a certain day; tops appeared on another. Roller skates had their place

A very young Michael Bond, 1926 (Photograph courtesy of Michael Bond)

in the calendar. Mine came from Woolworth's and cost sixpence each half. They seldom lasted a season and usually ended up sagging in the middle. Conkers heralded the approach of autumn.

Memory plays strange tricks, but the seasons also seemed more clearly defined. The winters were colder and there was always snow; ponds froze over and could be skated on. By contrast the summers were long and hot. I played endless games of cricket with my father in the local park. He did all the bowling and running for the ball, while I batted. He was a very kind and patient man and knew that the most important thing you can give a child is your time; a belief he must have been sorely tempted to forego after a hard day at the office when I stood, bat in hand, anxious to get going, watching him eat his "high tea." How he must have prayed for rain to stop play.

I had a reputation for being a good little boy, largely because I kept myself to myself and didn't say very much. But I used to think a lot, and it irritated me when perfect strangers took me at face value. One morning I was standing at the front door when the baker arrived. For some reason best known to myself I was carrying a large brick. When he patted me on the head and made the inevitable remark, I let go of the brick. It landed on his foot and produced a very satisfactory cry of pain. My mother stood up for me. Knowing her, she probably said he shouldn't have had his foot there anyway and that it served him right. Shortly after that we changed our baker—or he changed us.

My mother always saw things in black and white. In her later years, when colour television came along, she never entirely approved of it, although she was forced to admit it was very good for some things—like watching snooker, where you needed to see which ball was being played. But she still criticised it from time to time because the grass wasn't the right shade of green.

There were never any shades of grey in her life. If she went out after dark, which she rarely did, it was always "pitch black." Hot drinks became "stone cold" if they were left too long. If it rained, it rained "cats and dogs," and if a light was accidentally left on it was always "full on." Christmas presents had to be kept upright and not squeezed.

She was also a great believer in old-fashioned remedies for aches and pains, and looking back she was probably right; at least they were all tried and tested and none of them had any side effects. Calves' Foot Jelly cured most things, a nightly spoonful of a sickly chocolate-tasting substance called Virol built me up during the week, and on Friday night a dose of California Syrup of Figs prepared me for the Sunday lunch and ensured a constipation-free weekend. The state of one's bowels was very important in those days.

She also had a habit of coming out with statements which brooked no argument. Towards the end of her life, when she and my father were less active, I used to drive down to see them and take them for rides in the country; my father sitting in the front of the car smoking his pipe, so that it was often difficult to see where we were going, my mother sitting in the back with a bag of boiled sweets which she sucked rather noisily in between passing comments on the passing scene, or closing her eyes when we went down a steep hill.

"Don't like flowers much," she announced one day as we were passing through a particularly beautiful stretch of countryside. "The blessed petals fall off and make the place untidy."

On another occasion, thinking it would be a treat, I took them to the site of an old Roman villa. I parked the car near a group of houses and as my mother climbed out she looked around and said, "What a funny place to build a Roman villa—right next door to a housing estate!"

"I was lying awake last night thinking of these drives," she said on another occasion, when we were heading down the Portsmouth road towards the sea, "and I suddenly thought of all the murderers we must pass on the way. I hope you never give any of them lifts."

The latter remark probably stemmed from the fact that Mother was an avid reader of detective novels. Books were always part of the furniture and I was read to almost as soon as I was able to recognise sounds and never went to bed without a story. She belonged to a library and every Monday would go into Reading and return with half-a-dozen or so volumes which she devoured during the rest of the week, usually without comment, although she sometimes wrote to authors telling them she had enjoyed their latest work but that it was too short. Books by English writers like Freeman Wills Crofts, Edgar Wallace, and John Rhode were her favourites—she didn't hold much with American crime stories—they were too violent. When I started to read to myself my choice was more catholic—Sapper's *Bulldog Drummond,* and books about a character called "Biggles," plus innumerable readings of *The Swiss Family Robinson,* which I enjoyed because of all the practi-

Mother and Father on holiday (Photograph courtesy of Michael Bond)

cal advice it contained about things like making a pair of Wellington boots out of old socks and rubber solution; but I read everything she read too, and it doubtless sowed the seeds of my present interest in writing detective stories.

One day my father did me a very good deed which was to be of great benefit to me in later life; he introduced me to a weekly magazine called the *Magnet*. Until then, comics came and went; I had never been totally loyal to anyone particular publication, but used to oscillate, bestowing my favours on whichever happened to have the best free gift that week. The *Magnet* was something different. Set in a fictitious English public school called Greyfriars, its hero was a character named Billy Bunter, the epitome of all one shouldn't be, always borrowing money on the expectation of postal orders which never materialised, grossly overweight, lazy, and lying his way into and out of never-ending scrapes. But he inhabited a world full of wholly believable characters, whose reactions were so totally predictable it left one with a warm feeling of security and that all was for the best in the best of all possible worlds. I used to read it from cover to cover, including the advertisements for curing spots and increasing your height, until I felt I could have written it myself. Although I didn't realise it at the time, such dedication was a wonderful grounding for someone who in later life would be writing for a living. I still have a few of the original copies, and to meet someone who was also brought up on the *Magnet* is to establish an immediate rapport.

The *Magnet* remained my staple reading until war broke out and paper rationing brought its publication to an end. I learned later that Frank Richards, the author, who in his time must have written millions of words for a pittance, was a great gambler and spent what spare time he had popping over to France to play the tables.

Childhood holidays were taken at a place called Sandown, on the Isle of Wight. Armed with buckets and spades, we would set off by steam train in carriages decorated with sepia photographs and maps. An added excitement was catching the ferry across to the island via Portsmouth harbour, which in those days was always packed with ocean-going liners and naval craft of every description; it was the then equivalent of "going abroad"—a possibility which wouldn't have occurred to my parents in their wildest dreams, even if they had been able to afford it. My mother didn't really hold with such things.

I don't remember my father ever making any concession to being on the beach other than taking his shoes and socks off and rolling up the bottoms of his flannel trousers. In all the photographs still in my possession he is wearing a jacket and tie, often a waistcoat too, and smoking the inevitable pipe. More often than not he kept his hat on as well. Being a very polite man he liked to have something to raise when he met anyone he knew and he always felt lost without it. We used to

Sandown, Isle of Wight, 1930; Michael and his father (Photograph courtesy of Michael Bond)

stay at a "guest house" run by a Mrs. Gate who expected her guests to be out all day. It was situated on top of the cliffs overlooking the bay and my father would give me a piggyback up the long path home every evening. They were happy days.

*

My first encounter with the opposite sex came in the traditional shape of the girl next door. Her name was Sheila and if old photographs—sadly no longer in my possession—were anything to go by, we seemed to spend most of our time chatting across the garden fence. I was around eight at the time and I suppose she must have been a month or two younger. One picture showed her standing on a box, her silver blonde hair glowing in the evening sun, hanging on to my every word. From the expression on her face I was obviously on to a very good thing. It was only a matter of time and playing my cards right.

However, impatience must have got the better of me, for in the end I dealt myself a losing hand.

One day when my parents were out I invited her round to see my train set. Without a murmur, and with an innocence I have rarely encountered since, she followed me into the cupboard under the stairs. Once inside I shut the door and obeying what must have been very primitive instincts indeed, for I had no real idea *why* I was doing it, I removed my trousers.

Even Sheila sensed that all was not well, and to my horror she started to cry. No amount of bribing with offers of free lollipops until the end of time, or unlimited goes with my train set would make her stop.

It was the end of a beautiful friendship, and we were never allowed to talk to each other again.

My next adventure was with a girl called Patsy. Patsy? Sheila? I should have had more sense!

Even at the tender age of eight, Patsy had already built up quite a reputation in the neighbourhood. My mother used to say things like "You don't want to play with *that* girl . . . she's not nice . . ." But the plain fact was she struck me as being *very* nice, and I *did* want to play with her.

My big chance came one morning when she invited me up to her bedroom. We leaned out of the back window for a while exchanging such pleasantries as I could muster in those days, and then she disappeared.

When I looked round I found to my surprise that she had taken her knickers off and was sitting astride her potty doing what was known in polite circles as "big jobs." She seemed very pleased with the result and when she stood up you could see why. It was all curiously disturbing. Until then, going to the lavatory had always been a bit of a chore; I hadn't realised you could actually get pleasure from it. So when she invited me to have a go I needed no second bidding.

Unfortunately, just as I'd settled down and reached the point of no return, the door opened and her mother carne into the room. By this time Patsy was fully dressed and sitting demurely on her bed, leaving me to take the can for want of a better word.

Yet another beautiful friendship bit the dust, and by now my own reputation in the district was at almost as low an ebb as Patsy's.

Not surprisingly, these two events, following as they did closely on one another, put me off girls for quite a while; seven years to be precise. Apart from one entry in an early diary—"Went newting with Jesse—*super!*"—I contented myself with gazing furtively at the statuesque girls in Woolworth's while clutching a sixpence in my hot hand. They seemed too remote for words, and I would have run a mile if one of them had actually spoken to me.

Soon after that we moved away from the area to a larger house on a newly built estate. It had bay windows and the doors were varnished with imitation graining, two much sought-after embellishments in those days, for which one paid extra.

Perhaps in an effort to teach me the facts of life without actually mentioning the dreaded word "sex," I was given three guinea pigs. I called them Pip, Squeak, and Wilfred, after a cartoon series which was popular at the time. One of them, I was never quite sure which, let me down rather badly a few months later by producing a litter of baby guinea pigs. Perhaps whichever one it was had been as innocent as Sheila.

Binkie, "1/50 sec. at f/11 with Kodak Super XX" (Photograph courtesy of Michael Bond)

After the debacle with the guinea pigs I decided to devote my attention to a dog called Binkie. At least you knew where you stood with dogs. He remained my constant companion until I went into the Forces.

Anyway, by then I had other things to occupy my mind; school and hobbies. Hobbies consisted of photography, radio, marionettes, and cycling. For a while I was a very keen cyclist and was constantly setting forth on long trips with my best friend, Tim. A hundred miles a day was nothing, and with very little in the way of motorised traffic on the roads to impede our progress, the world was our oyster as we pedalled our way around the countryside armed with flasks of special liquid clipped to our dropped handlebars and saddlebags stuffed to capacity with camping equipment and other impedimenta.

Photography enjoyed a brief vogue and instead of putting titles under my work I put things like "1/100 sec. at f-4.5—weather cloudy."

By then I had also discovered films and whenever I could afford it I used to rush off with a friend to the local cinema. Reading had no less than nine in those days; one even had an organ which rose up through the floor and made the whole building shake when it was played. For one shilling and ninepence you entered a world of double features plus all the extras; the "shorts" with the Ritz Brothers or the Three Stooges, a cartoon, and the inevitable newsreel. And if you felt so inclined, which I often did, you could stay where you were and see it all over again.

Along with millions of others I fell in love many times over; Claudette Colbert one day, Deanna Durbin the next, believing that if only we could meet it would be love at first sight for them too. Hollywood was a wonderful dream factory.

But my two great interests, apart from the cinema, were building amplifiers and radio sets and constructing a mammoth marionette theatre complete with revolving stage and lighting equipment.

Radio was still in its infancy. The word "electronics" hadn't been invented, although it was just around the corner. I used to play around with ebonite and bits of wire and valves and large coils which had "Hear What the Wild Waves Are Saying" printed on the side. I can still remember the thrill of getting them to oscillate and the distinctive smell of ebonite when it was being cut.

The marionette theatre occupied first the garden shed, gradually forcing my long-suffering father to remove his tools as it expanded, and later the entire inside of the loft. I never did put on any shows—the excitement was in the building. Music Hall was still popular in those days and I used to go to the local Palace Theatre at every opportunity. I had no desire to be an actor, feeling myself much too shy to stand up before an audience. But on one occasion the curtain went up to reveal a stagehand and I decided that that was what I wanted to be when I grew up: a scene shifter. My parents greeted this news with a distinct lack of enthusiasm. My school fees were costing them money they could ill afford and it must have seemed a poor return.

School was very much of an intrusion into all these activities and I used to long for the holidays so that I could get on with things.

Being a day boy at a boarding school—and a Catholic one at that when I was Church of England—left me feeling a bit of an outsider and there were times when I did everything I could to avoid going. Little pills of soap covered with sugar was one method; another, much less successful because it required more skill, was to hit my knee with a stone in an effort to draw blood without inflicting too much pain—I usually ended up with badly bruised knees. To say that schooldays were among the least happy days of my life wouldn't be entirely true; there were moments of enormous fun, but on the whole I don't look back on them with any great pleasure. The statutory age for leaving was fourteen, and I couldn't wait for that day to arrive.

In any case, it was 1939 and war on Germany was about to be declared. There had been rumblings for some while; the newsreels were becoming gloomier and gloomier. One morning I arrived at school only to find my seat occupied by a large Dutch boy smoking a cigar—the first refugee I had ever encountered. Several of my form mates took advantage of the situation and produced cigarettes, for which they were speedily punished.

The day war was declared, having listened to Neville Chamberlain on the radio, I went out into the garden with my father and we made a sandbag out of a small

hessian bag filled with earth. It seemed rather futile, but it was a gesture. An air-raid warning sounded and we gazed up at the sky wondering if the heavens were about to open—I had seen H.G. Wells' *Things to Come*—but nothing happened. It was the start of what was to become known as "the phoney war."

When I left school I started work in a lawyer's office, carrying enormous piles of deed boxes up from the strong room in the morning and taking them back down again at night, licking stamps, delivering letters—which I always looked forward to because it meant I could call in at the local bookshop—operating the switchboard, and generally making myself useful. During the lunch hour when I was left in charge I used to read through the divorce files hoping I might find something juicy, but I rarely did, only a lot of sadness and bad feeling. For all of these things I was paid the princely sum of ten shillings a week and after a year I plucked up courage to ask for a raise. I was given an extra two-and-sixpence on the strict understanding that I wouldn't ask again for some time to come.

One day we stopped work half an hour early in order to celebrate the retirement at the age of sixty-five of a Mr. Jackson. Mr. Jackson had been with the firm all his life and had never married, probably because he had never been able to afford it. We had tea and cakes and he was given a gold watch. After that he said goodbye and we never saw him again. I resolved there and then that working in an office was not for me. Somehow or other life had to have more to offer. The thought of arriving in the world and departing again, leaving scarcely a ripple behind appalled me, but I had no very clear idea of what I wanted to do.

In desperation I replied to an advertisement in the local paper which said, quite simply, "Wanted: Someone interested in radio." To my great surprise it turned out to be the BBC who were opening up a small transmitter in the area and were in desperate need of staff.

I answered a few simple questions on things like Ohm's law and could I use a soldering iron and found myself with a new job. Which is how I came to meet Mrs. Chambers, an encounter for which my previous experiences with Sheila and Patsy had left me ill-prepared.

Mrs. Chambers was some twenty years my senior and it was part of her job to take me in hand and teach me all she knew, a task which she set about with enthusiasm once we got to know each other better. But that is another story.

*

Soon after, the war intervened in earnest. Early one afternoon four of us were on duty at the transmitter when we heard the sound of a plane approaching fast and low. One of the others looked out of the window and shouted, "Christ! It's a Heinkel." Before the rest of us had a chance to reply it happened. There was a violent explosion and we were thrown to the floor. It felt as though the whole building was about to collapse about our ears. We were on the fifth floor and I remember bracing myself for the long fall to come, convinced it was the end. Everything from that moment on seemed to take place in slow motion. Hardly had we recovered from the first explosion when there was a second, then a third and a fourth. It transpired later that the pilot was being chased home and seeing a likely target dropped everything en route. At the speed he was going it must have taken him only a matter of seconds, but at the time it seemed an eternity. Miraculously we survived, left suspended between the buildings on either side. Because of the angle of the trajectory the bottom half of the building had been literally blown away. I decided there and then that whatever way I was ultimately destined to go it wasn't by enemy bombing, but it wasn't until I managed to clamber down to the ground that I realised just how lucky we had been. The bottom floor was a restaurant and all those who had been inside when the bombs dropped were now in the basement covered by tons of rubble. The first person I saw was a girl with both her legs blown off. I can still see the look of mute despair in her eyes as she gazed up at me and I remember being unable to think of anything to say. As I clambered over the rubble I saw a movement and a hand came up clutching a pair of false teeth. It's strange the things one wants to save at such moments.

We quickly moved to a new site, a team of high-powered engineers arrived, and within two days we were on the air again.

Life with the BBC was very different to working in a lawyer's office; the BBC cast its net wider when choosing its staff, who seemed infinitely more colourful. One day I found myself working alongside someone who supplemented his income by writing short stories for one of the London evening papers. From time to time a cheque would arrive and he would take us all out for a drink. I used to look at him and wonder how he managed it! He wasn't at all my idea of how a writer should look. He made it sound as if the art of creation was very easy; a matter of tossing something off when the fancy took him, which perhaps he did, although I doubt it.

I decided I wanted to do something creative, but not having "lived" as he had—he'd spent some time in the Merchant Navy—it needed to be something other than writing. I decided to try my hand at drawing and after a lot of thought and lying awake at night, came up with a cartoon showing a man with two heads. He was sitting behind a desk and the caption read "I always say, Smithers, two heads are better than one."

I sent it off to *Punch*. There was nothing like starting at the top. It came back fairly promptly with the inevitable rejection slip, but whoever returned it had done a very nice thing. It had "Sorry—try again" written across it, which meant my creative enthusiasm wasn't entirely dampened.

I kept the whole thing secret. Admission of failure has never come very easily to me. I had a lovely grandfather on my mother's side, who spent his last years living with us. A printer's compositor by trade, he suffered from bad eyesight, but always bought his glasses from Woolworth's—sixpence each part. If he could read the price clearly they were fine. He wore a cap, had a large waxed moustache, and smelled of bay rum which he used on his hair.

Like most grandfathers, he doted on his grandson. He used to say with pride that I could do anything if I tried and there was no knowing where I would end up. It wasn't, and certainly isn't true, but he instilled in me a deep belief that it is possible to do most things if you work hard enough at them. Remembering his words, I bought myself a book on how to draw and resolved to try again one day.

However, before that happened a more serious diversion arrived on the scene in the slender shape of a girl I called then, and still think of as "N. K." She called me by my initials too, and for over a year we enjoyed a beautiful and totally platonic love affair. I did lots of "first things" with her. I went to my first symphony concert and visited my first London theatre. Over endless cups of coffee in our favourite coffee shop we set the world to rights. I added to my list of authors and discovered Eric Linklater, Somerset Maugham, Graham Greene, Dashiell Hammett, Raymond Chandler, Freud, Alexander Woollcott, Dorothy Parker, Robert Benchley, P.G. Woclehouse, and many others.

We exchanged locker keys at work and left each other books. Sometimes, if we were on different shifts, she would use up her meagre rations to bake me a treacle tart which she would leave for me. One day she bought me a record of Frank Sinatra singing "All or Nothing at All." Perhaps she was trying to tell me something . . . perhaps there is no such thing as a purely platonic relationship . . . but I know that I loved her very much and the moments we spent together were totally unique and carefree and unforgettable.

But once again the war intervened. On my seventeenth birthday I volunteered to become a pilot in the Royal Air Force and three months later a notice arrived telling me to report to an RAF intake centre in Regent's Park, London.

I said goodbye to my mother who, taking a black-and-white view of things as ever, was convinced she would never see me again. In a way she was right, for emotionally at least, that was when I left home.

My father, who was working in London by then, insisted on accompanying me, taking a later train to do so. This put me in a bit of a quandary because N.K. had promised to meet me on Paddington Station. She was waiting when the train arrived, wearing a light blue cloche hat and looking very pretty. My father raised his hat to her and I said goodbye to him. I expect he knew that although, God willing, I would always come back, life as we had known it together had come to an end and he must have been very sad.

N.K. and I had a coffee together and then we, too, said goodbye, although we were to write to each other every day for over a year.

So began a period in my life which was no worse than it was for many millions of others, and certainly better than it was for the many who died or were wounded or taken prisoner and suffered at the hands of the enemy.

Later that day, inducted, inoculated, uniformed, shorn of my hair, and shouted at, I marched off in ragged fashion to the Regent's Park Zoo to be fed—the RAF had taken over the restaurant. Queuing up at the counter with my plate I eyed some lumpy mashed potato uneasily and asked the WAAF behind the counter if she would mind giving me only one helping. She told me I would get what I was fucking given and I retired hurt. I had never heard a woman swear before, and as I sat down and looked out of the window it struck me that

the regular inmates of the zoo were faring rather better than I was. At least their keepers treated them with respect. I wondered if I had done the right thing.

I was posted to Scarborough on the east coast where I did press-ups on the cold wet beach watched over by unhappy looking seagulls, learned to swim on my back in a pool which before the war had been condemned and was now in an even worse state, drilled, marched, and was given an enthusiasm for mathematics by an elderly master from Eton who had been called up as an instructor. He turned what had previously been an extremely dull subject into one which had elegance and precision and above all was not one to be frightened of. In between whiles the great treat was to go off to the local amusement arcade and listen to the Mills Brothers singing "Paper Doll" on the juke box. I ate enormous quantities of peanut butter and drank vast amounts of beer, but despite all that I was fitter than I had ever been before.

*

Three months later I arrived at Perth in Scotland to begin my flying training. Clad in my issue wool-lined fly-

RAF training in Canada: Bond second from right, front row (Photograph courtesy of Michael Bond)

ing boots, sheepskin jacket, and goggles, I climbed into the rear cockpit of a Tiger Moth, fastened my safety belt, and, feeling a very gay dog indeed, exchanged the thumbs-up signal with my instructor in the front cockpit as we prepared for take-off. It was the last thumbs-up signal I was to give for quite a while.

The truth of the matter was I had never been up in an aeroplane. Some years before, when we'd been on holiday, my father had wanted to take me on a five-shilling joy trip he'd seen advertised, but my grandfather put his foot down saying that if man had been meant to fly God would have given him wings, and that if I was taken up he would leave home, so I didn't go.

Trundling along the runway, I realised the truth of his words. My instructor looked over his shoulder, probably intending to give me another of his ghastly thumbs-up signs, and stared at me in total disbelief as I leant over the side of the cockpit in order to be sick.

Several barrel rolls later I was wishing I was dead. Each time the plane turned upside-down I fell a few inches before the safety belt took up the strain. Looking at the ground far below, I felt like unfastening the buckle. At least the parachute would get me down quicker.

It was a depressing discovery, but even more dispiriting was the fact that the RAF were not disposed to take immediate action. So unconvinced were they of the need to do any such thing that they sent me out to Canada to carry on with my flying training, this time as a navigator—an even worse position in those preradar days. Every movement was transmitted via the pencil point as you tried to work out the aircraft's position on a chart.

It was the winter of 1943, which was a bad time for crossing the Atlantic Ocean in a crowded troopship. The weather was foul and the German U-boat campaign was at its height. Squatting gloomily behind a watertight door in the bowels of the ship, knowing that if we were torpedoed I would have to shut myself in and die a quick but horrible death, I added chronic seasickness to my growing list of deficiencies.

Six months and a good many flying hours later, having finally convinced the powers that be that no amount of pills would cure me, and that a navigator whose sole ambition in life was to get back down to earth again by the quickest possible route was not ideal material, I was sent back to England.

Sad in some ways, relieved in others, I found myself one bitterly cold December morning huddled over a coke stove in a Nissen hut on the Isle of Sheppey discussing which of two options to accept: a transfer to the Army or a job as a coal miner. I chose the former and was sent to Edinburgh where I exchanged my blue uniform for one of khaki.

In the event it turned out to be a wise choice. Contrary to expectations I actually enjoyed my time in the British Army and when the time came for demobilisation

even toyed with the idea of signing on. I moved around a lot, carrying everything I needed in my kitbag, and saw parts of the world—including my own country—I might not otherwise have seen. It taught me many probably quite useless things. I learned how to take a Vickers machine gun to pieces blindfold and put it back together again—I was in the Middlesex, an Infantry Support Regiment. In a perverse kind of way I even got pleasure out of polishing my boots until I could see my face in them, cleaning behind my cap badge as well as the front, marching and drilling, and making up my bed to the regulation pattern—if it wasn't exactly right the S.M. would hurl it to the floor with his pace-stick. Most of all it taught me disciplines which at times seem sadly lacking in today's world, and it taught me how to look after myself if need be.

One day, our training completed, we were told to assemble in the drill hall. There we were addressed by a brass hat who had come up from London especially to tell us about our posting. We were being sent to a British possession in the Indian Ocean. He painted a very rosy picture of what life there would be like, of how we were to consider ourselves, each one of us, ambassadors of our country; but above all how lucky we were to be going to such a wonderful place. He saluted us and left.

Our joy was short lived. Hardly had the sound of his staff car died away than the R.S.M. brought us to attention. "Take no bleedin' notice of what you 'as just 'eard," he bellowed, with what seemed an unnecessary degree of relish. "You lot is 'eading for Heegypt!"

That night we set off for Dover and early next morning boarded a cross-channel steamer for Calais. It was as I stepped off the boat onto French soil that I fell in love again, instantly and for ever; not with a girl this time, but with a country.

I still don't know quite what it is about France, but to go there still fills me with excitement and anticipation; even coming across a picture in a gallery is enough to set my heart fluttering with a mixture of remembered smells, of places visited, of meals eaten—not necessarily *haute cuisine,* but perhaps just bread and cheese and a bottle of wine. The French seem to be born with an understanding of what life is all about and I never leave their shores without a feeling of sadness which takes several days to get over.

The first journey across France by train gave me ample opportunity to study the countryside. It was the winter of 1945 and with the war barely over there was hardly a five-mile stretch of railway line left undamaged. It took several days to reach the south. Many of the carriages were without windows and we sat shivering in our greatcoats and blankets as we chugged slowly on our way.

The sun was shining in Toulon and there I visited my first cafe. Lighting was by candle, for there was no electricity, and there was hardly anything to eat, but I drank my first glass of wine. To order a sandwich seemed wrong when back at camp we had so much.

By contrast, when we arrived in Egypt we suddenly found ourselves in a land of extremes; of unbelievable poverty existing alongside untold wealth, for King Farouk was still in power and corruption was everywhere. Contact with the opposite sex if you were in the ranks was almost nonexistent. Most of the A.T.S. understandably gravitated toward the officers' clubs or Shepheard's Hotel, which was out of bounds to lesser mortals. True, dusky "maidens" beckoned to us through the bead curtains of local bars, and there seemed to be an inexhaustible supply of "young English virgin schoolteachers" on offer by local touts who for some obscure reason felt that had to be the height of an Englishman's desire, but since the M.O. had warned us that they were all "poxed up to the eyebrows" they were resistible—just.

I never went anywhere in the Forces without attending a lecture from the M.O. warning of the dangers of consorting with the local girls. He'd certainly been right in Toulon. On the boat trip to Port Said half the regiment seemed to go down with something or other, and lurid tales of the treatment they received put me off.

In between futile fatigues aimed at keeping us occupied—like picking up stones in the desert "because they made it look untidy," saluting anything that moved and whitewashing anything that didn't, I sat down one evening and sublimated my desires of the flesh by writing a short story set in a sleazy Cairo bar. I called it "Captain Hazel's Piece of String" and I sent it to a magazine called *London Opinion*.

Some weeks later a cheque for seven guineas arrived out of the blue. I wish now I'd had it framed—I might just as well have done; the Army Post Office didn't want to know about it; neither did any of the local Arab traders, but apart from my first book nothing before or since has quite equalled the thrill of that first sale.

This was it—I was a writer, fame and fortune awaited me.

Admittedly I wasn't quite on a par with my then hero, Ernest Hemingway. *He* was getting paid something like a dollar a word for his despatches. I decided to work hard at developing a simple style which made use of lots of small words.

I wrote home telling my parents the good news and shortly afterwards received a letter from my mother saying they had read the story and it was very nice, but they were a bit worried about me! It taught me the perils of writing in the first person.

More followed; short stories, articles, radio plays. Over the next ten years I spent most of my leisure time writing and learned the hard way that success doesn't come

easily. It was a good year if I sold one in twelve. I acquired an agent who had faith in me. Looking back, he must have lost money for the first few years: no wonder he didn't write to me very often. Every letter telling me he had sold a radio play to some far-flung station of the Empire must have cost him his ten per cent.

By then I had come out of the Army and returned to the BBC, first as an engineer working in a department responsible for monitoring foreign news broadcasts, then as a cameraman in television, and had married my first wife, Brenda.

They were the best of times and the worst of times; probably neither of us were really prepared for marriage, but we plunged into it because it was there and seemed the thing to do. Finding a home, let alone setting one up, was hard just after the war. We found ourselves on separate shifts, saying a quick "hello" and" goodbye" as we came and went. Gradually we drifted apart until the point came when there was really no going back, but I could never say "I wish it hadn't happened," and we are still good friends. If it hadn't happened we wouldn't have had our daughter, Karen, and that is impossible to picture. Life would not be the same without her. And if we hadn't had a daughter I wouldn't now be a grandfather to an equally lovely girl called Robyn who was born on Christmas Day, 1984.

Karen and Brenda: Graduation Day, Exeter University, 1979 (Photograph courtesy of Michael Bond)

Almost at the same time as Karen was born I had my first book published: *A Bear Called Paddington.* A year before—Christmas Eve 1957 to be exact—conscious that I hadn't bought my wife anything very exciting in the way of a present, I wandered into a London store looking for ideas and found myself in the toy department. On one of the shelves I came across a small bear looking, I thought, very sorry for himself as he was the only one who hadn't been sold.

I bought him and because we were living near Paddington station at the time, we christened him Paddington. He sat on a shelf of our one-roomed apartment for a while, and then one day when I was sitting in front of my typewriter staring at a blank sheet of paper wondering what to write, I idly tapped out the words "Mr. and Mrs. Brown first met Paddington on a railway platform. In fact, that was how he came to have such an unusual name for a bear, for Paddington was the name of the station."

It was a simple act and, in terms of deathless prose, not exactly earth shattering, but it was to change my life considerably. I carried on from where I had left off and by the end of the day I had completed the first chapter; by the tenth day I found myself with a book on my hands.

It went the rounds of various publishers and was finally taken by Collins, who liked it enough to commission a second, then a third, until finally a whole series emerged. Unwittingly, and without intending it, I had become a children's author, and for the next twenty-odd years that was how it was to be.

Much of my previous work for radio and television had been in the realms of fantasy; stories about young men who found themselves stranded in a small French village on the night of a full moon; there would be a statue of a beautiful girl which would briefly and miraculously come to life . . . .

They were usually returned with "Sorry, we don't take fantasy" scrawled over the rejection slip.

One of the nice things about writing for children is their total acceptance of the fantastic. Give a child a stick and a patch of wet sand and it will draw the outline of a boat and accept it as such. I did learn though, that to make fantasy work you have to believe in it yourself. If an author doesn't believe in his inventions and his characters nobody else will. Paddington to me is, and always has been, very much alive.

In 1965 I gave up working in television in order to become a full-time writer. I did so with a certain amount of regret for I had enjoyed my time there. During my last few years with the BBC I had been a senior cameraman with my own crew and enjoyed it so much there were times when I could hardly believe I was actually being paid to do it. I was lucky enough to work there during the days when television went out live and there

was a certain *cachet* about the job. It more than satisfied my boyhood ambition to work behind the scenes in "show business," and there was nothing to equal the thrill of doing a fast track in on a large camera crane and ending up sharply in focus. When you didn't the whole world collapsed, much as a pilot must feel after a bumpy landing. Paradoxically, swinging around on a crane all day cured me of airsickness. During my fifteen-year stay I worked with most of the big names and it taught me something I have since learned for myself; the more successful you are at something, the harder you have to work. When coffee break is called, the Yehudi Menuhins and Margot Fonteyns of this world carry on practising; they never let up.

*

In the autumn of 1981 my mother fell ill. At first it was just a case of her rheumatism being worse than usual, then she stopped going out for her usual rides. Boiled sweets remained uneaten, books were left unread. Soon it became clear that something was seriously wrong.

Mercifully, the end, when it came, was swift. Her worst fears were realised. She went into hospital and never came out again.

I took my father in to see her and he, ever unobservant and seeing the best in things, came out puffing his pipe saying, "I thought your mother was looking a little better today." But she wasn't. I have never seen anyone look so ill or change so much in such a short space of time. Three days later she was dead, riddled with bone cancer.

The hospital was staffed by nuns and they were wonderfully kind and reassuring. Just before the end when I went to see her she tried to form words with her lips but nothing happened. I often wonder what she wanted to say.

I put an announcement of her death in the *Daily Telegraph* and it would undoubtedly have confirmed her views on that otherwise excellent newspaper, which she had long since cancelled on account of the large number of misprints it contained.

True to form, they got her name wrong: they put *Francess* instead of *Frances*.

After she had been cremated I was offered her ashes and didn't like to say no. They were in a large brown plastic pot with a screw top and I put them in the car boot. It was the start of a series of mishaps that would have tried her patience sorely.

I had the romantic notion of scattering them on the mill stream at Newbury, outside the house where both she and I had been born and where once, when she was small, she had been tossed by a mad bull which had escaped from the market and was charging along the towpath. Emotionally, although she hadn't lived there for fifty years or so, she had never left the Newbury of her childhood.

My plan got off to a bad start. The very next day I was having lunch with an old friend and for some reason or other the conversation turned to things people keep in their car boot. I guessed the contents of hers correctly, but when it came to mine she failed miserably and was quite cross when I told her about my mother's ashes. It cast a gloom over the meal.

The following day the weather changed and for one reason and another the urn stayed where it was for several weeks. When I did find myself in the West Country the car broke down and I had to go back to London by train. I decided to put plan "B" into action and scatter the ashes over the railway line as we went through Newbury. But the carriage was crowded, so at the appropriate moment I went along to the toilet, only to discover the window was too small. By then it was too late.

When my car was ready for collection I drove back via Newbury, determined to do the deed come what may, and for the first time in some forty years made my way to West Mills. It wasn't quite as I remembered it. The mill house was still there and so was the lock-keeper's cottage, but the towpath was crowded and obviously used as a short cut from one part of the town to another. I hung around for a while furtively clutching a carrier bag containing the plastic pot, ignoring curious glances from passersby. Eventually there was a lull and I seized my opportunity. Undoing the screw top, I began empty-

ing the contents into the fast-flowing river. There were rather more ashes than I had expected and a large black cloud rose from the water and disappeared round the corner past the lock-keeper's cottage. Fearing that I was probably breaking all sorts of bylaws to do with pollution, I hastily replaced the cap and made my way back into town, where I wandered around for a while wondering whether or not to deposit the rest of the remains into a wastepaper bin. I'm sure that's what my mother would have done—I sensed how impatient she would have been by then, but it didn't seem right. In the end I drove a few miles out of town to Savernake Forest, a place she had often spoken of fondly and where she'd had many picnics as a child, and scattered the remaining ashes in a damp glade.

It had always been assumed, most of all by my mother, that my father would die before her. I think she always nursed plans of what she would do. They had married very young and she had devoted her life to looking after him. He never went outside the door without what she called a "square meal" inside him, and never had a loose button or an undarned sock. I doubt if he'd ever had to boil a kettle in his life, let alone an egg. In short, at the age of eighty-three he was ill-equipped to fend for himself.

Since we weren't in a position to have him live with us permanently, the first assumption led to a second. He would go into a home where he would be well looked

Robyn, Michael, Anthony, and Sue, Christmas 1985 (Photograph courtesy of Michael Bond)

after. But he would have none of that. He dug his heels in, and when my father dug his heels in there was no shifting him.

We fetched him up to London regularly at weekends and kept him well supplied with food. He developed a great liking for biscuits, which he said my mother had never bought him while she was alive, and he enjoyed a new lease of life, meeting new people he could tell his stories to, people who until then had only been names he'd heard me talk about.

He remained a civil servant until his death; always reading the small print. One Christmas, knowing his great liking for facts and figures, I bought him a copy of *The Guinness Book of World Records,* thinking it might be something he could dip into from time to time. The next time he came up he said he had got to page twenty-three and he was enjoying it very much indeed.

In his last years he often used to quote a mysterious "they." *They* say it's all going to happen in 1984. It was useless trying to explain that *1984* was the title of a book by George Orwell. "Ah!" was all he would say darkly. "That's next year, you know."

He didn't quite make it anyway. One evening some two years after my mother died, he folded his napkin after supper. It took him an agonisingly long time, for he was a very tidy man and liked to get it right, but we knew we mustn't interfere. Then, after shaking hands all round as he always did and thanking us for a lovely day, he tottered off to his room.

The next morning when he didn't appear for breakfast I went in to wake him and found him lying across the bed where he'd fallen. It was a strange feeling that suddenly I was the last in the line, with no-one to turn to.

A few days later I went through his belongings. His whole life was done up in neat piles; receipts, letters, official documents, certificates of birth and marriage, and last but not least, a list of addresses and telephone numbers of those who needed to be informed of his passing.

*

It's always hard to know where to end an autobiography. There is a point in one's life where things which happened before are in the past and can be talked about without fear of hurting anyone; after that the opposite is true.

If I seem to have dwelt a lot on others, my parents in particular, it's because I believe that although we have the power to shape our own destinies—put a hundred people in the same situation and they will go their different ways, we are in the end the sum of the people and events we meet on the way. If my mother hadn't read to me every night before I went to bed, if I hadn't

Michael Bond, 1984 (Photograph courtesy of Michael Bond)

been brought up in a house where books were part of the furniture, if I hadn't happened to be with my father when I passed a newsagent and been introduced to the *Magnet,* if I hadn't been to Mr. Jackson's leaving party, or answered an advertisement for the BBC, or fallen in love with N. K., I might not have become a writer.

Half of me always rebelled against my parents' conformity and wanted to escape, but they gave me many things for which I shall always be grateful.

For me, everything that happened before Karen was born, apart from work, is in the past. Other matters, like my eventual divorce and the bit in between that and re-marriage are still too recent and too personal.

It precludes talking about my son, Anthony, of whom I am very proud and have no fears for. It precludes talking about my second wife, Sue, who breathed fresh life into me at a time when nothing much seemed to matter. It precludes talking about many things, for the time being at least, but doubtless they will all turn up somewhere at some time. Writers tend to use anything and everything that happens to them. Life is their raw material.

I have never been a great one for going back. Perhaps that explains why, two or three years ago, when I was in Fortnum & Mason looking at some china and a woman came up to me and passed some quite innocuous and yet curiously phrased comment, I did nothing about it. I waited for a little while, feeling my heart pounding. I had a strange feeling that it was N.K. but when I looked around she had gone. I went outside into the street, but she was nowhere in sight. Perhaps, if it *was* her, she felt the same way too.

In recent years I have gone back to adult fiction, putting down on paper an idea which had been simmering away in my mind for some years. A long-time admirer of Georges Simenon and his wonderful creation, Inspector Maigret, I had been wanting to write about a detective who was all that Maigret wasn't; someone who solved his crimes by accident rather than design, and because humour is what I feel I am best at, they had to be humorous situations.

I had the name—Pamplemousse—and he was to have a dog called Pommes Frites that would help him in all his cases. Originally I planned to make him the last detective in Paris to ride a bicycle. I even bought myself a French machine with dropped handlebars and a ten-speed gear. But when I tried it out, the roads seemed bumpier than I'd remembered them, the hills were steeper, and the hard leather saddle was doing me no good at all. On my first outing I met the vicar who called out, "Ah, saving fuel, I see!" I put it back in the garage where it has remained ever since.

Then one day I was eating at a restaurant called "Pic" in Valence and I happened to order a dish called *Poulet de Bresse en Vessie*—a chicken from Bresse which is cooked in a pig's bladder. It was brought to the table, presented for approval, and then with due ceremony the head waiter picked up a knife to open up the outer casing. I suddenly wondered what would happen if, on cutting it open, he revealed not a chicken, but something else. . . .

In a flash it jelled. Monsieur Pamplemousse would be a defrocked ex-member of the Paris Sûreté turned food inspector. It would be a reason for his travelling all over France—something that had been a bit of a stumbling block with my original notion, and everywhere he went he could get involved in some kind of crime. Pommes Frites would act as his unofficial taster as well as helping him solve his cases. I couldn't wait to get back to England and start work.

Four books later I still look forward to writing the next one. There is the pre-planning to do; a new area of France to visit in order to get local colour. If, for example, I write something quite simple like "Monsieur Pamplemousse gazed out of the hotel window at Lake Geneva," it raises the immediate question—what does he see? Can he see across to the other side? What sort of boats are there?

And because he is, after all, a food inspector, there are meals to be eaten, local specialities to be sought out and tried, wines to be drunk.

Writing is a lonely occupation, but it's also a selfish one. When things get bad, as they do for everyone from time to time, writers are able to shut themselves away from it, peopling the world with their characters, making them behave the way they want them to behave, saying the things they want to hear. Sometimes they take over and stubbornly refuse to do what you tell them to do, but usually they are very good.

Sometimes I am Paddington walking down Windsor Gardens en route to the Portobello Road to buy his morning supply of buns, but if I don't fancy that I can always be Monsieur Pamplemousse, sitting outside a cafe enjoying the sunshine over a baguette split down the middle and filled with ham, and a glass of red wine. I wouldn't wish for anything nicer.

*

Bond contributed the following update to his essay in 2012:

The last paragraph feels as though it might have been written a million years ago, or only yesterday, which is equally nonsensical, of course. But the pace of life has

Paddington welcomes old and new friends. (Photograph courtesy of Michael Bond)

Anthony at the ready (Photograph courtesy of Michael Bond)

increased so much over the years, there are times when I need to put my thinking cap on to remember with any degree of certainty what happened twenty-four hours ago.

Looking back on my life, although I didn't realise it until long after the event, 1926 wasn't the best of times to be born. At midnight on May 5, the first general strike in Britain's history was called, and three years later the New York Stock Exchange suffered its worst day ever and crashed. October 29 became known as "Black Saturday."

The ripples from both these major events spread far and wide. Times were hard, but I had no reason to believe they were anything other than normal and my parents did all they could to make sure it stayed that way.

In those pre-television days, apart from the radio, my awareness of what was going on in the world was almost entirely derived from cinema newsreels. Toward the end of the thirties it seemed as though every time I went to the cinema, Hitler had invaded yet another European country. Whole families fled for their lives down country roads with all their worldly possession crammed into a pram, often with a baby perched on top. The images I saw then have remained with me. To my way of thinking, there are few sadder sights, and I have them very much in mind when I am writing about Paddington.

During my lifetime the world has become noticeably smaller, and with the growth of air travel few places are beyond the reach of anyone with the urge to travel. When I wrote the first "Paddington" book, I picked on Peru as being the land of his birth, partly because there were still bears living there, but also because it sounded remote and mysterious. I didn't dream that one day, not only would the Machu Picchu trail be alive to the sound

of voices as fans sought out where Paddington might have been born and brought up, but there would also be a bronze statue of him on the railway station that gave rise to his name.

All of which is very wonderful, but on the other side of the coin countries have lost their individuality and branches of Starbucks and Tesco pop up in the most surprising places. The plus side, from a writer's point of view, is that new markets have opened up, particularly in Eastern Europe and the Orient. Give that, and the rise of e-books, who knows where it will end?

I used to think that as I grew older I would spend the long winter evenings sticking boxfuls of photographs into albums, but I doubt if that will ever happen and by now most of them will have begun to fade anyway. However, science has come to my aid, as it has in so many other ways. With the invention of digital cameras I can now store as many pictures as I wish; all instantly retrievable at the press of a button. It's so much less time consuming and a great deal tidier.

All I know for certain is that I now have not one, but three lovely grandchildren; Harry and India arrived during the interim period, making a wonderfully varied trio with their elder sister, Robyn. My son, Anthony Barwell, rather than follow in his father's footsteps as a cameraman in television, is successfully ploughing his own furrow as a producer/director in a medium that has changed out of all recognition.

In 2008 Paddington celebrated his fiftieth anniversary with a long line of books, television programmes, and other activities to his credit. In 2011, another creation I fathered, a guinea-pig called Olga da Polga, celebrated her fortieth anniversary with a special edition of the first book in the series. And there are now seventeen "Monsieur Pamplemousse" books.

How and when did it all this happen? I sometimes ask myself. If my lovely grandfather could only see me now! Hopefully, to quote the poet Laurence Binyon, "Age shall not weary them."

I see writing as a job of work. It is what I do for a living. People who know exactly what being a bank manager involves, or an accountant (they don't, of course), tend to treat writers as though they have some God-given gift. At signing sessions they nudge each other as they draw near, and children especially become tongue tied when it's their turn.

The stock questions are a dead give-away. "How long does it take to write a book?" Answer: "As long as it takes." Or: "Where do you get all your ideas from?" Answer: "From the world around me." These answers sound most unsatisfactory; more like a brush off. The fact is that whatever you end up doing in life, your mind adjusts itself to the task in hand. A London taxi-driver, for example, after three years or so doing "the knowledge," has a comprehensive road map of the vast city implanted in his brain for ever more and thinks nothing of it.

Ideas don't grow on trees. If you are a writer, it isn't a case of wonderful things happening to you, the kind that never happen to other people, but your mind grows accustomed to making use of even the simplest events—a street sign, a snatch of overheard conversation: all is grist to the mill for use sooner or later. It's partly a matter of keeping your eyes open to the world around you. Most teenagers you see on the streets seem to be looking downwards rather than up, and if you take the Eurostar from London to Paris, their elders are often glued to their laptops rather than viewing the passing scene.

When I first had dreams of becoming a writer I spent hours gazing out of the window trying to think up plots. Plots came first, and characters took second place. Had I wished, I could literally have papered the walls with rejection slips.

A great many things came together when I wrote *A Bear Called Paddington,* but perhaps the most funda-mental thing of all was that the story was character driven, and in the words of Graham Greene: "Character is plot." If I were to add anything at all to his simple statement it would be a reminder that if an author doesn't believe in his character, why should anyone else?

There is more to it than that, of course. The great idea you wake up with in the early hours of the morning, or when you are out for a walk far from home—that wonderful moment when you can see it all in your mind's eye, picture the characters, hear every word of the dialogue—rapidly fade when the big moment of committing it to paper arrives. Somehow, the very first words are never quite how you had pictured them. It's when the hard work begins: a wearisome process of distillation.

I have always written to please myself on the basis that we all have a small voice deep inside us that says whether something is right or wrong, and you ignore it at your peril. Creating a well-finished story with a beginning, a middle, and an end is much like the work of a carpenter making a cabinet; there are no short cuts and real job satisfaction only comes with the final polish.

Sue with Olga da Polga (Photograph courtesy of Michael Bond)

It is nowhere as simple as that, of course. By the same token, a three-star Michelin chef will happily commit the list of ingredients for his or her recipe to a cookery book, along with full instructions on how to prepare their prize "signature dish," secure in the knowledge that very few readers—most of them lacking both "the passion" and the years spent slaving away in a hot kitchen—will come anywhere near emulating the same end result as they do, time after time. Getting to that point is a long, hard grind.

On the whole, most fictional characters are based on a real-life person, if only someone who briefly met up with the author and left an impression. By the time they have been played around with they are often far removed from the original. My lovely first agent, Harvey Unna, often remarked that people seldom recognise themselves anyway. I don't think he ever realised he was the role model for Paddington's best friend, Mr. Gruber, who runs an antique shop in the Portobello Road. Paradoxically it proves his point.

On the other hand, the bear who was my inspiration is nothing like the one in the books anyway—he is much too small for a start, but to me he is very real. He is with me in spirit while I am writing about his adventures, and I see the world with all its crazy manmade Health and Safety rules and regulations through his eyes, which act as yet another window on the world. Although by definition the books are classified as being meant for children, they aren't aimed at any particular age group. Most children hate being written down to and, provided the meaning is clear within the context, they often latch on to long words, even if they do mispronounce them; treating them with relish, as I did when I was small and "established" became "estuarated."

I also believe stories in picture books for younger children should be enjoyed as much by the person doing the reading as the one being read to, so they are always written with that in mind. I believe, as my father did, that the most precious thing you can give a small child is your time. Second only to that is a bedtime story last thing at night, so that it becomes a shared experience; one that will last a lifetime.

I consider myself lucky to be in a profession where you don't have to retire; publishers don't expect you to, loyal readers hope you won't, and I really don't know what I would do with myself if I did.

The passage of time in my life as a writer can really be measured by the changing tools of the trade: first the pen, then the upright Remington typewriter, followed by the IBM golf-ball with the best keyboard ever. Then a series of computers until, following the demise of Windows (XP still my favourite in the series), an Apple. I suppose each change affects a writer's style to a greater or lesser extent; one always hopes it's for the better.

The big plus about having a computer if you work at home is that you come downstairs in the morning, press a few buttons, and there are words on the screen. The days of staring at a blank sheet of paper in a typewriter are long since gone. Whole blocks of text can be moved around, reshaping things as you go, which is an enormous boon.

When things are going well, it's a wonderful way of earning a living. When they aren't, you need a very understanding partner. Even with the best will in the world, you know deep down you are hard to live with. But I am many times blessed in that respect. Not only does my wife, Sue, treat my gloomy moments with great fortitude, I value her opinion. She is an excellent proof reader and, being a good cook, she comes up with the kind of marmalade even Paddington would be hard put to find fault with.

I've just begun work on the eighteenth "Monsieur Pamplemousse" book. The opening chapter is complete. I'm not sure where he will take me, but it will be somewhere in France, so for the time being I shall be seeing the world through his eyes, along with those of his faithful hound Pommes Frites.

I look forward to yet another voyage of discovery. Who knows where it will end? For the time being I have absolutely no idea. That's one of the joys of writing!

* * *

BRIGHT, Alasdair

Personal

Born in England. *Hobbies and other interests:* Drawing wildlife.

Addresses

Home—Bedford, England. *E-mail*—info@brighcreative. co.uk.

Career

Illustrator. Royal Society for the Protection of Birds, Sandy, England, member of staff for eight years; freelance illustrator and designer, beginning 2001. *Exhibitions:* Work exhibited in galleries, including Bromham Mill Gallery, Bromham, England, 2009, and Eagle Gallery, Bedford, England, 2012.

Illustrator

Michael Morpurgo, *The Marble Crusher, and Other Stories,* Egmont (London, England), 2002, selection published as *The Marble Crusher,* 2007.

Jenny Oldfield, *Bright Eyes,* Hodder Children's Books (London, England), 2006.

Jenny Oldfield, *Dawn Light,* Hodder Children's Books (London, England), 2006.

Jenny Oldfield, *Midnight Snow,* Hodder Children's Books (London, England), 2006.

Jenny Oldfield, *Summer Shadows,* Hodder Children's (London, England), 2006.

Patricia Reilly Giff, *Big Whopper,* Yearling (New York, NY), 2010.

Patricia Reilly Giff, *Number One Kid,* Wendy Lamb Books (New York, NY), 2010.

Patricia Reilly Giff, *Flying Feet,* Yearling (New York, NY), 2011.

Patricia Reilly Giff, *Star Time,* Wendy Lamb Books (New York, NY), 2011.

Patricia Reilly Giff, *Bears Beware,* Wendy Lamb Books (New York, NY), 2012.

Patricia Reilly Giff, *Super Surprise,* Wendy Lamb Books (New York, NY), 2012.

Biographical and Critical Sources

PERIODICALS

Kirkus Reviews, July 15, 2010, review of *Number One Kid.*

School Library Journal, August, 2010, Amanda Moss Struckmeyer, review of *Number One Kid,* p. 76; July, 2011, Amy Commers, review of *Flying Feet,* p. 67.

ONLINE

Alasdair Bright Home Page, http://www.brightcreative.co.uk (August 1, 2012).

Circus of Illustration Web log, http://bedfordshireillustrators.tumblr.com/ (August 1, 2012), Marisa Straccia, interview with Bright.*

*   *   *

BURLEIGH, Robert 1936-

Personal

Born January 4, 1936, in Chicago, IL; married; children: three. *Education:* DePauw University, bachelor's degree, 1957; University of Chicago, M.A. (humanities), 1962.

Addresses

Home and office—Chicago, IL. *E-mail*—roburleigh@earthlink.net.

Career

Author and artist. Worked for Society of Visual Education as a writer and artist. *Exhibitions:* Work has appeared in group exhibitions and in solo exhibitions, under pseudonym Burleigh Kronquist, at ARC Gallery, Chicago, IL, 1988; Southport Gallery, Chicago, 1988,

Robert Burleigh (Photograph by Mike Burleigh. Reproduced by permission.)

1995; Artemisia Gallery, Chicago, 1992, 1994; University Club, Chicago, 1994; IDAO Gallery, Chicago, 1998, 1999, 2000; DePauw University Gallery, Greencastle, IN, 2002; O.K. Harris Works of Art, New York, NY, 2001, 2005; and Riverside Arts Center, Riverside, IL, 2006.

Member

Society of Children's Book Writers and Illustrators.

Awards, Honors

Orbis Pictus Award, 1992, for *Flight;* Notable Children's Book selection, American Library Association (ALA), Children's Choice selection, International Reading Association/Children's Book Council, and 100 Titles for Reading and Sharing selection and Books for the Teen Age selection, both New York Public Library, all 1997, all for *Hoops;* Notable Children's Trade Book in the Language Arts, 1998, for *Who Said That?;* Orbis Pictus Honor Book selection, 1999, for *Black Whiteness,* and 2005, for *Seurat and La Grande Jatte;* Best Children's Book selection, New York Society Literary Awards, 2001, for *Looking for Bird in the Big City;* Oppenheim Toy Portfolio Platinum Award, 2003, for *Earth from Above;* (with Ronde and Tiki Barber) Christopher Award, 2005, for *Game Day;* ALA Notable Book selection, 2005, for *Toulouse-Lautrec;* NAACP Image Award, 2005, for *Langston's Train Ride;* Notable Social-Studies Trade Book for Young People selection, 2009, National Council for the Social Studies/Children's Book Council

(CBC), 2009, for *Abraham Lincoln Comes Home;* Best Books selection, Bank Street College of Education, 2009, for *Clang! Clang! Beep! Beep!*; Outstanding Science Trade Book selection, National Science Teachers Association/CBC, 2010, for *One Giant Leap*, 2011, for *Into the Woods;* Prairie State Award, Illinois Reading Council, 2011.

Writings

A Man Named Thoreau, illustrated by Lloyd Bloom, Atheneum (New York, NY), 1985.

Flight: The Journey of Charles Lindbergh, illustrated by Mike Wimmer, Philomel (New York, NY), 1991.

Who Said That? Famous Americans Speak, illustrated by David Catrow, Holt (New York, NY), 1997.

Hoops, illustrated by Stephen T. Johnson, Silver Whistle (San Diego, CA), 1997.

Home Run: The Story of Babe Ruth, illustrated by Mike Wimmer, Silver Whistle (San Diego, CA), 1998.

Black Whiteness: Admiral Byrd Alone in the Antarctic, illustrated by Walter Lyon Krudop, Atheneum (New York, NY), 1998.

It's Funny Where Ben's Train Takes Him, illustrated by Joanna Yardley, Orchard (New York, NY), 1999.

Hercules, illustrated by Raul Colón, Silver Whistle (San Diego, CA), 1999.

Edna, illustrated by Joanna Yardley, Orchard (New York, NY), 2000.

Messenger, Messenger, illustrated by Barry Root, Atheneum (New York, NY), 2000.

Lookin' for Bird in the Big City, illustrated by Marek Los, Harcourt (San Diego, CA), 2001.

I Love Going through This Book, illustrated by Dan Yaccarino, HarperCollins (New York, NY), 2001.

Goal, illustrated by Stephen T. Johnson, Harcourt (San Diego, CA), 2001.

Chocolate: Riches from the Rainforest, Abrams (New York, NY), 2002.

Pandora, illustrated by Raul Colón, Harcourt (San Diego, CA), 2002.

The Secret of the Great Houdini, illustrated by Leonid Gore, Simon & Schuster (New York, NY), 2002.

Into the Air: The Story of the Wright Brothers' First Flight, illustrated by Bill Wylie, Silver Whistle (San Diego, CA), 2002.

Into the Woods: John James Audubon Lives His Dream, illustrated by Wendell Minor, Atheneum (New York, NY), 2003.

(Editor) *Earth from Above for Young Readers,* photographs by Yann Arthus Bertrand, illustrated by David Giraudon, Abrams (New York, NY), 2003.

(Editor) *Volcanoes: Journey to the Crater's Edge,* photographs by Philippe Bourseiller, illustrated by David Giraudon, Abrams (New York, NY), 2003.

(Editor) *The Sea: Exploring Life on an Ocean Planet,* photographs by Philip Plisson, illustrated by Emmanuel Cerisier, Abrams (New York, NY), 2003.

Amelia Earhart: Free in the Skies, illustrated by Bill Wylie, Silver Whistle (San Diego, CA), 2003.

Langston's Train Ride, illustrated by Leonard Jenkins, Orchard (New York, NY), 2004.

American Moments: Scenes from American History, illustrated by Bruce Strachan, Holt (New York, NY), 2004.

Seurat and La Grande Jatté: Connecting the Dots, Abrams (New York, NY), 2004.

(With Tiki and Ronde Barber) *By My Brother's Side,* illustrated by Barry Root, Simon & Schuster (New York, NY), 2004.

(With Tiki and Ronde Barber) *Game Day,* illustrated by Barry Root, Simon & Schuster (New York, NY), 2005.

Toulouse-Lautrec: The Moulin Rouge and the City of Light, Abrams (New York, NY), 2005.

(With Tiki and Ronde Barber) *Teammates,* illustrated by Barry Root, Simon & Schuster (New York, NY), 2006.

Paul Cézanne: A Painter's Journey, Abrams (New York, NY), 2006.

(With Jorge Posada) *Play Ball!,* Simon & Schuster (New York, NY), 2006.

Tiger of the Snows: Tenzing Norgay: The Boy Whose Dream Was Everest, illustrated by Ed Young, Atheneum (New York, NY), 2006.

Stealing Home: Jackie Robinson: Against the Odds, illustrated by Mike Wimmer, Simon & Schuster (New York, NY), 2007.

Napoleon: The Story of the Little Corporal, Abrams (New York, NY), 2007.

Fly, Cher Ami, Fly!: The Pigeon Who Saved the Lost Battalion, illustrated by Robert MacKenzie, Abrams (New York, NY), 2008.

Abraham Lincoln Comes Home, illustrated by Wendell Minor, Holt (New York, NY), 2008.

Clang! Clang! Beep! Beep! Listen to the City, illustrated by Beppe Giacobbe, Simon & Schuster (New York, NY), 2009.

One Giant Leap, illustrated by Mike Wimmer, Philomel (New York, NY), 2009.

Good-bye, Sheepie, illustrated by Peter Catalanotto, Marshall Cavendish Children (Tarrytown, NY), 2010.

Night Flight: Amelia Earhart Crosses the Atlantic, illustrated by Wendell Minor, Simon & Schuster Books for Young Readers (New York, NY), 2011.

The Adventures of Mark Twain by Huckleberry Finn, illustrated by Barry Blitt, Atheneum Books for Young Readers (New York, NY), 2011.

Flight of the Last Dragon, illustrated by Mary GrandPré, Philomel Books (New York, NY), 2012.

George Bellows: Painter with a Punch!, Abrams Books for Young Readers (Washington, DC), 2012.

If You Spent a Day with Thoreau at Walden Pond, illustrated by Wendell Minor, Christy Ottaviano Books (New York, NY), 2012.

How High Is the Sky? The Woman Who Measured the Stars, illustrated by Raúl Colón, Simon & Schuster Books for Young Readers (New York, NY), 2013.

OTHER

(With Mary Jane Gray) *Basic Writing Skills,* Society for Visual Education (Chicago, IL), 1976.

The Triumph of Mittens: Poems, Boardwell-Kloner (Chicago, IL), 1980.

Colonial America, illustrated by James Seward, Doubleday (Garden City, NY), 1992.

Writer and producer of over one hundred filmstrips and cassettes on educational subjects.

Adaptations

Abraham Lincoln Comes Home was adapted for both DVD and CD, Spoken Arts, 2009.

Sidelights

A writer of informational books of biography and history as well as a poet, Robert Burleigh is noted for introducing complex historical topics to young readers in an accessible and effective manner. Using a picture book format, the author presents facts about his subjects—often notable Americans such as Henry David Thoreau, Charles Lindbergh, Harry Houdini, Admiral Richard Byrd, and Jackie Robinson—in simple language and present-tense narration. Burleigh favors clipped, staccato texts in both his prose and his poetry, thereby expressing the ideas, drama, and importance of each of his topics in an evocative fashion. Reviewers have also noted the successful marriage of the author's texts with the illustrations of such artists as Lloyd Bloom, Ed Young, Raúl Colón, Beppe Giacobbe, and Wendell Minor. "While the subjects vary," Burleigh remarked on his home page, "my books are linked philosophically, stylistically and structurally by my wish to capture where possible the emotional intensity—the essence—of whatever the subject is."

Nineteenth-century writer and philosopher Henry David Thoreau is the subject of Burleigh's first illustrated biography. Considered a balanced overview of Tho-

Cover of Burleigh's picture-book biography **Napoleon,** *which features contemporary images of the nineteenth-century French emperor and his age.* (Painting by Jacques-Louis David. Copyright © 2007. Reproduced by permission of Abrams Books for Young Readers, an imprint of Abrams. All rights reserved.)

reau's life and influence, *A Man Named Thoreau* addresses its subject's time at Walden Pond, his love for nature, his literary works, and his advocacy of civil disobedience, among other topics. Burleigh presents Thoreau and his ideas by combining biographical facts with quotes from the philosopher's most popular work, *Walden.* Writing in *School Library Journal,* Ruth Semrau asserted that *A Man Named Thoreau* "unfolds new pleasures on every page" and provides young readers with an "exquisitely simple introduction to a difficult subject," while David E. White observed in *Horn Book* that the quotations "interspersed throughout the text . . . are beneficial in capturing the essence of this noted figure." A reviewer for the *Bulletin of the Center for Children's Books* also praised Burleigh's work in *A Man Named Thoreau,* declaring that to "have simplified concepts so much without distortion is a gift to the younger reader or listener."

Another nineteenth-century American is Burleigh's focus in *Into the Woods: John James Audubon Lives His Dream.* Here the author uses rhyming couplets to communicate the famous American naturalist's decision to give up a job in business in favor of wandering through the wilderness, painting and drawing the sights to be seen. A *Publishers Weekly* reviewer wrote of the book that Audubon's "philosophy wafts through the volume like a summer breeze," and a *Kirkus Reviews* critic called *Into the Woods* a "tribute" to Audubon and a "feast for bird lovers."

In the award-winning *Flight: The Journey of Charles Lindbergh* Burleigh takes to the skies, describing Lindbergh's famous non-stop flight from New York to Paris in 1927. Basing his text on the famed pilot's memoir *The Spirit of St. Louis* he focuses on Lindbergh's historic journey, which was undertaken when the aviator was twenty-five years old. Once again, the author was praised for successfully conveying a sophisticated concept—in this case the difficulty of, as *New York Times Book Review* contributor Signe Wilkinson explained, "staying awake, alert and in charge of a plane and one's life for two days and a very long, lonely night"—to an audience "too young to appreciate what pulling an all-nighter feels like." In *Horn Book* Ann A. Flowers remarked that Burleigh's use of the present tense "keeps the reader in suspense from the moment the plane takes off until [its arrival in] Paris" and deemed *Flight* "splendidly and excitingly presented." Burleigh's use of sentence fragments and single-sentence paragraphs "conveys the excitement of Lindbergh's historic flight," noted a critic in *Kirkus Reviews,* the reviewer recommending the picture book as one "that brings new life to one of the stories of the [twentieth] century."

Aviatrix Amelia Earhart is Burleigh's focus in the picture books *Amelia Earhart: Free in the Skies* and *Night Flight,* the latter illustrated by Minor. In *Night Flight* the years is 1932 and Earhart is about to embark on what will become the first solo flight across the Atlantic Ocean by a woman. Along with quotes from Earhart,

Burleigh's high-flying story in **Night Flight** *gains energy from Wendell Minor's detailed paintings.* (Illustration copyright © 2011 by Wendell Minor. Reproduced by permission of Simon & Schuster Books for Young Readers, an imprint of Simon & Schuster Children's Publishing Division.)

the author interjects "terse two-sentence stanzas . . . focused on the flight's trials," noted Karen Cruze in *Booklist,* and Minor's paintings in dynamic blues and reds "maintain tension by alternating between cockpit closeups" and images of Earhart's airborne plane. The combination of "gripping narrative and dynamic art immediately pull readers into the story," asserted a *Publishers Weekly* contributor in reviewing *Night Flight,* the critic concluding of storyhour audiences that "hearts will be racing."

In his picture book *Black Whiteness: Admiral Byrd Alone in the Antarctic* Burleigh chronicles the British explorer's incredible six-month stay alone in the Antarctic. Based on Byrd's daily journal and illustrated by Walter Lyon Krudop, *Black Whiteness* evokes the adventure's enduring hardships: sub-zero temperatures, continuous darkness with limited lighting equipment, and loneliness. "Burleigh's spare prose eloquently captures the spartan surroundings in which Byrd conducted daily meteorological studies," observed a critic in *Kirkus Reviews,* the writer going on to call the explorer's story "severe, often depressing, and always riveting."

Another story of snowbound adventure, Burleigh's *Tiger of the Snows: Tenzing Norgay: The Boy Whose Dream Was Everest* was described as "a stunning and lyrical ode to a contemplative man and his amazing achievement" by *School Library Journal* reviewer Be Astengo. The work examines the life of the Nepalese Sherpa who joined Sir Edmund Hillary as one of the first men to climb Mount Everest in 1953.

Shifting from adventure to sports, Burleigh crafts a picture-book look at one of baseball's most widely known heroes in *Home Run: The Story of Babe Ruth,* while in *Hoops* and *Goal* he describes basketball and soccer in verses that are filled with tactile imagery capturing the way each game feels to its players. "An ode to the game for older children, veteran players, and NBA fans," according to a *Publishers Weekly* reviewer, *Hoops* "will give language to teenagers' experience both on and off the court." A *Kirkus Reviews* critic noted that *Goal* uses soccer as a frame "to demonstrate the power of teamwork to achieve success" and dubbed Burleigh's book "a real winner."

Another baseball hero is Burleigh's focus in *Stealing Home: Jackie Robinson: Against the Odds,* which offers biographical information about the man who broke Major League Baseball's color barrier and depicts an electrifying moment from the 1955 World Series. "Burleigh's text features vivid, sharp images," noted GraceAnne A. DeCandido in her *Booklist* review of *Stealing Home.*

A classic American literary hero meets his maker in *The Adventures of Mark Twain by Huckleberry Finn,* a picture book in which fictional Huck Finn tells the story of Samuel Clemens, the author who created him out of a mix of real-life experiences and imagination. In a vernacular text that *Booklist* contributor Ian Chipman characterized as "undeniably cheery," Huck describes Clements' childhood in the American south, his work as a steamboat captain and newspaper journalist, and his adventures prospecting for gold and serving in the U.S. military prior to finding success as a writer and humorist. Cartoonist Barry Blitt captures the spirit of Burleigh's text with "exaggerated, tall-tale figures and period charm aplenty," according to Chipman, and a *Publishers Weekly* critic asserted that *The Adventures of Mark Twain by Huckleberry Finn* "begs to be read aloud with a backwoods twang."

Several of Burleigh's biographical picture books introduce readers to African-American culture. In *Lookin' for Bird in the Big City* a teenaged Miles Davis, trumpet in hand, makes music on the city streets as he goes in search of his hero, Charlie Parker. Here the author employs poetic language and rhythms to convey the flavor of jazz music and the enthusiasm Davis feels for it. "Words and art harmonize in this creatively imagined account," observed a *Publishers Weekly* reviewer, while *School Library Journal* contributor Mary Elam concluded that *Lookin' for Bird in the Big City* offers "a lovely and lyrical look at this all-American art form."

In *Langston's Train Ride* Burleigh chronicles a significant episode in the life of Harlem Renaissance writer Langston Hughes: a cross-country train ride during which Hughes composed his famous poem "The Negro Speaks of Rivers." Wendy Lukehart, writing in *School Library Journal,* applauded the author's "well-crafted, first-person narration" and a *Publishers Weekly* contributor predicted that *Langston's Train Ride* may well prompt readers "to reach out for their dreams."

In* Stealing Home *Burleigh joins artist Mike Wimmer in capturing a highlight in the career of baseball great Jackie Robinson. (Illustration copyright © 2007 by Mike Wimmer. All rights reserved. Reprinted with the permission of Simon & Schuster Books for Young Readers, an imprint of Simon & Schuster Children's Publishing Division.)

Burleigh, who paints under the pseudonym Burleigh Kronquist, has also produced picture-book biographies of celebrated French artists that are illustrated with reproductions of their paintings. Henri de Toulouse-Lautrec, the diminutive nineteenth-century painter, printmaker, draftsman, and illustrator, is the subject of *Toulouse-Lautrec: The Moulin Rouge and the City of Light.* "Burleigh confidently celebrates Lautrec's work and skill," observed Steev Baker in *School Library Journal.* In *Paul Cézanne: A Painter's Journey* the author examines the life of the famed post-impressionist. According to Regan McMahon in a review of *Paul Cézanne* for the *San Francisco Chronicle,* "Burleigh's excellent work is a complex portrait of a complex man, driven to paint no matter what other people thought of him and his art."

Some critics have particularly praised Burleigh's *The Secret of the Great Houdini,* which weaves the career of the American magician into a fictional story. Here Houdini's escape from a trunk hurled into deep water is described from the point of view of a youngster named Sam and his uncle Ezra, who have joined a crowd to watch the feat. While Sam and Uncle Ezra anxiously await Houdini's escape, Ezra tells Sam about Houdini's childhood and hardscrabble youth. Sam can hardly concentrate on what his uncle is saying, so terrified is he of

the possibility that Houdini will drown. "Burleigh achieves immediacy by writing his poetic text in the present tense," observed Marianne Saccardi in *School Library Journal.* Noting that "Houdini is a fascinating figure for all ages," a *Kirkus Reviews* critic added that Burleigh's "snapshot of one incredible feat . . . may spur further exploration, and inspiration," and *Booklist* reviewer Gillian Engberg declared that *The Secret of the Great Houdini* "captures the mystique of its famous subject."

Ancient Greece abounds with mythical tales about superhuman exploits and misadventures, and Burleigh shares two of these with younger readers in *Hercules* and *Pandora.* In *Hercules* the hero tests his mettle against supernatural challenges, ultimately descending to the underworld to battle the three-headed dog Cerberus. In *Booklist* Ilene Cooper liked the fact that *Hercules* uses "language that draws on the strength of its subject yet speaks in the lilt of poetry," and Stephanie Zvirin commented in the same periodical that *Hercules* would inspire young readers to search for other ancient myths about Hercules and other Greek gods, calling the book a "beautiful retelling."

Pandora puts a human face to the curious woman who, according to Greek myth, unleashed all the world's ills by opening a container. In his version of the story, Burleigh uses verse to illuminate how Pandora's curiosity becomes an obsession despite her understanding of the danger she faces by opening the jar. In a *School Library Journal* review of the work, Patricia Lothrop-Green praised "the graceful drama that unfolds" in the story, concluding: "This Pandora is tempting." Gillian Engberg of *Booklist* found *Pandora* to be "another fine retelling of a Greek myth."

In addition to his illustrated biographies, Burleigh has also created several stories for very young children. In *Goodbye Sheepie* he teams up with illustrator Peter Catalanotto to deal with a sensitive but important subject in a story about a young boy confronting the imminent death of the family dog. Noting that the author handles the theme of death and dying with great discretion, Kay Weisman recommended *Goodbye Sheepie* in her *Booklist* review as a "thoughtful" work that would be useful as a way to "spark discussions about death and funeral customs." "Burleigh looks at death without

blinking," asserted a *Publishers Weekly* contributor, and in *Goodbye Sheepie* he presents "a vision of death as not quite a final end."

Hitting the other end of the energy spectrum, *Clang! Clang! Beep! Beep! Listen to the City* features what *Booklist* critic Kristen McKulski characterized as a blend of "irresistible cityscapes and playful text." In a simple rhyming story full of onomatopoeia, Burleigh captures the energy of a bustling city from the ring of a morning's alarm clock through to the sibilant shushing of a parent to a child. Giacobbe contributes brightly colored, retro-styled paintings that employ "a vivid mix of primary and secondary colors to set the stage," according to *School Library Journal* contributor Lori A. Guenthner. While a *Kirkus Reviews* writer described *Clang! Clang! Beep! Beep!* as "a vivid sliver of city life," Guenthner recommended Burleigh's energetic story as a good choice "for children wanting to transport themselves to another place without the hassle of travel."

Burleigh teams up with artist Raúl Colón to tell a classic story of curiosity rewarded in the picture book **Pandora.** (Illustration copyright © 2002 by Raúl Colón. Reproduced by permission of Harcourt Mifflin Harcourt Publishing Company. All rights reserved.)

Burleigh pulls readers into the trenches of World War I in his picture book **Fly, Cher Ami, Fly!,** *featuring artwork by Robert MacKenzie.* (Illustration copyright © 2008 by Robert Mackenzie. Reproduced by permission of Abrams Books for Young Readers, an imprint of Abrams. All rights reserved.)

Burleigh offers slightly older readers a detailed look at a favorite confection in *Chocolate: Riches from the Rainforest.* This illustrated book covers many aspects of chocolate, from its history as a food of the Mayan and Aztec people to its transformational journey from cacao pod to candy bar. The author writes about the slave labor once used in the cacao and sugar industries, and about how Milton Hershey revolutionized the sale of milk chocolate from his factory in Pennsylvania. In a *School Library Journal* review, Augusta R. Malvagno praised the "delightful" book for its "kaleidoscope of fascinating information," while a contributor to *Kirkus Reviews* concluded that *Chocolate* is "a well-conceived and executed work on a subject of great interest."

Biographical and Critical Sources

PERIODICALS

Booklist, February 1, 1999, Stephanie Zvirin, review of *It's Funny Where Ben's Train Takes Him,* p. 979; August, 1999, Ilene Cooper, review of *Hercules,* p. 2050; March 15, 2000, Carolyn Phelan, review of *Edna,* p. 1377; May 15, 2000, Gillian Engberg, review of *Messenger, Messenger,* p. 1742, and Stephanie Zvirin, review of *Hercules,* p. 1758; February 15, 2001, Bill Ott, review of *Lookin' for Bird in the Big City,* p. 1152; June 1, 2001, Marta Segal, review of *I Love Going through This Book,* p. 1888; June 1, 2002, Gillian Engberg, review of *Pandora,* p. 1711; July, 2002, Gillian Engberg, review of *The Secret of the Great Houdini,* p. 1854; January 1, 2003, Julie Cummins, review of *Into the Woods: John James Audubon Lives His Dream,* p. 874; September 15, 2004, Hazel Rochman, review of *Langston's Train Ride,* p. 238; March 1, 2005, Carolyn Phelan, review of *Toulouse-Lautrec: The Moulin Rouge and the City of Light,* p. 1194; February 15, 2006, Gillian Engberg, review of *Paul Cézanne: A Painter's Journey,* p. 94; June 1, 2006, Gillian Engberg, review of *Tiger of the Snows: Tenzing Norgay: The Boy Whose Dream Was Everest,* p. 97; December 15, 2006, GraceAnne A. DeCandido, review of *Stealing Home: Jackie Robinson: Against the Odds,* p. 49; June 1, 2007, Hazel Rochman, review of *Napoleon: The Story of the Little Corporal,* p. 94; September 1, 2008, Randall Enos, review of *Fly, Cher Ami, Fly! The Pigeon Who Saved the Lost Battalion,* p. 101; December 1, 2008, Daniel Kraus, review of *One Giant Leap,* p. 67; June 1, 2009, Kristen McKulski, review of *Clang! Clang! Beep! Beep! Listen to the City,* p. 68; March 15, 2010, Kay Weisman, review of *Good-bye, Sheepie,* p. 47; February 1, 2011, Karen Cruze, review of *Night Flight: Amelia Earhart Crosses the Atlantic,* p. 69; February 15, 2011, Ian Chipman, review of *The Adventures of Mark Twain by Huckleberry Finn,* p. 64.

Bulletin of the Center for Children's Books, December, 1985, review of *A Man Named Thoreau,* p. 63.

Horn Book, March, 1986, David E. White, review of *A Man Named Thoreau,* pp. 215-216; November, 1991, Ann A. Flowers, review of *Flight: The Journey of Charles Lindbergh,* p. 752; March-April, 2011, Christine M. Heppermann, review of *Night Flight,* p. 136.

Kirkus Reviews, August 15, 1991, review of *Flight,* p. 1086; December 1, 1997, review of *Black Whiteness: Admiral Byrd Alone in the Antarctic,* p. 1773; February 1, 2001, review of *Goal,* p. 180; March 1, 2002, review of *Chocolate: Riches from the Rainforest,* p. 330; May 1, 2002, review of *Pandora,* p. 650; June 15, 2002, review of *The Secret of the Great Houdini,* p. 876; January 1, 2003, review of *Into the Woods,* p. 58; September 15, 2004, reviews of *By My Brother's Side,* p. 909, and *Langston's Train Ride,* p. 911; February 1, 2006, review of *Paul Cézanne,* p. 128; March 1, 2006, review of *Play Ball!,* p. 237; May 15, 2006, review of *Tiger of the Snows,* p. 514; May 1, 2007, review of *Stealing Home;* May 15, 2007, review of *Napoleon;* June 15, 2008, review of *Abraham Lincoln Comes Home;* August 15, 2008, review of *Fly, Cher Ami, Fly!;* April 1, 2009, review of *Clang! Clang! Beep! Beep!;* March 15, 2010, review of *Good-bye Sheepie;* February 1, 2011, review of *The Adventures of Mark Twain by Huckleberry Finn.*

New York Times Book Review, January 26, 1992, Signe Wilkinson, review of *Flight,* p. 21; November 8, 2009, Rich Cohen, review of *Listen to the City,* p. A&E 24.

Publishers Weekly, October 6, 1997, review of *Hoops,* p. 83; August 9, 1999, review of *Hercules,* p. 352; May

14, 2001, review of *Lookin' for Bird in the Big City,* p. 82; June 19, 2000, review of *Messenger, Messenger,* p. 54; June 4, 2001, review of *I Love Going through This Book,* p. 79; April 1, 2002, review of *Pandora,* p. 83; June 3, 2002, review of *The Secret of the Great Houdini,* p. 88; December 2, 2002, review of *Into the Woods,* p. 52; January 3, 2005, review of *Langston's Train Ride,* p. 54; January 9, 2006, review of *Play Ball!,* p. 53; December 11, 2006, review of *Stealing Home,* p. 69; June 5, 2006, review of *Tiger of the Snows,* p. 64; March 15, 2010, review of *Good-bye, Sheepie,* p. 50; December 20, 2010, review of *Night Flight,* p. 51; February 14, 2011, review of *The Adventures of Mark Twain by Huckleberry Finn,* p. 56.

San Francisco Chronicle, January 29, 2006, Regan McMahon, review of *Game Day,* p. M6; June 25, 2006, "An Artist's Life Is No Easy Path," p. M4.

School Library Journal, January, 1986, Ruth Semrau, review of *A Man Named Thoreau,* p. 64; October, 1999, Nina Lindsay, review of *Hercules,* p. 135; April, 2000, Kate McClelland, review of *Edna,* p. 92; April, 2001, Lee Bock, review of *Goal,* p. 129; June, 2001, Marianne Saccardi, review of *I Love Going through This Book,* and Mary Elam, review of *Lookin' for Bird in the Big City,* both p. 104; April, 2002, Augusta R. Malvagno, review of *Chocolate,* p. 129; May, 2002, Patricia Lothrop-Green, review of *Pandora,* p. 134; July, 2002, Marianne Saccardi, review of *The Secret of the Great Houdini,* p. 85; September, 2002, Dona Ratterree, review of *Into the Air,* p. 241; January, 2003, Laurie von Mehren, review of *Earth from Above for Young Readers,* p. 150; February, 2003, Robyn Walker, review of *Into the Woods,* p. 128; November, 2004,

Ann M. Holcomb, review of *By My Brother's Side,* p. 122; December, 2004, Wendy Lukehart, review of *Langston's Train Ride,* p. 127; May, 2005, Steev Baker, review of *Toulouse-Lautrec,* p. 146; January, 2006, Mary Hazelton, review of *Game Day,* p. 116; May, 2006, Marilyn Taniguchi, review of *Play Ball!,* p. 97; June, 2006, Be Astengo, review of *Tiger of the Snows,* p. 134; November, 2006, Rachel G. Payne, review of *Teammates,* p. 117; January, 2007, Marilyn Taniguchi, review of *Stealing Home,* p. 114; July, 2007, Ann W. Moore, review of *Napoleon,* p. 113; October, 2008, Miriam Lang Budin, review of *Fly, Cher Ami, Fly!,* p. 130; April, 2009, John Peters, review of *One Giant Leap,* p. 120; May, 2009, Lori A. Guenthner, review of *Clang! Clang! Beep! Beep!,* p. 71; October, 2009, MaryAnn Karre, review of *Abraham Lincoln Comes Here,* p. 58; April, 2010, Joan Kindig, review of *Good-bye, Sheepie,* p. 121; February, 2011, Wendy Lukehart, review of *Night Flight,* p. 94; March, 2011, Lucinda Snyder Whitehurst, review of *The Adventures of Mark Twain by Huckleberry Finn,* p. 178.

Teacher Librarian, June, 2000, Jessica Higgs, review of *Hercules,* p. 54.

ONLINE

Robert Burleigh Home Page, http://www.robertburleigh. com (August 1, 2012).

Burleigh Kronquist Web site, www.burleighkronquist.com (August 10, 2008).

Society of Children's Book Writers and Illustrators—Illinois Web site, http://www.scbwi-illinois.org/ (August 1, 2012), "Robert Burleigh."*

C

CHAPMAN, Lara

Personal

Married; children: one son, one daughter. *Education:* Bachelor's degree; teaching certification. *Hobbies and other interests:* Animals.

Addresses

Home—TX. *Agent*—Holly Root, Waxman Leavell Literary Agency, 80 5th Ave., Ste. 1101, New York, NY 10011.

Career

Novelist and educator. Teacher of fifth-grade English.

Member

Romance Writers of America (West Houston, TX, chapter).

Awards, Honors

RITA Award finalist, Romance Writers of America, 2012, and Young Adult selection, International Reading Association, both 2012, both for *Flawless.*

Writings

Flawless, Bloomsbury (New York, NY), 2011.

Biographical and Critical Sources

PERIODICALS

Bulletin of the Center for Children's Books, July-August, 2011, Karen Coats, review of *Flawless,* p. 513.
Kirkus Reviews, April 15, 2011, review of *Flawless.*
School Library Journal, June, 2011, Tina Zubak, review of *Flawless,* p. 513.
Voice of Youth Advocates, June, 2011, Jan Chapman, review of *Flawless,* p. 159.

ONLINE

Lara Chapman Home Page, http://larachapman.com (August 1, 2012).*

* * *

CLIFFORD, Leah 1981-

Personal

Born 1981, in OH. *Education:* Attended college. *Hobbies and other interests:* Travel.

Addresses

Home—OH. *Agent*—Rosemary Stimola, Stimola Literary Studio, 308 Livingston Ct., Edgewater, NJ 07020; info@stimolaliterarystudio.co.

Career

Writer. Worked as a flight attendant, cave tour guide, and waitress.

Writings

"TOUCH" YOUNG-ADULT NOVEL TRILOGY

A Touch Mortal, Greenwillow Books (New York, NY), 2011.
A Touch Morbid, Greenwillow Books (New York, NY), 2012.

Sidelights

In her debut novel *A Touch Mortal,* Leah Clifford "packs a paranormal story line with tension and romance," according to *Booklist* critic Frances Bradburn. The young-adult novel centers on Eden, a lonely and suicidal teen who discovers an instant connection with Az, the half-fallen angel she meets on the Jersey shore. As the pair fall in love, Az and his guardian angel Gabriel realize that Eden is pathless and faces grave danger from Luke, Az's cruel nemesis. To protect herself Eden must die, but after her suicide attempt she is transformed into a Sider, an immortal being. She also possesses the Touch, an unusual power that strips away morals and logic from mere mortals while releasing others like her from purgatory.

A writer in *Kirkus Reviews* remarked that Clifford offers an "intriguing twist on the paranormal" in *A Touch Mortal*, and several critics predicted that the novel's complex narrative will reward patient readers. "The suspense, drama, and tension of the [story's] second half explode," Alissa Lauzon commented in her *Voice of Youth Advocates* review, and Danielle Serra maintained in *School Library Journal* that *A Touch Mortal* "offer[s] . . . interesting twists and a movielike climax with sequel-justifying loose ends."

In Clifford's sequel, *A Touch Morbid*, Eden contracts a strange and terrible illness while searching with Az for Gabriel, who fell from the heavens trying to protect his friends from Luke. Meanwhile, Eden's friend Kristen suffers from a rapidly worsening mental illness, forcing the Siders to rely on Madeleine, an untrustworthy individual, in their fight against evil. "An intricately crafted plot, a dark edgy world, and dynamic, believable characters are the strengths of this story," Lauzon reported in her *Voice of Youth Advocates* appraisal of *A Touch Morbid.*

Biographical and Critical Sources

PERIODICALS

Booklist, March 15, 2011, Frances Bradburn, review of *A Touch Mortal,* p. 58; March 15, 2012, Frances Bradburn, review of *A Touch Morbid,* p. 60.
Kirkus Reviews, February 15, 2011, review of *A Touch Mortal;* January 15, 2012, review of *A Touch Morbid.*
School Library Journal, April, 2011, Danielle Serra, review of *A Touch Mortal,* p. 170.
Voice of Youth Advocates, June, 2011, Alissa Lazon, review of *A Touch Mortal,* p. 180; February, 2012, Alissa Lauzon, review of *A Touch Morbid,* p. 605.

ONLINE

Leah Clifford Home Page, http://www.leahclifford.com (August 1, 2012).
Leah Clifford Web log, http://leahclifford.wordpress com (August 1, 2012).*

*   *   *

CONVERSE, P.J.

Personal
Married.

Addresses
Home—Los Angeles, CA. *Agent*—George Nicholson, Sterling Lord Literistic, Inc., 65 Bleecker St., New York, NY 10012.

Career
Novelist. Teacher of English as a second language (ESL) in Hong Kong for two years.

Writings

Subway Girl, HarperTeen (New York, NY), 2011.

Sidelights

P.J. Converse wrote his debut novel, *Subway Girl,* after a stint teaching English as a second language (ESL) in Hong Kong. The title character is Amy Lee, who moves

Cover of Leah Clifford's young-adult fantasy romance A Touch Mortal, *the first novel in her "Touch" trilogy.* (HarperCollins Children's Books, 2011. Jacket illustration copyright © 2011 by Plush Studios/Getty Images. Reproduced by permission of Getty Images.)

to that teeming, cosmopolitan city from San Francisco after the end of her parents' marriage. Amy has a difficult time adjusting to her new life in Hong Kong, and her isolation is compounded by the fact that she barely speaks any Chinese. Her slightly punk-rock, nonconformist appearance attracts the interest of a group of teenage boys on the public transit system who dub her "Subway Girl." The story centers on Amy's friendship with one of those Chinese-American teens, Simon, who is on the verge of dropping out of school because he is failing English and his parents are unable to afford private tutors. After Simon approaches Amy and asks for help, their interaction is limited by their inability to communicate effectively. With practice and via e-mail, their conversation deepens and Simon learns that Amy has secret of her own: She is pregnant and does not possess the language skills needed to locate a clinic and deal with her condition.

Booklist contributor Courtney Jones found in *Subway Girl* "a mature, enthralling slice of Hong Kong life" and suggested that it fills the void of fictional "stories featuring characters of Asian descent" that avoid stereotypes. A reviewer for *Publishers Weekly* commended Converse for using "sometimes lyrical prose"

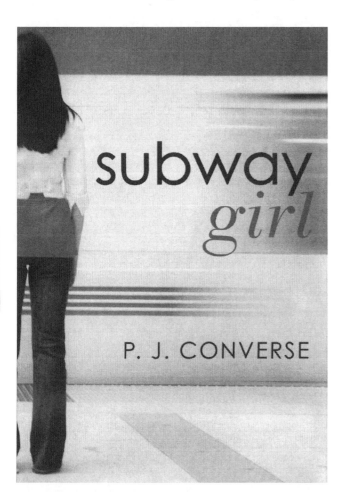

In Subway Girl *P.J. Converse takes readers to Hong Kong, where two teens work together to overcome the barrier of language and fit in with a new culture.* (HarperCollins Children's Books, 2011. Jacket cover copyright © 2011 by Plush Studios/Getty Images. Reproduced by permission of Getty Images.)

in weaving together "wanderlust, dreams, and the forces that both bring people together and pull them apart." Leah Sparks, writing in *Voice of Youth Advocates,* remarked that "Simon and Amy are likeable characters"; while their initial relationship is stifled by a language barrier, a genuine friendship leads to fluency in Converse's story. "As their relationship deepens," Sparks wrote, "so too does their understanding of each other's languages."

Biographical and Critical Sources

PERIODICALS

Booklist, May 1, 2011, Courtney Jones, review of *Subway Girl,* p. 84.
Bulletin of the Center for Children's Books, March, 2011, Karen Coats, review of *Subway Girl,* p. 324.
Kirkus Reviews, February 15, 2011, review of *Subway Girl.*
Publishers Weekly, January 17, 2011, review of *Subway Girl,* p. 50.
School Library Journal, June, 2011, Jennifer Rothschild, review of *Subway Girl,* p. 112.
Voice of Youth Advocates, April, 2011, Leah Sparks, review of *Subway Girl,* p. 54.

ONLINE

P.J. Converse Home Page, http://www.pjconverse.com (August 1, 2012).*

*   *   *

COOPER, Ilene 1948-

Personal

Born March 10, 1948, in Chicago, IL; daughter of Morris (a salesman) and Lillian Cooper (a homemaker). *Education:* University of Missouri, B.A.; Rosary College (River Forest, IL), M.L.S. *Religion:* Jewish. *Hobbies and other interests:* Knitting, traveling.

Addresses

Office—Booklist, American Library Association, 50 E. Huron, Chicago, IL 60611. *E-mail*—icooper@ala.org.

Career

Writer, editor, and librarian. Winnetka Public Library, Winnetka, IL, children's librarian, 1976-80; *Booklist* (magazine), Chicago, IL, children's book editor, beginning 1985. Consultant to *ABC Afterschool Specials,* ABC-TV, 1976-82.

Member

Society of Children's Book Writers and Illustrators.

Ilene Cooper (Photograph by Smith/Wright Photography. Reproduced by permission.)

Awards, Honors

Best Books designation, *Chicago Tribune,* 1995, for *Buddy Love—Now on Video;* Notable Social Studies Trade Books for Young People selection, Children's Book Council/National Council of Social Studies (CBC/ NCSS), and Best Books designation, *Chicago Tribune,* both 1997, both for *The Dead Sea Scrolls;* National Jewish Book Award for children's literature, 2003, for *Jewish Holidays All Year Round;* Notable Children's Books designation, American Library Association, and CBC/NCSS Notable Social Studies Trade Books for Young People selection, both 2003, and Society of Midland Authors Award for Juvenile Nonfiction, and Norman Sugarman Honor Book selection, both 2004, all for *Jack;* Prairie State Award for Excellence in Writing for Children, Illinois Reading Council, 2007; National Association Parenting Publications Gold Award, 2007, and Book Award for Best Children's Literature on Aging, Association for Gerontology in Higher Education, 2009, both for *The Golden Rule.*

Writings

PICTURE BOOKS

The Golden Rule, illustrated by Gabi Swiatkowska, Abrams Books (New York, NY), 2007.

Jake's Best Thumb, illustrated by Claudio Muñoz, Dutton (New York, NY), 2008.

NOVELS

The Winning of Miss Lynn Ryan, illustrated by Susan Magurn, Morrow (New York, NY), 1987.
Buddy Love—Now on Video, HarperCollins (New York, NY), 1995.
I'll See You in My Dreams, Viking Penguin (New York, NY), 1997.
Sam I Am, Scholastic Press (New York, NY), 2004.
Angel in My Pocket, Feiwel & Friends (New York, NY), 2011.

"KIDS FROM KENNEDY MIDDLE SCHOOL" NOVELSERIES

Queen of the Sixth Grade, Morrow (New York, NY), 1988.
Choosing Sides, Morrow (New York, NY), 1990.
Mean Streak, Morrow (New York, NY), 1991.
The New, Improved Gretchen Hubbard, Morrow (New York, NY), 1992.

"FRANCES IN THE FOURTH GRADE" CHAPTER-BOOKSERIES

Frances Takes a Chance, Bullseye Books (New York, NY), 1991.
Frances Dances, Bullseye Books (New York, NY), 1991.
Frances Four-Eyes, Bullseye Books (New York, NY), 1991.
Frances and Friends, illustrated by Vilma Ortiz, Bullseye Books (New York, NY), 1991.

"HOLLYWOOD WARS" NOVEL SERIES

My Co-Star, My Enemy, Puffin (New York, NY), 1993.
Lights, Camera, Attitude, Puffin (New York, NY), 1993.
Seeing Red, Puffin (New York, NY), 1993.
Trouble in Paradise, Puffin (New York, NY), 1993.

"HOLIDAY FIVE" NOVEL SERIES

Trick or Trouble, Viking (New York, NY), 1994.
The Worst Noel, Viking (New York, NY), 1994.
Stupid Cupid, Viking (New York, NY), 1995.
Star Spangled Summer, Viking (New York, NY), 1996.
No-Thanks Thanksgiving, Viking (New York, NY), 1996.

"ABSOLUTELY LUCY" CHAPTER-BOOK SERIES

Absolutely Lucy, illustrated by Amanda Harvey, Golden Books (New York, NY), 1999.
Lucy on the Loose, illustrated by Amanda Harvey, Golden Books (New York, NY), 2000.
Look at Lucy!, illustrated by David Merrell, Random House (New York, NY), 2009.
Lucy on the Ball, illustrated by David Merrell, Random House (New York, NY), 2011.

Little Lucy, illustrated by John Kanzler, Random House (New York, NY), 2011.

Lucy's Tricks and Treats, illustrated by David Merrell, Random House (New York, NY), 2012.

OTHER

Susan B. Anthony (biography), F. Watts (New York, NY), 1984.

(Editor, with Denise Wilms) *Guide to Non-Sexist Children's Books,* Volume II: *1976-1985,* Academy Chicago (Chicago, IL), 1987.

Jerry Pinkney: Achiever of Dreams, Harcourt (San Diego, CA), 1996.

The Dead Sea Scrolls, illustrated by John Thompson, Morrow (New York, NY), 1997.

Jewish Holidays All Year Round, illustrated by Elivia Savadier, Abrams Books (New York, NY), 2002.

The Annoying Team, illustrated by Colin Paine, Golden Books (New York, NY), 2002.

Jack: The Early Years of John F. Kennedy, Dutton (New York, NY), 2003.

Oprah Winfrey: A Twentieth-Century Life, Viking (New York, NY), 2007.

Writer for television series, including *American Playhouse* and *The Jeffersons;* author of teleplay *Under the Biltmore Clock,* 1983.

Sidelights

A distinguished critic of children's books who has served on the staff of *Booklist* magazine for more than twenty-five years, Ilene Cooper is also a popular writer for teen and preteen audiences. The author of the middle-grade novel *Angel in My Pocket* as well as the "Kids from Kennedy Middle School" and "Hollywood Wars" series, Cooper has also produced a critically acclaimed biography of the early life of John F. Kennedy. She has also researched and written several

Readers are introduced to the history of Jewish celebrations in Cooper's **Jewish Holidays All Year Round,** *a picture book featuring artwork by Elivia Savadier.* ("Ma'abarot in Grey" by Marcel Janco, c. 1950. Copyright © 1950 by The Jewish Museum, NY/Art Resource, NY; Artists Rights Society (ARS), New York/ADAGP, Paris. Reprinted with permission.)

works of nonfiction that follow her interest in women's history and her own religious roots.

Born in Chicago, Illinois, and a graduate of the University of Missouri, Cooper worked as a children's librarian before beginning her career as a critic/author. Her first work, *Susan B. Anthony,* appeared in 1984 and profiles the life of a nineteenth-century pioneer of the women's suffrage movement whose unstinting efforts helped win the vote for women. *Susan B. Anthony* led to Cooper's first novel for young readers, *The Winning of Miss Lynn Ryan.* Revolving around the efforts of a fifth-grade class to curry favor with a pretty and poised new teacher who demands perfection, *The Winning of Miss Lynn Ryan* illustrates how a teacher can "help her students see what is best in themselves or . . . stifle their better instincts," according to *Horn Book* contributor Nancy Vasilakis.

Cooper's popular novel series "Kids from Kennedy Middle School" delves into pre-teen politics. In *Queen of the Sixth Grade,* for example, Veronica Volner is the self-proclaimed queen of the school clique, and she commands that another girl, Robin, be cast out of the group when it becomes apparent that a boy Veronica likes favors Robin instead. "Sixth-grade meanness has rarely been better portrayed," commented Roger Sutton in his appraisal of *Queen of the Sixth Grade* in *Bulletin of the Center for Children's Books,* and a *Publishers Weekly* critic praised the story's mix of "snappy" dialog and "good" pacing. Nancy Vasilakis, writing in *Horn Book,* declared of the same novel that Cooper "probes with excellent understanding a specific problem of interpersonal relationships facing many schoolchildren."

The middle-school devilry continues in *Mean Streak* as testy Veronica attempts to hide her discombobulated home-life by causing problems for her romantic rivals, especially for Gretchen Hubbard, an overweight sixth grader. Now that she has alienated her best friends, Veronica has no one to turn to, however, when it appears that her divorced father is going to remarry. Writing in the *Bulletin of the Center for Children's Books,* Sutton remarked that while Veronica is portrayed as an unsavory character, in *Mean Streak* she is an engaging one that "captures our interest and sympathy, and . . . leaves us with some hope that she is capable of change."

In *Choosing Sides* the focus shifts to Jonathan Rossi, a sixth grader who is not only a good student but also a fine basketball player. Although Jon's dad pushes him to devote his free time to developing his game, just as his older brother has with football, the preteen has other interests. When a class assignment inspires a real passion in Jon, he learns to stand up for himself. Reviewing *Choosing Sides* in *School Library Journal,* Katharine Bruner commented that it is "heartening to find a protagonist who does not have to be antisports in order to enjoy music and literature."

In *The New, Improved Gretchen Hubbard* the formerly overweight Gretchen is suffering under the weight of

the nickname "Hippo Hubbard." After a Christmas-time crash diet and a makeover that includes a new hairstyle and updated wardrobe, Gretchen returns to school a changed girl and attracts the attention of a fifteen-year-old actor named Tim, who is working on a movie set. Unused to balancing schoolwork with a social life, she finds herself over her head, and her parents' impending divorce makes things worse. *The New, Improved Gretchen Hubbard* "realistically explores the changes that come from weight loss," observed Jana R. Fine in a *School Library Journal* review of Cooper's series finale. Fine also commended the "convincing" characters and "well-structured story line" in Cooper's novel.

In Cooper's four-volume "Frances in the Fourth Grade" series readers meet a bright and plucky fourth grader. *Frances Takes a Chance* finds the girl getting a new haircut as well as a new best friend, and her self-image continues to improve as her friendship with Polly Brock solidifies and helps her learn to be her own person. The everyday adventures of Frances continue in *Frances Dances, Frances Four-Eyes,* and *Frances and Friends.*

In Absolutely Lucy *Amanda Harvey illustrates Cooper's story about a shy boy who finds himself in an assortment of adventures thanks to his gregarious new puppy.* (Illustrations © 2000 by Amanda Harvey. Used by permission of Golden Books and imprint of Random House Children's Books, a division of Random House, Inc.)

A reviewer for *Publishers Weekly* described Cooper's stories in the series as "upbeat" and asserted that they present a "winning balance between Frances's home life and fourth grade year."

Cooper's "Hollywood Wars" books deal with the social pressures of teen life. In *My Co-Star, My Enemy* fifteen-year-old Alison suddenly finds herself cast in a plum role in a television show. Unfortunately, Alison's good luck attracts the animosity of fellow cast-member Jamie, also fifteen, whose six-year acting career seems to be near an end. In *Lights, Camera, Attitude* Alison prepares for her new television series while also dealing with a jealous boyfriend and a manipulative friend. *Seeing Red* finds her dealing with stage fright so that Jamie does not steal the limelight from her, while in *Trouble in Paradise* an overly zealous fan could prove a danger to Alison.

Another fan-pleasing series, Cooper's "Holiday Five" books, follows the lives of five friends who meet one summer at Camp Wildwood and agree to rejoin throughout the year on certain holidays. Cooper plots story lines around these holidays, dealing with realistic crises as they surface in the lives of these preteens. In *Trick or Trouble* Lia shares recent troubles with her camp friends before returning home at the end of the summer to find that her relationship with next-door neighbor and good friend Scott has changed. In *The Worst Noel* Kathy does not want to spend Christmas with her father and new family and opts instead to stay with friend Erin from summer camp. *Stupid Cupid* finds Maddy dealing with her widowed mother and her own excessive weight, while *Star Spangled Summer* finds the girls' long-awaited reunion at Camp Wildwood ruined when Jill, Erin, and Kathy are unable to attend. The "Holiday Five" series concludes with *No-Thanks Thanksgiving.*

Cooper has also turned her attention to younger readers in her "Absolutely Lucy" chapter-book series. In *Absolutely Lucy* Bobby has problems making friends until he gets a beagle puppy named Lucy for his eighth birthday and things begin to change in his life. *Lucy on the Loose* finds the rambunctious beagle lost after it chases a cat, and Bobby must overcome his shyness to ask strangers if they have seen his dog, while *The Annoying Team* deals with the theme of bullying. Maura Bresnahan, writing in *School Library Journal,* deemed *Absolutely Lucy* "entertaining and well plotted," while Zvirin noted in *Booklist* that *The Annoying Team* will "keep . . . readers well entertained."

Illustrated by Gabi Swiatkowska, Cooper's picture book *The Golden Rule* focuses on a grandfather as he explains the meaning of a biblical parable to his grandson, using examples from Christianity, Buddhism, and Islam, among other faiths. *Jake's Best Thumb,* which features artwork by Claudio Muñoz, centers on a little lad's proclivity for sucking on his thumb, much to the dismay of his family. A contributor in *Publishers Weekly*

An enthusiastic and imaginative young lad is the star of Cooper's story in Jake's Best Thumb, *which features illustrations by Claudio Muñoz.* (Illustration copyright © 2008 by Claudio Muñoz. Reproduced by permission of Dutton Children's Books, a division of Penguin Group (USA) Inc.)

predicted of *The Golden Rule* that many readers will appreciate the otherwise straightforward tone and universality of the material, and may well ponder the book's message," while a *Publishers Weekly* critic wrote that in *Jake's Best Thumb* Cooper makes "every word counts as she illuminates the various psychological dynamics."

Cooper is also known for her stand-alone novels. In *Buddy Love—Now on Video* a thirteen year old is able to combine his two main interests after his father buys a video recorder that helps him see his world differently and find new appreciation for his family. Older teens take center stage in the suspenseful *I'll See You in My Dreams,* in which sixteen-year-old Karen Genovese's dreams of a cute new boy at school begin to turn dark and ominous. "Cooper's sure touch paints the emotions of early adolescence accurately," noted *Voice of Youth Advocates* reviewer Faye H. Gottschall in a review of *Buddy Love—Now on Video,* while a *Kirkus Reviews* contributor described *I'll See You in My Dreams* as a fun book for teen readers that has "a spooky atmosphere and a few surprising plot twists."

Cooper tackles the issues of religion and interfaith marriage in *Sam I Am,* a middle-grade novel, while a mysterious coin changes the lives of four children in *Angel in My Pocket.* In the latter novel Bette is still mourning the loss of her mother two years earlier and struggling with her sister's departure for college when she finds a coin with an angel engraved on it. Soon, her circumstances soon take a turn for the better and she finds the courage to showcase her vocal talents at a school production. As the coin passes to three of Bette's classmates it brings further good fortune. "The children form an unlikely foursome, and each one develops as a character and a friend," Michele Shaw commented in a review of *Angel in My Pocket* for *School Library Journal,* and a *Publishers Weekly* critic noted of Cooper's story that "readers will be left contemplating the roles of luck, magic, and inner strength in the kids' transformed lives."

In *The Dead Sea Scrolls* Cooper explores the history behind the collection of religious documents discovered by a shepherd in 1947 in a cave on the shore of the Dead Sea. She recounts the efforts of scientists, translators, and scholars to authenticate and understand what many consider to be the most significant archaeological find of the twentieth century. Published to commemorate the fiftieth anniversary of the scrolls' discovery, the book benefits from research that ranges from studying the techniques of archaeologists and computer scientists to learning the history of Judeo-Christianity and the Middle East. In *The Dead Sea Scrolls* "this fascinating

Cooper once again captivates preteen readers with an engaging story in Angel in My Pocket, *a novel featuring cover art by Edwina White.* (Feiwel & Friends, 2010. Jacket illustration illustration by by Edwina White. Reproduced by permission of Feiwel & Friends, an imprint of Macmillan.)

story takes on new life," stated *Book Links* reviewer Judy O'Malley, and Jennifer M. Brabander wrote in *Horn Book* that the book "dynamically proves that biblical history is anything but dead." Patricia Lothrop-Green, writing in *School Library Journal,* asserted that Cooper acknowledges the "vitality" of the scrolls, and her "vivid descriptions . . . keep interest high."

Other nonfiction works by Cooper include *Jewish Holidays All Year Round* and *Jack: The Early Years of John F. Kennedy. Jewish Holidays* introduces readers to the Jewish calendar in a way that "strikes a tone both child-friendly and respectful," according to a *Publishers Weekly* critic. The author examines various holidays throughout the year, explains the significance of the rituals and traditions surrounding each, and suggests ways for families to celebrate them. Cooper visited the Jewish Museum in New York City in researching her book and was amazed at what she discovered. "I thought I knew something about Jewish holidays," she admitted to *Booklist* interviewer Zvirin. "But . . . there is always more to learn."

With *Jack* Cooper again turns her hand to biography, focusing on the childhood of eventually U.S. President John F. Kennedy, including his competition with his older brother, Robert, his trouble in school, and the illnesses that plagued him early on. "I . . . wanted to write about what it was like to be a child in this remarkable, yet highly pressurized, family," Cooper told Zvirin in another *Booklist* interview. A contributor to *Publishers Weekly* called *Jack* "an engaging overview" in which the author's use of "primary resources and photographs help capture the high pressured and privileged Kennedy lifestyle." In *Horn Book* Christine M. Heppermann praised Cooper's "revealing portrait" as "meticulously documented," while *School Library Journal* contributor Carol Fazioli cited the "lively style" of Cooper's biography.

"Kids always ask me where I get my ideas," Cooper once told *SATA.* "Most of them come from my own childhood and teenage years. Although many things have changed since I was young, the hopes and fears and feelings seem to remain the same."

Biographical and Critical Sources

PERIODICALS

Book Links, May, 1997, Judy O'Malley, review of *The Dead Sea Scrolls,* p. 16, and Ilene Cooper, discussion of *The Dead Sea Scrolls,* pp. 16-20.
Booklist, March 15, 2000, Stephanie Zvirin, review of *Absolutely Lucy,* p. 1376; October 1, 2000, Stephanie Zvirin, review of *Lucy on the Loose,* pp. 339, 350; May 1, 2001, Stephanie Zvirin, review of *I'llSee You in My Dreams,* p. 1610; June 1, 2002, Stephanie Zvirin, review of *The Annoying Team,* pp. 1719, 1721;

October 1, 2002, Stephanie Zvirin, review of *Jewish Holidays All YearRound,* p. 345; January 1, 2003, Stephanie Zvirin, reviews of *Jack: The Early Years of John F. Kennedy* and interview with Cooper, both p. 868; October 1, 2004, Stephanie Zvirin, review of *Sam I Am* and interview with Cooper, p. 344; January 1, 2007, Stephanie Zvirin, review of *Golden Rule* and *Oprah,* both p. 98; August 1, 2008, Stephanie Zvirin, review of *Jake's Best Thumb* and interview with Cooper, p. 77.

Bulletin of the Center for Children'sBooks, November, 1988, Roger Sutton, review of *Queen of the Sixth Grade,* p. 68; April, 1991, Roger Sutton, review of *Mean Streak,* p. 188; December, 1995, Roger Sutton, review of *Buddy Love—Now on Video,* pp. 123-124.

Horn Book, January, 1988, Nancy Vasilakis, review of *The Winning of Miss Lynn Ryan,* p. 62; January, 1989, Nancy Vasilakis, review of *Queen of theSixth Grade,* p. 68; September-October, 1997, Jennifer M. Brabander, review of *The Dead Sea Scrolls,* pp. 590-591; March-April, 2003, Christine M. Heppermann, review of *Jack,* pp. 222-223; November-December, 2004, Susan P. Bloom, review of *Sam I Am,* p. 705.

Kirkus Reviews, August 15, 1994, review of *Trick or Trouble,* p. 1142; June 1, 1997, review of *I'll See You in My Dreams,* p. 870; December 15, 2002, review of *Jack,* p. 1847; November 1, 2004, review of *Sam I Am,* p. 1048; February 1, 2007, review of *The Golden Rule,* p. 122; March 1, 2007, review of *Oprah Winfrey: Up Close,* p. 219; May 15, 2009, review of *Look at Lucy!*

New York Times Book Review, August 12, 2007, Julie Just, review of *The Golden Rule,* p. 17.

Publishers Weekly, October 14, 1988, review of *Queen of the Sixth Grade,* p. 77; June 14, 1991, reviews of *Frances Takes a Chance* and *Frances Dances,* both p. 47; May 10, 1993, review of *My Co-Star, My Enemy,* p. 72; July 4, 1994, review of *Trick or Trouble,* p. 64; October 16, 1995, review of *Buddy Love—Now on Video,* p. 62; June 2, 1997, review of *I'll See You in My Dreams,* p. 72; September 30, 2002, review of *Jewish Holidays All Year Round,* pp. 68-69; December 16, 2002, review of *Jack,* p. 69; December 20, 2004, review of *Sam I Am,* p. 60; January 29, 2007, review of *The Golden Rule,* p. 75; June 2, 2008, review of *Jake's Best Thumb,* p. 45; January 24, 2011, review of *Angel in My Pocket,* p. 153.

School Library Journal, May, 1990, Katharine Bruner, review of *Choosing Sides,* p. 103; October, 1992, Jana R. Fine, review of *The New, ImprovedGretchen Hubbard,* p. 114; August, 1994, Bonnie L. Raasch, review of *Trick or Trouble,* p. 154; February, 1995, Christina Dorr, review of *Stupid Cupid,* p. 96; May, 1996, Carrie A. Guarria, review of *Star Spangled Summer,* p. 110; June, 1997, Patricia Lothrop-Green, review of *The DeadSea Scrolls,* p. 133; March, 2001, Maura Bresnahan, review of *Absolutely Lucy,* p. 205; February, 2003, Carol Fazioli, review of *Jack,* p. 156; March, 2003, Martha Link, review of *Jewish Holidays All Year Round,* p. 216; October, 2004, Mara Alpert, review of *Sam I Am,* p. 160; March, 2011, Michele Shaw, review of *Angel in My Pocket,* p. 158.

Voice of Youth Advocates, April, 1996, Faye H. Gottschall, review of *Buddy Love—Now onVideo,* p. 24.

ONLINE

BookPage, http:/www.bookpage.com/ (December, 2002), Ron Kaplan, review of *Jewish Holidays AllYear Round.*

Ilene Cooper Home Page, http://www.ilenecooper.com (July 15, 2012).

Prairie Wind Web site, http://www.scbwi-illinois.org/pub/PrairieWind/ (spring, 2007), Sara Latta, "Pride of the Prairie: Ilene Cooper."*

*   *   *

COWHERD, Kevin

Personal

Married; children: three. *Hobbies and other interests:* Hiking, golf, travel.

Addresses

Home—Baltimore, MD. *Office*—Baltimore Sun, 501 N. Calvert St., Box 20104000, Baltimore, MD 21278. *E-mail*—wcowherd@baltsun.com.

Career

Syndicated columnist and author. *Baltimore Sun,* Baltimore, MD, feature writer and sports columnist, 1981-87, 2009—, and humor columnist, 1988-2009, all for print and online outlets.

Awards, Honors

Award for Excellence in Feature Writing, American Association of Sunday and Feature Editors, 1990.

Writings

MIDDLE-GRADE NOVELS

(Coauthor) Cal Ripken, Jr., *Hothead!,* Disney Hyperion (New York, NY), 2011.

(Coauthor) Cal Ripken, Jr., *Super-sized Slugger,* Disney Hyperion (New York, NY), 2012.

OTHER

Last Call at the 7-Eleven: Fine Dining at 2 A.M., the Search for Spandex People, and Other Reasons to Go on Living, Bancroft Press (Baltimore, MD), 1995.

When I Was Your Age, We Didn't Even Have Church: Chronicles of a Catholic Parent, illustrated by Jack Desrocher, Our Sunday Visitor (Huntington, IN), 1995.

Author of syndicated sports and humor columns beginning c. 1980s.

Adaptations

Hothead was adapted for audiobook, narrated by Cal Ripkin, Jr., Listening Library, 2011.

Biographical and Critical Sources

PERIODICALS

Booklist, February 15, 2011, Todd Morning, review of *Hothead!,* p. 73.

Journal of Adolescent & Adult Literacy, October, 2011, Suzan Bawolek, review of *Hothead!,* p. 166.

Publishers Weekly, September 11, 1995, review of *Last Call at the 7-Eleven: Fine Dining at 2 A.M., the Search for Spandex People, and Other Reasons to Go on Living,* p. 68; January 3, 2011, review of *Hothead!,* p. 51.

School Library Journal, April, 2011, Kim Dare, review of *Hothead!,* p. 182.

ONLINE

Baltimore Sun Online, http://www.baltimoresun.com/ (August 1, 2012), "Kevin Cowherd."*

D

DAVIES, Katie 1978-

Personal

Born 1978, in Newcastle upon Tyne, England; married Alan Davies (an actor), 2007; children: Susie. *Education:* Warwick University, degree; attended East 15 Acting School.

Addresses

Home—London, England.

Career

Writer. Worked as a literary agent; BBC Radio 4, performer on *One.*

Awards, Honors

Waterstone's Children's Book Prize, 2010, for *The Great Hamster Massacre.*

Writings

"GREAT CRITTER CAPERS" CHAPTER-BOOK SERIES

The Great Hamster Massacre, illustrated by Hannah Shaw, Simon & Schuster (London, England), 2010, Beach Lane Books (New York, NY), 2011.
The Great Rabbit Rescue, illustrated by Hannah Shaw, Simon & Schuster (London, England), 2010, Beach Lane Books (New York, NY), 2011.
The Great Cat Conspiracy, illustrated by Hannah Shaw, Simon & Schuster (London, England), 2011, Beach Lane Books (New York, NY), 2012.

OTHER

Author of sketches for *One,* BBC Radio 4. Contributor to periodicals, including *Spectator* and *Idler.*

Sidelights

British author Katie Davies explores the subject of death, albeit in a humorous manner, in her debut children's book *The Great Hamster Massacre.* Part of her "Great Critter Capers" series and based on an actual event from Davies' childhood, the story concerns a girl's investigation into the bizarre passing of her pet Russian Dwarf hamsters. "I haven't got an agenda in writing about death," Davies remarked in a London *Guardian* interview with Michelle Pauli. "I think that around seven you start to hear of someone who has died or you have a pet that died and you can't hide that from children, however you might choose to explain it."

In *The Great Hamster Massacre* readers are introduced to nine-year-old Anna, an animal lover who convinces her mother to purchase a pair of female hamsters. When one of the hamsters becomes pregnant, the family realizes they actually have a mating pair and soon they are the proud owners of eight newborns. When Anna makes a terrible discovery one morning—all of the babies are dead and one of the adult hamsters is missing—she ignores the obvious conclusion and begins searching for the killer with the help of younger brother Tom and best friend Suzanne. "What follows is an interesting take on how children deal with grief and shock, with a refreshing lack of condescension toward Anna, and by extension, young readers," observed *School Library Journal* critic Heather Talty in her review of *The Great Hamster Massacre.*

Davies received the prestigious Waterstone's Children's Book Prize for *The Great Hamster Massacre,* which features comical, black-and-white illustrations by Hannah Shaw. According to Nicolette Jones in the London *Sunday Times,* the tale "has the ring of truth," and *Booklist* contributor Linda Sawyer described it as "an interesting mix of British humor and serious issues." A writer in *Kirkus Reviews* also applauded *The Great Hamster Massacre,* stating that "Anna's fountain of ideas convincingly tracks the busy 9-year-old mind down to the smallest, delightful detail."

Katie Davies teams up with artist Hannah Shaw to create the whimsical artwork in **The Great Hamster Massacre.** (Illustration copyright © 2011 by Hannah Shaw. Reproduced by permission of Beach Lane Books, an imprint of Simon & Schuster Children's Publishing.)

Anna and her cohorts make a return appearance in *The Great Rabbit Rescue,* which has "the same hilarious and heartwarming tones as its predecessor," as a critic stated in the *Liverpool Echo.* Upon learning that he will move in with his father, Joe-down-the-street asks Anna to look after his pet rabbit, which he must leave behind. Anna, Suzanne, and Tom take turns guarding the creature, but when it falls ill they surmise that it must be lonely for Joe and they plot a complicated reunion. "Readers will enjoy Anna's narration, which has an animated, slightly rambling style," Amy Holland commented in her *School Library Journal* review of *The Great Rabbit Rescue.* A *Kirkus Reviews* contributor maintained that in "this gentler sequel" Davies' "laconic style and deadpan humor" is "well-matched to the chapter-book format."

The Great Cat Conspiracy, the third installment in Davies' "Great Critter Capers" series, finds Anna and friends looking into the strange disappearance of a number of local felines. The girls' sleuthing leads them to the home of an elderly woman with a penchant for collecting things that do not belong to her, cats included. "There are quite a few laugh out loud moments," observed Marie Imeson in her *School Librarian* appraisal of *The Great Cat Conspiracy.*

Biographical and Critical Sources

PERIODICALS

Booklist, July 1, 2011, Linda Sawyer, review of *The Great Hamster Massacre,* p. 60.
Children's Bookwatch, October, 2011, review of *The Great Hamster Massacre.*
Evening Standard (London, England), March 1, 2010, Liz Hoggard, "Katie Davies: My Life Married to Alan Davies, London's Funniest Man."
Guardian (London, England), February 10, 2010, Michelle Pauli, "*Great Hamster Massacre* Wins Waterstone's Children's Books Prize."

Kirkus Reviews, April 1, 2011, review of *The Great Hamster Massacre*; November 15, 2011, review of *The Great Rabbit Rescue.*
Liverpool Echo, January 17, 2011, review of *The Great Rabbit Rescue,* p. 11.
School Librarian, summer, 2010, Marie Imeson, review of *The Great Hamster Massacre,* p. 98; summer, 2011, Marie Imeson, review of *The Great Cat Conspiracy,* p. 98.
School Library Journal, September, 2011, Heather Talty, review of *The Great Hamster Massacre,* p. 116; January, 2012, Amy Holland, review of *The Great Rabbit Rescue,* p. 72.
Sunday Times (London, England), January 10, 2010, Nicolette Jones, review of *The Great Hamster Massacre,* p. 50.

ONLINE

Katie Davies Home Page, http://www.katiedaviesbooks. com (August 1, 2012).*

*   *   *

DOMINY, Amy Fellner 1964-

Personal

Born March 25, 1964, in Redwood City, CA; married; husband's name Jake; children: two. *Education:* Arizona State University, B.S. (advertising), 1987, M.F.A. (playwriting), 2004.

Addresses

Home—Phoenix, AZ. *Agent*—Caryn Wiseman, Andrea Brown Literary Agency; caryn@andreabrownlit.com. *E-mail*—amy@amydominy.com.

Career

Playwright and novelist. Worked as an advertising copywriter.

Member

Society of Children's Book Writers and Illustrators.

Awards, Honors

Sydney Taylor Notable Book selection, Association of Jewish Libraries, 2012, for *OyMG.*

Writings

OyMG, Walker (New York, NY), 2011.
Audition and Subtraction, Walker (New York, NY), 2012.

Also author of plays for children.

Sidelights

Amy Fellner Dominy explores themes of self-identity, anti-Semitism, and family heritage in *OyMG,* her first young-adult novel. The work centers on Ellie Taylor, an ambitious teen who fights prejudice while earning a scholarship to an elite prep school. "I think the original inspiration for *OyMG* comes from something that happened to me when I was a teenager," Dominy remarked on her home page. "I was fired from a babysitting job when the family found out I was Jewish. Up until then, I'd always taken pride in my differences but I also wanted to be liked and accepted. It really shook me. I knew I wanted to write a story about a Jewish girl who is tested about her identity."

Born in California in 1964, Dominy moved several times with her family before settling in Tempe, Arizona, at age eight. An excellent student, she played in

Dominy weaves a Jewish perspective into her humorous coming-of-age story in **OyMG,** *which focuses on a teen's battle against discrimination while working toward her dreams.* (Jacket illustration photographs by Rubberball/ Mark Andersen/Getty Images; cover illustration by Danielle Delaney. Reproduced by Walker & Company, a division of Bloomsbury Publishing, Inc.)

Amy Fellner Dominy (Photograph by Sonya Sones. Reproduced by permission.)

the marching band and performed in school plays. After graduating from college, Dominy spent some twenty years in the advertising business, writing print ads, radio spots, and commercials for television. Wanting to tell her own tales, however, she earned a master's degree in playwriting from Arizona State University in 2004. As she recalled on her home page, "Playwriting experience led me to a publisher who wanted me to write Reader's Theater scripts for kids. So I did. And that led me to writing short stories for teens. And that gave me the confidence to try my hand at writing a full-length novel."

Ellie, the protagonist in *OyMG,* loves to argue, especially with her equally opinionated Jewish grandfather. A skilled orator, Ellie plans to attend the Christian Society Speech and Performing Arts Camp over the summer, hoping to win a private scholarship to Benedict's Conservatory, a prestigious private school with an outstanding debate team. At camp Ellie meets Devon Yeats, a talented debater with good looks to match. The two quickly hit it off, although Ellie grows worried after Devon admits that his grandmother, the scholarship's benefactor, is prejudiced against Jews. Now Ellie must decide if landing a spot at Benedict's is worth denying her religion.

Feeling different from one's peers is a key theme in *OyMG,* Dominy told *Journal of Adolescent & Adult Literature* interviewer Allison Wimmer. "For Ellie in this story, that difference is her religion and cultural heritage," the author noted. "It's central to the storyline, but it's also the crux of a larger question for Ellie; namely, a search for identity and an acceptance of who she is and who she wants to be."

In her *Booklist* review of *OyMG,* Ilene Cooper stated that Dominy "does a good job . . . discussing beliefs, personal responsibility, and how to do the 'right' thing." "This lighthearted book is an excellent balance of humor along with a serious message," Wimmer reported of the debut novel, and a contributor for *Kirkus Reviews* predicted of *OyMG* that "readers who like their frothy romance with a bracing dash of serious social issues will be clamoring for seconds."

In *Audition and Subtraction* Dominy also explores themes of identity as her teen protagonist Tatum Austin finds her relationships disintegrating all around her. Tatum's parents have separated, her best friend has fallen for a cute new student, and longtime buddy Aaron is now acting like he might want to be more than just friends. In reviewing Dominy's second novel, a *Kirkus Reviews* contributor cited the narrator's "authentic voice" and concluded that *Audition and Subtraction* touches on a key element of adolescence: that "newly developing boy/girl connections inevitably affect the life-defining girl/girl friendships that preceded them."

Biographical and Critical Sources

PERIODICALS

Booklist, July 1, 2011, Ilene Cooper, review of *OyMG,* p. 56.
Bulletin of the Center for Children's Books, May, 2011, Claire Gross, review of *OyMG,* p. 414.
Journal of Adolescent & Adult Literacy, November, 2011, Allison Wimmer, review of *OyMG,* p. 257, and interview with Dominy, p. 258.
Kirkus Reviews, April 15, 2011, review of *OyMG;* August 1, 2012, review of *Audition and Subtraction.*
School Library Journal, June, 2011, Susan Riley, review of *OyMG,* p. 116.

ONLINE

Amy Fellner Dominy Home Page, http://amydominy.com (July 15, 2012).
Cynsations Web log, http://cynthialeitichsmith.blogspot.com/ (May 19, 2011), Cynthia Leitich Smith, interview with Dominy.

DOWNING, Johnette

Personal

Female. *Education:* Southeastern Louisiana University, B.A.

Addresses

Home and office—New Orleans, LA. *E-mail*—info@johnettedowning.com.

Career

Singer, songwriter, and author. Isidore Newman School, New Orleans, LA, member of staff for fourteen years. Musical performer; recordings include (with Dickie Knicks) *New Moon: Music for Little Folk,* 1990, *Music Time,* 1992, *From the Gumbo Pot,* 1998, *Wild and Woolly Wiggle Songs,* 2001, *Silly Sing Along,* 2002, *The Second Line: Scarf Activity Songs,* 2003, and *Fins and Grins,* 2006, and (with Jimmy LaRocca's Original Dixieland Jazz Band) *Dixieland Jazz for Children,* 2007.

Member

National Association of Recording Arts and Sciences, Society of Children's Book Writers and Illustrators, Haiku Society of America, Independent Children's Artist Network (cofounder and vice president), New Orleans Haiku Society (cofounder).

Awards, Honors

Six Parents' Choice awards; two Parent's Guide to Children's Media awards; four National Parenting Publications awards; four iParenting Media awards; Family Choice award; Family Review Center award; Imagination Award; Haiku International Association Award honorable mention.

Writings

A Squirrel Jumped out of a Tree, Colonial Press, 1990.
Today Is Monday in Louisiana, illustrated by Deborah Ousley Kadair, Pelican Publishing (Gretna, LA), 2006.
(Adapter) *Down in Louisiana,* illustrated by Deborah Ousley Kadair, Pelican Publishing (Gretna, LA), 2007.
(Adapter) *Chef Creole,* illustrated by Deborah Ousley Kadair, Pelican Publishing (Gretna, LA), 2009.
(Adapter) *Today Is Monday in Texas,* illustrated by Deborah Ousley Kadair, Pelican Publishing (Gretna, LA), 2010.
(Adapter) *Today Is Monday in New York,* illustrated by Deborah Ousley Kadair, Pelican Publishing (Gretna, LA), 2011.
Why the Oyster Has the Pearl, illustrated by Bethanne Hill, Pelican Publishing (Gretna, LA), 2011.
(Adapter) *Why the Possum Has a Large Grin: A Choctaw Tale,* illustrated by Christina Wald, Pelican Publishing (Gretna, LA), 2012.

Today Is Monday in Kentucky, illustrated by Deborah Ousley Kadair, Pelican Publishing (Gretna, LA), 2012.

Lyricist on recordings, including *New Moon: Music for Little Folk,* 1990, *Music Time,* 1992, *From the Gumbo Pot,* 1998, *Wild and Woolly Wiggle Songs,* 2001, *Silly Sing Along,* 2002, *The Second Line: Scarf Activity Songs,* 2003, *Fins and Grins,* 2006, and *Dixieland Jazz for Children,* 2007.

Contributor of poetry to anthologies, including *Katrina-ku: Storm Poems,* New Orleans Haiku Society, 2006, and to periodicals such as *Frogpond, bottle rockets, World Haiku, Nisqually Delta Review,* and *YAWP.* Contributor of articles to *Pass It On!* and *Applause!*

SELF-ILLUSTRATED

(Adapter) *My Aunt Came Back from Louisiane,* Pelican Publishing (Gretna, LA), 2008.
Why the Crawfish Lives in the Mud, Pelican Publishing (Gretna, LA), 2009.
(Adapter) *There Was an Old Lady Who Swallowed Some Bugs,* Pelican Publishing (Gretna, LA), 2010.
Amazon Alphabet, Pelican Publishing (Gretna, LA), 2011.

Sidelights

Louisiana-based singer/songwriter Johnette Downing has performed her music all over the world. Praised as

Johnette Downing shares the beauty and uniqueness of her home state in her song book **Down in Louisiana,** *featuring collage art by Doborah Ousley Kadair.* (Illustration copyright © 2007 by Deborah Ousley Kadair. Reproduced by permission of Pelican Publishing Co., Inc.)

a "seasoned and engaging performer" by Paul Shackman in *Booklist,* Downing has also written more than a dozen books for young readers. In her music, as well as in picture books such as *Today Is Monday in Louisiana, Why the Crawfish Lives in the Mud,* and *My Aunt Came Back from Louisiane* she focuses on sharing the colorful musical and literary heritage of her home state with children.

Today Is Monday in Louisiana, Downing's adaptation of a popular song, introduces a new variety of Louisiana food for each day of the week. As the cumulative song moves on from day to day, each new verse repeats the previous meal, giving readers and listeners a chance to chime with the refrain from memory. As a *Publishers Weekly* critic maintained, "keeping with the spirit of the culture it celebrates," Downing's book includes a recipe and a full description of each dish, encouraging young readers to continue their discovery of the region's cuisine. The "rhythmic, repetitive text will appeal to children," predicted a *Kirkus Reviews* contributor, and Judith Constantinides commented in *School Library Journal* that *Today Is Monday in Louisiana* will make "a pleasing addition to Louisiana lore and a fun, light note" for possible school projects on the state.

In a companion volume, *Today Is Monday in New York,* Downing turns the spotlight on the Empire State and its culinary delights, including Nathan's hot dogs and buffalo wings. "A fun twist on a classic" was how Kris Hickey described *Today Is Monday in New York* in her review for *School Library Journal.*

In *Down in Louisiana* Downing introduces young readers to another traditional Louisiana song while also presenting a rhyming tour of the state's landscape. The book serves as both an introduction to the marshes, wetlands, and bayous of Louisiana and a counting game wherein young readers are encouraged to determine the number of native animals that appear on each page. A wide variety of unusual creatures—from alligators and armadillos to crawfish and pelicans—are pictured in illustrations by Deborah Ousley Kadair, each in their natural environment. Downing adapts "Aiken Drum," another familiar tune, in her picture book *Chef Creole,* a work that is "always welcome for storytimes," according to Constantinides.

Downing has a number of self-illustrated titles to her credit, among them *Amazon Alphabet, There Was an Old Lady Who Swallowed Some Bugs, My Aunt Came Back from Louisiane,* and *Why the Crawfish Lives in the Mud.* She explores the wonders of the rainforest in *Amazon Alphabet,* "a colorful introduction to the Amazon River watershed area," according to Frances E. Millhouser in *School Library Journal.*

In *There Was an Old Lady Who Swallowed Some Bugs* a woman's unusual diet includes fleas, slugs, and even a poached roach, and audiences "will find sly humor and a bit of the unexpected presented with bold art" in

Downing takes on both author and illustrator duties in her regional-themed abecedarian **Amazon Alphabet.** (Copyright © 2011 by Johnette Downing. Reproduced by permission of Pelican Publishing Co., Inc.)

each turn of the page, according to Mary Elam in *School Library Journal*. In *My Aunt Came Back from Louisiane*, a Louisiana-centric take on a favorite children's song, the title character returns from a visit to the Pelican State with a variety of gifts, such as red beans from New Orleans and a baguette from Lafayette. Reviewing *My Aunt Came Back from Louisiane*, Constantinides praised the "simple, colorful collages" that enliven Downing's story.

Downing's original pourquoi tale, *Why the Crawfish Lives in the Mud*, also features her original collage illustrations. After Crab catches a fish for dinner, Crawfish mocks his friend's efforts, telling Crab that a much bigger meal can be found down in the bayou. The fib works, but when an angry Crab returns from his futile quest, Crawfish must retreat into a precarious position. A writer in *Kirkus Reviews* described the work as a "trickster tale jazzed up with Cajun French phrases," and Constantinides applauded *Why the Crawfish Lives in the Mud* as a "humorous choice for storytimes."

Biographical and Critical Sources

PERIODICALS

Booklist, November 1, 2003, Paul Shackman, review of *The Second Line: Scarf Activity Songs*, p. 524; February 1, 2006, Paul Shackman, review of *Music Time*, p. 77; April 1, 2007, Paul Shackman, review of *Fins and Grins*, p. 86.

Children's Bookwatch, January, 2007, review of *Fins and Grins;* April, 2008, sound recording review of *Dixieland Jazz for Children*.

Kirkus Reviews, October 15, 2006, review of *Today Is Monday in Louisiana*, p. 1069; September 1, 2008, review of *My Aunt Came Back from Louisiane*; October 15, 2009, review of *Why the Crawfish Lives in the Mud*; February 1, 2011, review of *Amazon Alphabet*.

Publishers Weekly, February 2, 2004, "Sing, Play, Learn," p. 30; October 16, 2006, review of *Today Is Monday in Louisiana*, p. 52.

School Library Journal, February, 2004, Beverly Bixler, review of *The Second Line*, p. 77; December, 2005, Stephanie Bange, review of *Music Time*, p. 86; December, 2006, Judith Constantinides, review of *Today Is Monday in Louisiana*, p. 96; May, 2007, Kirsten Martindale, review of *Fins and Grins*, p. 75; November, 2007, Judith Constantinides, review of *Down in Louisiana*, p. 106; July, 2008, Stephanie Bange, review of *Dixieland Jazz for Children*, p. 60; February, 2009, Judith Constantinides, review of *My Aunt Came Back from Louisiane*, p. 91; March, 2009, Judith Constantinides, review of *Chef Creole*, p. 134; January, 2010, Judith Constantinides, review of *Why the Crawfish Live in the Mud*, p. 72; January, 2011, Mary Elam, review of *There Was an Old Lady Who Swallowed Some Bugs*, p. 74; May, 2011, Kris Hickey, review of *Today Is Monday in New York* p. 95; June, 2011, Frances E. Millhouser, review of *Amazon Alphabet*, p. 102.

ONLINE

Johnette Downing Home Page, http://www.johnette downing.com (July 15, 2012).

Johnette Downing Web log, http://johnettedowning. blogspot.com (July 15, 2012).

Pelican Publishing Web site, http://www.pelicanpub.com/ (July 15, 2012), "Johnette Downing."*

*   *   *

DRAPER, Penny 1957-

Personal

Born 1957, in Toronto, Ontario, Canada; married; children: one son, one daughter. *Education:* Trinity College, University of Toronto, B.A. (literature); attended Storytellers School of Toronto.

Addresses

Home—Victoria, British Columbia, Canada. *E-mail*—penny@pennydraper.ca.

Career

Author, bookseller, and storyteller. University of Victoria Bookstore, Victoria, British Columbia, Canada, textbook manager. Professional storyteller at schools, libraries, conferences, and festivals for fifteen years.

Awards, Honors

Geoffrey Bilson Award finalist, Silver Birch Award finalist, Ontario Library Association, and Diamond Willow Award finalist, all 2006, all for *Terror at Turtle Mountain;* Silver Birch Award finalist, 2007, for *Peril at Pier Nine;* Bolen Books Children's Prize, and Moonbeam Award, both 2009, and Red Cedar Award nominee, 2010-11, all for *Graveyard of the Sea;* Saskatchewan Book Award, 2011, for *Ice Storm.*

Writings

"DISASTER STRIKES" NOVEL SERIES

Terror at Turtle Mountain, Coteau Books (Regina, Saskatchewan, Canada), 2006.
Peril at Pier Nine, Coteau Books (Regina, Saskatchewan, Canada), 2007.
Graveyard of the Sea, Coteau Books (Regina, Saskatchewan, Canada), 2008.
A Terrible Roar of Water, Coteau Books (Regina, Saskatchewan, Canada), 2010.
Ice Storm, Coteau Books (Regina, Saskatchewan, Canada), 2011.
Day of the Storm, Coteau Books (Regina, Saskatchewan, Canada), 2012.

Sidelights

A professional storyteller, Penny Draper is also the author of several award-winning stories in the "Disaster Strikes" novel series, which offers fictional accounts of actual events from Canadian history. In *Terror at Turtle Mountain* Draper reimagines the Frank Slide, a deadly avalanche that occurred on April 29, 1903, and killed more than ninety people in Frank, a small coal-mining town located in what is now Alberta. In the novel Nathalie Vaughan, a thirteen year old, bravely joins a group of rescue workers searching for survivors following the massive rockslide. *"Terror at Turtle Mountain* epitomizes the Canadian survival story," Los Brymer remarked in the *Canadian Review of Materials,* and "through the fears, hopes, wishes, resolve, pluck, and heroics of a believable adolescent protagonist, Draper humanizes and brings to life a snippet of Canadian history."

In *Peril at Pier Nine* Draper recalls the tragic 1949 fire that engulfed the S.S. *Noronic,* a passenger cruise ship on the Great Lakes. The book's protagonist, a talented and ambitious young sailor named Jack Gordon, longs for adventure at sea and dreams of one day captaining the *Noronic.* After the ship docks at Toronto's Ward Island, Jack notices a fire raging on board and he commandeers the island's only motorboat as part of a daring mission to save the *Noronic*'s passengers. "Readers will appreciate the fast paced action of the story," Anne Hatcher predicted in *Resource Links,* and *Canadian Review of Materials* critic Georgie Perigny described *Peril at Pier Nine* as "a quick, entertaining read."

Based on two shipwrecks from the early 1900s, *Graveyard of the Sea* concerns twelve-year-old Nell Baker, who lives with her father in an isolated lighthouse located on Canada's west coast. When a government official visits the lighthouse, announcing that it will soon be equipped with a telegraph, Nell decides to teach herself Morse Code. Her new skills pay off when a ship runs aground and she is able to relay a distress message, although the rescue ultimately fails. When a second ship also runs into trouble, Nell must act quickly to help the sailors after she discovers that the telegraph lines are down. *Graveyard of the Sea* "is a well-

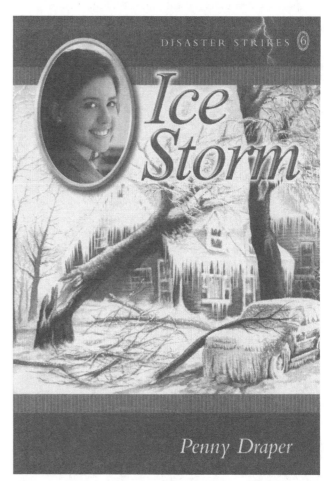

Cover of Penny Draper's historical novel Ice Storm, *which features cover art by Aries Cheung.* (Jacket illustration © 2011 by Aries Cheung. Reproduced by permission of Coteau Books.)

constructed, fun read that will be enjoyed by fans of historical fiction," Jeannine Stickle observed in her review of Draper's novel for the *Canadian Review of Materials.*

A devastating tsunami that struck Newfoundland's Burin Peninsula in 1929 is the focus of *A Terrible Roar of Water.* The real-life disaster is seen through the eyes of twelve-year-old Murphy whose uncle, a fisherman, has raised him since the death of his father. Murphy's small community is caught unawares when three massive waves, triggered by a small earthquake, wreak havoc on the region. In *Resource Links* Victoria Pennell commented that "readers who are familiar with Draper's other books will enjoy the drama and history for which she is noted."

Draper looks at another incredible meteorological event in *Ice Storm.* In January 1998, a major winter storm coated parts of the northwestern United States and Canada with more than three inches of accumulated ice, knocking out power to millions of people and causing billions of dollars of property damage. In the novel Alice must fend for herself while her father helps restore power to the area; Alice's cousin Sophie remains in her care while her family works feverishly to save their dairy cows. Calling *Ice Storm* "an unusual story of survival," a critic in *Kirkus Reviews* further noted that "Draper covers the terror and impact of the storm."

Biographical and Critical Sources

PERIODICALS

Canadian Review of Materials, June 23, 2006, Lois Brymer, review of *Terror at Turtle Mountain*; November 23, 2007, Georgie Perigny, review of *Peril at Pier Nine*; September 25, 2009, Jeannine Stickle, review of *Graveyard of the Sea.*
Kirkus Reviews, March 1, 2011, review of *Ice Storm.*
Resource Links, June, 2006, Victoria Pennell, review of *Terror at Turtle Mountain*, p. 5; February, 2008, Anne Hatcher, review of *Peril at Pier Nine*, p. 7; December, 2009, Victoria Pennell, review of *A Terrible Roar of Water*, p. 13.
School Library Journal, October, 2006, Kristen Oravec, review of *Terror at Turtle Mountain*, p. 150.

ONLINE

Coteau Books Web site, http://coteaubooks.com/ (July 15, 2012), "Penny Draper."
Penny Draper Home Page, http://www.pennydraper.ca (July 15, 2012).*

*　　*　　*

DROUHARD, Brianne 1980-

Personal

Born 1980. *Education:* California Institute of the Arts, B.F.A. (animation), 2002.

Addresses

Home—CA. *E-mail*—brianne@briannedrouhard.com.

Career

Illustrator and animator. Storyboard artist; character and animator for television programs, including *Teen Titans,* 2004-06, *Class of 3000,* 2006-07, *Transformers: Animated,* 2007-09, *Avengers: Earth's Mightiest Heroes,* 2010, *New Teen Titans,* 2011-12, and *Super Best Friends Forever,* 2012. *Exhibitions:* Work included in group shows at galleries in Los Angeles, CA.

Writings

SELF-ILLUSTRATED

Billie the Unicorn, Immedium (San Francisco, CA), 2011.

Adaptations

Billie the Unicorn was adapted as an interactive app for iPhone and iPad.

Sidelights

In addition to her work as an animator and character designer for children's television programs, Brianne Drouhard is also the author and illustrator of *Billie the Unicorn.* Showcasing Drouhard's colorful, motion-filled art, *Billie the Unicorn* introduces a big-eyed, blue unicorn with a yearning for adventure that many children can relate to.

The title character in *Billie the Unicorn* lives in a cornfield where all the plants look the same. Although the young unicorn is first enticed by the nearby forest, where her cousins are able to grow colorful flowers amid a variety of undergrowth plants, another garden soon captures her imagination. After she hears about the queen's amazing castle and its vast and colorful gardens, Billie is determined to see it, but a difficult predicament ultimately causes the young unicorn to reconsider what matters most in her life. "Drouhard's background in animation is apparent in [the] fantastic, rainbow-sparkly spreads" in *Billie the Unicorn,* wrote a *Kirkus Reviews* writer, the critic adding that the story's central dilemma is lightened by art with "an Alice-in-Wonderland whimsy."

Biographical and Critical Sources

PERIODICALS

Children's Bookwatch, August, 2011, review of *Billie the Unicorn.*
Kirkus Reviews, April 1, 2011, review of *Billie the Unicorn.*

School Library Journal, September, 2011, Linda Ludke, review of *Billie the Unicorn,* p. 120.

ONLINE

Brianne Drouhard Home Page, http://www.brianne drouhard.com (August 1, 2012).
Brianne Drouhard Web log, http://potatofarmgirl.blogspot. com (August 1, 2012).*

* * *

DUNNING, Joan 1948-

Personal

Born 1948; children: two. *Education:* University of California, Santa Barbara, B.A..

Addresses

Home—Arcata, CA. *E-mail*—joandunning@gmail.com.

Career

Artist, writer, and naturalist. Fine-art painter; float designer for Rose Bowl Parade, Pasadena, CA. *Exhibitions:* Works included in gallery shows and private collections.

Awards, Honors

Award for designing Rose Bowl Parade float for City of Los Angeles; Bookbuilders of Boston Award, c. 1985, for *The Loon: Voice of the Wilderness;* AAAS/Subaru SB&F Prize for Excellence in Science Books, and Northern California Book Award in Children's Literature (younger readers category), both 2012, both for *Seabird in the Forest;*

Writings

SELF-ILLUSTRATED

The Loon: Voice of the Wilderness, Yankee Books (Dublin, NH), 1985.
Secrets of the Nest: The Family Life of North American Birds, Houghton Mifflin (Boston, MA), 1994.
From the Redwood Forest: Ancient Trees and the Bottom Line: A Headwaters Journey, photographs by Doug Thron, Chelsea Green Publishing (White River Junction, VT), 1998.
Seabird in the Forest: The Mystery of the Marbled Murrelet, Boyds Mills Press (Honesdale, PA), 2011.

ILLUSTRATOR

Sneed B. Collard III, *Leaving Home,* Houghton Mifflin (Boston, MA), 2002.

Sidelights

Joan Dunning shares her love of the environment, particularly the old-growth forests of the Northern California, in books such as *Secrets of the Nest: The Family Life of North American Birds* and the award-winning *Seabird in the Forest: The Mystery of the Marbled Murrelet.* A painter, writer, and naturalist, Dunning strives to balance art with science in all her creative work. "I believe that children deserve a good story," she told Gary Graham Hughes in an Environmental Protection Information Center Web site interview. "I like fuzzy, lovable, appealing images. I believe they are good for children's souls." "On the other hand," she continued, "I am devoted to the elegance and discipline of science; I love the reality of nature and the challenge of walking that fine line between anthropomorphizing and presenting delicious information and images that instantly magnetize children to the natural world."

Dunning's first book, *The Loon: Voice of the Wilderness,* was published in the mid-1980s and immediately became something of a nature classic, selling well over 100,000 copies following its author's appearance on the popular NPR radio program "All Things Considered." Illustrated with detailed pen-and-ink drawings and watercolor plates, *The Loon* prompted *New York Times Book Review* contributor Allen Lacy to dub it "a fine piece of natural history" that "is also poetic and deeply moving."

In *Secrets of the Nest* Dunning explores the remarkable diversity of bird nesting habits, discussing the nests' locations, colors, and sizes as well as how a variety of birds build their nests and care for their young. Among the birds Dunning examines are Harris's hawks, which nest in cacti, and kingfishers, which tunnel into the soil of steep riverbanks. "Each section is illustrated with lovely pen-and-ink drawings as sensitive to detail as Dunning's prose," Virginia Dwyer commented in her *Booklist* review of *Secrets of the Nest,* while a *Publishers Weekly* critic predicted that "this study will appeal equally to the novice and the seasoned birder." *Secrets of the Nest* also contains Dunning's watercolor plates of many of the birds discussed.

Seabird in the Forest was Dunning's first book to be illustrated with original oil paintings, and here her focus is on the marbled murrelet. A seabird that nests on the upper limbs of trees in old-growth forests along the Pacific Coast, the marbled murrelet returns to the same tree year after year. There the female lays a single egg; to feed the chick, adult murrelets make long flights back to the ocean to fish. "The text runs beneath expressive illustrations, with close-ups of adult birds and their chick as well as landscapes suggesting their contrasting worlds," a writer stated in appraising *Seabird in the Forest* for *Kirkus Reviews,* and a *Publishers Weekly* critic applauded the "verdant, rain-muted paintings" that depict the murrelet and its habitat. In the words of *School Library Journal* contributor Margaret Bush, Dunning's "large, glossy volume effectively describes the unfamiliar bird and the redwood ecosystem."

Joan Dunning shares her love of nature in the art and story for her picture book Seabird in the Forest: The Mystery of the Marbled Murelet. (Copyright © 2011 by Joan Dunning. Reproduced by permission of Boyds Mills Press, Inc.)

Dunning has also provided the artwork for *Leaving Home,* a picture book about animal maturation that features a text by Sneed B. Collard III. "In a series of richly colored watercolor paintings, Dunning portrays a wide array of species," remarked Carolyn Phelan in a review of *Leaving Home* for *Booklist,* and Louise L. Sherman wrote in *School Library Journal* that the artist's technique of depicting "most of the animals . . . breaking through into the pastel border that frames each illustration" effectively reinforces the theme of Collard's work.

"I have always wanted to write and illustrate books since I was a little girl," Dunning told *SATA.* "I have been inspired by the books of Holling C. Holling, who wrote and illustrated *Minn of the Mississippi,* about a tiny snapping turtle that floats the length of the Mississippi River. I was inspired by the way he included sketches of scientific information in the margins of his books and I have done the same in my books. I was also inspired by the illustrations of N.C. Wyeth of books like *Treasure Island* and *Kidnapped.* Wyeth showed me that children's books can be illustrated in beautiful, detailed oil paintings that honor children with the time and attention that has gone into their creation. Another of my favorite author/illustrators and role models is Beatrix Potter, creator of *Peter Rabbit.*

"I have always loved trees. When I was a teenager, I had a tree nursery. I took the native trees that I grew and planted them up in the San Gabriel Mountains behind my city of Pasadena. Now I live on the edge of a giant redwood forest. When I look out my kitchen window, there are huge trees just a few feet away and deer

and other wild animals pass by. I am not against logging, but I think that forests should not be cut faster than they grow. This is called 'sustainability'. I also do not believe that any more ancient, old-growth trees should be cut anywhere in the world. In North America less than 4 percent of our ancient forests remain standing.

"I have loved to draw and paint ever since I was a child, and I believe anyone can learn to draw. My father was a photographer and I used to work with him in his darkroom. My mother used to correct high-school English papers and she taught me how to write. My children are both artists and they love the natural world."

Biographical and Critical Sources

PERIODICALS

Booklist, March 15, 1994, Virginia Dwyer, review of *Secrets of the Nest: The Family Life of NorthAmerican Birds,* p. 1312; March 1, 2002, Carolyn Phelan, review of *Leaving Home,* p. 1137; April 15, 2011, Carolyn Phelan, review of *Seabird in the Forest: The Mystery of theMarbled Murrelet,* p. 51.
Children's Bookwatch, July, 2011, review of *Seabird in the Forest.*
Kirkus Reviews, February 1, 2002, review of *Leaving Home,* p. 178; March 1, 2011, review of *Seabird in the Forest.*
New York Times Book Review, June 2, 1985, Allen Lacy, review of *The Loon: Voice of the Wilderness.*
Publishers Weekly, February 14, 1994, review of *Secrets of the Nest,* p. 74; September 28, 1998, review of *From the Redwood Forest: Ancient Treesand the Bottom Line: A Headwaters Journey,* p. 82; April 4, 2011, review of *Seabird in the Forest,* p. 52.
School Library Journal, April, 2002, Louise L. Sherman, review of *Leaving Home,* p. 129; May, 2011, Margaret Bush, review of *Seabird in the Forest,* p. 95.
Sierra, November, 1998, Bob Schildgen, review of *From the Redwood Forest,* p. 76.

ONLINE

California Readers Web site, http://www.californiareaders.org/ (April, 2011), Bonnie O'Brian, "Meet Joan Dunning."
Environmental Protection Information CenterWeb site, http://www.wildcalifornia.org/ (July 5, 2011), Gary Graham Hughes, "Meet Joan Dunning."

*   *   *

DUTTON, Mike

Personal

Married; children: one son.

Addresses

Home—Berkeley, CA. *Office*—Google, Inc., 1600 Amphitheatre Pkwy., Mountain View, CA 94043. *E-mail*—mike@duttonart.net.

Career

Illustrator and comics artist. Google, Inc., doodler.

Illustrator

Lesléa Newman, *Donovan's Big Day,* Tricycle Press (Berkeley, CA), 2011.

Sidelights

Mike Dutton made his debut as a children's book illustrator with *Donovan's Big Day,* a picture book whose author, Lesléa Newman, gained a measure of notoriety as the author of 1989's groundbreaking *Heather Has Two Mommies.* One of the most controversial titles in contemporary American children's literature, *Heather Has Two Mommies* features a story about a child who is raised by same-sex parents, and *Donovan's Big Day* shares that perspective.

Donovan's Big Day focuses on a boy who is anticipating a major event in his young life. After Donovan eats breakfast with his grandparents, he carefully dresses for his role as ring-bearer in a wedding ceremony, although the identities of the betrothed remains a surprise until the story's end. In *Booklist* Hazel Rochman commended" Dutton's digitally touched gouache artwork, which keeps the focus on Donovan's role in the blissfully happy event." A *Publishers Weekly* contributor echoed Rochman's sentiment, asserting that the first-time illustrator's images "are bright and upbeat, clearly empathizing with the green-eyed hero's seriousness and pride." Assessing *Donovan's Big Day* for *School Library Journal,* Donna Cardon also appreciated the way in which Dutton's "illustrations capture Donovan's excited, self-conscious expressions as he moves carefully through his tasks."

In addition to his work in book illustration, Dutton works at Web giant Google, Inc., where he is part of a team of "doodlers" who create new iterations of the Google corporate logo. Google Doodles appear on the search page for one day only and celebrate holidays, birthdays of notable persons, or special events around the world.

Mike Dutton's illustration projects include capturing the joy of a family event in Lesléa Newman's **Donovan's Big Day.** (Illustration copyright © 2011 by Mike Dutton. Reproduced by permission of Tricycle Press, an imprint of Random House Children's Books, a division of Random House, Inc.)

Biographical and Critical Sources

PERIODICALS

Booklist, April 1, 2011, Hazel Rochman, review of *Donovan's Big Day,* p. 73.
Publishers Weekly, February 21, 2011, review of *Donovan's Big Day,* p. 130.
School Library Journal, April, 2011, Donna Cardon, review of *Donovan's Big Day,* p. 150.

ONLINE

Mike Dutton Home Page, http://duttonart.net (August 1, 2012).
Mike Dutton Web log, http://duttonart.tumblr.com (August 1, 2012).*

F-G

FORSHAY, Christina

Personal
Born in CA; married; husband a firefighter; children: two. *Education:* California State University, Long Beach, B.F.A. (illustration), 2002.

Addresses
Agent—The Bright Agency, 435 E. 14th St., Ste. 11F, New York, NY 10009; mail@thebrightagency.com. *E-mail*—christina@christinaforshay.com.

Career
Illustrator.

Member
Society of Children's Book Writers and Illustrators.

Awards, Honors
V/SB Artworks Event Portfolio Contest winner, Society of Children's Book Writers and Illustrators (SCBWI), 2007; SCBWI-L.A. People's Choice Portfolio Award and Illustrator's Day Professional's Choice Portfolio Award, both 2010; SCBWI-Orange County Editor's Day Portfolio Award, L.A. Scholarship Award, and Illustration Mentorship Award, all 2011.

Illustrator
Kristyn Crow, *The Really Groovy Story of the Tortoise and the Hare,* Albert Whitman (Chicago, IL), 2011.

Also illustrator of *Toad's Road Code,* written by Leyland Perree.

Sidelights
Illustrator Christina Forshay provides the artwork for *The Really Groovy Story of the Tortoise and the Hare,* Kristyn Crow's contemporary retelling of Aesop's clas-

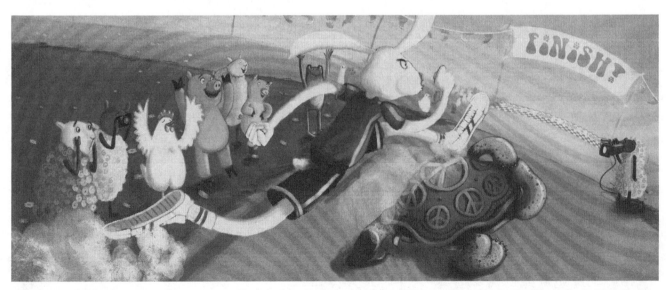

Christina Forshay helps put a new spin on an age-old tale in the artwork she contributes to Kristyn Crow's **The Really Groovy Story of the Tortoise and the Hare.** (Illustration copyright © 2011 by Christina Forshay. Reproduced by permission of Albert Whitman & Company.)

sic fable. In this updated version the mismatched duo's chance encounter at the fairgrounds sets the stage for their epic showdown. Hare, a trash-talking city dweller, is installed as the overwhelming pre-race favorite because no one believes that Tortoise, a mellow country boy, could possibly keep pace with his fleet-footed opponent. Inevitably, however, cocky Hare finds a way to foul up before crossing the finish line in second place.

Forshay's computer-generated artwork was cited by critics as a highlight of *The Really Groovy Story of the Tortoise and the Hare.* Her "illustrations, in saturated opaque colors in cheerful hues, offer amusing comic modeling in her animal cast," Hope Morrison remarked in the *Bulletin of the Center for Children's Books,* and a writer in *Kirkus Reviews* applauded the "positive energy that oozes from each spread." Other critics noted Forshay and Crow's visual and verbal references to the 1970s. "Readers will enjoy the details, such as the peace signs on Tortoise's shell," C.J. Connor reported in *School Library Journal,* and a *Publishers Weekly* online contributor reported that Forshay's "hallucinogenic moiré backgrounds amplify Hare's panic once he realizes that he's underestimated his competition."

Biographical and Critical Sources

PERIODICALS

Bulletin of the Center for Children's Books, April, 2011, Hope Morrison, review of *The Really Groovy Story of the Tortoise and the Hare,* p. 367.
Kirkus Reviews, February 1, 2011, review of *The Really Groovy Story of the Tortoise and the Hare.*
School Library Journal, February, 2011, C.J. Connor, review of *The Really Groovy Story of the Tortoise and the Hare,* p. 78.

ONLINE

Christina Forshay Home Page, http://www.christina forshay.com (July 15, 2012).
Publishers Weekly Online, http://www.publishersweekly. com/ (May 9, 2011), review of *The Really Groovy Story of the Tortoise and the Hare.**

* * *

GIBSON, Amy

Personal

Married; children: three. *Education:* Stanford University, B.A.; Santa Clara University, M.A. (education), CLAD teaching credential.

Addresses

Office—Digital Media Academy, 718 University Ave., Ste. 115, Los Gatos, CA 95032. *E-mail*—amy@ amygibson.com.

Career

Author and educator. Digital Media Academy, Los Gatos, CA, director. Worked at a high-tech company for four years; former elementary-school teacher.

Writings

Around the World on Eighty Legs, illustrated by Daniel Salmieri, Scholastic Press (New York, NY), 2011.
Split! Splat!, illustrated by Steve Björkman, Scholastic Press (New York, NY), 2012.

Sidelights

Amy Gibson introduces young readers to a host of creatures both unusual and familiar in *Around the World on Eighty Legs,* her debut picture book. Featuring humorous verse descriptions of more than fifty animals, the work focuses on unusual inhabitants of Africa, Asia, Australia, South America, and the Arctic and Antarctic. Among the creatures profiled are the hoatzin, an Ecuadorian bird known for its peculiar odor; the pangolin, a scaly, anteater-like mammal from Africa; and the takin, a hoofed creature resembling a goat or antelope.

"Instructional and entertaining, the poems nicely balance information with humor and wordplay," a critic observed in reviewing *Around the World on Eighty Legs* for *Publishers Weekly.* "Along with all the humor and fun, kids will pick up plenty of information," *Booklist* critic Hazel Rochman stated, and a writer for *Kirkus Reviews* maintained that readers "will go on quite a journey" in the pages of Gibson's picture book.

Gibson extols the virtues of spring weather in *Split! Splat!,* "an onomatopoetic praise song to rain and mud," according to a *Kirkus Reviews* contributor. Her story here centers on a young girl who frolics outdoors as a gentle rain falls, joining in messy, muddy play with her neighbors and her dog. Writing in *Booklist,* Carolyn Phelan noted that Gibson's "text is playful," and the *Kirkus Reviews* critic described *Split! Splat!* as "good sloshy fun."

Biographical and Critical Sources

PERIODICALS

Booklist, February 1, 2011, Hazel Rochman, review of *Around the World on Eighty Legs,* p. 64.
Horn Book, March-April, 2011, Susan Dove Lempke, review of *Around the World on Eighty Legs,* p. 132; March 15, 2012, Carolyn Phelan, review of *Split! Splat!,* p. 66.
Kirkus Reviews, February 1, 2011, review of *Around the World on Eighty Legs;* January 15, 2012, review of *Split! Splat!*
Publishers Weekly, January 3, 2011, review of *Around the World on Eighty Legs,* p. 50.
School Library Journal, February, 2011, Marilyn Taniguchi, review of *Around the World on Eighty Legs,* p. 96; March, 2012, Keisha M. Miller, review of *Split! Splat!,* p. 124.

ONLINE

Amy Gibson Home Page, http://www.amygibson.com (July 15, 2012).*

*   *   *

GÖRRISSEN, Janina 1984-

Personal

Born April 30, 1984, in Frankenthal, Rhineland-Palatinate, Germany; married Marc Rueda (an illustrator). *Education:* Attended Escola Joso (Barcelona, Spain), 2003-06.

Addresses

Home—Niederkirchen, Rhineland-Palatinate, Germany. *E-mail*—jgoerrissen@gmx.net.

Career

Illustrator. Artil Studio, Rhineland-Palatinate, Germany, co-founder with husband Marc Rueda.

Illustrator

Laurie Faria Stolarz, *Black Is for Beginnings,* graphic-novel adaptation by Barbara Randall Kesel, Flux (Woodbury, MN), 2009.

Evonne Tsang, *I Love Him to Pieces,* Graphic Universe (Minneapolis, MN), 2011.

Janina Görrissen creates the comic-book-style artwork that Brings to life Evonne Tsang's story in **My Boyfriend Is a Monster: I Love Him to Pieces.**

Ann Kerns, *I Date Dead People,* Graphic Universe (Minneapolis, MN), 2012.

Sidelights

Artist Janina Görrissen illustrates graphic novels for young-adult readers and she made her U.S. debut creating the artwork for Laurie Faria Stolarz's *Black Is for Beginnings,* Born in Germany, Görrissen attended art school in Barcelona, Spain. She and her husband, fellow artist Marc Rueda, now have their own illustration firm, Artil Studio.

A horror/romance involving a couple who can foretell the future, *Black Is for Beginnings* finds Stacey and Jacob living in different locales now that their intense relationship has flamed out. In Stolarz' tale readers learn that a series of calamitous events are tied to the couples' unusual psychic gifts. Daniel Kraus, reviewing the novel for *Booklist,* asserted that Görrissen's artwork for *Black Is for Beginnings* "reflects the schizophrenia of Stacey's and Jacob's lives . . . and takes full advantage of unusual panel construction."

Görrissen earned solid reviews for her first entry in the "My Boyfriend Is a Monster" series of graphic novels. Collaborating with Evonne Tsang on *I Love Him to Pieces,* she was tasked with visually depicting the emerging romance between an unlikely pair: Dicey is a talented baseball player who is teamed with Jack, an introspective Goth, on a class assignment. The two begin dating, but their bliss is interrupted when a renegade fungus begins turning residents of their Florida home town into zombies. Jack succumbs, but his parents are scientists and have an anti-zombie drug on hand; Dicey's job now is to transport him to his parents safely, without being eaten by zombies herself. "So vivacious are Jack and Dicey in Görrissen's black-and-white art that readers will forgive the indistinct depictions of violence," remarked a *Kirkus Reviews* contributor in reviewing the graphic novel. A critic for *Publishers Weekly* also commended the drawings in *I Love Him to Pieces,* writing that "Görrissen's artwork is slick and attractive, and she clearly has a skill for facial expressions."

Görrissen is also the illustrator of the graphic comichorror novel *I Date Dead People,* which features a text by Ann Kerns. In this tale, young Nora finds teen romance with Tom, the ghost who inhabits her family's century-old house. Snow Wildsmith, a contributor to *Booklist,* predicted that readers familiar with the previous "My Boyfriend Is a Monster" books are likely to "welcome the return of Görrissen's appealingly rounded and cheerful art."

Biographical and Critical Sources

PERIODICALS

Booklist, October 1, 2009, Daniel Kraus, review of *Black Is for Beginnings,* p. 33; March 15, 2011, Francisca Goldsmith, review of *I Love Him to Pieces,* p. 32; May 15, 2012, Snow Wildsmith, review of *I Date Dead People,* p. 43.

Bulletin of the Center for Children's Books, July-August, 2011, April Spisak, review of *I Love Him to Pieces,* p. 542.
Kirkus Reviews, March 15, 2011, review of *I Love Him to Pieces.*
Publishers Weekly, April 4, 2011, review of *I Love Him to Pieces,* p. 55.
School Library Journal, July, 2011, Alana Joli Abbott, review of *I Love Him to Pieces,* p. 123.

ONLINE

Janina Görrissen Home Page, http://www.jgoerrissen.com (August 1, 2012).
Janina Görrissen Web log, http://jgoerrissen.blogspot.com (August 1, 2012).*

* * *

GREENWOOD, Diana 1956-

Personal

Born 1956, in Minneapolis, MN; children: one daughter. *Education:* Degree (business). *Religion:* Presbyterian.

Addresses

Home—Napa Valley, CA. *Agent*—Jen Rofé, Andrea Brown Literary Agency, 1076 Eagle Dr., Salinas, CA 93905.

Career

Editor and novelist. Retail interior designer; journalist and copywriter.

Member

Society of Children's Book Writers and Illustrators.

Writings

Insight, Zondervan (Grand Rapids, MI), 2011.

Contributor to Web log *The Mixed-Up Files of Middle Grade Authors.*

Sidelights

Diana Greenwood was born in Minnesota but spent time in Winnipeg, Manitoba, as well as California during her formative years. Jobs in commercial interior design and work as a copy editor and lifestyle writer occupied Greenwood's hours in between honing her fiction-writing skills until the Michigan-based publisher Zondervan agreed to take on her novel, *Insight.*

In *Insight* Greenwood blends paranormal mystery with Christian revelation. Set in 1940s Wisconsin, her story's narrator is Elvira, the daughter of a family blighted by alcoholism and poverty. Elvira's father departs to fight in World War II, leaving behind a pregnant wife, and he never returns home. Elvira's little sister Jessie is born after a perilous labor and she does not speak until she is four years old. As Elvira eventually realizes, Jessie is gifted with what appear to be extrasensory powers, including future sight and the ability to sense others' thoughts. The girls' mother, meanwhile, is depressed and perennially short tempered. When Jessie convinces her mom that her husband is waiting for them out West the woman seeks the help of an itinerant preacher and prepares both daughters for their transformative road trip to California. In the end, Elvira comes to better understand her sister's gifts and her own faith with the help of this minister.

"While Christian beliefs flavor this effort, they never overpower the narrative but are instead organic to it," noted a *Kirkus Reviews* contributor in appraising Greenwood's debut. Writing for *School Library Journal*, Mahnaz Dar remarked of *Insight* that "Elvira's descriptions of her strained familial relationships and pain over her father's absence will resonate with readers."

Biographical and Critical Sources

PERIODICALS

Kirkus Reviews, April 15, 2011, review of *Insight.*
School Library Journal, August, 2011, Mahnaz Dar, review of *Insight,* p. 102.

ONLINE

Diana Greenwood Home Page, http://www.dianagreenwood.com (August 1, 2012).*

* * *

GRIFFIN, Molly Beth 1982-

Personal

Born October 7, 1982, in Minneapolis, MN; children: Jasper. *Education:* Grinnell College, B.A. (English); Hamline University, M.F.A. (writing for children and young adults). *Hobbies and other interests:* Cooking, reading, hiking.

Addresses

Home—Minneapolis, MN. *E-mail*—mollybethgriffin@gmail.com.

Career

Writer and educator. Loft Literary Center, Minneapolis, MN, teacher; manuscript critique and writing mentor.

Awards, Honors

Barbara Kneutson Award, Hamline University, 2011, for *Loon Baby;* artist initiative grant, Minnesota State Arts Board, 2012; Milkweed Prize for Children's Literature, 2012, for *Silhouette of a Sparrow.*

Writings

Loon Baby, illustrated by Anne Hunter, Houghton Mifflin Books for Children (Boston, MA), 2011.
Silhouette of a Sparrow, (young-adult novel), Milkweed Editions (Minneapolis, MN), 2012.

Sidelights

In her debut picture book *Loon Baby,* Molly Beth Griffin explores a common childhood fear—separation from a parent—while centering on the loving relationship between a young bird and its mother. Based in Minnesota, where she teaches and mentors other writers, Griffin has also produced the award-winning young-adult novel *Silhouette of a Sparrow,* which a *Kirkus Reviews* contributor described as "a sweet, quiet coming-of-age story" that is set against the backdrop of Jazz-Age America. As Griffin's sixteen-year-old heroine discovers romantic love and gains a sense of her life's purpose, her "familial and identity struggles will resonate with contemporary teens," according to a *Publishers Weekly* critic. "Though my writing reaches across all age groups and genres," the author commented to *SATA,* "it all demonstrates my passion for exploring young people's changing relationship to the natural world."

Secure in their cozy nest in the great north woods, Baby Loon and Mama Loon venture out one day to the middle of a small lake, searching for dinner when readers first encounter them in *Loon Baby.* When Mama Loon dives beneath the waves and fails to return immediately, her floating fledging grows concerned. After paddling about for some time, tiny Loon Baby bravely puts his head beneath the surface, attempting his very first dive while trying to spot his parent. When it begins raining, the young waterfowl resorts to a tried-and-true method to attract Mama Loon's 's attention: emitting a loud, plaintive wail.

Loon Baby earned praise for its simple but effective narrative and comforting message. "This gentle story of a young bird's fears . . . offers reassurance to children in a similar situation," observed *School Library Journal* critic Susan Scheps. A reviewer in *Publishers Weekly* stated that "Griffin does a good job of keeping the story's action and tension manageable," and a *Kirkus Reviews* writer maintained that *Loon Baby* is "guaranteed to hit the mark with anyone who's ever felt lost and alone."

Biographical and Critical Sources

PERIODICALS

Booklist, February 15, 2011, Patricia Austin, review of *Loon Baby,* p. 77.

Molly Beth Griffin introduces readers to life in a coastal ecosystem in her picture book **Loon Baby,** *which features artwork by Anne Hunter.* (Illustration copyright © 2011 by Anne Hunter. Reproduced by permission of Houghton Mifflin Harcourt Publishing Company. All rights reserved.)

Kirkus Reviews, February 15, 2011, review of *Loon Baby;* August 1, 2012, review of *Silhouette of a Sparrow.*
Publishers Weekly, August 6, 2012, review of *Silhouette of a Sparrow,* p. 57
School Library Journal, May, 2011, Susan Scheps, review of *Loon Baby,* p. 78.

ONLINE

Molly Beth Griffin Home Page, http://mollybethgriffin.com (July 15, 2012).
Publishers Weekly Online, http://www.publishersweekly.com/ (May 9, 2011), review of *Loon Baby.*

*   *   *

GRIMARD, Gabrielle 1975-

Personal

Born 1975, in Montreal, Quebec, Canada; married; husband a boat builder; children: two. *Education:* Attended Concordia University.

Addresses

Home—Montreal, Quebec, Canada. *Agent*—Lori Nowicki, Painted Words, 310 W. 97th St., Apt. 24, New York, NY 10025-6127.

Career

Illustrator. Worked as a fine-art painter and muralist, 1998-2001.

Awards, Honors

Great Books for Children selection, Canadian Toy Testing Council, 2007, for *L'arbre à chats* by Nancy Montour.

Illustrator

Claire Dumont and Suzanne Lacoursière, *Conduis mes pas vers la paix: le pardon,* Médiaspaul (Montreal, Quebec, Canada), 2003, translated by Gisèle Larocque as *Jesus Gives Us Peace: The Sacrament of Reconciliation,* Pauline Books & Media (Boston, MA), 2006.

Maryse Pelletier, *La chasse aux moules,* La Courte Échelle (Montreal, Quebec, Canada), 2003.

Maryse Pelletier, *La chasse aux flèches,* La Courte Échelle (Montreal, Quebec, Canada), 2004.

Ania Kazi, *Monsieur Alphonse et le secret d'Agathe,* Dominique et Cie. (Saint-Lambert, Quebec, Canada), 2004.

Maryse Pelletier, *La chasse au plomb,* La Courte Échelle (Montreal, Quebec, Canada), 2004.

Bernadette Renaud, *Pas de chouchous!,* Éditions du Renouveau pédagogique (Saint-Lambert, Quebec, Canada), 2004.

Milda Castillo and others, *L'accident Hugo,* Éditions de l'Hôpital Sainte-Justine (Montreal, Quebec, Canada), 2005.

Christine Bonenfant, *La fabrique de contes,* Éditions P. Tisseyre (Saint-Lambert, Quebec, Canada), 2005.

Sylvie Roberge, *Le cirque,* Dominique et Cie. (Saint-Lambert, Quebec, Canada), 2005.

Christine Bonenfant, *La fabrique de contes. II,* Éditions P. Tisseyre (Saint-Lambert, Quebec, Canada), 2006.

Charles Perrault, *Cendrillon,* retold by Anique Poitras, Éditions Imagine (Montreal, Quebec, Canada), 2006.

Sylvie Roberge, *La magie,* Dominique et Cie. (Saint-Lambert, Quebec, Canada), 2006.

Isabel Fonte, *Crimson Pete and the Missing Treasure,* music by Glenn Morley and Mark Shekter, Tormont (Montreal, Quebec, Canada), 2006.

Lorna Mulligan, *Le trésor des pirates: histoire avec autocollants,* French translation by Nathalie Vallière, Tormont (Montreal, Quebec, Canada), 2006.

Nancy Montour, *L'arbre à chats,* Dominique et Cie. (Saint-Lambert, Quebec, Canada), 2007.

Sylvie Roberge and Jacques Pasquet, *Les jeux de ficelle,* Dominique et Cie. (Saint-Lambert, Quebec, Canada), 2007.

Sonia Sarfati, *Xavier et la porte qui n'existe pas,* Dominique et Cie. (Saint-Lambert, Quebec, Canada), 2007.

Sylvie Roberge, *Les jeux de ficelles,* Dominique et Cie. (Saint-Lambert, Quebec, Canada), 2007.

Sylvie Roberge, *Les marionettes,* Dominique et Cie. (Saint-Lambert, Quebec, Canada), 2007.

Sylvie Roberge and Nancy Montour, *Les papillons,* Dominique et Cie. (Saint-Lambert, Quebec, Canada), 2008.

Marie Lasnier, *Tatiana au pays du vent,* Dominique et Cie. (Saint-Lambert, Quebec, Canada), 2008.

Sophie Morissette, *Hourra! tout un plat!,* Éditions du Renouveau pédagogique (Saint-Laurent, Quebec, Canada), 2008.

Elaine Arsenault, *La prophétie d'Ophélia,* translation by Caroline LaRue, Dominique et Cie. (Saint-Lambert, Quebec, Canada), 2008.

Andrée Poulin, *La plus belle robe du royaume,* Bayard Canada (Montreal, Quebec, Canada), 2008.

Elaine Arsenault, *Le destin de Ballanika,* translation by Caroline LaRue, Dominique et Cie. (Saint-Lambert, Quebec, Canada), 2008.

Elaine Arsenault, *La quête de Lily,* translation by Caroline LaRue, Dominique et Cie. (Saint-Lambert, Quebec, Canada), 2008.

Michel Noël and Sylvie Roberge, *Eskoumina: L'amour des petits Fruits,* Hurtubise (Montreal, Quebec, Canada), 2008.

Ingrid Lee, *Maybe Later,* Orca Book Publishers (Custer, WA), 2008.

Marie Lasnier, *Une famille tricotée serré,* Dominique et Cie. (Saint-Lambert, Quebec, Canada), 2009.

Sonia Sarfati, *Xavier et le livre de lumière,* Dominique et Cie. (Saint-Lambert, Quebec, Canada), 2009.

Sylvie Roberge, *Casse-Noisette, l'histoire d'un ballet,* Dominique et Cie. (Saint-Lambert, Quebec, Canada), 2009.

Andrée Poulin, reteller, *Blanche-Neige* (based on a story by the Brothers Grimm), Éditions Imagine (Montreal, Quebec, Canada), 2009.

Karen Kingsbury, *The Princess and the Three Knights,* ZonderKidz (Grand Rapids, MI), 2009.

Sylvie Roberge, *Les échecs,* Dominique et Cie. (Saint-Lambert, Quebec, Canada), 2010.

Alain M. Bergeron, *La classe de Madame Caroline,* Dominique et Cie. (Saint-Lambert, Quebec, Canada), 2010.

Dominique Demers, *Aujourd'hui, peut-être,* Dominique et Cie. (Saint-Lambert, Quebec, Canada), 2010, translated by Sheila Fischman as *Today, Maybe,* Orca Book Publishers (Victoria, British Columbia, Canada), 2011.

Karen Kingsbury, *Brave Young Knight,* Zonderkidz (Grand Rapids, MI), 2011.

Dominique Demers, *Le noël du petit Gnouf,* Dominique et Cie. (Saint-Lambert, Quebec, Canada), 2011.

Mireille Messier, *Fatima et les voleurs de clémentines,* Éditions de la Bagnole (Outremont, Quebec, Canada), 2011.

Paule Brièpre, *Maman solo,* Imagine (Montreal, Quebec, Canada), 2011.

Linda Wilscam, *Picotine et l'homme aux ballons,* Québec Amérique (Montreal, Quebec, Canada), 2012.

Lili Chartrand, *Monsieur Fred,* Dominique et Cie. (Saint-Lambert, Quebec, Canada), 2012.

Dominique Demers, *Le petit Gnouf. No 2,* Dominique et Cie. (Saint-Lambert, Quebec, Canada), 2012.

Also illustrator of paper-doll sets featuring stories by Melody N. Chanted,Peter Pauper Press, 2011.

Sidelights

Gabrielle Grimard is a prolific illustrator of children's books published in both Canada and the United States. Living and working in the Francophone Quebec city of Montreal, Grimard is particularly adept at creating images for folk tales and stories of a religious nature. She studied art at Concordia University in Montreal and forged a career as a muralist and solo artist before becoming a book illustrator. Her first illustration project, Claire Dumont and Suzanne Lacoursière's *Conduis mes pas vers la paix: le pardon,* was published in 2003.

One of Grimard's first English-language illustration projects, *The Princess and the Three Knights,* is a story by successful Christian-novel writer Karen Kingsbury that finds a royal monarch determined to find a worthy mate for his cherished daughter. Several knights show their interest, but all must undergo character tests in order to prove themselves fit for marriage into the royal family. In a second collaboration, *Brave Young Knight,* a rostoer of ambitious young men continue their competition for the royal daughter.

Grimard's art "adheres closely to fairy-tale conventions," asserted Gillian Engberg in reviewing *The Princess and the Three Knights* for *Booklist,* the critic predicting that the book's "bright, attractive scenes will easily hold children's attention." Appraising *Brave Young Knight,* a *Publishers Weekly* reviewer remarked on the artist's unique style, noting that "patchwork lawn, layered hills, and geometrical patterns on lattices, fabric, and woodwork decorate Grimard's medieval village scenes."

During her career Grimard has collaborated with author Dominique Demers on *Today, Maybe,* a picture book that has been translated from the original French by Sheila Fischman. In Demers' whimsical story a young girl wills herself to stop growing and ensconces herself in an isolated forest hut to await a special visitor, her sole companion a bird. A succession of visitors discovers the girl in her hideout, but she deflects threats from a wolf, a witch, a band of pirates, and even a tempting proposal from a prince in order to greet her mysterious guest. Although Demers' story generates "feeling of thinness," according to *Canadian Review of Materials* contributor Andrea Galbraith, Grimard's "beautiful, warm illustrations greatly add to the text" in *Today, Maybe,* and in *Quill & Quire* Gwyneth Evans wrote that "the mood of Demers's poetic story" is beautifully matched by Grimard's images, with their rich colours, exquisite and sometimes quirky details." For *Booklist* critic Thom Barthelmess, Demers and Grimard's collaborative effort stands as "a work of clever, poetic sweetness, with familiar folktale imagery giving way to tender surprise."

Biographical and Critical Sources

PERIODICALS

Booklist, September 1, 2009, Gillian Engberg, review of *The Princess and the Three Knights,* p. 102; April 15, 2011, Thom Barthelmess, review of *Today, Maybe,* p. 61.
Canadian Review of Materials, February 4, 2011, Andrea Galbraith, review of *Today, Maybe.*
Kirkus Reviews, March 1, 2011, review of *Today, Maybe;* March 15, 2011, review of *Brave Young Knight.*
Publishers Weekly, February 21, 2011, review of *Today, Maybe,* p. 132; February 28, 2011, review of *Brave Young Knight,* p. 53.
Quill & Quire, March, 2011, Gwyneth Evans, review of *Today, Maybe.*

*   *   *

GULLEDGE, Laura Lee 1979-

Personal

Born 1979, in VA. *Education:* James Madison University, B.A. (studio art/education), 2001; M.A. (art education), 2002.

Addresses

Home—Brooklyn, NY. *Agent*—Dan Lazar, Writers House, 21 W. 26th St., New York, NY 10010. *E-mail*—lauraleegulledge@gmail.com.

Career

Educator and author/illustrator. Louisa County Public Schools, Mineral, VA, middle-school art teacher, 2002-04; volunteer art teacher in Accra, Ghana, 2007. Freelance scenic painter and event producer; presenter at workshops. *Exhibitions:* Work exhibited in solo and group shows at galleries in Brooklyn, NY, and elsewhere.

Member

Animamus Art Salon.

Awards, Honors

CYBILS Award finalist, 2011, and Eisner Award nomination for Best Lettering, and YALSA Great Graphic Novels for Teens listee, American Library Association, both 2012, all for *Page by Paige.*

Writings

SELF-ILLUSTRATED

Page by Paige (graphic novel), Amulet Books (New York, NY), 2011.

Contributor of online comics to *Daily Cross Hatch* and *Acti-i-Vate Webcomix Collective;* contributor to periodicals, including *Madison Magazine* and *Washington Post.*

Sidelights

Laura Lee Gulledge fictionalizes her own coming-of-age experiences in her self-illustrated graphic novel *Page by Paige.* A graduate of James Madison University, Gulledge taught middle-school art for several years while developing a career path as creative as she was. In addition to her work as a comic artist, she also designs and crafts stage sets, presents workshops, and plans large-scale public events in and around her adopted city of Brooklyn.

In *Page by Paige* readers meet Paige Turner, a teen who has just moved with her family from Virginia to New York City. Along with the typical adolescent worries about fitting in with friends, Paige also has to learn to navigate an alien landscape as well as a teen culture that is very different from the one back home. *Page by*

Laura Lee Gulledge taps the challenges of her own teen years in her self-illustrated graphic-novel memoir **Page by Paige.**

Paige is framed as the young woman's sketchbook and captures her big dreams of becoming an artist as well as her little dreams of making friends, finding a boyfriend, and keeping family relationships on an even keel while she gradually asserts her independence.

Calling *Page by Paige* a "strong debut," Elaine Gass Hirsch added in *Voice of Youth Advocates* that "Gulledge's emotive illustrations help to convey the ups and downs of young adulthood." With its "expressive" black-and-white art and its focus on what a *Kirkus Reviews* critic characterized as "an artistic introvert," the work allows readers to understand Paige's "innermost thoughts, even as they join her quest for identity and belonging."; As Francesca Goldsmith wrote in *Booklist,* the central character "serves as a reflection of and inspiration to readers who might see themselves as nascent artists." *Page by Paige* "gets it right," Stephen Burt announced in reviewing Gulledge's graphic-novel memoir for *Rain Taxi* online. "It's the kind of teen story that goes with an indie-pop soundtrack," Burt added, noting that the author/illustrator "shows a faultless sympathy with her characters" and "her visual style fits their moody innocence, their optimism, and their fears."

Biographical and Critical Sources

PERIODICALS

Booklist, March 15, 2011, Francisca Goldsmith, review of *Page by Paige,* p. 34.
Horn Book, July-August, 2011, Tanya D. Auger, review of *Page by Paige,* p. 148.
Kirkus Reviews, April 1, 2011, review of *Page by Paige.*
Publishers Weekly, February 7, 2011, review of *Page by Paige,* p. 59.
School Library Journal, July, 2011, Barbara M. Moon, review of *Page by Paige,* p. 121.
Voice of Youth Advocates, August, 2011, Elaine Gass Hirsch, review of *Page by Paige,* p. 268.

ONLINE

Laura Lee Gulledge Home Page, http://www.cobald designs.biz (August 1, 2012).
Laura Lee Gulledge Web log, http://whoislauralee.blogspot (August 1, 2012).*

H

HALE, Nathan

Personal

Married; children: two.

Addresses

Home—Provo, UT. *Agent*—Kid Shannon, 630 9th Ave., Ste. 707, New York, NY 10036. *E-mail*—nathan@ spacestationnathan.com.

Career

Author and illustrator. Chase Studios (natural-history exhibit company), Cedarcreek, MO, former staff artist.

Awards, Honors

Notable Book selection, American Library Association (ALA), and Great Graphic Novel for Teens selection, YALSA/ALA, both 2008, both for *Rapunzel's Revenge* by Shannon and Dean Hale.

Writings

SELF-ILLUSTRATED

The Devil You Know, Walker & Company (New York, NY), 2005.
Yellowbelly and Plum Go to School, Putnam (New York, NY), 2007.
The Twelve Bots of Christmas, Walker & Co. (New York, NY), 2010.

SELF-ILLUSTRATED; "NATHAN HALE'S HAZARDOUS TALES" GRAPHIC NOVEL SERIES

One Dead Spy, Harry N. Abrams (New York, NY), 2012.
Big Bad Ironclad, Harry N. Abrams (New York, NY), 2012.

ILLUSTRATOR; "JUNGLE BOOK" SERIES BASED ON THE WORK OF RUDYARD KIPLING

Mowgli's Big Birthday, adapted by Diane Namm, Sterling Publishing (New York, NY), 2006.
Mowgli Knows Best, adapted by Diane Namm, Sterling Publishing (New York, NY), 2007.
The Boy and His Sled Dog, adapted by Diane Namm, Sterling Publishing (New York, NY), 2010.
The Brave Little Seal, adapted by Diane Namm, Sterling Publishing (New York, NY), 2010.

ILLUSTRATOR

Shannon Hale and Dean Hale, *Rapunzel's Revenge,* Bloomsbury (New York, NY), 2008.
Anne Muecke, *The Dinosaurs' Night before Christmas,* Chronicle Books (San Francisco, CA), 2008.
Jill Santopolo, *The Nina, the Pinta, and the Vanishing Treasure,* Orchard Books (New York, NY), 2008.
Dan McCann, *Balloon on the Moon,* Walker & Company (New York, NY), 2008.
Jill Santopolo, *The Ransom Note Blues,* Orchard Books (New York, NY), 2009.
Candace Ryan, *Animal House,* Walker Books for Young Readers (New York, NY), 2010.
Shannon Hale and Dean Hale, *Calamity Jack,* Bloomsbury (New York, NY), 2010.
L.A. Peacock, *Panic in Pompeii,* Scholastic (New York, NY), 2011.
Rick Walton, adaptor, *Frankenstein,* Feiwel & Friends (New York, NY), 2012.

Contributor of artwork to *Cricket* magazine.

Adaptations

The Devil You Know was produced as a filmby 21 Laps.

Sidelights

Utah artist Nathan Hale transitioned from work as an artist for Chase Studios, a company that creates natural-history exhibits for museums across the United States, to a full-time job as a book illustrator and author. Illustration work came first and included a job creating art for Shannon and Dean Hale's quirky graphic novels *Rapunzel's Revenge* and *Calamity Jack,* both which recast traditional fairy-tale characters in stories set in an alternate version of the Old West. In *Rapunzel's Revenge* "Hale's detailed, candy-colored artwork demands close viewing," asserted a *Publishers Weekly* critic, while Tina Coleman commented in *Booklist* on his talent for creating "expressive characters and lending a wonderful sense of place to the [story's] fantasy landscape." Describing *Calamity Jack* as a "steampunk-flavored fairy tale," Anita L. Burkham also praised Hale's art in her *Horn Book* review by noting that his "adrenaline-fueled action sequences, . . . shifts in perspective, and sound effects . . . drive the story forward."

Hale's original picture books include *The Devil You Know, Yellowbelly and Plum Go to School,* and *The Twelve Bots of Christmas,* as well as the multi-volume "Nathan Hale's Hazardous Tales" graphic novels, which salt true stories from history with a liberal layer of humor and invention. In *The Devil You Know* the Fell family finds that the house they have just moved into is haunted. The troublesome demon who lives with them skis down the stairs and otherwise drives the family crazy with its noisy antics. Along comes Ms. Phisto, who claims she does "minor-demon removal" and "light housekeeping." The family signs her up to remove the

Anne Meucke's quirky version of a favorite holiday tale in The Dinosaurs' Night before Christmas *gains a dose of humor from Hale's amusing art.* (Illustration copyright © 2008 by Nathan Hale. Used by permission of Chronicle Books LLC., San Francisco. Visit ChronicleBooks.com.)

demon, but they soon regret the decision when Ms. Phisto turns out to be a more-serious nuisance. "Think *Amityville Horror* with a happy ending," stated a critic for *Publishers Weekly,* the reviewer praising "Hale's considerable visual talents." "This spirited romp will appeal to readers who are not afraid of a little magic and mayhem," predicted Joy Fleishhacker in her *School Library Journal* review of *The Devil You Know.*

Yellowbelly and Plum Go to School finds Yellowbelly, a cat-like monster, and his best friend, a purple teddy bear named Plum, preparing for their first day at school. Yellowbelly enjoys the new adventure until he misplaces Plum in the schoolyard. A frantic search recovers the missing bear, but only after several other students use poor Plum as a Frisbee and a basketball. Fleishhacker noted that young readers "will relate to Yellowbelly's childlike characteristics and be amused by his humorously exaggerated behavior and not-too-frightening appearance," and a *Kirkus Reviews* critic wrote that "Hale makes a common premise uncommonly appealing with illustrations that feature a gloriously multi-species cast." A reviewer for *Publishers Weekly* called *Yellowbelly and Plum Go to School* "heartwarming and clever" and concluded that Hale's "tale of friendship and loyalty will have readers awaiting more from this likable twosome."

In *The Twelve Bots of Christmas* Hale re-wires a traditional holiday song, going hi-tech in a story that introduces a robotic version of Santa Claus and trades in Santa's sleigh for a sleek new space ship (with robotic reindeer, of course). No drummers drumming or ladies dancing here; instead, as Hale's lyrics play out from one to a dozen readers meet an ever-increasing gathering of robotic creatures, all which enjoy a colorful celebration on the book's final pages. Hale's computer-generated illustrations serve as a "subtle homage to everything from *Star Wars* to *Dr. Who,*" according to Mara Alpert in *School Library Journal,* the critic predicting that readers will enjoy examining the artwork's "fun details." Using what a *Kirkus Reviews* critic described as "dark, edgy hues," *The Twelve Bots of Christmas* is a good choice for children "who like electronics, robots, tools and gears," while in *Horn Book* Chelsey G.H. Philpot praised the work as an "imaginative variation" on the well-known song that includes "plenty of fun . . . for techies."

In "Nathan Hale's Hazardous Tales" even reluctant readers are compelled to turn the pages as Hale weaves the events of history into a graphic-novel story. In *One Dead Spy* he plays on his name by focusing on the famous colonial patriot Nathan Hale, who was hanged in 1776 after being convicted of spying for General George Washington's colonial army. Hoping to delay his execution Scheherazade style, Hale enthralls the hangman with the history stories that make up the "Hazardous Tales" series. In *Big Bad Ironclad!* Hale focuses on the epic seagoing battle between the metal-coated warship the USS *Monitor* and the Confederate Navy's *Virginia*

Hale puts a futuristic spin on the holiday season in his self-illustrated picture book The Twelve Bots of Christmas. (Copyright by Nathan Hale. Reproduced by permission of Walker & Company, an imprint Bloomsbury USA.)

that took place in 1861. "Livelier than the typical history textbook," *Big Bad Ironclad!* also takes a "sillier" approach than the typical children's book, according to a *Kirkus Reviews* writer, resulting in a work that "will appeal to both history buffs and graphic-novel enthusiasts." Appraising the series concept, another contributor to *Kirkus Revies* noted of *One Dead Spy* that Hale's "innovative approach to history . . . will have young people reading with pleasure."

Biographical and Critical Sources

PERIODICALS

Booklist, September 1, 2008, Tina Coleman, review of *Rapunzel's Revenge,* p. 100; November 15, 2008, Ilene Cooper, review of *The Dinosaurs'Night before Christmas,* p. 49; October 1, 2009, Eva Volin, review of *Calamity Jack,* p. 41.

Horn Book, March-April, 2010, Anita L. Burkam, review of *Calamity Jack,* p. 56; November-December, 2010, Chelsey G.H. Philpot, review of *The Twelve Bots of Christmas,* p. 63.

Kirkus Reviews, June 15, 2007, review of *Yellowbelly and Plum Go to School;* November 1, 2008, review of *The Dinosaurs' Night before Christmas;* December 1, 2009, review of *Calamity Jack;* June 15, 2010, review of *Animal House;* September 1, 2010, review of *The Twelve Bots of Christmas;* July 15, 2012, review of *Big Bad Ironclad!*

Publishers Weekly, August 1, 2005, review of *The Devil You Know,* p. 65; June 18, 2007, review of *Yellowbelly and Plum Go to School,* p. 52; August 4, 2008, review of *Rapunzel's Revenge,* p. 63.

School Librarian, summer, 2010, Andy Sawyer, review of *Calamity Jack,* p. 112.

School Library Journal, August, 2005, Joy Fleishhacker, review of *The Devil You Know,* p. 96; August, 2007, Joy Fleishhacker, review of *Yellowbellyand Plum Go to School,* p. 81; January, 2010, Eric Norton, review of *Calamity Jack,* p. 128; July, 2010, Rachel Kamin, review of *The Boy and His Sled Dog,* p. 62; August, 2010, Jasmine L. Precopio, review of *Animal House,* p. 85; October, 2010, Mara Alpert, review of *The Twelve Botsof Christmas,* p. 71.

ONLINE

Kid Shannon Web site, http://www.kidshannon.com/ (April 5, 2008), "Nathan Hale."

Nathan Hale Home Page, http://www.spacestationnathan.com (August 1, 2012).

Nathan Hale Web log, http://spacestationnathan.blogspot.com (August 1, 2012).*

*   *   *

HARRINGTON, Kim 1974-

Personal

Born 1974; married; children: one son. *Education:* B.A. (marketing); M.B.A.

Addresses

Home—MA. *E-mail*—kimharringtonbooks@yahoo.com.

Career

Writer.

Awards, Honors

Quick Pick for Reluctant Young Adult Readers designation, American Library Association, 2011, for *Clarity.*

Writings

The Dead and Buried, Point (New York, NY), 2013.

"CLARITY" YOUNG-ADULT NOVEL SERIES

Clarity, Point (New York, NY), 2011.
Perception, Point (New York, NY), 2012.

"SLEUTH OR DARE" MIDDLE-GRADE NOVEL SERIES

Partners in Crime, Scholastic (New York, NY), 2012.
Sleepover Stakeout, Scholastic (New York, NY), 2012.
Framed and Dangerous, Scholastic (New York, NY), 2012.

Sidelights

A sixteen year old with unusual psychic abilities joins a murder investigation in *Clarity,* Kim Harrington's first novel for a young-adult audience. In addition to *Clarity* and its sequel, *Perception,* Harrington has also tantalized preteen mystery fans with her "Sleuth or Dare" novels featuring likeable seventh-grade sleuths Norah and Darcy.

Clarity focuses on Clarity "Clare" Fern who, like the other members of her family, possesses a supernatural gift: she can recount people's histories simply by touching an object in their possession. When a tourist is murdered in Eastport, the Cape Cod town where Clare's family lives, the police ask the teen to help solve the crime. The situation grow even more complicated after Clare learns that her brother has become a prime suspect in the murder and that she must work the case with Justin, her cheating ex-boyfriend, as well as with Gabriel, the handsome son of Eastport's new detective.

"Harrington's well-developed characters and tight plot are simultaneously charming, realistically complex, and intriguing," a critic stated in a *Publishers Weekly* review of *Clarity,* and a *Kirkus Reviews* writer called Clare "an appealing character with whom readers easily can identify." *Clarity* is a good choice for "kids who love all things paranormal or who just appreciate a good whodunit," Gina Bowling concluded in her *School Library Journal* review of Harrington's Y.A. debut.

When readers reconnect with Clare in *Perception,* the teen is still torn by her romantic feelings for both Justin and Gabriel when she begins receiving messages from a secret admirer. After a student goes missing and is thought to be murdered, Clare's admirer turns menacing and she must now use her powers to uncover the truth about a strange new series of unfolding events. Writing in *School Library Journal,* Krista Welz applauded *Perception,* describing Clare as "a strong female lead who, throughout the story, gains confidence and depth."

Biographical and Critical Sources

PERIODICALS

Booklist, March 15, 2011, Angela Leeper, review of *Clarity,* p. 54; February 15, 2012, Michael Cart, review of *Perception,* p. 54; May 1, 2012, Carolyn Phelan review of *Partners in Crime,* p. 158.
Bulletin of the Center for Children's Books, March, 2011, Claire Gross, review of *Clarity,* p. 330.
Kirkus Reviews, February 1, 2011, review of *Clarity.*
Publishers Weekly, January 24, 2011, review of *Clarity,* p. 155.
School Library Journal, March, 2011, Gina Bowling, review of *Clarity,* p. 162; March, 2012, Krista Welz, review of *Perception,* p. 158.
Voice of Youth Advocates, April, 2012, Donna Miller, review of *Perception,* p. 73.

ONLINE

Kim Harrington Home Page, http://www.kimharrington books.com (July 15, 2012).
Kim Harrington Web log, http://kimharrington.blogspot.com (July 15, 2012).

* * *

HAUTMAN, Pete 1952-
(Peter Murray)

Personal

Born September 29, 1952, in Berkeley, CA; son of Thomas Richard and Margaret Elaine (an artist) Hautman; married Mary Louise Logue (a writer). *Education:* Attended Minneapolis College of Art and Design, 1970-72, and University of Minnesota, 1972-76.

Cover of Kim Harrington's young-adult novel Clarity, *featuring cover art by Sarah Howell.* (Jacket illustration copyright © 2011 by Sarah Howell. Reproduced by permission of Scholastic, Inc.)

Addresses

Home—Golden Valley, MN; and Stockholm, WI. *Agent*—Jennifer Flannery, Flannery Literary, 1140 Wickfield Ct., Naperville, IL 60563-3300; FlanLit@aol. com. *E-mail*—pete@petehautman.com.

Career

Writer. Worked in freelance marketing and design, and as a sign painter, graphic artist, and pineapple slicer.

Member

Mystery Writers of America.

Awards, Honors

New York Times Notable Book designation, 1993, for *Drawing Dead,* and 1996, for *The Mortal Nuts;* Edgar Allan Poe Award nomination, Mystery Writers of America, and Best Books for Young Adults designation, American Library Association (ALA), both 1996, both for *Mr. Was;* ALA Quick Picks for Reluctant Young-Adult Readers designation, 1998, for *Stone Cold;* Minnesota Book Award for Best Popular Novel, 1999, for *Mrs. Million;* Children's Choices selection, International Reading Association/Children's Book Council, and ALA Popular Paperbacks for Young Adults designation, both 2001, both for *Hole in the Sky;* ALA Best Books for Young Adults designation, and Minnesota Book Award, both 2003, both for *Sweetblood;* National Book Award for Young People's Literature, 2004, and ALA Best Books for Young Adults designation, both for *Godless;* ALA Best Books for Young Adults designation and Quick Picks for Reluctant Young-Adult Readers designation, both 2005, both for *Invisible;* ALA Best Books for Young Adults designation, 2006, for *Rash;* Minnesota Book Award finalist, and ALA Quick Picks for Reluctant Young-Adult Readers designation, both 2010, both for *Blank Confession; Los Angeles Times* Book Prize, 2011, for *The Big Crunch.*

Writings

YOUNG-ADULT FICTION

Mr. Was, Simon & Schuster (New York, NY), 1996.
Stone Cold, Simon & Schuster (New York, NY), 1998, published as *No Limit,* Simon Pulse (New York, NY), 2005.
Hole in the Sky, Simon & Schuster (New York, NY), 2001.
Sweetblood, Simon & Schuster (New York, NY), 2003.
Godless, Simon & Schuster (New York, NY), 2004.
Invisible, Simon & Schuster (New York, NY), 2005.
Rash, Simon & Schuster (New York, NY), 2006.
All-In, Simon & Schuster (New York, NY), 2007.
(Editor) *Full House: Ten Stories about Poker,* Putnam (New York, NY), 2007.
How to Steal a Car, Scholastic Press (New York, NY), 2009.

Blank Confession, Simon & Schuster (New York, NY), 2010.
The Big Crunch, Scholastic Press (New York, NY), 2011.
The Obsidian Blade (first book in "Klaatu Diskos" trilogy), Candlewick Press (Somerville, MA), 2012.
What Boys Really Want, Scholastic Press (New York, NY), 2012.

"BLOODWATER MYSTERIES" NOVEL SERIES; WITH WIFE, MARY LOGUE

Snatched, Putnam (New York, NY), 2006.
Skullduggery, Putnam (New York, NY), 2007.
Doppelganger, Putnam (New York, NY), 2008.

FOR CHILDREN; NONFICTION; UNDER NAME PETER MURRAY

Beavers, Child's World (Mankato, MN), 1992.
Black Widows, Child's World (Mankato, MN), 1992.
Dogs, Child's World (Mankato, MN), 1992.
Planet Earth, Child's World (Mankato, MN), 1992.
The Planets, illustrated by Anastasia Mitchell, Child's World (Mankato, MN), 1992.
Rhinos, Child's World (Mankato, MN), 1992.
Silly Science Tricks, Child's World (Mankato, MN), 1992, published as *Silly Science Tricks: With Professor Solomon Snickerdoodle,* illustrated by Anastasia Mitchell, 1993.
Snakes, Child's World (Mankato, MN), 1992.
Spiders, Child's World (Mankato, MN), 1992.
The World's Greatest Chocolate Chip Cookies, illustrated by Anastasia Mitchell, Child's World (Mankato, MN), 1992.
The World's Greatest Paper Airplanes, illustrated by Anastasia Mitchell, Child's World (Mankato, MN), 1992.
You Can Juggle, illustrated by Anastasia Mitchell, Child's World (Mankato, MN), 1992.
Your Bones: An Inside Look at Skeletons, illustrated by Viki Woodworth, Child's World (Mankato, MN), 1992.
The Amazon, Child's World (Mankato, MN), 1993.
Beetles, Child's World (Mankato, MN), 1993.
Chameleons, Child's World (Mankato, MN), 1993.
The Everglades, Child's World (Mankato, MN), 1993.
Frogs, Child's World (Mankato, MN), 1993.
Gorillas, Child's World (Mankato, MN), 1993.
Hummingbirds, Child's World (Mankato, MN), 1993.
Parrots, Child's World (Mankato, MN), 1993.
Porcupines, Child's World (Mankato, MN), 1993.
The Sahara, Child's World (Mankato, MN), 1993.
Saturn, Child's World (Mankato, MN), 1993.
Sea Otters, Child's World (Mankato, MN), 1993.
The Space Shuttle, Child's World (Mankato, MN), 1993.
Tarantulas, Child's World (Mankato, MN), 1993.
Science Tricks with Air, illustrated by Anastasia Mitchell, Child's World (Mankato, MN), 1995, published as *Professor Solomon Snickerdoodle's Air Science Tricks,* 1995.

Science Tricks with Light, illustrated by Anastasia Mitchell, Child's World (Mankato, MN), 1995, published as *Professor Solomon Snickerdoodle's Light Science Tricks,* Child's World (Plymouth, MN), 1999.

Professor Solomon Snickerdoodle Looks at Water, illustrated by Anastasia Mitchell, Child's World (Mankato, MN), 1995, published as *Professor Solomon Snickerdoodle's Water Science Tricks,* 1998.

Dirt, Wonderful Dirt!, illustrated by Penny Dann, Child's World (Mankato, MN), 1995.

Make a Kite!, illustrated by Penny Dann, Child's World (Mankato, MN), 1995.

The Perfect Pizza, illustrated by Penny Dann, Child's World (Mankato, MN), 1995.

Sitting Bull: A Story of Bravery, Child's World (Mankato, MN), 1996.

Cactus, Child's World (Mankato, MN), 1996.

Orchids, Child's World (Mankato, MN), 1996.

Roses, Child's World (Plymouth, MN), 1996.

Earthquakes, Child's World (Plymouth, MN), 1996.

Mushrooms, Child's World (Plymouth, MN), 1996.

Hurricanes, Child's World (Plymouth, MN), 1996.

Tornadoes, Child's World (Plymouth, MN), 1996.

Volcanoes, Child's World (Plymouth, MN), 1996.

Deserts, Child's World (Plymouth, MN), 1997.

Lightning, Child's World (Plymouth, MN), 1997.

Mountains, Child's World (Plymouth, MN), 1997.

Rainforests, Child's World (Plymouth, MN), 1997.

Redwoods, Child's World (Plymouth, MN), 1997.

Prairies, Child's World (Plymouth, MN), 1997.

Floods, Child's World (Plymouth, MN), 1997.

Scorpions, Child's World (Plymouth, MN), 1997.

Pigs, Child's World (Chanhassen, MN), 1998.

Snails, Child's World (Chanhassen, MN), 1998.

Sheep, Child's World (Chanhassen, MN), 1998.

Curiosity: The Story of Marie Curie, illustrated by Leon Baxter, Child's World (Plymouth, MN), 1998.

Perseverance: The Story of Thomas Alva Edison, illustrated by Robin Lawrie, Child's World (Plymouth, MN), 1998.

Dreams: The Story of Martin Luther King, Jr., illustrated by Robin Lawrie, Child's World (Plymouth, MN), 1999.

A Sense of Humor: The Story of Mark Twain, illustrated by Robin Lawrie, Child's World (Chanhassen, MN), 1999.

Copper, Smart Apple Media (North Mankato, MN), 2001.

Silver, Smart Apple Media (North Mankato, MN), 2001.

Oil, Smart Apple Media (North Mankato, MN), 2001.

Diamonds, Smart Apple Media (North Mankato, MN), 2001.

Gold, Smart Apple Media (North Mankato, MN), 2001.

Iron, Smart Apple Media (North Mankato, MN), 2001.

Apatosaurus, Smart Apple Media (North Mankato, MN), 2001.

Stegosaurus, Smart Apple Media (North Mankato, MN), 2001.

Pterodactyls, Smart Apple Media (North Mankato, MN), 2001.

Tyrannosaurus Rex, Smart Apple Media (North Mankato, MN), 2001.

Triceratops, Smart Apple Media (North Mankato, MN), 2001.

Velociraptor, Smart Apple Media (North Mankato, MN), 2001.

ADULT NOVELS

Drawing Dead, Simon & Schuster (New York, NY), 1993.

Short Money, Simon & Schuster (New York, NY), 1995.

The Mortal Nuts, Simon & Schuster (New York, NY), 1996.

Ring Game, Simon & Schuster (New York, NY), 1997.

Mrs. Million, Simon & Schuster (New York, NY), 1999.

Rag Man, Simon & Schuster (New York, NY), 2001.

Doohickey, Simon & Schuster (New York, NY), 2002.

The Prop, Simon & Schuster (New York, NY), 2006.

Sidelights

Pete Hautman is a versatile and prolific writer who has produced critically acclaimed fiction for both adult and

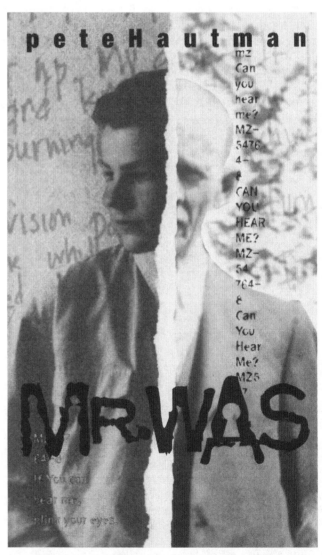

Cover of Pete Hautman's award-winning young-adult novel **Mr. Was,** *which takes readers on a trip through time.* (Jacket illustration design and illustration by Sammy Yuen Jr. (NY, 1996). Reproduced by permission of Simon Pulse, an imprint of Simon & Schuster Children's Publishing Division.)

teen readers. Lauded by critics for his imaginative, action-filled plots, Hautman's novels include *Mr. Was, Blank Confession,* and *The Big Crunch,* the last a recipient of the *Los Angeles Times* Book Prize. Under the pseudonym Peter Murray, Hautman has also published numerous works of juvenile nonfiction covering everything from dinosaurs to weather to biographies of notable Americans.

In 1992, after working for almost twenty years in advertising and design, Hautman left that field to begin his second career as a freelance author. "It has turned out to be a happy decision," he once told *SATA.* "I live in a large house in south Minneapolis with mystery writer, poet, and children's author Mary Logue, and a cat named Ubik. We spend part of each summer at our second home, an old farmhouse in Stockholm, Wisconsin. Both Mary and I write every day, and we like it. We act as each other's editor, critic, and cheerleader."

Hautman's YA debut, *Mr. Was,* is a serious tale that mixes contemporary elements with time travel. Taking place in the author's home state of Minnesota, the story focuses on teenager Jack Lund as he moves with his widowed dad into his late grandfather's home. While the house seems forbidding, it contains a portal that takes Jack back to 1940, allowing him to escape his brutal father's alcoholism and the death of his mother. Further twists to the plot ensue when Jack's new job as a farmhand causes him to come face to face with the young woman who will one day become his grandmother—as long as his presence in the past does not disrupt his own future. Other adventures take Jack from rural Minnesota to the World War II battlefield of Guadalcanal as *Mr. Was* plays out.

"Ingenious plotting and startling action combine to make [*Mr. Was*] . . . a riveting read," a *Publishers Weekly* contributor enthused, the reviewer adding that Hautman's plot is "sophisticated" without becoming "overwhelming," and is "mined with surprises that explode like fireworks."

Gambling-addicted teen Denn Doyle is the troubled protagonist of *Stone Cold,* a novel by Hautman that has been more-recently released as *No Limit.* In this story Denn brushes aside the concerns of family and friends who realize that his compulsion to play poker is becoming increasingly destructive and remains hooked on the sense of power the game gives him. Poker and the wealth it promises become the center of Denn's life, and soon he loses interest in his landscaping business, his family, and even his girlfriend.

Stone Cold is "enthralling reading," wrote *Horn Book* contributor Nancy Vasilakis, the critic adding that the novel's "final devastating scene will . . . leave readers with something to think about." A *Publishers Weekly* critic called Hautman's story "swift and salacious," noting that it "compellingly echoes gambling's siren call."

Booklist contributor Roger Leslie found "Denn's first-person narration . . . brisk and engaging" and the novel builds intrigue by focusing on "the interesting intricacies of addiction" rather than arguing against gambling. "Hautman knows the world of cards and the world of adolescence; this is a compelling read," concluded Paula Rohrlick in her *Kliatt* review of *Stone Cold.*

Denn's story continues in *All-In,* as the now-seventeen-year-old poker prodigy finally strikes it rich. When he falls for card dealer Cattie Hart, however, his luck changes for the worse; Cattie secretly works for Artie Kingston, Denn's nemesis, and the teen soon finds himself in desperate financial straits. Hoping to avoid returning home penniless, Denn tries to attract the financing that will enable him to enter Artie's million-dollar, winner-take-all poker tournament. Writing in *Booklist,* Ian Chipman praised *All-In,* stating that Hautman "call[s] the action with all the deftness of a dealer flipping cards: sharp, fast, and effortless."

Taking place in the near future, *The Hole in the Sky* centers on four teenagers who number among the few survivors of an influenza outbreak that has depopulated most of Earth. Sixteen-year-old Ceej Kane and his sister Harryette now live with their uncle near the Grand Canyon. When Harryette and his uncle both disappear, Ceej and friend Tim go in search of them and are attacked by the Kinka—a cult-like group believing itself to be chosen by an angry God and charged with eliminating all other survivors. Fleeing into the wilderness, Ceej and Tim meet Bella, a mysterious Hopi girl who agrees to help them.

While noting that the story's mysticism—involving Native American beliefs regarding the existence of a magical path leading to a new world—"may displease those who like their speculative fiction to remain realistic," a *Horn Book* contributor praised *The Hole in the Sky* for its "intense action and fascinating premise." Reviewing the work for *Booklist,* Roger Leslie complimented the author, noting that he "promises much and delivers impressively." "Hautman writes lyrically about the Grand Canyon, and the tense plot will keep readers turning the pages," Rohrlick predicted in her review of *The Hole in the Sky* for *Kliatt.*

Sweetblood introduces readers to a diabetic teenager named Lucy who writes a school report linking vampire legends to her chronic disease. Lucy is depressed and lonely when she comes into contact with a group of Goth students, including one who thinks he is a vampire. As the teen sinks further into despair, she begins looking for a new way to view life. Debbie Carton, writing in *Booklist,* noted "Lucy's clever, self-deprecating" narration, while a *Kirkus Reviews* contributor called *Sweetblood* "an original and powerful tale."

Hautman's award-winning YA novel *Godless* focuses on Jason Bock, a bright teenager who, along with his equally gifted friend Shin, creates graphic novels. The pair's creative output takes a surprising turn after they create a new religion that they intend as a spoof of Catholicism. Their new faith, based on the spirituality of water, soon begins to take on a life of its own as other teens become believers and follow Jason to "worship" at the local watertower. A terrible accident and the realization that Shin has actual begun to believe what the two of them invented finally force Jason to address the consequences of his actions.

The topic of religion, both as it derived and is practiced, looms large over the course of *Godless*. The tone of the novel changes from fairly light-hearted to deep and complex; according to Joel Shoemaker in *School Library Journal*, "While chuckling aloud may be common in the early chapters, serious issues dominate the latter stages of the book." Hautman explained that his novel is not about God; "It's about how people—teenagers in particular—deal with the questions that arise when their faith has been shaken," he explained on his home page. "Inventive, frequently funny and sometimes scary, this YA novel has a lot to offer readers," wrote Claire Rosser in *Kliatt*, and a *Kirkus Reviews* contributor praised Hautman's story as "thought-provoking and unique."

In *Invisible* Doug claims to be "invisible" because of the way he is treated by a teacher and ignored by a girl he has a crush on. The only positive relationship he has is the one he shares with his best friend, Andy, a popular athlete. As the story unfolds, readers perceive that Doug behaves like a stalker and has numerous emotional problems. His relationship with Andy is also complex and its layers are revealed as readers discover the events shaping Doug's life. A *Kirkus Reviews* contributor called *Invisible* a "haunting, lonely tale," while a *Publishers Weekly* contributor noted that "the strength of Hautman's painfully sad novel is the wisecracking but clearly unreliable voice of its narrator." Susan Riley, writing in *School Library Journal*, commented that, "with its excellent plot development and unforgettable, heartbreaking protagonist, this is a compelling novel of mental illness." According to Ilene Cooper in *Booklist*, "the chilling but ambiguous denouement" of *Invisible* "is definitely unsettling."

Rash is set in the futuristic United Safer States of America, where doing anything dangerous is against the law and people have to wear helmets even while walking along a sidewalk. When hot-tempered Bo Marsten gets into a fight which results in his arrest, he winds up in a rehabilitation factory where he is forced to join an illegal football team. "This thought-provoking and highly entertaining dystopian fantasy is certain to spark discussion among teens," predicted a *Publishers Weekly* contributor, and a *Kirkus Reviews* critic wrote of *Rash* that Hautman's "bitingly funny and unexpectedly heartwarming [depiction of] Bo's coming-of-age is a winner."

A bored suburban teen opts for a life of crime in *How to Steal a Car*, a "sharply observed, subversive coming-

of-age tale," according to a contributor in *Kirkus Reviews*. After finding a pair of lost keys in a mall parking lot, Kelleigh Monahan impulsively takes the owner's car for a joy ride, an illogical but thrilling act that leads her to join a ring of auto thieves. Critics praised the work, especially secondary characters such as Kelleigh's philandering father, a defense attorney who frees a rapist on a technicality. "This tight, slim book is a moral briar patch that might leave some grasping for purpose," maintained Daniel Kraus in *Booklist*, and Adrienne L. Strock noted in *School Library Journal* that Hautman draws Kelleigh as "an empty, judgmental girl who seeks to fill her life's voids with cheap thrills."

Hautman explores the issue of bullying in *Blank Confession*, "a taut mystery that's nearly impossible to put down," in the view of a critic in *Publishers Weekly*. The work opens as sixteen-year-old Shayne Blank walks into his local police station and confesses to a murder. Shayne's description of the crime alternates with flashbacks from Mikey Martin, a vulnerable high-school junior who draws the ire of his sister's menacing, drug-dealing boyfriend. An unlikely friendship between Mikey and Shayne, who views himself as the boy's protector, ultimately results in a violent confrontation. According to *Horn Book* reviewer Lauren Adams, in *Blank Confession* "Hautman draws us into a side of teenage life darkened by drugs, and . . . asks whether violence can ever be justified."

Hautman offers a tender love story in *The Big Crunch*, which centers on June, a high-school junior. Thanks to her father's career, June is entering her sixth school in four years and is wary of forming any lasting attachments. June's new classmate Wes has just ended a romantic relationship and vows to remain single for a time, but when he literally collides with June in the school hallway the two teens are instantly drawn to one another. "Showing his range, Hautman . . . writes a love story that's affecting despite, or perhaps because of, its ordinariness," explained a critic in *Publishers Weekly*, and *Voice of Youth Advocates* contributor Lynn Evarts described *The Big Crunch* as "simple, poignant, and very, very real."

In *What Boys Really Want* a feud between longtime friends threatens to ruin their once-close relationship. When Adam Merchant decides to pen a self-help book for his high-school classmates, he plagiarizes material from the blog of best friend Lita Wolz, a teen who dispenses dating advice as the sassy "Miz Fitz." When Lita discovers Adam's treachery, conflict erupts. "This is fresh, realistic YA fiction at its best," remarked Amy Pickett in a *School Library Journal* review of *What Boys Really Want*. A reviewer in *Publishers Weekly* observed that "Hautman captures the angst, awkwardness, and joy of crushes and first dates with humor and heart," and Kraus called *What Boys Really Want*, "fun, sarcastic, blundering, preposterous, but every bit still a romance."

Cover of Hautman's young-adult novel The Big Crunch, *a romantic story featuring cover art by Frank Stockton.* (Jacket illustration copyright © 2011 by Frank Stockton. Reproduced by permission of Scholastic, Inc.)

In addition to his solo books, Hautman has collaborated with wife Mary Logue on the "Bloodwater Mysteries" series of novels. Geared toward younger readers, series opener *Snatched* introduces readers to Roni Delicata and Brian Bain, two teen detectives determined to solve the mystery of their classmate's disappearance. As B. Allison Gray wrote in her *School Library Journal* review of the book, the coauthors "are able to manage the rapid unfolding of the plot while still allowing for character development," while Christine M. Heppermann called Roni and Brian a "younger, hipper Holmes and Watson" in her *Horn Book* review.

In *Skullduggery* Brian and Roni help a local archaeologist save a Native American burial ground from greedy developers. Rohrlick commented that "this amiable mystery offers humor and surprising turns of events," and a contributor in *Kirkus Reviews* remarked that "the adventures of these meddlesome junior sleuths . . . are quite entertaining." Roni becomes convinced that she has spotted a younger version of Brian on a missing-persons Web site in *Doppelganger,* the third installment

in the "Bloodwater Mysteries" series. Rohrlick offered praise for this "well-plotted and suspenseful tale" by the husband-and-wife team, and *Booklist* critic Carolyn Phelan applauded the novel's "smart dialogue, quick pacing, and likable protagonists."

Biographical and Critical Sources

PERIODICALS

Booklist, October 1, 1993, Donna Seaman, review of *Drawing Dead,* p. 253; April 1, 1996, Thomas Gaughan, review of *The Mortal Nuts,* p. 1346; September 15, 1996, Laura Tillotson, review of *Mr. Was,* p. 230; October 1, 1997, David Pitt, review of *Ring Game,* p. 310; September 15, 1998, Roger Leslie, review of *Stone Cold,* p. 218; April 15, 2001, Roger Leslie, review of *Hole in the Sky,* p. 1554; September 1, 2001, Joanne Wilkinson, review of *Rag Man,* p. 56; September 1, 2002, Joanne Wilkinson, review of *Doohickey,* p. 62; May 1, 2003, Debbie Carton, review of *Sweetblood,* p. 1595; June 1, 2004, Ilene Cooper, review of *Godless,* p. 1730; June 1, 2005, Ilene Cooper, review of *Invisible,* p. 1784; March 1, 2006, Frank Sennett, review of *The Prop,* p. 71; May 1, 2007, Carolyn Phelan, review of *Skullduggery,* p. 44, and Ian Chipman, review of *All-In,* p. 85; May 1, 2008, Carolyn Phelan, review of *Doppelganger,* p. 46; August 1, 2009, Daniel Kraus, review of *How to Steal a Car,* p. 57; October 1, 2010, Daniel Kraus, review of *Blank Confession,* p. 82; January 1, 2011, Gillian Engberg, review of *The Big Crunch,* p. 88; December 15, 2011, Daniel Kraus, review of *What Boys Really Want,* p. 56.

Entertainment Weekly, July 26, 1996, Gene Lyons, review of *The Mortal Nuts,* p. 51.

Horn Book, November, 1998, Nancy Vasilakis, review of *Stone Cold,* p. 730; May, 2001, review of *Hole in the Sky,* p. 325; July-August, 2003, Lauren Adams, review of *Sweetblood,* p. 458; July-August, 2004, Deirdre F. Baker, review of *Godless,* p. 453; May-June, 2005, Betty Carter, review of *Invisible,* p. 325; May-June, 2006, Vicky Smith, review of *Rash,* p. 319; July-August, 2006, Christine M. Heppermann, review of *Snatched,* p. 442; November-December, 2009, Christine M. Heppermann, review of *How to Steal a Car,* p. 675; November-December, 2010, Lauren Adams, review of *Blank Confession,* p. 93; January-February, 2011, Christine M. Heppermann, review of *The Big Crunch,* p. 95; May-June, 2012, Lauren Adams, review of *The Obsidian Blade,* p. 85.

Journal of Adolescent & Adult Literacy, February, 2005, James Blasingame, interview with Hautman, p. 438.

Kirkus Reviews, August 15, 2001, review of *Rag Man,* p. 1149; August 15, 2002, review of *Doohickey,* p. 1163; June 1, 2003, review of *Sweetblood,* p. 805; May 1, 2004, review of *Godless,* p. 442; May 15, 2005, review of *Invisible,* p. 590; January 15, 2006, review of *The Prop,* p. 55; April 15, 2006, review of *Snatched,* p. 407; June 1, 2006, review of *Rash,* p. 573; April

15, 2007, review of *Skullduggery*; March 1, 2008, review of *Doppleganger*; August 15, 2009, review of *How to Steal a Car*; October 1, 2010, review of *Blank Confession*; November 15, 2010, review of *The Big Crunch*; December 1, 2011, review of *What Boys Really Want.*

Kliatt, May, 2003, Claire Rosser, review of *Sweetblood,* p. 10; May, 2004, Claire Rosser, review of *Godless,* p. 8; September, 2004, Claire Rosser, review of *Sweetblood,* p. 20; July, 2005, Paula Rohrlick, review of *No Limit,* pp. 21; November, 2005, Claire Rosser, review of *Godless,* p. 14, and Paula Rohrlick, review of *Hole in the Sky,* p. 20; May, 2007, Paula Rohrlick, review of *Skullduggery,* p. 13; July, 2007, Paula Rohrlick, review of *All-In,* p. 16; March, 2008, Paula Rohrlick, review of *Doppelganger,* p. 14.

Library Journal, October 1, 1993, Erna Chamberlain, review of *Drawing Dead,* p. 126; January, 1996, Paul Kaplan, review of *Short Money,* p. 176; May 1, 1996, Rex E. Klett, review of *The Mortal Nuts,* p. 136; October 1, 1997, Jo Ann Vicarel, review of *Ring Game,* p. 122; April 1, 1999, Thomas L. Kilpatrick, review of *Mrs. Million,* p. 128.

New York Times Book Review, November 7, 1993, Marilyn Stasio, review of *Drawing Dead,* p. 24; May 21, 1995, Marilyn Stasio, review of *Short Money,* p. 39; June 23, 1996, Marilyn Stasio, review of *The Mortal Nuts,* p. 28; November 9, 1997, Marilyn Stasio, review of *Ring Game,* p. 29; April 9, 2000, John D. Thomas, review of *Mrs. Million,* p. 223; October 14, 2001, Marilyn Stasio, review of *Rag Man,* p. 26.

People, August 5, 1996, J.D. Reed, review of *The Mortal Nuts,* p. 32.

Publishers Weekly, August 30, 1993, review of *Drawing Dead,* p. 74; March 27, 1995, review of *Short Money,* p. 78; October 28, 1996, review of *Mr. Was,* p. 83; September 1, 1997, review of *Ring Game,* p. 94; October 12, 1998, review of *Stone Cold,* p. 78; February 8, 1999, review of *Mrs. Million,* p. 196; May 14, 2001, review of *Hole in the Sky,* p. 83; August 13, 2001, review of *Rag Man,* p. 281; August 12, 2002, review of *Doohickey,* p. 274; June 2, 2003, review of *Sweetblood,* p. 53; June 28, 2004, review of *Godless,* p. 51; June 27, 2005, review of *Invisible,* p. 65; January 16, 2006, review of *The Prop,* p. 35; May 8, 2006, review of *Rash,* p. 66, and Sue Corbett, interview with Hautman, p. 67; September 14, 2009, review of *How to Steal a Car,* p. 50; November 15, 2010, review of *Blank Confession,* p. 59; November 29, 2010, review of *The Big Crunch,* p. 51; December 12, 2011, review of *What Boys Really Want,* p. 70.

School Library Journal, October, 1996, John Peters, review of *Mr. Was,* p. 147; September, 1998, Joel Shoemaker, review of *Stone Cold,* p. 203; June, 2001, Steven Engelfried, review of *Hole in the Sky,* p. 149; July, 2003, Lynn Evarts, review of *Sweetblood,* p. 130; August, 2004, Joel Shoemaker, review of *Godless,* p. 123; June, 2005, Susan Riley, review of *Invisible,* p. 160; June, 2006, B. Allison Gray, review of *Snatched,* p. 158; July, 2008, Sheila Fiscus, review of *Doppelganger,* p. 99; November, 2009, Adrienne L. Strock, review of *How to Steal a Car,* p. 108; Decem-

ber, 2010, Lalitha Nataraj, review of *Blank Confession,* p. 114; February, 2011, Shawna Sherman, review of *The Big Crunch,* p. 109; January, 2012, Amy Pickett, review of *What Boys Really Want,* p. 116.

Voice of Youth Advocates, October, 2004, Jamie S. Hansen, review of *Godless,* p. 298; February, 2011, Lynn Evarts, review of *The Big Crunch,* p. 554; April, 2012, Rachel Wadham, review of *The Obsidian Blade,* p. 74.

ONLINE

BookPage Web site, http://www.bookpage.com/ (June 1, 2005), Linda M. Castellito, interview with Hautman.
Pete Hautman Home Page, http://www.petehautman.com (July 15, 2012).
Pete Hautman Web log, http://petehautman.blogspot.com (July 15, 2012).*

*   *   *

HÉNAFF, Carole 1973-

Personal

Born 1973, in Orange, France. *Education:* Studied theatrical literature (Paris, France); studied illustration and graphic design (Barcelona, Spain). *Hobbies and other interests:* Travel.

Addresses

Home—Barcelona, Spain. *Agent*—Marlena Agency, marlena@marlenaagency.com. *E-mail*—carolehenaff@gmail.com.

Career

Illustrator and graphic designer. Peret Studio, Barcelona, Spain, graphic designer for four years; freelance designer.

Illustrator

Susie Morgenstern, *Les dues meitats de l'amistat,* translated from the French by Enric Tudó i Rialp, Cruïlla (Barcelona, Spain), 2006.

Paula Carballeira, *Smara,* Kalandraka Ediciones Andalucía (Seville, Spain), 2006.

Sin Título, Blur (Madrid, Spain), 2007.

La lletera (adapted from a story by La Fontaine), Cruïlla (Barcelona, Spain), 2007.

Camille Meyer, editor, *Poètes en exil,* Mango (Paris, France), 2007.

Paul Bakolo Ngoi, *Quién ha lído alguna vez roncar a un plátano?,* Edelvives (Madrid, Spain), 2008.

Jesús Ballaz, *El anillo fulgurante,* Edelvives (Madrid, Spain), 2010.

Jesús Ballaz, *L'anell fulgurant,* Baula (Barcelona, Spain), 2010.

Wafa' Tarnowska, *The Arabian Nights,* Barefoot Books (Cambridge, MA), 2010.

Hugh Lupton and Daniel Morden, *The Adventures of Achilles,* Barefoot Books (Cambridge, MA), 2012.

Biographical and Critical Sources

PERIODICALS

Booklist, January 1, 2011, Hazel Rochman, review of *The Arabian Nights,* p. 78.
Kirkus Reviews, November 15, 2010, review of *The Arabian Nights.*
School Library Journal, February, 2011, C.J. Connor, review of *The Arabian Nights,* p. 131.

ONLINE

Carole Hénaff Home Page, http://www.carolehenaff.com (August 1, 2012).
Carole Hénaff Web log, http://carolehenaff.blogspot.com (August 1, 2012).*

* * *

HEYER, Carol 1950-

Personal

Born February 2, 1950, in Cuero, TX; daughter of William Jerome (a metallurgist and craftsman) and Merlyn Mary (an entertainer and artist) Heyer; children: one. *Education:* Attended Moorpark College; California Lutheran University, B.A., 1974. *Hobbies and other interests:* Interior decorating, gardening.

Addresses

Home—Thousand Oaks, CA. *E-mail*—carolheyer@gmail.com.

Career

Author and illustrator of children's books. Lynn-Davis Productions (film production company; then Lynn-Wenger Productions), Westlake Village, CA, staff artist and writer, 1982-88; Touchmark, Thousand Oaks, CA, founder, writer, and illustrator, beginning 1988. Hollywood Film School, artist, 1986-88.

Member

Society of Children's Book Writers and Illustrators, Association of Science-Fiction and Fantasy Artists, Society of Illustrators—Los Angeles.

Awards, Honors

Magazine Merit Award, Society of Children's Book Writers and Illustrators, 1988, for cover illustration of *Dragon;* International Reading Association (IRA)/Children's Book Council (CBC) Choice selection, 1989, for *Beauty and the Beast,* 1990, for *Excalibur;* awards from Prints Regional Design Competition, Spectrum International Competition for Fantastic Art, and Society of Illustrators; two Chesley Award nominations, Carnegie Art Institute; Best Cover Art award, *Aboriginal Science Fiction;* (with Scott Goto) Buckeye Children's Book Award, North Carolina Children's Book Award, Monarch Award, Colorado Children's Book Award, Maryland Black-Eyed Susan Book Award, IRA/CBC Teachers' Choice selection, and several children's choice awards, all 2005, all for *Once upon a Cool Motorcycle Dude* by Kevin O'Malley.

Writings

SELF-ILLUSTRATED

(Reteller) *Beauty and the Beast,* Ideals Publishing (Milwaukee, WI), 1989.
The Easter Story, Ideals Publishing (Milwaukee, WI), 1989.
(Reteller) *Excalibur,* Ideals Publishing (Milwaukee, WI), 1990.
The Christmas Story, Ideals Publishing (Milwaukee, WI), 1991.
(Reteller) *Robin Hood,* Ideals Publishing (Milwaukee, WI), 1993.
(Reteller) *The Sleeping Beauty in the Wood,* Ideals Children's Books (Nashville, TN), 1996.
The First Easter, Ideals Children's Books (Nashville, TN), 2002.
The First Christmas, Ideals Children's Books (Nashville, TN), 2003.
Humphrey's First Christmas, Ideals Children's Books (Nashville, TN), 2007.
The Little Shepherd's Christmas, Ideals Children's Books (Nashville, TN), 2011.
Humphrey's First Palm Sunday, Ideals Children's Books (Nashville, TN), 2012.

ILLUSTRATOR

Katherine Zwers and John Tobin, *A Star in the Pasture,* Ideals Publishing (Milwaukee, WI), 1988.
Katherine Zwers and John Tobin, *The Golden Easter Egg,* Ideals Publishing (Milwaukee, WI), 1989.
Stephen Cosgrove, *The Dream Stealer,* Graphic Arts Center (Portland, OR), 1989.
Stephen Cosgrove, *Prancer,* Graphic Arts Center (Portland, OR), 1989.
Rapunzel, Ideals Publishing (Milwaukee, WI), 1992.
C.F. Alexander, *All Things Bright and Beautiful,* Ideals Publishing (Milwaukee, WI), 1992.
O. Henry, *The Gift of the Magi,* Ideals Children's Books (Nashville, TN), 1994.
Pamela Kennedy, reteller, *A Christmas Carol* (based on Charles Dickens' novel), Ideals Children's Books (Nashville, TN), 1995.

Laurence Pringle, *Dinosaurs! Strange and Wonderful,* Boyds Mills Press (Honesdale, NY), 1995.

Ellen Jackson, *Here Come the Brides,* Walker (New York, NY), 1998.

Anna Sewell, *Black Beauty,* Ideals Children's Books (Nashville, TN), 2000.

Sonia Black, *Let's Read about . . . Abraham Lincoln,* Scholastic (New York, NY), 2002.

Henry Winkler and Lin Oliver, *Day of the Iguana,* Grosset & Dunlap (New York, NY), 2003.

Henry Winkler and Lin Oliver, *I Got a "D" in Salami,* Grosset & Dunlap (New York, NY), 2003.

Sonali Fry, *Let's Read about . . . George W. Bush,* Scholastic (New York, NY), 2003.

Henry Winkler and Lin Oliver, *The Zippity Zinger,* Grosset & Dunlap (New York, NY), 2004.

(With Scott Goto and Kevin O'Malley) Kevin O'Malley, *Once upon a Cool Motorcycle Dude,* Walker & Company (New York, NY), 2005.

Sarah Albee, reteller, *The Crow and the Pitcher: A Tale about Problem Solving* (based on a story by Aesop), Reader's Digest Young Families (Pleasantville, NY), 2007.

(With Scott Goto and Kevin O'Malley) Kevin O'Malley, *Once upon a Royal Superbaby,* Walker & Co. (New York, NY), 2010.

Contributor of illustrations to periodicals, including *Aboriginal Science Fiction, Alfred Hitchcock's Mystery, Amazing Stories, Dragon, Dungeon, Ellery Queen's Mystery, Isaac Asimov's Science Fiction, Realms of Fantasy,* and *Science Fiction Age.*

OTHER

(With Charles Davis) *Thunder Run* (screenplay), Cannon, 1986.

Carol Heyer retells the story of King Arthur's acquisition of his famous sword in **Excalibur,** *pairing her text with her sumptuous paintings.* (Copyright © 1991 by Carol Heyer. Ideals Children's Books, 1991. Reproduced by permission of Carol Heyer.)

Adaptations

Prancer was adapted as a film, produced by Rafaella De Laurentis, Orion Films, 1989.

Sidelights

While growing up in Thousand Oaks, California, Carol Heyer developed her skill as an artist by spending time sketching camels at Jungleland, a local wildlife park that housed many of the animals used in Hollywood films. While Heyer would grow up to become a professional artist—her work has appeared in advertising, films, and printed books as well as on cards and other gift items—her long-held love of camels eventually inspired her original self-illustrated stories *Humphrey's First Christmas* and *Humphrey's First Palm Sunday.* Geared for the holiday season, the first picture book introduces a camel named Humphrey whose caravan stops at a starlit manger on the night of the Christ Child's birth; the curious camel also meets up with Jesus several years later in *Humphrey's First Palm Sunday.* While animals are featured in several of her illustration projects for children's books, Heyer is best known for her fantasy illustrations.

"I particularly enjoy writing and illustrating fantasy," Heyer once told *SATA.* "In that genre there are no limits to what can be imagined, no physical laws that must be obeyed. Wizards can defy gravity and float, and dragons can be horrible monsters or cuddly companions. The only limits are those one sets for oneself, and I have never enjoyed doing that." Supernatural creatures grace the pages of *Excalibur* and *Robin Hood,* both which feature Heyer's art alongside her original retellings of classic fairytales and myths. In *Excalibur* she shares the legend of King Arthur and how he earned the right to the sword Excalibur. While *Bulletin of the Center for Children's Books* critic Kathryn Pierson Jennings described the storys as "a good blend of contemporary and legendary language," *School Library Journal* contributor George Delalis claimed that the strength of *Excalibur* comes from Heyer's "dark and brooding pencil and acrylic illustrations." The author/illustrator draws on traditional sources in her version of *Robin Hood,* in which she recounts the exploits of the man who redistributed the money of the wealthy into the hands of the poor, all the while outwitting the Sheriff of Nottingham. Shirley Wilton, writing in *School Library Journal,* remarked that "the realistic, full-color illustrations" in this work "are steeped in medieval atmosphere . . . and richly colored with acrylic paints and pencils."

Other books featuring paintings by Heyer include Pamela Kennedy's retelling of Charles Dickens' classic tale *A Christmas Carol* as well as Ellen Jackson's *Here Come the Brides* and Laurence Pringle's science book *Dinosaurs! Strange and Wonderful.* Kennedy introduces *A Christmas Carol* to a younger set of readers in a picture-book format that received much praise from reviewers. According to a *Publishers Weekly* critic, "Heyer's accomplished art justifies yet another version of this classic." In the retelling, Kennedy stayed close to Dickens' original story, noted *Booklist* critic Kay Weisman, the critic adding that the illustrator's "vibrant acrylic paintings add elegance to the presentation."

In *Dinosaurs!* Pringle explores the characteristics of eleven prehistoric creatures while also introducing the role paleontologists play in discovering more about these sometimes-large and sometimes-small beasts. Predicting that the book's attractive cover illustration will attract young dino-fans, *Booklist* contributor Carolyn Phelan added that Heyer's interior pictures "offer eye-catching views of dinosaur days and intriguing illustrations of paleontologists at work." A critic reviewing *Dinosaurs!* for *Publishers Weekly* asserted that "Heyer's detailed acrylics . . . offer an up-to-date representation of what the 'terrible lizards' may well have looked like."

Featuring a text by Kevin O'Malley, *Once upon a Cool Motorcycle Dude* and *Once upon a Royal Superbaby* allowed Heyer to work in collaboration with fellow illustrator Scott Goto as well as O'Malley to create an entertaining visual narrative. In the first book, two classmates team up on a storytelling project, but during their presentation the tale swings wildly as it alternates between the efforts of Princess Tenderheart to recover the beloved ponies that have been stolen by a local giant and the bravado of a tattooed motorcyclist who cruises in to battle said giant. The dual—and dueling—narratives are illustrated by Heyer and Goto in turn, producing what a *Kirkus Reviews* critic described as a "disarming, funny and not agenda-driven dig at the hot-button issue of gender difference." While a *Publishers Weekly* critic characterized *Once upon a Cool Motorcycle Dude* as a "great conversation starter about issues of gender stereotyping, and the benefits of teamwork," *Once upon a Royal Superbaby* reunites the creative team, as well as the young narrators, in a second bout of skewed storytelling. Complete with Heyer's pastel-toned acrylic paintings, which capture Queen Tenderheart's part in the tale with "airy delicacy," this quirky sequel "illustrates the value of collaborative effort," according to a *Kirkus Reviews* writer.

"For me," Heyer once told *SATA,* "writing and art have been inextricably bound. When I worked in advertising I wrote copy and did design work; in the film industry, I had the opportunity to do both writing and art direction; and now in children's books I am able to write and illustrate. I have found it impossible to write without seeing an illustration and equally impossible to do a painting and not be able to write a story around it. Visualization is the key to both writing and art. Making a character, place, or thing real and believable is the goal of both arts; to achieve an intensity in both my writing and my art is paramount. In color and character, intensity is emotion and emotion is remembrance. It is for this the writer/artist strives. To impart some part of this passion to the reader/viewer is the ultimate goal."

Biographical and Critical Sources

PERIODICALS

Booklist, March 15, 1995, Carolyn Phelan, review of *Dinosaurs! Strange and Wonderful,* p. 1332; November 15, 1995, Kay Weisman, review of *A Christmas Carol,* p. 564; May 1, 1998, Ilene Cooper, review of *Here Come the Brides,* p. 1514; November 1, 2010, Laura Tillotson, review of *Once upon a Royal Superbaby,* p. 74.

Bulletin of the Center for Children's Books, January, 1992, Kathryn Pierson Jennings, review of *Excalibur,* p. 128.

Kirkus Reviews, March 15, 2005, review of *Once upon a Cool Motorcycle Dude,* p. 356; July 15, 2010, review of *Once upon a Royal Superbaby.*

Publishers Weekly, January 2, 1995, review of *Dinosaurs!,* p. 77; September 18, 1995, review of *A Christmas Carol,* p. 96; February 21, 2005, review of *Once upon a Cool Motorcycle Dude,* p. 175.

School Library Journal, January, 1992, George Delalis, review of *Excalibur,* p. 103; November, 1993, Shirley Wilton, review of *Robin Hood,* p. 116; March, 1995, Diane Nunn, review of *Dinosaurs!,* p. 199; October, 1995, review of *A Christmas Carol,* p. 37; September, 2010, Kim T. Ha, review of *Once upon a Royal Superbaby,* p. 132.

Ventura County Star, November 26, 2011, Jeffrey Dransfeldt, profile of Heyer.

ONLINE

Carol Heyer Home Page, http://www.carolheyer.com (August 1, 2012).

* * *

HOSFORD, Kate 1966(?)-

Personal

Born c. 1966, in Farmington, ME; married; children: two sons. *Education:* Amherst College, B.A., 1988; Pratt Institute, degree, 2000; Vermont College of Fine Arts, M.F.A., 2011.

Addresses

Home—Brooklyn, NY. *Agent*—Adams Literary, 7845 Colony Rd., C4 No. 215, Charlotte, NC 28226.

Career

Social worker, educator, and author/illustrator. Worked as an elementary-school teacher.

Writings

Big Bouffant, illustrated by Holly Clifton-Brown, Carolrhoda Books (Minneapolis, MN), 2011.

Big Birthday, illustrated by Holly Clifton-Brown, Carolrhoda Books (Minneapolis, MN), 2012.

Infinity and Me, illustrated by Gabi Swiatkowska, Carolrhoda Books (Minneapolis, MN), 2012.

Sidelights

Kate Hosford's career as a children's book author evolved from her work as an illustrator. A teacher and social worker, Hosford began writing original stories to showcase her work as an artist, and in the process she "gradually discovered that I preferred the writing to the illustrating," she recalled to Cynthia Leitich Smith on the *Cynsations* Web log. Hosford eventually enrolled in a two-year program at the Vermont College of Fine Arts and earned an M.F.A. degree in the school's Writing for Children and Young Adults program.

Hosford's first book, *Big Bouffant,* was sparked by the word "bouffant," a formal updo popular with women during the 1960s that involved teasing the hair high on top of the head and holding it all in place with hairspray. In the story, Annabelle is dismayed by the standard ponytails and braided pigtails her classmates wear on the first day of school. When she sees a photograph of her grandmother sporting an immense bouffant, the little girl decides that a new hairdo will help her stand out among her friends. Annabelle's mom expresses her

The little girl in Kate Hosford's Big Bouffant *has fun standing out from the crowd as she comes to life in Holly Clifton-Brown's whimsical art.* (Illustration copyright © 2011 by Holly Clifton-Brown. Reproduced by permission of Carolrhoda, an division of Lerner Publishing Group. All rights reserved. No part of this excerpt may be used or reproduced in any manner whatsoever without the prior written permission of Lerner Publishing Group, Inc.)

doubts, but the little girl persists and her bouffant quickly becomes a hot new trend at school. Reviewing Hosford's debut in *School Library Journal,* Melissa Smith asserted that illustrator Holly Clifton-Brown's choice of palette and her incorporation of "colorful patterns result in rich illustrations that carry Annabelle's exuberance and determination through the pages."

Clifton-Brown also provided the artwork for Hosford's second picture book, *Big Birthday.* Again, Annabelle is determined to stand out from the crowd. Bored with her usual birthday party at the zoo, the girl decides that the moon would be a much-better venue. When her exasperated parents comply and hire a rocket ship with a crew, Annabelle realizes that the long trip into space is tedious and the fun of floating around in zero-gravity wears off quickly. Moreover, her guests cannot eat her birthday cake on the moon because they must keep their space helmets fastened. "Hosford's rhyming text is fun to read, and kids will enjoy hearing about a great idea gone wrong," asserted Catherine Callegari in her *School Library Journal* review of *Big Birthday.*

As a child, Hosford was a fan of Kay Thompson's precocious heroine Eloise and her adventures at the posh Plaza Hotel; she devoured the "Pippi Longstocking" tales by Astrid Lindgren; and she also felt a kinship with the plucky Canadian orphan in Lucy Maud Montgomery's *Anne of Green Gables.* "All of these girls went their own way without worrying too much about what other people thought," Hosford reflected in her Cynsations interview. "I probably based my main character, Annabelle, on this type of girl."

Biographical and Critical Sources

PERIODICALS

Kirkus Reviews, March 1, 2011, review of *Big Bouffant;* February 15, 2012, review of *Big Birthday.*
School Library Journal, April, 2011, Melissa Smith, review of *Big Bouffant,* p. 146; April, 2012, Catherine Callegari, review of *Big Birthday,* p. 136.

ONLINE

Cynsations Web log, http://cynthialeitichsmith.blogspot. com/ (April 28, 2011), Cynthia Leitich Smith, interview with Hosford.
Kate Hosford Home Page, http://khosford.com (August 1, 2012).*

J-K

JAFFE, Michele 1970-
(Michele Sharon Jaffe)

Personal

Born 1970, in Los Angeles, CA. *Education:* Harvard University, B.A., 1991, Ph.D. (comparative literature), 1998.

Addresses

Home—Las Vegas, NV. *E-mail*—michele@michelejaffe. com.

Career

Huntington Library, San Marino, CA, staff member; Harvard University, Cambridge, MA, instructor in Shakespearean literature.

Writings

FOR YOUNG ADULTS

Bad Kitty, HarperCollins (New York, NY), 2006.
Kitty Kitty, HarperTeen (New York, NY), 2008.
Catnipped (graphic novel), illustrated by Lince, Tokyopop/ Harper Collins (Los Angeles, CA), 2008.
Rosebush, Razorbill (New York, NY), 2010.
Ghost Flower, Razorbill (New York, NY), 2012.

Contributor to anthology *Prom Nights from Hell,* HarperCollins (New York, NY), 2007.

"ARBORETTI FAMILY SAGA"; FOR ADULTS

The Stargazer, Pocket Books (New York, NY), 1999.
The Water Nymph, Pocket Books (New York, NY), 2000.
Lady Killer, Ballantine Books (New York, NY), 2002.
Secret Admirer, Ballantine Books (New York, NY), 2002.

ADULT NOVELS

Bad Girl, Ballantine Books (New York, NY), 2003.
Loverboy, Ballantine Books (New York, NY), 2004.

OTHER

The Story of O: Prostitutes and Other Good-for-Nothings in the Renaissance, Harvard University Press (Cambridge, MA), 1999.

Sidelights

Although Michele Jaffe earned a Ph.D. in comparative literature with the intention of becoming a teacher, she quickly fled academia in favor of a career as a fiction writer that would allow her to incorporate the historical research that she loved. Set during the Renaissance, Jaffe's "Arboretti Family Saga" novels—*The Stargazer, The Water Nymph, Lady Killer,* and *Secret Admirer*— follow the romantic exploits of six male cousins, while *Loverboy* moves into mystery as she details the exploits of an F.B.I. agent battling a modern-day serial killer. while these books are for adults, Jaffe also focuses on teen readers, winning fans with *Bad Kitty* and its sequels as well as the teen thrillers *Rosebush* and *Ghost Flower.*

In *The Stargazer* Jaffe transports readers to Venice, where Isabella Bellochio has been stabbed with a dagger belonging to aristocrat Ian Foscari. When Ian witnesses Bianca pulling the dagger from Isabella's lifeless body, he assumes her to be the killer until her heartfelt protestations of innocence convince him to give her a week to prove her innocence. Because she is confined to his castle, Ian covers up the arrangement by introducing Bianca as his fiancée, which pleases his family. The daughter of a doctor, Bianca agrees to the ruse as long as she can perform an autopsy on her murdered friend. As Bianca and Ian work to find the true murderer, they fall passionately in love.

The Water Nymph is set in Elizabethan England as Crispin Foscari, Earl of Sandal, is dismissed from the queen's secret service after being accused of treason. With only two weeks to uncover the identity of his accuser, the earl meets Sophie Champion, a businesswoman with questions about the suspicious death of her father, and the two develop a mutual admiration and love for each other.

Sixteenth-century London is the setting for *Secret Admirer* and *Lady Killer*, the two other novels in Jaffe's "Arboretti Family Saga." In the first, Lady Tuesday Arlington finds that painting the scenes of her frightening nightmares helps her to deal with them, but these same dream paintings incriminate her as a killer when her husband is found murdered. Convinced of her innocence, Investigator Lawrence Pickering also falls in love with Lady Tuesday, thereby attracting the ire of the real killer. As *Lady Killer* opens, it is three years since Miles Loredon killed the vampire of London in front of numerous witnesses. When Lady Clio Thornton finds the body of a woman that appears to have the marks of a vampire bite, she approaches Miles with her

Cover of Michele Jaffe's young-adult novel **Bad Kitty,** *which chronicles the first case of teen sleuth Jasmine Callihan.* (Jacket art © 2006 by Beci Orpin. Reproduced by permission of HarperCollins Children's Books, a division of HarperCollins Publishers.)

findings. As Clio and Miles work to solve the case, they fall in love, despite the fact that Miles is betrothed to Clio's cousin.

Booklist contributor Patty Engelmann concluded of *The Stargazer* that "Jaffe's characters are intriguing, and the plot's many twists and turns are wonderfully entertaining." Also writing in *Booklist,* Margaret Flanagan described *The Water Nymph* as "fast-paced historical fiction fairly crackling with passion and suspense." Discussing *Secret Admirer* in *Romantic Times* online, Kathe Robin claimed that Jaffe "creates a masterful and highly suspenseful mystery with enough red herrings and stunning surprises to keep any fan enthralled," and the same critic dubbed *Lady Killer* "a compelling, hard-to-put-down read."

In *Loverboy* readers meet Imogen Page, a federal agent who sees life differently due to an unusual medical condition called synesthesia. Because she has the ability to translate what she sees and hears into tastes, Imogen is unusually sensitive to her surroundings and she uses her gift as head of the F.B.I.'s Cognitive Sciences unit, which is on the trail of a brutal serial killer known as Loverboy. After kidnaping his victim, the brazen five-time killer creates collages of his planned crime scene and then sends them to police in advance of his deadly attack. When a brilliant nuclear physicist seems to be the subject of a collage received by Las Vegas police, Imogen must channel her gift in hopes of deciphering the clues imbedded in the sinister work. A *Kirkus Reviews* writer called *Loverboy*'s female sleuth "smart, tough, and cute as a button," while *Booklist* critic Joanne Wilkinson asserted that Jaffe's story is enlivened by "fascinating secondary characters, plenty of sprightly sexual banter, . . . and plot twists aplenty."

Seventeen-year-old Californian Jasmine Callihan narrates *Bad Kitty,* Jaffe's first novel for teen readers. *Bad Kitty.* Jasmine's dream has always been to become a detective, and her wish comes true during a family vacation at Las Vegas's Venetian Hotel when she finds herself knee-deep in mystery. Following an attack by a frightened three-legged cat, the accident-prone teen disrupts a nearby wedding celebration, then becomes enmeshed in a murder that points a guilty finger at the husband of a famous fashion model. Helped by the model's eight-year-old son, as well as by her three newly arrived best friends, the teen sets to work, her amusing banter fueling Jaffe's high-energy plot.

Noting the presence of a suitable love interest and the appeal of Jaffe's "quirky characters" in *Bad Kitty,* a *Publishers Weekly* reviewer predicted that teen mystery fans "will likely find themselves quickly clawing their way through this fun novel." Jasmine's unique narrative voice is "the book's greatest asset," asserted a *Kirkus Reviews* writer, the critic adding that a sometimes-confusing storyline "manages to hang onto its fizz until the enjoyably twisty ending." In addition to the "hilarious dialogue" among the teen friends, readers "will be entertained by Jaffe's inclusion of footnotes to the plot twists on each page," wrote *School Library Journal* contributor Kathryn Childs, the critic assuring that *Bad Kitty* provides "plenty of amusement" for mystery buffs.

Jasmine's adventures continue in *Kitty Kitty* as well as in the graphic novel *Catnipped,* the latter which features artwork by Lince. In *Kitty Kitty* Jasmine is spending her senior year in Venice, Italy, and she misses her friends and her dishy new boyfriend, Jack. Although she hoped to convince her father to let her jet to Los Angeles for a visit, she senses a mystery when classmate Arabella dies and the police rule the young woman's death a suicide. Soon Jasmine is back in detective mode, joined by her loyal friends and determined to ferret out the facts linking a missing heiress, a handsome gondolier, and a squirrel costume. *Catnipped* continues Jasmine's adventures, this time while the teen is hoping to meet up with Jack at a local shopping mall.

In *Booklist* Stephanie Zvirin described *Kitty Kitty* as a "frenzied combination of chick lit, mystery, and sparkling fun" which is enlivened by Jasmine's "wildly colorful personality." For Amy S. Pattee, reviewing Jaffe's story in *School Library Journal,* the story plays out in a series of "red herrings and unexpected twists that will intrigue fans of the genre," and Andrea Lipinski predicted in the same periodical that *Catnipped* "will be especially appreciated by fans of Jaffe's novels" due to its mix of "lively and fun" manga-style art and quirky teen banter.

In *Rosebush* and *Ghost Flower* Jaffe turns again to the thriller genre, this time spinning a story that finds pretty and popular New Jersey high schooler Jane Freeman waking up in a hospital bed in the I.C.U. unable to talk. All Jane remembers of the night before is joining her boyfriend at a party, but paramedics found her near a rosebush, the victim of a supposed hit-and-run accident. As memories slowly begin to drift back, threatening letters from an anonymous admirer also appear in Jane's hospital room, but the psychiatrist assigned to her case is quick to dismiss the teen's growing premonition of evil as the symptoms of a closed-head injury.

While noting that *Rosebush* mines the successful recipe for YA thrillers that include "rich girls with evil hearts," a *Publishers Weekly* critic asserted that the novel "distinguishes itself . . . in character development." "Fear and anticipation stalk this thriller," announced a *Kirkus Reviews* writer, the critic describing *Rosebush* as "cleverly written with a finger on the pulse of the target audience," and in *Booklist* Lynn Rutan wrote that Jaffe's "insecure" heroine "grows believable as she takes on the mystery" of her accident. In prose that is "at once poetic, harrowing, and poignant," according to *Voice of Youth Advocates* contributor Suzanne Osman, *Rosebush* will appeal to teens who "relish chilling suspense . . . and intricate relationships between friends, family mem-

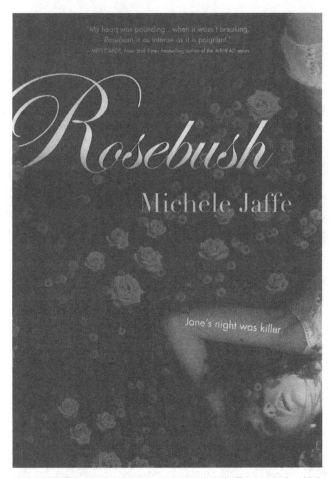

Cover of Jaffe's novel **Rosebush,** *a young-adult thriller in which a high schooler recovers from a traffic accident only to face something even more horrific.* (Jacket illustration photograph by Shavaughn Murphy. Reproduced by permission of Razorbill, an imprint of Penguin Group (USA), Inc.)

bers, and boyfriends," and Jessie Spalding characterized it in *School Library Journal* as a murder mystery with "a suspenseful modern twist."

Another teen mystery unfolds in *Ghost Flower* as foster teen Eve Brightman moves to a small Arizona town and finds work at a local coffee shop. Approached by two teens from the area, Eve agrees to be part of their scheme to gain control of a large inheritance. Aurora Silverton, the cousin of Bridgette and Bain Silverton, has been missing for three years, and Eve looks enough like Aurora to successfully impersonate her for three months, until the day of Aurora's eighteenth birthday when the inheritance will fall to her control. Although Eva enjoys stepping into Aurora's life, the ghostly best friend of the missing teen quickly alerts her that there is much more to this situation than she ever expected, including a threat to her own life.

Praising *Ghost Flower* as "a compellingly sinister page-turner," a *Kirkus Reviews* writer added that "tension builds rapidly and effectively . . . as unanswered questions pile up." "Sinister details . . . and an intriguing story line" will appeal to teen fans of "tense, dark thrillers with paranormal overtones," predicted *Booklist* contributor Julie Trevelyan, while a *Publishers Weekly* reviewer recommended that readers of *Ghost Flower* "withhold trust" from Jaffe's street-wise and "unreliable narrator."

Biographical and Critical Sources

PERIODICALS

Booklist, May 1, 1999, Patty Engelmann, review of *The Stargazer,* p. 1581; June 1, 2000, Margaret Flanagan, review of *The Water Nymph,* p. 1857; May 1, 2004, Joanne Wilkinson, review of *Loverboy,* p. 1510; January 1, 2006, Krista Huntley, review of *Bad Kitty,* p. 84; May 1, 2008, Stephanie Zvirin, review of *Kitty Kitty,* p. 48; January 1, 2011, Lynn Rutan, review of *Rosebush,* p. 98; May 1, 2012, Julie Trevelyan, review of *Ghost Flower,* p. 48.

Bulletin of the Center for Children's Books, April, 2006, Karen Coats, review of *Bad Kitty,* p. 359.

Kirkus Reviews, April 15, 2000, review of *The Water Nymph,* p. 511; April 1, 2004, review of *Loverboy,* p. 288; January 15, 2006, review of *Bad Kitty,* p. 86; October 15, 2010, review of *Rosebush;* March 1, 2012.

Library Journal, May 1, 1999, Kim Uden Rutter, review of *The Stargazer,* p. 110; May 15, 2000, Kim Uden Rutter, review of *The Water Nymph,* p. 125.

Publishers Weekly, June 7, 1999, review of *The Stargazer,* p. 71; June 21, 1999, "Love Ain't What It Used to Be," p. 26; May 1, 2000, review of *The Water Nymph,* p. 50; May 20, 2002, reviews of *Lady Killer* and *Secret Admirer,* both p. 53; May 3, 2004, review of *Loverboy,* p. 168; January 30, 2006, review of *Bad Kitty,* p. 71; November 1, 2010, review of *Rosebush,* p. 45; February 27, 2012, review of *Ghost Flower,* p. 91.

Renaissance Quarterly, autumn, 2000, David Marsh, review of *The Story of O: Prostitutes and Other Good-for-Nothings in the Renaissance,* p. 906.

School Library Journal, February, 2006, Kathryn Childs, review of *Bad Kitty,* p. 132; August, 2008, Amy S. Pattee, review of *Kitty Kitty,* p. 124; January, 2009, Andrea Lipinski, review of *Catnipped,* p. 132; April, 2011, Jessie Spalding, review of *Rosebush,* p. 176.

Seventeenth-Century News, fall, 2000, Edward H. Thompson, review of *The Story of O,* pp. 232-235.

Voice of Youth Advocates, February, 2006, Amy Alessio, review of *Bad Kitty,* p. 487; February, 2011, Suzanne Osman, review of *Rosebush,* p. 555.

ONLINE

Beatrice Online, http://www.beatrice.com/ (September 5, 2002), interview with Jaffe.

Michele Jaffe Home Page, http://http://www.michelejaffe.com (August 1, 2012).

Romance Reader Online, http://www.theromancereader.com/ (September 5, 2002), Cathy Sova, review of *The Stargazer.*

Romantic Times Online, http://www.romantictimes.com/ (September 5, 2002), Kathryn Falk, review of *The Stargazer;* Kathe Robin, reviews of *The Stargazer, The Water Nymph, Secret Admirer,* and *Lady Killer.*

*   *   *

JAFFE, Michele Sharon
See JAFFE, Michele

*   *   *

JOHNSON, J.J. 1973-

Personal

Born 1973, in Norwich, NY; married. *Education:* Binghamton University, degree; Harvard University, M.Ed.

Addresses

Home—Durham, NC. *E-mail*—jj@jjjohnsonauthor.com.

Career

Writer. Former internship coordinator for The Learning Web and Youth Advocacy.

Member

Society of Children's Book Writers and Illustrators.

Awards, Honors

Parent's Choice Silver Honor selection, 2011, and Amelia Bloomer listee, American Library Association, 2012, both for *This Girl Is Different.*

Writings

This Girl Is Different (young-adult novel), Peachtree Publishers (Atlanta, GA), 2011.

Sidelights

This Girl Is Different, the debut young-adult novel by J.J. Johnson, centers on Evensong "Evie" Sparkling Morningdew, an opinionated and strong-willed home-schooled student who decides to spend her senior year at a public school. According to Johnson, *This Girl Is Different* was inspired in part by U.S. President Barack Obama's 2008 presidential campaign. Noting that Obama, the son of a Kenyan father and an American mother, had an unusual upbringing and spent some of his childhood in Indonesia, Johnson began contemplating the notion of the outsider. "I was thinking about change and the system, and speaking your mind . . .," she told Zack Smith in an *Independent Weekly* online interview. "I was thinking, 'What if you grew up outside the system? What if you viewed high school through different eyes?'"

Raised in a geodesic dome by her hippie mother, Evie longs for a taste of conventional schooling and perhaps a dash of romance before heading to Cornell University. Once she enters her local public high school, however, she is shocked at the injustices students must endure, from dirty restrooms and non-recyclable cafeteria dishware to social cliques and domineering teachers. Hoping to affect change, Evie and two friends start a blog, the People's Lightning to Undermine True Oppression (PLUTO), which soon enjoys a loyal and rabid following. When her classmates begin using PLUTO to nurse grudges and spread rumors, some of which prove damaging to students and teachers alike, Evie must re-examine her beliefs and redistribute responsibility for the status quo.

Reviewing *This Girl Is Different* in *Booklist*, Courtney Jones noted that "Evie is a strong yet vulnerable hero-

Cover of J.J. Johnson's young-adult novel This Girl Is Different, *which follows a home-schooled teen on her journey into public-school territory.* (Jacket illustration copyright © 2011 by Peachtree. Reproduced by permission Peachtree Publishers.)

ine," and Rhona Campbell observed in *School Library Journal* that the novel's protagonist "does undergo a degree of character reform through the process." According to a reviewer in *Publishers Weekly,* Johnson's "smart first novel will likely spark discussions about authority abuse and crossing boundaries."

Biographical and Critical Sources

PERIODICALS

Booklist, May 1, 2011, Courtney Jones, review of *This Girl Is Different,* p. 84.
Kirkus Reviews, March 15, 2011, review of *This Girl Is Different.*
Publishers Weekly, February 21, 2011, review of *This Girl Is Different,* p. 134.
School Library Journal, July, 2011, Rhona Campbell, review of *This Girl Is Different,* p. 100.

ONLINE

Independent Weekly Online (NC), http://www.indyweek. com/ (April 27, 2011), Zach Smith, interview with Johnson.
J.J. Johnson Home Page, http://www.jjjohnsonauthor.com (July 15, 2012).*

* * *

KOSS, Amy Goldman 1954-

Personal

Born January 26, 1954, in Detroit, MI; daughter of Max (a juke box man) and Harriet (a teacher) Goldman; married Mitchell Koss (a television news producer), August, 1982; children: two. *Education:* Attended Lansing Community College and Wayne State University.

Addresses

Home—Glendale, CA. *Agent*—Linda Pratt, Wernick & Pratt Agency; info@wernickpratt.com. *E-mail*—amygkoss@sbcglobal.net.

Career

Writer. Teacher of writing.

Member

Authors Guild, Society of Children's Book Writers and Illustrators, Children's Authors Network, Children's Literature Council of Southern California.

Awards, Honors

John Burroughs Award listee, 1989, for *Curious Creatures in Peculiar Places*; Children's Books of the Year selection, Bank Street College of Education, 1998, for

Amy Goldman Koss (Photograph by Clara Rodriguez. Reproduced by permission.)

How I Saved Hanukkah; Best Books selection, *School Library Journal,* 1999, for *The Ashwater Experiment;* Notable Book selection, Association of Jewish Libraries, 2001, for *Stolen Words;* Best Book for the Teen Age selection, New York Public Library, and International Reading Association (IRA) Children's Choice and Young-Adult Choice selections, both 2001, and Land of Enchantment Award, Maude Hart Lovelace Award, and Garden State Teen Book Award, all 2003, all for *The Girls;* Quick Picks for Reluctant Readers selection, American Library Association (ALA), 2006, for *Poison Ivy;* ALA Best Book for Young Adults selection, and Recommended listee, New York Public Library, both 2006, and several state book awards, 2008, all for *Side Effects.*

Writings

PICTURE BOOKS; SELF-ILLUSTRATED

What Luck! A Duck!, Price, Stern, Sloan (Los Angeles, CA), 1987.
Where Fish Go in Winter, and Answers to Other Great Mysteries, Price, Stern, Sloan (Los Angeles, CA), 1987.
Curious Creatures in Peculiar Places, Price, Stern, Sloan (Los Angeles, CA), 1989.
City Critters around the World, Price, Stern, Sloan (Los Angeles, CA), 1991.

INTERMEDIATE NOVELS

The Trouble with Zinny Weston, Dial (New York, NY), 1998.
How I Saved Hanukkah, illustrated by Diane deGroat, Dial (New York, NY), 1998.
The Ashwater Experiment, Dial (New York, NY), 1999.
The Girls, Dial (New York, NY), 2000.
Smoke Screen, Pleasant Company Publications (Middleton, WI), 2000.
Stranger in Dadland, Dial (New York, NY), 2001.
Stolen Words, Pleasant Company Publications (Middleton, WI), 2001.
Strike Two, Dial (New York, NY), 2002.
The Cheat, Dial (New York, NY), 2003.
Gossip Times Three, Dial (New York, NY), 2003.
Kailey, illustrated by Philip Howe, Pleasant Company Publications (Middleton, WI), 2003.
Poison Ivy, Roaring Brook Press (New Milford, CT), 2006.
Side Effects, Roaring Brook Press (New Milford, CT), 2006.
The Not-$o-Great Depression: In Which the Economy Crashes, My Sister's Plans Are Ruined, My Mom Goes Broke, My Dad Grows Vegetables, and I Do Not Get a Hamster, Roaring Brook Press (New York, NY), 2010.

Sidelights

Amy Goldman Koss is known for her ability to look at the problems and adventures of middle graders with an insightful and realistic eye while also introducing realistic characters who hold readers' attention. Koss began her publishing career as an author and illustrator of picture books with rhyming texts before shifting her focus to longer fiction for preteens. In such novels as *The Trouble with Zinny Weston, How I Saved Hanukkah, The Girls, Strike Two,* and *Poison Ivy* she blends humor with realistic situations to sensitively convey the ups and downs of growing up.

In Koss's debut novel *The Trouble with Zinny Weston* fifth-grader Ava tells the story of how she became fast friends with newcomer Zinny Weston, and how everything went wrong after Zinny's mother drowned a raccoon in a garbage can because it killed all the fish in her backyard pond. Ava and her veterinarian parents are devoted animal lovers while Zinny and her mother view wild creatures as dirty and detestable; when Zinny's mom is reported to the animal protection agency Ava becomes the prime suspect. "Koss clearly knows the dynamics of middle-school friendship and how small misunderstandings can explode into war," wrote a contributor to *Publishers Weekly* in a review of *The Trouble with Zinny Weston,* while other critic noted that Ava's consideration of the moral dilemma involved provides readers with a good exposition of this sensitive issue. "Middle-graders will enjoy this first novel for the friend/enemy drama . . . and for the sympathetic open discussion of animal rights," predicted Hazel Rochman in her critique of the story for *Booklist. The Trouble with Zinny Weston* ends with a "believable" resolution to Ava and

Zinny's problem, noted Mary M. Hopf in *School Library Journal,* and "readers will enjoy meeting these characters."

In *How I Saved Hanukkah* fourth-grader Marla Feinstein is not looking forward to the holiday season. Everyone else in her class celebrates Christmas, but Marla's mother will not let them hang lights on the house because they are Jewish. On the other hand, Mrs. Feinstein is not interested in staging a festive Hanukkah celebration either, and Mr. Feinstein is out of town on business. It is up to Marla and her friend Lucy to inspire Mrs. Feinstein to celebrate the holidays with potato pancakes (latkes), playing the dreidel game, and dancing the hora. "A witty, warmly realized cast" makes *How I Saved Hanukkah* "fresh and believable," wrote a reviewer in *Publishers Weekly,* and Eva Mitnick likewise predicted in *School Library Journal* that Koss's "fun and breezy tone and affectionately drawn characters will appeal to readers."

Although Hillary, the narrator of *The Ashwater Experiment,* is only twelve years old, she has attended eighteen schools while following her parents as they make and sell knickknacks at craft fairs around the country. Faced with the prospect of spending nine consecutive months in Ashwater, California, where she and her parents will house-sit for a family on sabbatical, the preteen is dubious that the next few months will be any different. Because of her peripatetic lifestyle, Hillary prefers to live in a fantasy where the outside world is merely a set put before her by "the Watchers," beings who are interested in her responses to a variety of situations. The girl's "Watchers" fantasy is "a comic expression of the loneliness Hillary cannot express," observed a reviewer for *Publishers Weekly,* and a *Kirkus Reviews* critic remarked of *The Ashwater Experiment* that "undercurrents of humor, and characters who seem typecast initially but develop surprising complexities, give this bittersweet tale unusual depth." A *Horn Book* was also impressed by the novel, writing that here "Koss artfully sidesteps the predictable and crafts a truly original piece of fiction brimming with humor and insight."

In *The Girls* Maya is deeply hurt when the other girls in her clique suddenly turn on her and she is ostracized from their ranks. Although she is clueless about why this happened, Maya realizes that only Candace decides who is in and who is out. Told in multiple narratives, *The Girls* takes the reader into the psyche of young women in a complex social web, and Gillian Engberg predicted in her *Booklist* review that "readers, particularly girls, weathering the agonizing, variable minefields of cliques will easily find themselves in this taut, authentic story." Susan Oliver, writing in *School Library Journal,* predicted of *The Girls* that Koss's "provocative page-turner will be passed from one girl to the next like a note with the latest gossip."

Smoke Screen deals with another adolescent problem: the damaging results of a seemingly harmless lie. When Mitzi's heartthrob Mike comes to talk with her she has a speck of something in her eye and tears are running down her cheek. Anxious to inspire his concern and attentiveness, she tells him that she is crying because her mother, who has just stopped smoking, is sick. This simple fib begins to take on embarrassing and disastrous consequences, however, when Mitzi's story gains dramatic heft and circulates around school. *Smoke Screen* treats readers to "a snappy read with appealing characters," according to *Booklist* contributor Anne O'Malley, while Shilo Halfen, writing in *School Library Journal,* noted that "short chapters and sparkling dialogue will appeal to even the most reluctant readers."

Koss focuses on a preteen boy in *Stranger in Dadland,* which finds twelve-year-old John heading off for a week-long California vacation with his father. This is the first time father and son have gone anywhere together, but they find themselves on their own after John's older sister Liz backs out. In California things begin to go downhill: a new girlfriend monopolizes

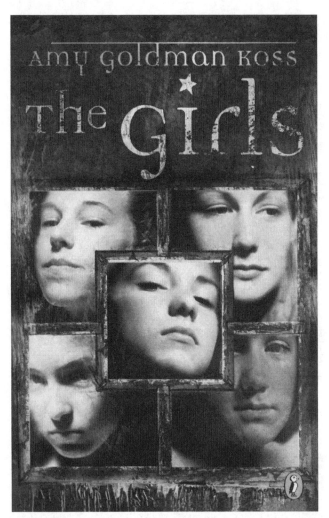

Koss explores the inner dynamics of middle-school cliques in The Girls, *which focuses on the strength of personality and the true meaning of friendship.* (Jacket copyright © 2000 by Cliff Nielsen. Reproduced by permission of Dial Books for Young Readers, a division of Penguin Group (USA) Inc.)

A twelve year old is determined to build a relationship with his dad despite the distractions the season has in store in Koss's novel **Stranger in Dadland.** (Jacket art copyright © 2001 by Jesse Reisch. Reproduced by permission of Dial Books for Young Readers, a division of Penguin Group (USA) Inc.)

Dad's time and the man's job takes up whatever time is left. After John has a skateboarding accident things start getting better and father and son begin to learn elemental truths about one another. Sharon Grover, reviewing *Stranger in Dadland* for *School Library Journal,* suggested that "many kids . . . will understand and appreciate John's predicament," and in *Booklist* Ilene Cooper wrote that the novel's "first-person dialogue crisply captures John's angst." In *Publishers Weekly* a reviewer remarked that "Koss is hilarious on Los Angeles," and her young narrator's "delivery proves once again the author's unusual insight into middle-graders and their concerns."

In *Stolen Words* eleven-year-old Robyn Gittleman goes on vacation to Vienna, Austria, with her parents, hoping for a distraction from a recent family tragedy. Since Aunt Beth died in an automobile accident Robyn's mother has suffered from depression. Robyn brings the journal Aunt Beth gave her and plans to record the activities of their trip, but the day they arrive in Vienna the family's luggage is stolen. With a new diary in hand, she begins collecting not only her own impressions of

Austria but also everyone's attempt to come to terms with Aunt Beth's death. *Booklist* reviewer Shelle Rosenfeld called *Stolen Words* an "engaging read" that "realistically depict[s] the grieving-healing process," and in *Publishers Weekly* a critic noted that the "particularly insightful portrayals of Robyn's anger and internal conflicts find an almost ideal counterbalance in her mordant wit and candor."

When readers meet them in *Strike Two,* cousins Gwen and Jess are as close as sisters. Their respective fathers are twins who both work for the *Press Gazette,* which sponsors the softball team the girls play on. When the newspaper's labor union calls a strike everything changes: Gwen's father is now out of work while Jess's father, part of management, works long hours and is never home. Worst of all for Gwen is the dissension on the softball team when strike problems show up on the field and her friendship with Jess is threatened. Lee Bock, writing in *School Library Journal,* found that "Koss has created realistic characters that young people will both recognize and relate to."

The Cheat concerns eighth-grader Jake, a smart but unpopular student who gives the pretty and popular Sarah the answers to an upcoming geography test. This attempt to win her favor backfires when Sarah and two of her friends are sent home from school for cheating. When she refuses to tell on Jake, the boy has a decision to make: will he step forward on his own and accept the consequences? A critic for *Kirkus Reviews* called *The Cheat* "provocative and disturbing," while Frances Bradburn noted in *Booklist* that Koss's "message is obvious, but not cloyingly so." Lynne T. Burke, in a review for *Reading Today,* concluded that *The Cheat* "packs a powerful punch."

In *Gossip Times Three* best friends Abby, Bess, and Cristy have a falling out after Bess begins to date Zack, a boy she knows Abby has a crush on. Soon Cristy finds herself in the middle of the dispute, and Koss's story, told by an anonymous narrator, reads like an English school paper. *Gossip Times Three* "openly addresses questions of theme, plot, and foreshadowing and offers readers alternative scenarios and explanations of the characters' motivations," according to *School Library Journal* contributor Laurie von Mehren. "Koss understands the dynamics of junior high friendships, attractions and cliques, and she develops the ramifications of the romantic triangle with easy authenticity," asserted a critic for *Publishers Weekly.*

The titular ten-year-old protagonist of *Kailey* lives in California and enjoys exploring the tide pools along the coastline. When a development threatens the shoreline, Kailey decides to take action. She organizes a protest that leads the developer to compromise, building his proposed shopping mall but preserving the tide pools that the girl loves. Chris Sherman, reviewing *Kailey* for *Booklist,* wrote that Koss's nature-themed story "offers good character development, lots of conflict, excellent description, and a realistic conclusion."

Koss interweaves eight different narrators in a chronicle of one girl's effort to stop bullying in *Poison Ivy*. Ivy has few friends in school and she is a favorite target of friends Ann, Sophia, and Benita. When her teacher, Mrs. Gold, suggests that the class hold a mock trial, Ivy steps forth and demands that her three tormenters be judged by their peers. Together with several other students who assume the roles of defense counsel, jurors, and prosecution, *Poison Ivy* features a strong message: "beauty, popularity, and fear are the trinity by which girls rule," according to *Booklist* critic Krista Hutley. Beginning with what a *Publishers Weekly* contributor described as a "fascinating premise," Koss's story provides "a study in superficiality and spite," according to the critic. Framed as a trial transcription, *Poison Ivy* "delivers the crushing and thoughtless cruelty of adolescents with great accuracy," according to a *Kirkus Reviews* contributor, and in *Horn Book* Lelac Almagor asserted that "the novel's pessimism is offset by its honesty and by the unforgettable voice of Poison Ivy herself."

A boy hoping for popularity gets into unforseen trouble after he helps classmates on a test in Koss's novel **The Cheat.** (Cover art copyright © 2003 by Cliff Nielsen. Reproduced by permission of Dial Books for Young Readers, a division of Penguin Group (USA) Inc.)

Izzy is fifteen years old when readers meet her in *Side Effects,* but her life does not hold the promise typical of her age. Izzy has stage IV Hodgkin's lymphoma, a cancer that requires a difficult course of treatment if it is to be overcome. In what a *Publishers Weekly* contributor described as a "candid, often comical narrative," Izzy shares the stages of her disease from diagnosis through chemotherapy, with its range of unpleasant side effects, and then recounts the difficulties dealing with confused classmates upon her return to school. *Side Effects* "will certainly open readers' eyes to the tribulations of young cancer patients and how to offer support," asserted the *Publishers Weekly* reviewer, and in *Booklist* Frances Bradburn praised Koss for her decision not "to glamorize Izzy's illness or treatment." *Side Effects* is based on "solid research into various Children's Hospital patients and their treatments," explained *School Library Journal* reviewer Rhonda Campbell, "but it's not too heavy, complex, or long."

Koss taps into an anxiety shared by both parents and children in the archly titled *The Not-$o-Great Depression: In Which the Economy Crashes, My Sister's Plans Are Ruined, My Mom Goes Broke, My Dad Grows Vegetables, and I Do Not Get a Hamster.* California ninth-grader Jacki has grown up assuming that her adult life will be much like that of her comfortably affluent parents, but that all changes when her mother is laid off from her well-paying job. While the family must adjust to no more restaurant dinners, private school, or private swimming pool, this economic fallout is one of several problems for Jacki, who is also dealing with a new crush and a broken leg that is keeping her couch-bound. Woven into Koss's lesson on economic realities are "a variety of . . . recessionary experiences" that include "a visit to a food kitchen," according to *Voice of Youth Advocates* critic Erin Wyatt. "As ever, Koss's writing is smooth, and the dialogue [in *The Not-$o-Great Depression*] keeps things moving briskly," according to Goldsmith, while a *Kirkus Reviews* writer cited the story for treating readers to "a cast of charming characters and a semi-happy ending."

"I assumed that when I grew up I'd get some miserable job doing something awful and I'd only get to draw pictures and make up stories in my teeny bits of free time," Koss once told *SATA*. "My dad's life was like that. He hated his job as a juke box man so he played violin, painted spooky pictures, and built ornate furniture on his weekends. Perhaps that's why I was a lousy student and never prepared much for adulthood. That is, I went to lots and lots of college, but never graduated and I had many jobs, but no career.

"It didn't occur to me that writing and drawing could be my REAL work until I married a guy who believed it was worth risking humiliation to try to do what we WANTED to with our lives. I figured if he could, I could—so, I began submitting work and getting countless letter-bomb rejections.

Koss chronicles the fallout of the financial recession in her middle-grade novel **The Not-$o-Great Depression,** *which features cover art by* **Stephanie Power.** (Jacket illustration illustration © 2010 by Stephanie Power. Reproduced by permission of Henry Holt & Company, LLC.)

"But eventually my drawings, poems, articles, and short stories found their way into newspapers and literary magazines. That was a relief. Then I got my first picture book published and that felt great!

"I spent the next few years writing and illustrating picture books in verse until I started having babies and got so fat my hand could barely hold my drawing pens.

"I took a few years off to change diapers and push strollers then began my rejection collection ALL OVER AGAIN. After eons of disappointment, I was finally yanked out of the slush pile by a fabulous editor at Dial Books for Young Readers. She suggested that I try writing intermediate novels. And that's exactly what I've been doing ever since. And I LOVE it, especially when my characters become so real that I feel them crowding around my computer, scrutinizing what I say about them.

"Now, I write all day while my kids are in school, and I sometimes sneak in a few hours after everyone else has gone to bed. I know mine is a weird, isolated life—but I also know it's absolutely PERFECT for me."

Biographical and Critical Sources

PERIODICALS

Booklist, May 15, 1998, Hazel Rochman, review of *The Trouble with Zinny Weston,* p. 1626; March 1, 2001, Ilene Cooper, review of *Stranger in Dadland,* p. 1278; September 15, 2001, Shelle Rosenfeld, review of *Stolen Words,* p. 223; November 1, 2001, Francisca Goldsmith, review of *Strike Two,* p. 475; January 1, 2003, Frances Bradburn, review of *The Cheat,* p. 890; December 1, 2003, Chris Sherman, review of *Kailey,* p. 667; February 15, 2006, Krista Hutley, review of *Poison Ivy,* p. 93; September 15, 2006, Frances Bradburn, review of *Side Effects,* p. 55; March 15, 2010, Francisca Goldsmith, review of *The Not-$o-Great Depression,* p. 44.

Buffalo News, August 15, 2000, Jean Westmoore, review of *The Girls,* p. N7; May 15, 2001, Jean Westmoore, review of *Stranger in Dadland,* p. N12; September 10, 2003, Jean Westmoore, review of *The Cheat,* p. N5.

Horn Book, July-August, 1999, review of *The Ashwater Experiment,* p. 385; March, 2001, review of *Stranger in Dadland,* p. 210; July-August, 2003, Lauren Adams, review of *Gossip Times Three,* p. 461; March-April, 2006, Lelac Almagor, review of *Poison Ivy,* p. 190; May-June, 2010, Chelsey G.H. Philpot, review of *The Not-$o-Great Depression,* p. 83.

Journal of Adolescent and Adult Literacy, November, 2002, review of *The Girls,* p. 214.

Kirkus Reviews, May 1, 1999, review of *The Ashwater Experiment;* August 1, 2002, review of *Where Fish Go in Winter, and Other Great Mysteries,* p. 1134; December 15, 2002, review of *The Cheat,* p. 1851; June 15, 2003, review of *Gossip Times Three,* p. 860; February 15, 2006, review of *Poison Ivy,* p. 185; September 1, 2006, review of *Side Effects,* p. 906; April 15, 2010, review of *The Not-$o-Great Depression.*

Kliatt, September, 2003, Claire Rosser, review of *Gossip Times Three,* p. 8.

People, January 8, 1990, Ralph Novak, review of *Curious Creatures in Peculiar Places,* p. 29.

Publishers Weekly, June 29, 1998, review of *The Trouble with Zinny Weston,* p. 59; September 28, 1998, review of *How I Saved Hanukkah,* p. 54; June 14, 1999, review of *The Ashwater Experiment,* p. 71; October 15, 2001, review of *Stolen Words,* p. 73; December 9, 2002, review of *The Cheat,* p. 85; July 7, 2003, review of *Gossip Times Three,* p. 73; September 22, 2003, review of *Kailey,* p. 104; February 27, 2006, review of *Poison Ivy,* p. 61; December 11, 2006, review of *Side Effects,* p. 71; May 3, 2010, review of *The Not-$o-Great Depression,* p. 54.

Reading Today, August-September, 2003, Lynne T. Burke, review of *The Cheat,* p. 32.

School Library Journal, July, 1998, Mary M. Hopf, review of *The Trouble with Zinny Weston,* p. 96; October, 1998, Eva Mitnick, review of *How I Saved Hanukkah,* p. 38; August, 1999, p. 158; March, 2001, Sharon Grover, review of *Stranger in Dadland,* p. 252; September, 2001, Lee Bock, review of *Strike Two,* p. 226;

September, 2003, Laurie von Mehren, review of *Gossip Times Three*, p. 216; March, 2006, Jennifer Ralston, review of *Poison Ivy*, p. 225; September, 2006, Rhona Campbell, review of *Side Effects*, p. 209; May, 2010, Emily Chornomaz, review of *The Not-$o-Great Depression*, p. 118.

Voice of Youth Advocates, August, 2010, Erin Wyatt, review of *The Not-$o-Great Depression*, p. 250.

ONLINE

Amy Goldman Koss Home Page, http://www.amygoldmankoss.net (August 1, 2012).*

* * *

KOZLOWSKY, M.P.

Personal

Married; children: one daughter. *Education:* Bachelor's degree.

Addresses

Home—New York, NY.

Career

Author and educator. Taught high-school English for three years.

Writings

Juniper Berry (middle-grade novel), illustrated by Erwin Madrid, HarperCollins (New York, NY), 2011.

Biographical and Critical Sources

PERIODICALS

Booklist, March 1, 2011, Thom Barthelmess, review of *Juniper Berry*, p. 60.
Bulletin of the Center for Children's Books, May, 2011, April Spisak, review of *Juniper Berry*, p. 425.
Kirkus Reviews, March 1, 2011, review of *Juniper Berry*.
Publishers Weekly, March 21, 2011, review of *Juniper Berry*, p. 77.
School Library Journal, August, 2011, Kim Dare, review of *Juniper Berry*, p. 109.

ONLINE

M.P. Kozlowsky Home Page, http://www.mpkozlowsky.com (August 1, 2012).

KUJAWINSKI, Peter 1974-

Personal

Born 1974, in Chicago, IL; married Celia Rose (a singer and songwriter); children: two. *Education:* Georgetown University, degree, 1996; Institut d'Études Politiques de Paris, certificate of studies, 1996; École Nationale d'Administration, degree, 2003.

Addresses

Home—Port-au-Prince, Haiti. *E-mail*—peterkujawinski @gmail.com.

Career

Writer and diplomat. U.S. Department of State, foreign service officer in Tel Aviv, Israel, Paris, France, and New York, NY, 2006-09, political counselor in Port-au-Prince, Haiti, 2010-12, U.S. consul general for Alberta, Saskatchewan, and the Northwest Territories, 2012—.

Writings

"DORMIA" NOVEL SERIES

(With Jake Halpern) *Dormia*, Houghton Mifflin (Boston, MA), 2009.
(With Jake Halpern) *World's End*, Houghton Mifflin (Boston, MA), 2011.

OTHER

Contributor to *International Herald Tribune*.

Sidelights

Peter Kujawinski, a U.S. diplomat who has served in Israel, France, and Haiti, is the coauthor of *Dormia* and *World's End*, the first two novels in the "Dormia" fantasy series for middle graders. Interestingly, Kujawinski and coauthor Jake Halpern completed their first manuscript while living in different parts of the world—Kujawinski in France and Halpern in New Mexico—but exchanged text via e-mail on a daily basis. "We just passed the thing back and forth like a cyber football," Kujawinski recalled on the *World of Dormia* Web site. "I would go out for drinks at a local bistro, come home late, burn the midnight oil in Paris, hammer out a new chapter, and then fire the thing across the globe to Jake."

In *Dormia* Kujawinski and Halpern introduce Alfonso Perplexon, a twelve-year-old Minnesotan who can perform incredible feats of physical dexterity—such as climbing tall trees and walking on power lines—while sleepwalking. When Alfonso's long-lost Uncle Hill appears, the preteen discovers the source of his powers: his ancestors are from the land of Dormia, where they practice "wakeful sleeping." Hill informs Alfonso that the hidden kingdom is in grave danger from the Dragoonya, and the pair must travel to the Ural Mountains to deliver a Dormian bloom, a mystical plant that Alfonso has been nurturing in his sleep.

Critiquing *Dormia* in *Booklist,* Cindy Welch praised the novel for its "old-fashioned storytelling, . . . where action supports story development rather than substituting for it." Beth L. Meister commented in *School Library Journal* that Kujawinski and Halpern "provide a wealth of detail, bringing locales as exotic as a cave city and a decaying icebreaker ship to life," and a *Publishers Weekly* reviewer noted that the authors "offer some compelling battle scenes."

Set three years after the events in *Dormia, World's End* chronicles Alfonso's dangerous journey to the ancient Dormian city of Jasper, where his father went missing years earlier. "Intricately developed and interweaving plotlines, strong characterizations, and a zestfully imagined fantasy world make for a pleasurably meandering and satisfying read," remarked *School Library Journal* critic Hayden Bass. According to Mary Ann Darby in *Voice of Youth Advocates,* "Halpern and Kujawinski develop both the characters and mythology of Dormia more fully this time, especially the older and wiser Alfonso."

Biographical and Critical Sources

PERIODICALS

Booklist, July 1, 2009, Cindy Welch, review of *Dormia,* p. 60.
Publishers Weekly, May 25, 2009, review of *Dormia,* p. 58.
School Library Journal, February, 2011, Hayden Bass, review of *World's End,* p. 108.
Voice of Youth Advocates, August, 2009, Mary Ann Darby, review of *Dormia,* p. 237; December, 2010, Mary Ann Darby, review of *World's End,* p. 471.

Cover of **World's End,** *a futuristic fantasy by Jake Halepern and Peter Kujawinski that features artwork by John Rocco.* (Jacket illustration © 2010 by John Rocco. Reproduced by permission of Houghton Mifflin Harcourt Publishing Company. All rights reserved.)

ONLINE

Peter Kujawinski Home Page, http://peterkujawinski.com (July 15, 2012).
World of Dormia Web site, http://worldofdormia.com/ (July 15, 2012).

L

LAYNE, Steven L.

Personal

Born in Crawfordsville, IN; married Deborah Dover, 1987; children: Grayson, Victoria, Jackson, Candace. *Education:* Judson College, B.A. (psychology), 1987; Northern Illinois University, M.S.Ed., 1992, Ed.D. (reading education), 1996. *Hobbies and other interests:* Reading, writing, teaching, singing, tennis, volleyball, playing with his kids.

Addresses

Home—St. Charles, IL. *Office*—Department of Education, Judson University, 1151 N. State St., Elgin, IL 60123-1498. *E-mail*—slayne@judsonu.edu.

Career

Educator and writer. Former counselor at an impatient psychiatric unit; former fifth-grade teacher in Carpentersville, IL, then Oak Brook, IL; Judson College, Elgin, IL, associate professor, then professor of education and literature, 2004—. Member of board, Northern Illinois Reading Council, and Literacy Volunteers of America Fox Valley Affiliate. Member, DuPage Literacy Roundtable.

Member

International Reading Association (member of board of directors, 2011-14), College Reading Association, National Council of Teachers of English, National Council for the Social Studies, Society of Children's Book Writers and Illustrators, Assembly on Literature for Adolescents, Children's Literature Assembly, Illinois Reading Council (member of committees; president, 2005-06), Northern Illinois Reading Council, Special Interest Group Network on Adolescent Literature, Alpha Upsilon Alpha.

Awards, Honors

Literacy Award, Alpha Upsilon Alpha Honor Society of the International Reading Association, 1995-96; Outstanding Research Award, Northern Illinois University Alumni Council/College of Education, 1997; Winn Research Award, 1997; named Illinois Reading Teacher of the Year, 1999; ICARE Reading Award, 2000; National Educator Award, Milken Family Foundation, 2001; Edwin A. Hoey Award, National Council of Teachers of English, 2001; Missouri Library Association Best of the Best designation, and Hal Clement Award for Best New Science-Fiction Novel for Young Adults, both 2001, and International Reading Association (IRA) Young-Adult Choice designation, and Texas Lone Star Top-20 listee, both 2003, all for *This Side of Paradise;* IRA/ Children's Book Council Children's Choice Award designation, 2002, for *The Teachers' Night before Christmas,* and 2004, for *My Brother Dan's Delicious; Learning* magazine Teachers' Choice selection, 2006, for *T Is for Teachers;* Distinguished Alumni Award, Judson University, 2009; inducted into Illinois Reading Council Hall of Fame, 2010.

Writings

PICTURE BOOKS

Thomas's Sheep and the Great Geography Test, illustrated by Perry Board, Pelican Publishing (Gretna, LA), 1998.

The Teacher's Night before Christmas, illustrated by James Rice, Pelican Publishing (Gretna, LA), 2001.

My Brother Dan's Delicious, illustrated by Chuck Galey, Pelican Publishing (Gretna, LA), 2003.

Thomas's Sheep and the Spectacular Science Project, illustrated by Perry Board, Pelican Publishing (Gretna, LA), 2004.

The Principal's Night before Christmas, illustrated by James Rice, Pelican Publishing (Gretna, LA), 2004.

(With wife Deborah Dover Layne) *T Is for Teachers: A School Alphabet,* illustrated by Doris Ettlinger, Sleeping Bear Press (Chelsea, MI), 2005.

Over Land and Sea: A Story of International Adoption, illustrated by Jan Bower, Pelican Publishing (Gretna, LA), 2005.

The Preacher's Night before Christmas, illustrated by Carol Benioff, Pelican Publishing (Gretna, LA), 2006.

Love the Baby, illustrated by Ard Hoyt, Pelican Publishing (Gretna, LA), 2007.

(With wife Deborah Dover Layne) *P Is for Princess: A Royal Alphabet,* illustrated by Robert Papp and Lisa Papp, Sleeping Bear Press (Chelsea, MI), 2007.

(With wife Deborah Dover Layne) *Number One Teacher: A School Counting Book,* illustrated by Doris Ettlinger, Sleeping Bear Press (Chelsea, MI), 2008.

Teachers' Night before Halloween, illustrated by Ard Hoyt, Pelican Publishing (Gretna, LA), 2008.

(With wife Deborah Dover Layne) *W Is for Windy City: A Chicago Alphabet,* illustrated by Michael Hays and Judy MacDonald, Sleeping Bear Press (Ann Arbor, MI), 2010.

Share with Brother, illustrated by Ard Hoyt, Pelican Publishing (Gretna, LA), 2011.

Stay with Sister, illustrated by Ard Hoyt, Pelican Publishing (Gretna, LA), 2012.

NOVELS

This Side of Paradise, North Star Books (St. Charles, IL), 2001.

Mergers, Pelican Publishing (Gretna, LA), 2006.

Paradise Lost, Pelican Publishing (Gretna, LA), 2011.

OTHER

Life's Literary Lessons: Poems for Teachers, International Reading (Newark, DE), 2001.

Verses for Dad's Heart, illustrated by Gail Greaves Klinger, Pelican Publishing (Gretna, LA), 2004.

Verses for Mom's Heart, illustrated by Gail Greaves Klinger, Pelican Publishing (Gretna, LA), 2005.

Igniting a Passion for Reading: Successful Strategies for Building Lifetime Readers, foreword by Gail Boushey and Joan Moser, Stenhouse Publishers (Portland, ME), 2009.

Contributor to books and to journals, including *Illinois Reading Council Journal, Reading Teacher, Reading Horizons,* and *Contemporary Education.*

Adaptations

My Brother Dan's Delicious, Love the Baby, and *This Side of Paradise* were adapted for audiobook, 2009.

Sidelights

A noted literacy consultant, Steven L. Layne has written works for readers of all ages, among them his award-winning teen novel *This Side of Paradise* and *The Teachers' Night before Christmas,* a picture book for children. Layne has also authored several inspirational books for teachers, parents, and adult caretakers as well as producing *Over Land and Sea: A Story of International Adoption.* In each of his books, as well as in his work as a professor of education and literature, his

primary focus is on building lifetime readers. "Just as the writer in me is trying to reach lots of different kinds of readers," Layne explained to a *Reading Today* interviewer, "the teacher in me is trying to reach lots of different kids."

Layne was challenged to write his first novel for young adults by several students in an eighth-grade class he was teaching in the late 1990s. Praised as a "taut SF thriller" by a *Kirkus Reviews* contributor, *This Side of Paradise* finds Jack Barrett struggling under the thumb of his perfectionist father. When a job change prompts Mr. Barrett to move the family to a seemingly perfect gated community run by his new corporate employer, the high-school junior realizes that something is eerily wrong. When his mother and younger brother disappear after the move to Paradise, Jack is determined to discover the source of the hold someone—or some thing— has on his dad. He is aided in his quest by a new love interest as well as his motorcycle-riding grandmother. The *Kirkus Reviews* critic praised Jack as "a likeable teenager, with an appealing self-deprecating tone" and Jack's nemesis as "genuinely chilling," while in *Booklist* Hazel Rochman favorably cited the teen narrator's "wry contemporary voice."

In *Paradise Lost,* a sequel to *This Side of Paradise,* Jack must again confront Adam Eden, his father's nefarious alter ego and a man bent on creating a perfect society. Upon returning to school in the fall, Jack grows suspicious when he discovers that the school wallflower has undergone a stunning physical transformation. The

A young boy's fascination with the space program influences his dreams in Steven L. Layne's **Thomas's Sheep and the Spectacular Science Project,** *featuring illustrations by Perry Board.* (Illustration copyright © 2004 by Perry Board. All rights reserved. Reproduced by permission of Pelican Publishing Co., Inc.)

Doris Ettlinger creates the entertaining and detailed illustrations that capture the action in Layne's concept book in **T Is for Teachers.** (Illustration copyright © 2005 by Doris Ettlinger. All rights reserved. Reproduced by permission of the illustrator.)

teen's worst fears are confirmed when he hears that Eden has been spotted in the area, and then Jack's brother vanishes and his grandmother is poisoned. "Younger teens may enjoy the action-packed story line that keeps them guessing," Kimberly Castle remarked in her *School Library Journal* review of *Paradise Lost.* Jamie Hansen, writing in *Voice of Youth Advocates,* also complimented Layne's novel, stating that the "futuristic thriller ensures an abundance of teen appeal with plenty of violent action and liberal dollops of ribald slapstick humor."

With *Mergers,* another work aimed at young adults, Layne explores a world in which racial differences among humans have been obliterated through genetic engineering. Dirk is part of a small group of teens living in hiding because they exhibit the racial features that are now forbidden. Each of the teens has a special power: African-born Nicci can move time, Hispanic Mateo is a shapeshifter, Asian Keiko can heal with her touch, and Caucasian Dirk can read the thoughts of others. When they use their powers to travel into the past in an effort to stop the technology that will culminate in this homogenous future society, the teens attract the attention of someone who has expected their arrival and is now determined to stop them. In *Voice of Youth Advocates,* a reviewer described the storyline of *Mergers* as "the Hardy Boys with a more serious twist."

Turning to younger children, Layne has collaborated with wife Deborah Dover Layne on the picture book *T Is for Teachers: A School Alphabet,* a guidebook for young schoolgoers featuring engaging illustrations by Dorris Ettlinger. Geared for slightly older readers and animated by Perry Board's colorful cartoon-style illustrations, *Thomas's Sheep and the Spectacular Science Project* and *Thomas's Sheep and the Great Geography Test* find a young boy aided by a flock of fact-finding sheep while tackling taxing tests and creating well-done classroom presentations.

Layne addresses the familiar childhood issue of sibling rivalry in *Love the Baby*, in which a young rabbit becomes jealous of the parental attention given to the newborn in his household. Their relationship changes dramatically, however, when the baby wakes one night and Older Brother is the only one to answer its cries. "The short, simple text flows smoothly and uses repetition to keep the focus on the theme," Martha Topol explained in her review of *Love the Baby* for *School Library Journal.* Layne's bunny siblings make a return appearance in *Share with Brother,* a story about "the concept of getting along together, even when it isn't fun," according to a reviewer in *Children's Bookwatch.*

Biographical and Critical Sources

PERIODICALS

Booklist, February 1, 2002, Hazel Rochman, review of *This Side of Paradise,* p. 934; April 1, 2007, Stephanie Zvirin, review of *Love the Baby,* p. 58.

The universal toddler fear of not having it all is at the core of Layne's picture book **Share with Brother,** *featuring artwork by Ard Hoyt.* (Illustration copyright © 2011 by Ard Hoyt. Reproduced by permission of Pelican Publishing Co., Inc.)

Children's Bookwatch, July, 2008, review of *Number One Teacher: A School Counting Book*; February, 2011, review of *Share with Brother.*

Kirkus Reviews, October 15, 2001, review of *This Side of Paradise,* p. 1486; November 15, 2010, review of *Share with Brother.*

Publishers Weekly, May 4, 1998, review of *Thomas's Sheep and the Great Geography Test,* p. 215; September 24, 2001, review of *The Teacher's Night before Christmas,* p. 57.

Reading Today, August, 2001, review of *Life's Literary Lesson: Poems for Teachers,* p. 32; December, 2005, "Teacher, Author, Leader," p. 29.

Reviewer's Bookwatch, May, 2005, Kimberly Hutmacher, review of *T Is for Teachers: A School Alphabet.*

School Library Journal, September, 1998, Kathy Piehl, review of *Thomas's Sheep and the Great Geography Test,* p. 175; January, 2002, Joel Shoemaker, review of *This Side of Paradise,* p. 136; May, 2003, Kathleen Whalin, review of *My Brother Dan's Delicious,* p. 122; July, 2004, Sally R. Dow, review of *Verses for Dad's Heart,* p. 124; June, 2005, Deborah Vose, review of *Over Land and Sea: A Story of International Adoption,* p. 120; August, 2005, Corrina Austin, review of *T Is for Teachers,* p. 114; July, 2006, Tasha Saecker, review of *Mergers,* p. 106; July, 2007, Martha Topol, review of *Love the Baby,* p. 80; March, 2011, Kimberly Castle, review of *Paradise Lost,* p. 165.

Voice of Youth Advocates, February 1, 2002, review of *This Side of Paradise,* p. 447; May 1, 2006, review of *Mergers;* April, 2011, Jamie Hansen, review of *Paradise Lost,* p. 83.

ONLINE

Children's Book Council Web site, http://www.cbcboks.org/cbcmagazine/ (June 13, 2006), Steven L. Layne, "Looking Back. . . ."

Judson College Web site, http://www.judsoncollege.edu/ (June 13, 2006), "Steve Layne."

School Library Journal Web log, http://blog.schoollibraryjournal.com/practicallyparadise/ (December 7, 2009), Diane Kelly, interview with Layne.

Steven L. Layne Home Page, http://www.stevelayne.com (July 15, 2012).*

*   *   *

LEAVITT, Lindsey 1980-

Personal

Born August 17, 1980; married; children: three daughters. *Education:* Attended Brigham Young University.

Addresses

Home—Las Vegas, NV. *Agent*—The Greenhouse Literary Agency, 11308 Lapham Dr., Oakton, VA 22124. *E-mail*—contact@lindseyleavitt.com.

Career

Novelist and educator. Former elementary-grade teacher in Murray, UT.

Member

Society of Children's Book Writers and Illustrators.

Writings

YOUNG-ADULT NOVELS

Sean Griswold's Head, Bloomsbury (New York, NY), 2011.

"PRINCESS FOR HIRE" NOVEL SERIES

Princess for Hire, Disney/Hyperion Books (New York, NY), 2010.

The Royal Treatment, Disney/Hyperion Books (New York, NY), 2011.

A Farewell to Charms, Disney/Hyperion Books (New York, NY), 2012.

Sidelights

Lindsey Leavitt writes the appealing "Princess for Hire" series of 'tween novels. Leavitt's titular heroine is Desi Bascomb, a girl who bolts from her job as a costumed groundhog in her boring Idaho hometown after answering an advertisement that reads "Princess for Hire." In the first book in the series, which is also titled *Princess for Hire,* Meredith runs the mysterious Façade Agency, which helps real-life princesses when they need a break from their glamorous royal lives. Meredith providesone such client with Desi, and the substitution is accomplished with the help of some magic makeup and a giant bubble that teleports Desi back and forth to her new job. Although the groundhog loves her job, there is a downside: a princess for hire is barred from genuinely interacting or forging real relationships with the people she meets during her work as a princess substitute.

"Leavitt's debut novel has an entertaining premise that would be right at home as a TV movie," asserted a *Publishers Weekly* contributor in reviewing Leavitt's first "Princess for Hire" installment. Reviewing the book in *School Library Journal,* Shari Fesko called *Princess for Hire* "a fast-paced and humorous read with a dash of romance" and predicted that "it's sure to leave readers longing for the next installment."

Desi returns in *The Royal Treatment,* which finds her happy to learn that Meredith is bumping her up a pay grade to that of a Level-Two Princess. When the girl lands the coveted role of Titania in her high school's production of Shakespeare's *A Midsummer Night's Dream,* the real-life princess she is currently surrogating becomes enmeshed in a tabloid scandal and does not want to return to her own life. Imprisoned in an overtime shift that may never end, Desi worries that she may also be giving up her chance at real-world stardom. "Leavitt keeps the story dancing along with breathless, wish-fulfillment glee," remarked a contributor to *Kirkus Reviews,* the critic adding of *The Royal Treatment* that "Desi's character stands out with her unsinkable confidence."

A Las Vegas, Nevada, native, Leavitt attended Brigham Young University and then married her high-school lab partner. She worked as an elementary school teacher before becoming a writer. In an interview with Liesl Shurtliff for the *Deseret News,* she described her early teen years as "angstsville" and a time when she was "awkward and unsure." By creating an alternate persona for Desi, as stealth princess, Leavitt hopes to help readers create their own transformative bubble to navigate new worlds. As she told Shurtliff, "Listening to yourself, to your own advice, takes courage and Desi finds that courage through walking in other girls' shoes. Er, heels."

Cover of Lindsay Leavitt's humorous young-adult novel Sean Griswold's Head, *in which a troubled teen fixates on something to help her gain perspective on her problems.* (Jacket photographs by Krystian Kaczmarski (boy); Dietmar Klement (green board); Carolina K. Smith (ledge). Reproduced by permission of Bloomsbury USA.)

In addition to her fanciful "Princess for Hire" stories, Leavitt has also authored the young-adult novel *Sean Griswold's Head,* which introduces a focused, driven, and successful student athlete named Payton Gritas. Payton is devastated to learn that her father has been diagnosed with multiple sclerosis, but she even more traumatized by the fact her parents and older brothers have attempted to keep this news from her. Torn by anger and grief, she stops speaking to her family, quits the basketball team, and allows her grades to plummet. A sympathetic guidance counselor attempts to help Payton by recommending that she start a journal and focus on something other than her father's plight. Payton's focus becomes Sean Griswold, the boy who has occupied the desk in front of her every year since third grade. Although best friend Jac is supportive of the journaling idea, it soon brings Payton a host of new worries.

"Payton is likable and the writing brisk and amusing," noted a *Kirkus Reviews* writer in appraising *Sean Griswold's Head.* In *School Library Journal,* Adrienne L. Strock cited the story's "likable characters" and commended Leavitt's method of handling of serious illness as "refreshing and realistic without being overwrought with angst."

Biographical and Critical Sources

PERIODICALS

Booklist, March 1, 2011, John Peters, review of *Sean Griswold's Head,* p. 61.
Bulletin of the Center for Children's Books, February, 2011, Kate Quealy-Gainer, review of *Sean Griswold's Head,* p. 284.
Deseret News, May 14, 2011, Liesl Shurtliff, "Leavitt Delivers a Tween Treat with New Novel."
Kirkus Reviews, February 15, 2011, review of *Sean Griswold's Head;* April 1, 2011, review of *The Royal Treatment.*
Publishers Weekly, February 15, 2010, review of *Princess for Hire,* p. 132; January 31, 2011, review of *Sean Griswold's Head,* p. 51.
School Library Journal, May, 2010, Shari Fesko, review of *Princess for Hire,* p. 118; March, 2011, Adrienne L. Strock, review of *Sean Griswold's Head,* p. 165.
Voice of Youth Advocates, April, 2011, Debbie Wenk, review of *Sean Griswold's Head,* p. 62.

ONLINE

Lindsey Leavitt Home Page, http://lindseyleavitt.com (August 1, 2012).*

*   *   *

LOOK, Lenore

Personal

Born in Seattle, WA; married; children: two daughters. *Education:* Princeton University, bachelor's degree, 1984.

Addresses

Home—Randolph, NJ.

Career

Author and journalist. Reporter for *Los Angeles Times* and *Trenton Sun,* Trenton, NJ. Also worked as a model and actress, appearing on television programs such as *Sesame Street.*

Member

Society of Children's Book Writers and Illustrators.

Awards, Honors

Notable Social Studies Trade Books for Young Readers selection, Children's Book Council/National Council for the Social Studies, 1999, for *Love as Strong as Ginger;* Notable Book for Children selection, *Smithsonian* magazine, 2001, Notable Children's Book designation, American Library Association (ALA), and Charlotte Zolotow Award highly commended title, Cooperative Children's Book Center (CCBC), all for *Henry's First-Moon Birthday* ; Manoa Award for Best American Essays, 2001, for "Facing the Village"; Notable Children's Book designation, ALA, 2004, for *Ruby Lu, Brave and True;* Choices selection, CCBC, and Notable Children's Book designation, ALA, both 2006, both for *Ruby Lu, Empress of Everything;* Notable Children's Book designation, ALA, 2006, for *Uncle Peter's Amazing Chinese Wedding.*

Writings

Love as Strong as Ginger, illustrated by Stephen T. Johnson, Atheneum (New York, NY), 1999.
Henry's First-Moon Birthday, illustrated by Yumi Heo, Atheneum (New York, NY), 2001.
Uncle Peter's Amazing Chinese Wedding, illustrated by Yumi Heo, Atheneum (New York, NY), 2006.
Polka Dot Penguin Pottery, illustrated by Yumi Heo, Schwartz & Wade Books (New York, NY), 2011.

Contributor of essays and articles to *Princeton Alumni Weekly, Publishers Weekly,* and *Race and Races: Cases for a Diverse America.*

"RUBY LU" CHAPTER-BOOK SERIES

Ruby Lu, Brave and True, illustrated by Anne Wilsdorf, Atheneum (New York, NY), 2004.
Ruby Lu, Empress of Everything, illustrated by Anne Wilsdorf, Atheneum (New York, NY), 2006.
Ruby Lu, Star of the Show, illustrated by Stef Choi, Atheneum (New York, NY), 2011.

"ALVIN HO" CHAPTER-BOOK SERIES; ILLUSTRATED BY LEUYEN PHAM

Alvin Ho: Allergic to Girls, School, and Other Scary Things, Schwartz & Wade Books (New York, NY), 2008.

Alvin Ho: Allergic to Camping, Hiking, and Other Natural Disasters, Schwartz & Wade Books (New York, NY), 2009.
Alvin Ho: Allergic to Birthday Parties, Science Projects, and Other Man-made Catastrophes, Schwartz & Wade Books (New York, NY), 2010.
Alvin Ho: Allergic to Dead Bodies, Funerals, and Other Fatal Circumstances, Schwartz & Wade Books (New York, NY), 2011.

Adaptations

Henry's First-Moon Birthday was adapted for videocassette Books in the "Alvin Ho" series have been adapted as audiobooks.

Sidelights

Author Lenore Look draws on her experiences growing up as a Chinese American, as well as those as an American visiting China, to tell stories that balance the sometimes-competing themes of individuality and tradition. Each of Look's picture books "emphasizes its main character's attempt to achieve a healthy balance

Cover of Lenore Look's chapter book **Ruby Lu, Brave and True,** *featuring artwork by Anne Wilsdorf.* (Aladdin Paperbacks, 2004. Cover illustration copyright © 2004 by Anne Wilsdorf. Reproduced by permission of Aladdin Paperbacks, an imprint of Simon & Schuster Children's Publishing Division.)

between independence and connection to family," wrote April Spisak in the *Bulletin of the Center for Children's Books* online. Look is also the author of the "Ruby Lu" and "Alvin Ho" series of chapter books for young readers, both which have been praised for their insightful explorations of childhood as well as their humorous, rapid-fire plots.

Look's first picture book, *Love as Strong as Ginger,* draws on memories of the author's grandmother, who worked in a factory in Seattle during the 1960s and 1970s. Set in that era, the story focuses on the relationship between young Katie and her grandmother, GninGnin, and Katie's understanding of the hard work GninGnin must perform in order to earn a living. "The words are simple. The facts are stark," wrote Hazel Rochman in her *Booklist* review, concluding that *Love as Strong as Ginger* "is a fine addition to the realistic stories of coming to America." A *Horn Book* critic called the book a "powerfully felt evocation of the dreams that can sustain one generation with hope of a better life for the next." While Look "doesn't flinch from describing the harsh conditions . . . her story focuses on the strength and dreams of the women who work there," wrote a *Publishers Weekly* contributor of the work, which features illustrations by Stephen T. Johnson.

Both *Henry's First-Moon Birthday* and *Uncle Peter's Amazing Chinese Wedding* follow Jen's struggles to deal with the changes occurring in her life. In *Henry's First-Moon Birthday* she helps prepare for her baby brother's one-month birthday celebration. Although jealous that the baby receives all the attention, she realizes by day's end that he will one day be glad she was in charge of his party. In *Uncle Peter's Amazing Chinese Wedding* Jen is once again envious, this time because Uncle Peter's fiancée is taking all her usually doting uncle's attention. Initially intending to disrupt the celebration, Jen changes her mind after she is invited to help coordinate wedding festivities by both bride and groom.

"Jen's chatty narration infuses the book with . . . cozy immediacy," wrote Gillian Engberg in her *Booklist* review of *Henry's First-Moon Birthday,* and Jennifer Mattson noted in the same periodical that "references to Chinese traditions emerge naturally throughout" *Uncle Peter's Amazing Chinese Wedding.* Although a *Publishers Weekly* critic also noted the cultural appeal of Look's story, the reviewer added that the real draw comes from the "true-to-life voice . . . [in which] Jen conveys real feeling."

Look's almost-eight-year-old heroine has her first adventure in *Ruby Lu, Brave and True.* With a mother who studies Chinese fan dancing, a dad who loves board games, and a mischievous little brother named Oscar, Ruby's family life is as exciting as her time at Chinese school. Considered "plucky" by a *Publishers Weekly*

A geeky preteen hoping to avoid all thing unpleasant is Look's hero in a series of books illustrated by LeUyen Pham that include **Alvin Ho: Allergic to Girls, School, and Other Scary Things.** (Illustration copyright © 2008 by LeUyen Pham. Reproduced by permission of Schwartz & Wade Books, an imprint of Random House Children's Books, a division of Random House, Inc.)

critic and "refreshingly feisty" by a contributor to *School Library Journal,* Look's protagonist fills "the need for a recurring Asian American character," according to *Booklist* contributor Terry Glover. Debbie Stewart, writing in *School Library Journal,* called *Ruby Lu, Brave and True* "funny and charming," adding that a favorite magic trick of Ruby's is featured in flip-book format on the corner pages. Look also provides a glossary, enabling readers to research terms related to Chinese culture.

Ruby's cousin Flying Duck is visiting from China in *Ruby Lu, Empress of Everything.* Although she immediately feels a kinship with her cousin, the changes the boy brings to the Lu household make her feel out of place: the family begins to speak Cantonese at home and now eats with chopsticks. When Flying Duck teaches Oscar Chinese sign language and begins to understand the toddler faster than does Ruby, the girl's frustration peaks. Ruby is "as spunky as Ramona and as moody as Judy," according to *Horn Book* critic Jennifer M. Brabander, comparing Look's heroine to the beloved fictional heroines of Beverly Cleary and Megan McDonald respectively. "Ruby Lu invites readers into a contemporary world that honors differences while ultimately celebrating universal moments of childhood," wrote Julie R. Ranelli in her *School Library Journal* review of *Ruby Lu, Empress of Everything.*

Ruby's family experiences some difficult times as the youngster enters third grade in *Ruby Lu, Star of the Show.* When Ruby's father loses his job, each member of the household is forced to make a number of sacrifices: Ruby cannot take her new dog, Elvis, to obedience school and her mother must take a minimum-wage position at the mall to help pay the bills. Ruby must also adjust to the unorthodox methods of her stay-at-home dad, who becomes increasingly frustrated by his situation. Noting that the work still includes moments of humor, a writer in *Kirkus Reviews* reported that "Look provides some real insight into the struggles a family faces when its main breadwinner is out of work," and Stacy Dillon, writing in *School Library Journal,* called *Ruby Lu, Star of the Show* "a fun easy chapter book despite the heavier issues."

Look tackles childhood issues from a male perspective in her "Alvin Ho" series, featuring the adventures of a bright but neurotic Chinese-American youngster. "'Alvin' is about the perils of childhood and how being a boy is all about survival," Look stated in a *Powell's Books* interview. In *Alvin Ho: Allergic to Girls, School, and Other Scary Things* readers meet the second grader as he faces a most-unusual problem: He becomes so anxious at school that he cannot bring himself to speak. To combat his fears, Alvin visits with a psychotherapist who finally draws the lad out of his shell, helping Alvin begin an unlikely friendship with a classmate. "Look's . . . intuitive grasp of children's emotions is rivaled only by her flair for comic exaggeration," a reviewer commented in *Publishers Weekly,* and *Horn Book* contributor Jennifer M. Brabander observed that the author "acknowledges kids' troubles while lightening them in a funny yet respectful way."

Alvin dreads an upcoming trip with his father and sister in *Alvin Ho: Allergic to Camping, Hiking, and Other Natural Disasters,* the second work in the series. Upon learning that he will spend some time in the Great Outdoors, a panic-stricken Alvin turns to his older brother, who orders survival gear from the Internet, and his uncle, who instructs him in camping lore. "Look's pitch-perfect descriptions and phrasing add to the overall humor and heart of the story," Nicole Waskie remarked in *School Library Journal,* and Brabander maintained that

the author "takes familiar kid traumas and troubles and ramps them up a notch, leaving them easily recognizable to young readers but a whole lot funnier."

In *Alvin Ho: Allergic to Birthday Parties, Science Projects, and Other Man-made Catastrophes* the perpetually nervous second-grader must endure a class field trip to the houses of deceased authors Louisa May Alcott and Ralph Waldo Emerson in his hometown of Concord, Massachusetts. A critic in *Kirkus Reviews* wrote that "Alvin proves an engaging narrator, whose imagination runs wild to hilarious effect." The protagonist's inability to talk at school leads to a gross misunderstanding about his grandfather in *Alvin Ho: Allergic to Dead Bodies, Funerals, and Other Fatal Circumstances.* "Alvin's frenetic first-person voice . . . is engaging and real, often laugh-out-loud funny," observed another *Kirkus Reviews* contributor of this installment in Look's series.

Although Look covers a variety of themes in both her picture books and chapter books, Spisak cited a unifying factor: "It's clear that her books reflect her own understanding, and yet with their focus on home, family, and culture they manage to be universal as well as personal."

Look's hapless preteen returns to the relief of fans in Alvin Ho: Allergic to Birthday Parties, Science Projects, and Other man-Made Catastrophes, *featuring Pham's humorous illustrations.* (Illustration copyright © 2010 by LeUyen Pham. Reproduced by permission of Schwartz & Wade Books, an imprint of Random House Children's Books, a division of Random House, Inc.)

Biographical and Critical Sources

PERIODICALS

Booklist, October 15, 1999, Hazel Rochman, review of *Love as Strong as Ginger,* p. 443; April 1, 2001, Gillian Engberg, review of *Henry's First-Moon Birthday,* p. 1470; January 1, 2004, Terry Glover, review of *Ruby Lu, Brave and True,* p. 878; December 15, 2005, Jennifer Mattson, review of *Uncle Peter's Amazing Chinese Wedding,* p. 47; February 15, 2006, Cindy Dobrez, review of *Ruby Lu, Empress of Everything,* p. 104; July 1, 2008, Jennifer Mattson, review of *Alvin Ho: Allergic to Girls, School, and Other Scary Things,* p. 61; February 1, 2011, Linda Perkins, review of *Ruby Lu: Star of the Show,* p. 78; October 15, 2011, Courtney Jones, review of *Alvin Ho: Allergic to Dead Bodies, Funerals, and Other Fatal Circumstances,* p. 47.

Bulletin of the Center for Children's Books, April, 2004, Karen Coats, review of *Ruby Lu, Brave and True,* p. 336; January, 2006, Elizabeth Bush, review of *Uncle Peter's Amazing Chinese Wedding,* p. 215; May, 2006, Karen Coats, review of *Ruby Lu, Empress of Everything,* p. 410.

Childhood Education, winter, 2001, Debora Wisneski, review of *Henry's First-Moon Birthday,* p. 111, annual, 2006, Lea Lee, review of *Uncle Peter's Amazing Chinese Wedding,* p. 303.

Horn Book, May, 1999, review of *Love as Strong as Ginger,* p. 318; May-June, 2006, Jennifer M. Brabander, review of *Ruby Lu, Empress of Everything,* p. 322; July-August, 2008, Jennifer M. Brabander, review of *Alvin Ho: Allergic to Girls, School, and Other Scary Things,* p. 453; September-October, 2009, Jennifer M. Brabander, review of *Alvin Ho: Allergic to Camping, Hiking, and Other Natural Disasters,* p. 567; September-October, 2010, Jennifer M. Brabander, review of *Alvin Ho: Allergic to Birthday Parties, Science Projects, and Other Man-Made Catastrophes,* p. 82; March-April, 2011, Jennifer M. Brabander, review of *Ruby Lu, Star of the Show,* p. 120; September-October, 2011, Jennifer M. Brabander, review of *Alvin Ho: Allergic to Dead Bodies, Funerals, and Other Fatal Circumstances,* p. 91.

Kirkus Reviews, December 1, 2005, review of *Uncle Peter's Amazing Chinese Wedding,* p. 1277; March 1, 2006, review of *Ruby Lu, Empress of Everything,* p. 234; June 15, 2008, review of *Alvin Ho: Allergic to Girls, School, and Other Scary Things*; May 15, 2009, review of *Alvin Ho; Allergic to Camping, Hiking, and Other Natural Disasters*; September 1, 2010, review of *Alvin Ho* ; January 15, 2011, review of *Ruby Lu, Star of the Show*; August 15, 2011, review of *Alvin Ho: Allergic to Dead Bodies, Funerals, and Other Fatal Circumstances.*

Publishers Weekly, May 24, 1999, review of *Love as Strong as Ginger,* p. 79; April 9, 2001, review of *Henry's First-Moon Birthday,* p. 73; January 19, 2004, review of *Ruby Lu, Brave and True,* p. 76; December 5, 2005, review of *Uncle Peter's Amazing Chinese Wedding,* p. 54; April 3, 2006, review of *Ruby Lu, Empress of Everything,* p. 76; July 7, 2008, review of *Alvin Ho: Allergic to Girls, School, and Other Scary Things,* p. 58.

School Library Journal, July, 1999, Margaret A. Change, review of *Love as Strong as Ginger,* p. 76; June, 2001, Alice Casey Smith, review of *Henry's First-Moon Birthday,* p. 126; February, 2004, Debbie Stewart, review of *Ruby Lu, Brave and True,* p. 116; March, 2005, Kathleen T. Isaacs, review of *Ruby Lu, Brave and True,* p. 68; January, 2006, Maura Bresnahan, review of *Uncle Peter's Amazing Chinese Wedding,* p. 106; August, 2008, Faith Brautigam, review of *Alvin Ho: Allergic to Girls, School, and Other Scary Things,* p. 96; July, 2009, Nicole Waskie, review of *Alvin Ho: Allergic to Camping, Hiking, and Other Natural Disasters,* p. 66; March, 2011, Stacy Dillon, review of *Ruby Lu, Star of the Show,* p. 128; October, 2011, Maryann H. Owen, review of *Polka Dot Penguin Pottery,* p. 112.

ONLINE

Bulletin of the Center for Children's Books Online, http://bccb.lis.uiuc.edu/ (November, 2006), April Spisak, "Rising Star: Lenore Look."

Powell's Books Web site, http://www.powells.com/ (June 23, 2009), "Kids' Q&A: Lenore Look."

Random House Web site, http://www.randomhouse.com/ (August 1, 2012), "Lenore Look."*

*   *   *

LYNCH, Chris 1962-

Personal

Born July 2, 1962, in Boston, MA; son of Edward J. (a bus driver) and Dorothy (a receptionist) Lynch; married Tina Coviello (a technical support manager), August 5, 1989 (marriage ended) partner's name Jules; children: Sophia, Walker. *Education:* Suffolk University, B.A. (journalism), 1983; Emerson University, M.A. (professional writing and publishing), 1991. *Hobbies and other interests:* Running.

Addresses

Home—Ayrshire, Scotland. *Agent*—Fran Lebowitz, Writers House, 21 W. 26th St., New York, NY 10010.

Career

Writer and educator. Proofreader of financial reports, 1985-89. Teacher of writing at Emerson University, 1995, and Vermont College, beginning 1997; Lesley University, Cambridge, MA, instructor in low-residency M.F.A program. Conducted a writing workshop at Boston Public Library, summer, 1994.

Member

Authors Guild, Author's League of America.

Chris Lynch (Photograph by Jeff Thiebauth. Reproduced by permission.)

Awards, Honors

American Library Association (ALA) Best Books for Young Adults and Quick Picks for Reluctant Young-Adult Readers citations, 1993, for *Shadow Boxer,* 1994, for *Iceman* and *Gypsy Davey,* and 1996, for *Slot Machine;* Best Books of the Year designation, *School Library Journal,* 1993, for *Shadow Boxer;* Blue Ribbon Award, *Bulletin of the Center for Children's Books,* 1994, for *Iceman* and *Gypsy Davey;* Editors' Choice award, *Booklist,* 1994, for *Gypsy Davey;* Dorothy Canfield Fisher Award finalist, Book of the Year award, *Hungry Mind Review,* and Young Adults' Choice citation, International Reading Association, all 1997, all for *Slot Machine;* Michael L. Printz Honor Book designation, and ALA Best Book for Young Adults designation, both 2002, both for *Freewill;* National Book Award nomination, 2005, for *Inexcusable.*

Writings

Shadow Boxer, HarperCollins (New York, NY), 1993.
Iceman, HarperCollins (New York, NY), 1994.
Gypsy Davey, HarperCollins (New York, NY), 1994.
Slot Machine, HarperCollins (New York, NY), 1995.
Political Timber, HarperCollins (New York, NY), 1996.
Extreme Elvin (sequel to *Slot Machine*), HarperCollins (New York, NY), 1999.
Whitechurch, HarperCollins (New York, NY), 1999.
Gold Dust, HarperCollins (New York, NY), 2000.
Freewill, HarperCollins (New York, NY), 2001.

All the Old Haunts (stories), HarperCollins (New York, NY), 2001.
Who the Man, HarperCollins (New York, NY), 2002.
The Gravedigger's Cottage, HarperCollins (New York, NY), 2004.
Inexcusable, Atheneum Books for Young Readers (New York, NY), 2005.
Me, Dead Dad, and Alcatraz (sequel to *Extreme Elvin*), HarperCollins (New York, NY), 2005.
Sins of the Fathers, HarperTempest (New York, NY), 2006.
The Big Game of Everything, HarperTeen (New York, NY), 2008.
Hothouse, HarperTeen (New York, NY), 2010.
Angry Young Man, Simon & Schuster/BFYR (New York, NY), 2011.
Kill Switch, Simon & Schuster Books for Young Readers (New York, NY), 2012.
Pieces, Simon & Schuster Books for Young Readers (New York, NY), 2013.

Contributor of short stories to anthologies, including *Ultimate Sports,* edited by Donald Gallo, Delacorte, 1995, *Night Terrors,* edited by Lois Duncan, Simon & Schuster, 1996, *Guys Write for Guys Read,* Viking, 2004; and *No Such Thing as the Real World,* Harper-Collins, 2009. Contributor of stories and articles to periodicals, including *Signal, School Library Journal,* and *Boston* magazine.

Authors work has been translated into several languages, including Italian and Taiwanese.

"BLUE-EYED SON" NOVEL SERIES

Mick, HarperCollins (New York, NY), 1996.
Blood Relations, HarperCollins (New York, NY), 1996.
Dog Eat Dog, HarperCollins (New York, NY), 1996.

"HE-MAN WOMAN-HATERS CLUB" SERIES; FOR YOUNG READERS

Johnny Chesthair, HarperCollins (New York, NY), 1997.
Babes in the Woods, HarperCollins (New York, NY), 1997.
Scratch and the Sniffs, HarperTrophy (New York, NY), 1997.
Ladies' Choice, HarperTrophy (New York, NY), 1997.
The Wolf Gang, HarperCollins (New York, NY), 1998.

"CYBERIA" NOVEL SERIES

Cyberia, Scholastic Press (New York, NY), 2008.
Monkey See, Monkey Don't, Scholastic Press (New York, NY), 2009.
Prime Evil, Scholastic Press (New York, NY), 2010.

"VIETNAM" NOVEL SERIES

I Pledge Allegiance, Scholastic Press (New York, NY), 2012.
Sharpshooter, Scholastic Press (New York, NY), 2012.
Free-fire Zone, Scholastic Press (New York, NY), 2012.

Sidelights

An American author of teen fiction who now makes his home in Scotland, Chris Lynch creates realistic and compelling novels featuring young people wading through the muddy waters of adolescence on their way to adulthood. Indeed, confused and misunderstood teens have become Lynch's stock in trade; these youths populate the pages of his ground-breaking novels *Shadow Boxer, Iceman,* and *Hothouse* as well as his "Blue-Eyed Son" and "Vietnam" series. Episodic and fast paced, Lynch's stories question the male stereotypes of macho identity and inarticulate violence. His youthful outsider characters are often athletes and wannabe athletes as well as kids who have been churned up and spit out by "the system." Their stories reveal what it means to be young and urban and male in America, warts and all.

"Growing up I listened way too much to the rules as they were handed down," Lynch recalled in an interview for *Authors and Artists for Young Adults (AAYA).* Although he was raised in Boston, the fifth of seven children in a stable family, his Jamaica Plains neighborhood was transitioning from an Irish stronghold to Hispanic during his childhood. After Lynch's father died when the future author was five years old, his mother was left to raise her children alone and finances became somewhat strained. "She did a good job of covering it up, but things were pretty lean back then," Lynch remembered. "We were definitely a free cheese family, though I never felt deprived as a kid."

A somewhat reclusive child, Lynch attended primary and secondary levels Catholic schools, and while grammar school was enjoyable, high school was a different matter. "I hated high school—every minute. It was rigid, kind of a factory. An all-boys' football factory. Nothing like the arts was encouraged in any way." Although Lynch played street hockey, football, and baseball as a child, during high school he stopped playing as a way of rebelling against the pro-sports culture. "I'm not against all athletics," he explained in his *AAYA* interview, because "sports has a tremendous potential for channeling energy. But . . . it mostly encourages the macho ethos and schools let athletes run wild."

Although Lynch dropped out of high school in his junior year, he eventually enrolled at Boston University, where he studied political science. A journalism course sparked his interest in writing, and after transferring to Suffolk University, he majored in the subject. After graduation, Lynch spent six years working at odd jobs such as painting houses, driving a moving van, and proofreading financial reports. While pursuing a master's program in professional writing and publishing at Boston's Emerson University, he took a children's writing class from Y.A. author Jack Gantos, and it was here that Lynch began what became his first published novel, *Shadow Boxer.* "We were supposed to write five pages on a childhood incident," the author recalled in *AAYA.* "I had a vague idea of writing about some things my brother and I had done in our youth, but as soon as I sat down with it, I was off to the races. The stuff just poured out."

Shadow Boxer is a story of two brothers learning to deal with life after the death of their father, a journeyman boxer. Fourteen-year-old George becomes the man of the house after his father dies, a casualty of years of battering he endured in the boxing ring. George's mother is bitter and hates the sport that cost her husband his life, but George's younger brother, Monty, wants to follow in his father's footsteps. Monty begins to train at the local gym with his uncle, and when George tries to discourage him from this path it exacerbates the boys' sibling rivalry. Told in brief, episodic vignettes with urban slang, the novel reaches its climax when Monty is shown a video of one of the brutal beatings his father took in the ring.

Reviewing *Shadow Boxer* in *Horn Book,* Peter D. Sieruta wrote that Lynch captures, "with unflinching honesty," the novel's working-class Boston setting. While the book's episodic style, with short, terse paragraphs, weakens the plot, according to Sieruta, several chapters of the novel "read like polished short stories and are stunning in their impact." Tom S. Hurlburt, writing in *School Library Journal,* dubbed *Shadow Boxer* "a gritty, streetwise novel that is much more than a sports story," and several critics recommended that Lynch's style—creating a series of brief, hard-hitting vignettes that reveal character—makes the novel accessible to reluctant readers.

In *Iceman* Lynch tells the story of a troubled youth for whom violence on the ice is a much-needed release. Fourteen-year-old Eric is a hockey player with a reputation as a fine shooter and a strong defensive player with a penchant for hitting. Known as the "Iceman" due to his antics on the ice, Eric actually seems to enjoy hurting people. His only friends are his older brother Duane, whose act of trading his skates for a guitar impresses Eric, and the local embalmer, McLaughlin, who also impresses Eric with his devotion to his work. The source of Eric's rage comes from his dysfunctional family: his mother, a former nun, continually spouts verses from the Bible while his father only seems interested in Eric when the boy is doing damage on the ice. As his actions on the ice become increasingly violent, Eric is soon shunned by even his own teammates. McLaughlin gives the teen some comfort in his world of death, and Eric considers a future in mortuary science until a shocking observation prompts the teen to face his current problems.

Randy Brough, reviewing *Iceman* for *Voice of Youth Advocates,* remarked that Lynch's "novel of disaffected adolescence" is "as satisfying as a hard, clean hip check." Jack Forman, while noting the book's appeal to hockey enthusiasts in his *School Library Journal* review, also pointed out that *Iceman* "is no advertisement for the sport." Stephanie Zvirin, summed up the effect of the novel in *Booklist*, wrote that Lynch's "totally unpredictable novel . . . is an unsettling, complicated portrayal of growing up in a dysfunctional family" as well as "a thought-provoking book guaranteed to compel and touch a teenage audience."

A reviewer for *Publishers Weekly* called *Whitechurch* an "unsettling, coolly polished" story that again demonstrates Lynch's "profound understanding of society's casualties, misfits and losers." In the novel, teens Pauly, Oakley, and Lilly must learn to navigate the treacherous shoals that exist in their dilapidated New England town in a series of interconnecting short stories. Seemingly trapped in the dead-end environment of Whitechurch, each teen finds his or her own way to break out of the stagnant environment. A reviewer for *Horn Book* wrote of *Whitechurch* that the "sharply evoked characters and their complex relationship are the novel's greatest strengths."

Praised by *School Library Journal* critic Michael McCullough for containing "some of the best sports writing readers will ever find in a YA novel," *Gold Dust* is set in Boston during the 1975 school-busing integration controversy. In Lynch's story, seventh-grade baseball fan Richard Moncrief dreams of transforming the new transfer student from Dominica into a first-rate baseball player. The two plan to team up and become the adolescent equivalents of Boston Red Sox players Fred Lynn and Jim Rice, dubbed the "Gold Dust Twins" during the 1975 season. However, Richard soon realizes that his new teammate, Napoleon "Charlie" Ellis, is a difficult friend to have, because Charlie's actions force the white boy to address the racial tensions in his Boston neighborhood. Lauren Adams, writing in *Horn Book,* noted that "Lynch's provocative novel tells a piece of the city's history and the more intimate story of a transforming friendship." *Gold Dust* "is a wonderful baseball book," declared *Booklist* contributor Debbie Carton, and a *Publishers Weekly* critic dubbed the story's denouement "as honest as it is heartbreaking."

Lynch's award-winning novel *Freewill* is considered something of a departure from the author's usual style: it is written in the form of a mystery and utilizes second-person narration. Having lost his father and stepmother in a strange accident, Will is sent to a special school where a sudden rash of suicides forces the reader to wonder if Will is not responsible. One of the teen's wood carvings is found at the scene of each of these suicides, attracting the police's suspicious and also drawing the attention of a weird group of hangers-on. Finally, Will's grandfather helps the boy unravel the mystery and find out what is really going on. Described by Adams as an "unsettling narrative," *Freewill* is a "dark, rich young-adult novel that offers something to think about as well as an intriguing story," according to *Booklist* contributor Susan Dove Lempke.

Lynch's protagonist in *Who the Man* is deeply misunderstood. Thirteen-year-old Earl is physically mature for his age and people assume he is older and more emotionally mature than his years. Because of his size, Earl is constantly teased by his classmates and his frustration results in fist fights and, ultimately, suspension from school. Readers soon realize that Earl's problems do not end at school; at home the teen silently watches the disintegration of his parent's marriage and witnesses his father contemplate an extramarital affair. In *Booklist* Ed Sullivan wrote that in *Who the Man* "Lynch challenges readers to consider gender stereotypes . . . as he follows a young man's painful journey toward self-discovery." Similarly, a *Publishers Weekly* reviewer acknowledged Lynch for his "hypnotic voice," and deemed *Who the Man* is a "striking chronicle of a painful transition from boyhood to manhood."

Booklist reviewer Gillian Engberg called *Inexcusable* a "bone-chilling" and "daring story [that] is told in the defensive voice of the accused rapist." In the novel, which was nominated for a National Book Award, high-school senior and popular football player Keir Sarafian is accused of rape. Lynch's readers initially enter the story believing Keir's narration of events, but his viewpoint comes into question when he begins to recognize certain things about himself. Paula Rohrlick remarked in *Kliatt* that "Keir is a good example of an unreliable narrator, whose version of reality and sense of himself . . . are dangerously off base." In the view of a *Publishers Weekly* critic, in *Inexcusable* "Lynch makes it nearly impossible for readers to see the world in black-and-white terms," and the novel is "guaranteed to prompt heated discussion."

Three thirteen year olds living in a working-class Boston neighborhood are captivated by the energy of their charismatic new parish priest in Lynch's novel *Sins of the Fathers*. Drew, the narrator, as well as Skitz and Hector have been friends forever, and they all serve at altar boys at Blessed Sacrament. When Father Mullarkey joins the church, he is a welcome counterpoint to the two staid, older priests that the boys nickname Fathers Blarney and Shenanigan because the younger man shares the same love of rock music that the boys do. While the pragmatic Drew credits Father Mullarkey with helping him to see the world in a new way, he also realizes that Hector's increasingly strange behavior may be the consequence of an inappropriate relationship with one of the three parish priests. While noting that the theme of sexual abuse is treated by Lynch with subtlety, Paula Rohrlick added in *Kliatt* that *Sins of the Father* is a story "related with rare wit and candor." Grounded in the boys' strong friendship, the novel "conveys . . . the damage that young people can be subjected to when adult influence goes unchecked," according to *School Library Journal* critic Carolyn Lehman.

In his "Blue-eyed Son" novel trilogy, Lynch returns to the mean streets of Boston to explore latent and sometimes overt racism. In *Mick* a fifteen year old sees his predominately Irish neighborhood becoming racially mixed as African Americans, Hispanics, and Asians move in. Although Mick disagree with his friends and older brother Terry's plans to disrupt the upcoming St. Patrick's Day parade by harassing gay and Cambodian marchers, he participates in their activities and when he throws an egg at a Cambodian marcher Mick's action is caught on television. Now hailed as a hero in the local bar, Mick becomes a pariah at school. Soon only the mysterious Toy remains his friend, and Mick begins to sever ties with his close-knit Irish neighborhood and hang out with a group of Latinos instead. Ultimately, Mick's behavior has consequences that are meted out by an angry Terry.

In *Blood Relations* Mick struggles to find himself, forming a brief liaison with beautiful Evelyn and finally ending up in the bed of Toy's mother, while in *Dog Eat Dog* he and Terry face off for a final showdown while Toy comes out of the closet as a homosexual. "With realistic street language and an in-your-face writing style . . . Lynch immerses readers in Mick's world," Kelly Diller wrote in a review of *Mick* for *School Library Journal.* According to Diller, Lynch has created a "noble anti-hero" in his series opener. Reviewing *Blood Relations* for *School Library Journal,* Kellie Flynn commented that "this story moves quickly, Mick's serio-comic edginess is endearing, and the racism theme is compelling." Flynn's comment that the series concept makes the ending of *Blood Relations* something of a let-down was echoed by Elizabeth Bush, who wrote in *Bulletin of the Center for Children's Books* that, "when the finish finally arrives, the unrelenting brutalities of the earlier volumes will leave the audience virtually unshockable."

Two high-school friends react to the deaths of their fathers in Lynch's *Hothouse,* which a *Kirkus Reviews* writer described as "a concise exploration of manhood, heroism and the psychology of a small . . . town." Russell and DJ are both stunned when their firefighter dads are killed inside a burning building, and their shared grief tightens the bond of their friendship. As the son of fallen local heroes, the two teens are treated with compassion and respect by their neighbors and even as heroes themselves. Then an investigation into the deadly fire finds that drub abuse was a factor in the firemen's deaths and everything Russ and DJ once held as true is shattered.

A record of events as preceived by Russ, an aspiring firefighter himself, *Hothouse* highlights "the garrulous slaps and punches that make up many male relationships," noted Daniel Kraus in his *Booklist* review of Lynch's novel. In *Publishers Weekly* a critic maintained that the author "expertly explores the gap between public perception and reality," while Betty Carter wrote in *Horn Book* that the "search for two fathers' legacies and two boys' futures" become intertwined within concerns over "self-doubt, . . . ethics, . . . and personal responsibility." Praising *Hothouse* as "a satisfying read," Angie Hammond added in her *Voice of Youth Advocates*

Cover of Lynch's novel Hothouse, *which finds two teens dealing with the tragic death of their firefighter dads.* (HarperCollins Children's Books, 2010. Jacket illustration illustration © 2010 by Sean Freeman. Reproduced by permission of Sean Freeman.)

appraisal that "Weaving tough topics, such as death, friendship, family, school, and identity into a seamless story truthfully portrayed has become Lynch's standard."

Narrated by Robert, the older half-brother of seventeen-year-old Alexander, *Angry Young Man* captures the frustrations of a young man who is desperate to belong. Raised by their single mom, the boys have grown up in financial uncertainty due to their mother's precarious job as a waitress. Despite such circumstances, Robert has lined up a job that allows him to attend community college, and with a nice girlfriend he seems to be laying the foundation of a stable future. Not so, Alexander, who prefers to be called Xan to set himself apart. Without his older brother's athletic talent, high academic standing, and large group of friends, Xan has always felt overlooked and inadequate . . . until he discovered a like-minded group of teens who channel their insecurities and frustrations into activism of a destructive nature.

In *Angry Young Man* "Lynch tells an exquisite tale of acceptance, belonging, and familial love," according to

Voice of Youth Advocates contributor Devin Burritt. Robert "narrates with a cerebral wit and detachment" that reflects his ability to rise above his family's circumstances," noted a *Publishers Weekly* contributor, resulting in a story that "can be brutal and ugly, yet isn't devoid of hope," according to the critic. Framed by a "complex sibling relationship," in the opinion of *Booklist* reviewer Ian Chipman, Lynch's novel illustrates how Robert and Xan can "have drastically different interpretations" of the same childhood environment, and Robert's "dry and sardonic wit makes him a likable and charming" narrator, according to Ryan Donovan in his *School Library Journal* review.

Another teen begins to question his family background in *Kill Switch,* which focuses on the close relationship between high-school senior Daniel and Daniel's ageing grandfather. During the teen's final summer before college Da begins to show signs of dementia, and every hour spent with the elderly man now seems precious. The timeworn stories of Da's youth start to gain unpleasant new details, however, as the man regales his grandson with stories of overthrowing foreign governments and tracking down wayward scientists with the help of covert operatives. The fact that Da used to work for the government gives these stories a veneer of truth; or is it just that the old man is going senile? In *Booklist* Chipman praised *Kill Switch* as vintage Lynch: "a compact, frayed nerves bundle of brilliance," according to the critic, while Dean Schneider concluded in *Horn Book* that the author's "spare prose" crystalizes "the complicated relationship of grandfather, son, and grandson."

In *I Pledge Allegiance* readers meet Morris, Rudi, Ivan, and Beck, whose stories play out in Lynch's "Vietnam" novel series. After Rudi is drafted, his three best friends decided to go to their local Boston recruitment office and sign up to join the U.S. military as well, each in a different branch of the armed forces. Morris describes his time in the U.S. Navy in *I Pledge Allegiance,* allowing readers to experience life aboard the USS *Boston* and the crew's efforts to support ground forces facing enemy fire in the jungles bordering the Meikong river Delta. *Sharpshooter* finds Ivan trained as a U.S. Army sniper. He intended to follow in the heroic path of his dad, a World War II veteran, but standing face to face with the enemy in the jungles of Southeast Asia causes the teen to rethink his views on courage and honor. Rudi narrates *Free-fire Zone* and here he shares his insecurities with readers while describing his experiences on the battlefield as a U.S. Marine.

"Lynch puts his readers in the center of intense conflict," noted Todd Morning in a *Booklist* review of *I Pledge Allegiance,* while in *Publishers Weekly* a critic noted that the story also touches on themes such as "racial unrest in the Navy" as well as "battles, tragedies, and inability to explain the horrors of war." *Sharpshooter* "brilliantly captures the war in small details," asserted Morning in appraising the second "Vietnam"

novel, and a *Kirkus Reviews* writer concluded of Lynch's series that it "gains richness from the multiple narratives" and ranks among "the best Vietnam War novels" written for young adults.

In addition to his hard-hitting novels for older teens, Lynch also addresses younger readers in several works of fiction. *Slot Machine* is a boys-at-summer-camp comedy about an overweight youth who resists all attempts to turn him into a jock. Thirteen-year-old Elvin Bishop is attending a Christian Brothers summer camp, with its heavy emphasis on sports as preparation for high school—the coaches literally 'slot' young athletes for specific sports. Friends with Mike, who seems to fit in anywhere, and Frank, who sells his soul to fit in, Elvin endures torment but steers a middle course and finally finds a niche for himself with the help of an arts instructor.

According to Stephanie Zvirin, writing in *Booklist, Slot Machine* is a "funny, poignant coming-of-age story." While noting Lynch's ability to write broad, physical comedy as well as dark humor, Zvirin concluded that "this wry, thoughtful book speaks with wisdom and heart to the victim and outsider in us all." Maeve Visser Knoth, writing in *Horn Book,* also noted the use of humor and sarcasm in this "biting, sometimes hilarious novel," as well as the serious purpose in back of it all. "Lynch writes a damning commentary on the costs of conformity and the power gained by standing up for oneself," the critic concluded.

Lynch reprises Elvin in the novels *Extreme Elvin* and *Me, Dead Dad, and Alcatraz.* In *Extreme Elvin* the teen is a freshman at a Catholic all-boys high school. As a *Publishers Weekly* critic noted, the novel's "wisecracking, irrepressible" character is "just as funny—and perhaps even more likable" in this new installment as the "pudgy hero has one scatological misadventure after the next." In the book, the newly girl-crazy Elvin gains a terrible reputation for his eternal hemorrhoids before being tricked into believing he has caught a sexually transmitted disease from holding hands. In the end, the young teen goes against his buddies' advice, opting to date the plump girl he really likes instead of a pretty but standoffish thinner girl. The *Publishers Weekly* critic deemed *Extreme Elvin* "witty and knowing."

Elvin is fourteen years old in *Me, Dead Dad, and Alcatraz,* and now he meets his uncle Alex, who he had been told was dead. As the teen learns, his mother lied about the relative's demise in order to hide the truth: that Alex has been serving a prison term for theft. Comedic stories unfold as Elvin's uncle attempts to become a father figure for the boy, with disastrous results. *School Library Journal* critic Miranda Doyle predicted that readers "will identify with Elvin's outsider status and enjoy his hilarious missteps on the path to adulthood," while *Booklist* critic Michael Cart called Elvin "the quintessential adolescent male—worried about sex, personal identity, and just about everything." Paula Rohrlick, writing in *Kliatt,* called *Me, Dead Dad, and Alcatraz* a "funny and poignant novel" that will appeal to "Elvin's fans."

Described by *Horn Book* contributor Claire E. Gross as an "oddball futuristic conspiracy-adventure story," Lynch's *Cyberia* is the first installment in a science-fiction series for middle graders. In the novel, Zane possesses a technologically advanced communications device, which has been given him by his workaholic single dad to keep Zane entertained while he is home alone. The device allows the boy to communicate with his dog Hugo, and when the pup recounts stories of animal abuse Zane is inspired to become an animal rights advocate. Family veterinary Dr. Gristle seems to be the key to the reported mistreatment of a local group of greyhound race dogs, and in order to help Zane must override the monitoring system—including a microchip implanted in his ankle—that keeps him under constant surveillance.

Reviewing *Cyberia,* Gross cited "the tenderness" that characterizes Zane's relationship with Hugo as well as the "hefty dose of dry situational comedy" Lynch stirs into his story. This "very funny book occasionally strikes notes of unexpected poignancy," wrote *Booklist* contributor Daniel Kraus, and a *Publishers Weekly* ob-

Cover of Lynch's young-adult novel The Big Game of Everything, *which finds a teen learning to appreciate his quirky relatives while working in the family business.* (Jacket photograph by Maurice Harmon/ Graphistock Photography/Veer. Used by permission of HarperTeen, a division of Harper-Collins Publishers.)

served of *Cyberia* that the author also explores a serious theme: "the double edge of technology that offers shortcuts but erodes independence."

Zane is living a life of true captivity when readers rejoin him in *Monkey See, Monkey Don't.* His efforts to stop the maniacal veterinarian Dr. Gristle having been discovered, the boy has been locked into his room for two months, and his problems do not end when he is finally released. Fortunately, the loyal pup Hugo remains vigilant and aids the boy in his attempt to help several animals in distress. Yet another animal needs Zane's assistance in series installment *Prime Evil.*

Reviewing *Monkey See, Monkey Don't* in *Booklist,* Daniel Kraus praised Lynch for his "affecting understanding of the bond between humans and animals, describing Hugo as an "irresistible" series character. Lynch's use of "short, direct narration and dry dialogue keep the action zipping along," observed Claire E. Gross in her *Horn Book* appraisal of the same novel, and "Zane's sudden unreliability as a narrator adds . . . interest." The "Cyberia" series "finishes . . . with another fun science-fiction adventure," noted Jessica Miller in reviewing *Prime Evil* for *School Library Journal,* the critic citing the novel for its "slapstick humor and . . . interesting plot."

Union Jack, the middle-grade hero in *The Big Game of Everything,* reacts to the name his hippy parents gave him by renaming himself Onion Jock. Although Jock is looking forward to a summer spent outside, working at his grandfather's golf course, he dreads having to deal with his mischievous brother Egon, his boy-crazy sister Meredith, and his totally laid-back parents. At sibling tensions begin to escalate Grampus becomes openly curmudgeonly and expresses discontent with entire the family as well as with his seemingly comfortable life. It soon becomes clear to Jock that the materialistic retirees who daily play their way through Grampus's golf course may be exacerbating the older man's unhappiness and pushing him toward senility.

Reviewing *The Big Game of Everything* for *Horn Book,* Adams wrote that the "motley group of eccentric characters" Lynch allows to roam, club in hand, "on a giant [golf-course] playground" provides readers with "a welcome [fictional] getaway." For Rohrlick, *The Big Game of Everything* is "an affirmation of the value of family" in which Lynch's "dialogue is often a delight," and in *School Library Journal* Jeffrey Hastings dubbed the novel a "funny and thoughtful" exploration of what is most important in life as seen "through the eyes of a teenage boy."

Written for even-younger readers, Lynch's "He-Man Woman-Haters Club" novels employ the same broad humor as the "Elvin" books to poke fun at the stereotypes of younger adolescent boys. Lincoln—also known as Johnny Chesthair—decides to start a club in his uncle's garage and invites as members wimpy Jerome, wheelchair-bound Wolfgang, and huge Ling-Ling. Later members include a guitarist named Scratch and Cecil, a boy who is "gentle and synaptically challenged," according to *Booklist* contributor Randy Meyer in a review of *Scratch and the Sniffs.* Each of the original members takes a turn narrating a book in the five-volume series, each title involving the humorous undoing of these would-be heroes. Reviewing *The Wolf Gang,* Shelle Rosenfeld concluded in *Booklist* that "Lynch's presentation of the boys' seesawing view of girls as enemies or attractions is dead-on, as is his portrayal of the ties of friendship that bind—and survive even the toughest tests in the end."

As a writer, Lynch avoids studying a story's "why's too closely," as he told an interview for *Teenreads.com.* "I want to tell realistic stories, which I think come with their own messages built into them without my having to preach. Specifically, the issue of substance abuse—like violence, or racism—is a fact of our lives, and the only way I can contribute anything is merely to chronicle the facts of lives as I see them."

Biographical and Critical Sources

BOOKS

Authors and Artists for Young Adults, Gale (Detroit, MI), Volume 19, 1996, Volume 44, 2002.
Children's Literature Review, Volume 58, Gale (Detroit, MI), 2000.
St. James Guide to Young-Adult Writers, 2nd edition, St. James Press (Detroit, MI), 1999.

PERIODICALS

Booklist, December 15, 1993, Gary Young, review of *Shadow Boxer,* p. 747; February 1, 1994, Stephanie Zvirin, review of *Iceman,* p. 1001; September 1, 1995, Stephanie Zvirin, review of *Slot Machine,* p. 74; October 15, 1996, Anne O'Malley, review of *Political Timber,* p. 4141; April 15, 1997, Randy Meyer, review of *Scratch and the Sniffs,* pp. 1429-1430; August, 1998, Shelle Rosenfeld, review of *The Wolf Gang,* pp. 2006-2007; September 1, 2000, Debbie Carton, review of *Gold Dust,* p. 116; May 15, 2001, Susan Dove Lempke, review of *Freewill,* p. 1745; November 15, 2002, Ed Sullivan, review of *Who the Man,* p. 588; September 1, 2005, Michael Cart, review of *Me, Dead Dad, and Alcatraz,* p. 111; September 15, 2005, Gillian Engberg, review of *Inexcusable,* p. 55; September 1, 2008, Ian Chapman, review of *The Big Game of Everything,* p. 110; September 15, 2008, Daniel Kraus, review of *Cyberia,* p. 50; January 1, 2010, Daniel Kraus, review of *Monkey See, Monkey Don't,* p. 86; May 15, 2010, Daniel Kraus, review of *Hothouse,* p. 36; January 1, 2011, Ian Chipman, review of *Angry Young Man,* p. 92; Daniel Kraus, review of *Prime Evil,* p. 106; October 15, 2011, Todd Morning, review

of *I Pledge Allegiance,* p. 46; March 1, 2012, Ian Chipman, review of *Kill Switch,* p. 76, and Todd Morning, review of *Sharpshooter,* p. 83.

Bulletin of the Center for Children's Books, November, 1994, Elizabeth Bush, review of *Gypsy Davey,* p. 93; April, 1996, Elizabeth Bush, reviews of *Mick, Blood Relations,* and *Dog Eat Dog,* p. 270; September, 2008, April Spisak, review of *Cyberia,* p. 33; December, 2008, Deborah Stevenson, review of *The Big Game of Everything,* p. 162; December, 2010, Ruth Cox Clark, review of *Hothouse,* p. 456; February, 2011, Elizabeth Bush, review of *Angry Young Man,* p. 284; December, 2011, Elizabeth Bush, review of *I Pledge Allegiance,* p. 214.

Horn Book, May-June, 1994, Patty Campbell, "The Sand in the Oyster," pp. 358-362; November-December, 1995, Maeve Visser Knoth, review of *Slot Machine,* pp. 746-747; November-December, 1995, Peter D. Sieruta, review of *Shadow Boxer,* pp. 745-746; March-April, 1997, Elizabeth S. Watson, review of *Political Timber,* p. 201; July-August, 1999, review of *Whitechurch,* p. 469; November-December, 2000, Lauren Adams, review of *Gold Dust,* p. 758; July-August, 2001, Lauren Adams, review of *Freewill,* p. 457; September-October, 2001, review of *All the Old Haunts,* p. 588; July-August, 2004, Laurence Adams, review of *The Gravedigger's Cottage,* p. 456; January-February, 2006, Betty Carter, review of *Inexcusable,* p. 83, and Christine M. Hepperman, review of *Me, Dead Dad, and Alcatraz,* p. 84: September-October, Lauren Adams, review of *The Big Game of Everything,* p. 592; January-February, 2009, Claire E. Gross, review of *Cyberia,* p. 96; November-December, 2009, Claire E. Gross, review of *Monkey See, Monkey Don't,* p. 678; September-October, 2010, Betty Carter, review of *Hothouse,* p. 83; March-April, 2012, Dean Schneider, review of *Kill Switch,* p. 113.

Kirkus Reviews, October 15, 2001, review of *All the Old Haunts,* p. 1488; August 15, 2005, review of *Me, Dead Dad, and Alcatraz,* p. 918; September 1, 2010, review of *Hothouse*; February 15, 2012, review of *Sharpshooter.*

Kliatt, May, 2004, Michele Winship, review of *The Gravedigger's Cottage,* p. 10; September, 2005, Paula Rohrlick, review of *Me, Dead Dad, and Alcatraz,* p. 10; November, 2005, Paula Rohrlick, review of *Inexcusable,* p. 8; September 8, 2008, Paula Rohrlick, review of *Sins of the Fathers,* p. 14.

Publishers Weekly, October 21, 1996, review of *Political Timber,* p. 84; January 11, 1999, review of *Extremely Elvin,* p. 73; May 10, 1999, review of *Whitechurch,* p. 69; August 21, 2000, review of *Gold Dust,* p. 74; October 29, 2001, review of *All the Old Haunts,* p. 65; November 11, 2002, review of *Who the Man,* p. 65; October 17, 2005, review of *Inexcusable,* p. 69; October 23, 2006, review of *Sins of the Fathers,* p. 53; September 8, 2008, review of *Cyberia,* p. 51; September 13, 2010, review of *Hothouse,* p. 47; December 20, 2010, review of *Angry Young Men,* p. 54; October 24, 2011, review of *I Pledge Allegiance,* p. 54.

School Library Journal, September, 1993, Tom S. Hurlburt, review of *Shadow Boxer,* p. 252; March, 1994,

Jack Forman, review of *Iceman,* p. 239; March, 1996, Kelly Diller, review of *Mick,* pp. 220-221; March, 1996, Kellie Flynn, review of *Blood Relations,* p. 221; October, 2000, Michael McCullough, review of *Gold Dust,* p. 164; November, 2001, Angela J. Reynolds, review of *All the Old Haunts,* p. 160; September, 2005, Miranda Doyle, review of *Me, Dead Dad, and Alcatraz,* p. 207; September, 2006, Carolyn Lehman, review of *Sins of the Fathers,* p. 211; October, 2008, Jeffrey Hastings, review of *The Big Game of Everything,* p. 152; January, 2010, Necia Blundy, review of *Monkey See, Monkey Don't,* p. 106; September, 2010, Allison Tran, review of *Hothouse,* p. 157; February, 2011, Ryan Donovan, review of *Angry Young Man,* p. 113, Jessica Miller, review of *Prime Evil,* p. 114; January, 2012, Chris Shoemaker, review of *I Pledge Allegiance,* p. 120.

Voice of Youth Advocates, December, 1993, John R. Lord, review of *Shadow Boxer,* p. 295; April, 1994, Randy Brough, review of *Iceman,* p. 28; December, 1994,

Keith W. McCoy, review of *Gypsy Davey,* p. 277; October, 2010, Angie Hammond, review of *Hothouse,* p. 352; December, 2010, Ruth Cox Clark, review of *Hothouse,* p. 456; February, 2011, Devin Burritt, interview with Lynch, p. 18, and Ryan Donovan, review of *Angry Young Man,* p. 113; February, 2012, Ann Reddy Damon, review of *I Pledge Allegiance,* p. 595.

ONLINE

HarperCollins Web site, http://www.harperchildren.com/ (December 10, 2009), "Chris Lynch."

National Book Award Web site, http://www.nationalbook. org/ (December 20, 2009), "Chris Lynch."

Simon & Schuster Web site, http://authors/simonand schuster.com/ (August 1, 2012), "Chris Lynch."

Teenreads.com, http://www.teenreads.com/ (December 20, 2009), interviews with Lynch.*

M

MAI-WYSS, Tatjana 1972-

Personal

Born 1972, in Switzerland; married; children: one. *Education:* Northern Illinois University, B.F.A. (illustration and French).

Addresses

Home—Clemson, SC. *Agent*—Red Fox Literary, 129 Morrow Ave., Shell Beach, CA 93449; info@ redfoxliterary.com. *E-mail*—tatjanamaiwyss@hotmail. com.

Career

Illustrator. Taylor Studios, Rantoul, IL, museum fabricator and muralist, 1996; freelance illustrator, 1998—. Arts Center, Clemson, SC, program coordinator and instructor, 2011—.

Awards, Honors

Giverny Award, 2011, for *A Tree for Emmy* by Mary Ann Rodman.

Illustrator

Hy Conrad, *Whodunit Crime Puzzles,* Sterling Publishing (New York, NY), 2002.

Hy Conrad, *Whodunit Crime Mysteries,* Sterling Publishing (New York, NY), 2003.

Scott Thomas, *The Yawn Heard 'round the World,* Tricycle Press (Berkeley, CA), 2003.

Jim Sukach, *Wicked Whodunits,* Sterling Publishing (New York, NY), 2005.

Andrea Cheng, *The Lemon Sisters,* Putnam (New York, NY), 2006.

Barbara Bottner, *You Have to Be Nice to Someone on Their Birthday,* Putnam (New York, NY), 2007.

Sherry Shahan, *That's Not How You Play Soccer, Daddy!,* Peachtree Publishing (Atlanta, GA), 2007.

Carol Ann Williams, *Booming Bella,* Putnam (New York, NY), 2008.

Mary Ann Rodman, *A Tree for Emmy,* Peachtree Publishing (Atlanta, GA), 2009.

Eugene Gagliano, *My Teacher Dances on the Desk* (poems), Sleeping Bear Press (Chelsea, MI), 2009.

Melinda Long, *The Twelve Days of Christmas in South Carolina,* Sterling Publishing (New York, NY), 2010.

Taryn Souders, *Whole-y Cow! Fractions Are Fun,* Sleeping Bear Press (Ann Arbor, MI), 2010.

Jerry Pallotta, *A Giraffe Did One,* Sleeping Bear Press (Ann Arbor, MI), 2011.

Lesley Simpson, *A Song for My Sister,* Random House (New York, NY), 2012.

Sidelights

Born in Switzerland, Tatjana Mai-Wyss is an illustrator who works primarily in watercolor, gouache, colored pencil, and collage. Her art has graced the pages of more than a dozen children's books, including Scott Thomas's *The Yawn Heard 'round the World,* Sherry Shahan's *That's Not How You Play Soccer, Daddy!,* and Taryn Souders' *Whole-y Cow! Fractions Are Fun.*

The Yawn Heard 'round the World, the debut project for both Mai-Wyss and Thomas, centers on a young girl's efforts to avoid bedtime. Although Sara maintains that she is not the least bit sleepy, the huge yawn she subsequently emits takes on a life of its own, infecting her family members before spreading to Europe, Asia, and South America. "Mai-Wyss uses her charming watercolors to great effect," a writer noted in *Kirkus Reviews,* and a *Publishers Weekly* critic observed that the book's "spry illustrations remain consistently energized." *The Yawn Heard 'round the World* treats readers to "an imaginative romp with creatively detailed art," Mary Elam concluded in *School Library Journal.*

Mai-Wyss also provided the illustrations for Andrea Cheng's *The Lemon Sisters,* a "charming intergenerational story," according to Ilene Cooper in *Booklist.* The work concerns an octogenarian's relationship with a trio of young and energetic neighbor girls, and "Mai-Wyss brings out the shared feelings of fun and delight

Tatjana Mai-Wyss adds an element of fun to Taryn Souders' math lessons in **Whole-y Cow! Fractions Are Fun.** (Illustration copyright © 2010 by Tatjana Mai-Wyss. Reproduced by permission of Sleeping Bear Press, an imprint of The Gale Group.)

in her delicate watercolors," in Cooper's opinion. In *You Have to Be Nice to Someone on Their Birthday,* a tale by Barbara Bottner, a girl's upcoming celebration is ruined by the arrival of her horrid cousins, her mother's forgetfulness, and an unfortunate run-in with a teacher. A contributor in *Kirkus Reviews* remarked that "Mai-Wyss's busy paintings are full of sly jokes" that enliven Bottner's story.

A boy and his father take very different approaches to a favorite game in Shahan's *That's Not How You Play Soccer, Daddy!* Mikey, a serious-minded team captain, has his sights firmly set on winning a big game while his affable dad prefers having fun to competing with others. Mai-Wyss's watercolor-and-collage illustrations for *That's Not How You Play Soccer, Daddy!* "keep the action moving," Blair Christolon wrote in her review of the picture book for *School Library Journal.*

In *Booming Bella,* a story by Carol Ann Williams, a girl's clamorous voice prevents a terrible mistake from occurring during her class field trip. "Mai-Wyss's appealing illustrations depict Bella as an ebullient blonde miss who even dresses loudly," according to a *Kirkus Reviews* writer, and Maura Bresnahan reported in *School Library Journal* that the girl's "irrepressible personality shines through in the active cartoon illustrations." "Bright, breezy, expressive, cartoon-style watercolors capture Bella's exuberance," commented *Booklist* reviewer Patricia Austin in her upbeat appraisal of *Booming Bella.*

Mai-Wyss employs collage techniques in creating the illustrations for Mary Ann Rodman's *A Tree for Emmy.* Here the narrative focuses on a girl's search for a wild mimosa tree like the one growing in her grandmother's yard. A critic in *Kirkus Reviews* praised the "vibrant" artwork in the picture book and Elam remarked that the illustrations "feature lively cartoon figures and depict Emmy's vibrant world." In *Whole-y Cow!* Souders introduces a barnyard animal with a yen for fractions. Mai-Wyss's "cow is wonderfully wacky" noted a *Kirkus Reviews* contributor, the critic also observing that "illustrations make the book come alive."

Biographical and Critical Sources

PERIODICALS

Booklist, November 1, 2002, Diane Foote, review of *Whodunit Crime Puzzles,* p. 490; April 1, 2003, Stephanie Zvirin, review of *The Yawn Heard 'round the World,* p. 1404; December 15, 2005, Ilene Cooper, review of *The Lemon Sisters,* p. 49; September 1, 2007, Hazel Rochman, review of *That's Not How You Play Soccer, Daddy!,* p. 137; June 1, 2008, Patricia Austin, review of *Booming Bella,* p. 86; May 15, 2009, Carolyn Phelan, review of *A Tree for Emmy,* p. 47.

Bulletin of the Center for Children's Books, April, 2007, Deborah Stevenson, review of *You Have to Be Nice to Someone on Their Birthday,* p. 324.

Kirkus Reviews, April 1, 2003, review of *The Yawn Heard 'round the World,* p. 541; December 15, 2005, review of *The Lemon Sisters,* p. 1319; January 15, 2007, review of *You Have to Be Nice to Someone on Their Birthday,* p. 70; May 15, 2008, review of *Booming Bella*; February 15, 2009, review of *A Tree for Emmy*; August 15, 2010, review of *Whole-y Cow! Fractions Are Fun.*

Publishers Weekly, January 20, 2003, review of *The Yawn Heard 'round the World,* p. 80.

School Library Journal, May, 2003, Mary Elam, review of *The Yawn Heard 'round the World,* p. 130; January, 2006, Blair Christolon, review of *The Lemon Sisters,* p. 93; October, 2007, Blair Christolon, review of *That's Not How You Play Soccer, Daddy!,* p. 125; July, 2008, Maura Bresnahan, review of *Booming Bella,* p. 84; March, 2009, Mary Elam, review of *A Tree for Emmy,* p. 126; November, 2010, Loreli E. Stochaj, review of *Whole-y Cow!,* p. 94.

ONLINE

Tatjana Mai-Wyss Home Page, http://tatjanawyss.blogspot.com (July 15, 2012).*

* * *

MANDELSKI, Christina 1970-

Personal

Born 1970; married; children: two daughters. *Education:* B.A. (creative writing). *Hobbies and other interests:* Cooking.

Addresses

Home—Houston, TX. *Agent*—Danielle Chiotti, Upstart Crow Literary, P.O. Box 25303, Brooklyn, NY 11202; danielle@upstartcrowliterary.com. *E-mail*—contact@christinamandelski.com.

Career

Novelist. Presenter at schools.

Writings

The Sweetest Thing, Egmont USA (New York, NY), 2011.

Sidelights

Looking back on her life, Christina Mandelski can recognize that she was destined to become a writer: a bookworm as a child, she wrote fanciful stories about her school friends and then graduated to stints on the school newspaper and yearbook in both junior high and high school. Mandelski kept her momentum in college, where she majored in creative writing, but life had other plans after that, at least for a few years. However, while raising her own two daughters she decided to put her writing dreams to the test and the result was her young-adult novel *The Sweetest Thing.*

In *The Sweetest Thing* readers meet Sheridan Wells, a Midwest high-school sophomore who lives with her dad, a talented chef and restaurant owner, now that her mom has left home. With her father busy angling for a spot on a reality cooking show, Sheridan feels as though she must deal with her typical teen worries on her own. Baking and decorating cakes allows her some solace however, because it is something that her mother used to do when she lived at home. Thinking that Mom might be the one to help her navigate boyfriend problems and the like, Sheridan gets best friend Jack to help her find the missing woman and convince her to return home. Romantic entanglements, ailing relatives, and even a scary mishap all figure into the plot of Mandelski's story, which "explores the need to embrace the reality rather than the fantasy of love," according to a *Kirkus Reviews* writer.

Cover of Christina Mandelski's young-adult coming-of-age novel **The Sweetest Thing,** *which finds a teen using cooking to bond with her absent and very-much-missed mom.* (Jacket illustration image © 2011 by Christina Kilgore. Reproduced by permission of Egmont USA.)

Praising Sheridan as a "likeable protagonist [who] is talented and funny," KaaVonia Hinton-Johnston added in *Voice of Youth Advocates* that *The Sweetest Thing* will appeal to "readers who like contemporary realistic fiction with a little romance." The novel's most engaging scenes" focus on the young woman's love of the baker's art, noted the *Kirkus Reviews* critic, "and they showcase the intrinsic rewards of a job well done."

Biographical and Critical Sources

PERIODICALS

Bulletin of the Center for Children's Books, June, 2011, Deborah Stevenson, review of *The Sweetest Thing,* p. 478.
Kirkus Reviews, April 15, 2011, review of *The Sweetest Thing.*
Publishers Weekly, March 21, 2011, review of *The Sweetest Thing,* p. 78.
School Library Journal, Richelle Roth, review of *The Sweetest Thing,* p. 102.
Voice of Youth Advocates, June, 2011, KaaVonia Hinton-Johnson, review of *The Sweetest Thing,* p. 168.

ONLINE

Christina Mandelski Home Page, http://www.christina mandelski.com (August 1, 2012).*

* * *

McDONALD, Megan 1959-

Personal

Born February 28, 1959, in Pittsburgh, PA; daughter of John (an ironworker) and Mary Louise (a social worker) McDonald; married Richard Haynes. *Education:* Oberlin College, B.A., 1981; University of Pittsburgh, M.L. S., 1986.

Addresses

Home—Sebastopol, CA.

Career

Children's book author and librarian. Carnegie Library, Pittsburgh, PA, children's librarian, 1986-90; Minneapolis Public Library, Minneapolis, MN, children's librarian, 1990-91; Adams Memorial Library, Latrobe, PA, children's librarian, 1991-94; storyteller and freelance writer.

Member

American Library Association, Society of Children's Book Writers and Illustrators.

Megan McDonald (Courtesy of Megan McDonald.)

Awards, Honors

Children's Choice selection, International Reading Association/Children's Book Council (IRA/CBC), 1991, and *Reading Rainbow* book selection, Public Broadcasting System, both for *Is This a House for Hermit Crab?*; Notable Children's Trade Book in the Field of Social Studies designation, National Council for the Social Studies/CBC, 1992, for *The Potato Man*; Judy Blume Contemporary Fiction Award, Society of Children's Book Writers and Illustrators, 1993, for *The Bridge to Nowhere*; Carolyn W. Field Award, 1993, for *The Great Pumpkin Switch*; Beverly Cleary Children's Choice selection, and Garden State Children's Book Award for Younger Fiction, both 2003, both for *Judy Moody*; Notable Children's Books designation, American Library Association (ALA), Oppenheim Toy Portfolio Gold Award, and IRA/CBC Children's Choice selection, all c. 2001, all for *Judy Moody Gets Famous!*; IRA/CBC Children's Choice selection, Amelia Bloomer Project listee, ALA, Oppenheim Toy Portfolio Gold Award, and Best of the Best listee, Chicago Public Library, all 2002, all for *Judy Moody Saves the World!*; Children's Trade Hardcover Merit Award, New York Book Show, 2003, for *Judy Moody Predicts the Future*; Best of the Best listee, Chicago Public Library, and Parents' Choice Awards Recommended title, both 2005, both for *Stink: The Incredible Shrinking Kid*; IRA/CBC Children's

Choice selection, 2005, for *Judy Moody Declares Independence;* Best Children's Books of the Year selection, Bank Street College of Education, 2005, for *Saving the Liberty Bell;* ALA Notable Children's Books designation, and One Hundred Titles for Reading and Sharing listee, New York Public Library, both 2008, both for *The Hinky-Pink;* Best of the Best listee, Chicago Public Library, 2009, for *Judy Moody and Stink: The Mad, Mad, Mad, Mad Treasure Hunt;* Best Children's Books of the Year selection, Bank Street College of Education, and National Parenting Publications Award, both 2009, both for *It's Picture Day Today!;* numerous other honors.

Writings

FOR CHILDREN

Is This a House for Hermit Crab?, illustrated by S.D. Schindler, Orchard (New York, NY), 1990.

The Potato Man, illustrated by Ted Lewin, Orchard (New York, NY), 1991.

Whoo-oo Is It?, illustrated by S.D. Schindler, Orchard (New York, NY), 1992.

The Great Pumpkin Switch, illustrated by Ted Lewin, Orchard (New York, NY), 1992.

Insects Are My Life, illustrated by Paul Brett Johnson, Orchard (New York, NY), 1995.

My House Has Stars, illustrated by Peter Catalanotto, Orchard (New York, NY), 1996.

Tundra Mouse: A Storyknife Book, illustrated by S.D. Schindler, Orchard (New York, NY), 1997.

The Bone Keeper, illustrated by G. Brian Karas, DK Ink (New York, NY), 1999.

The Night Iguana Left Home, illustrated by Ponder Goembel, DK Ink (New York, NY), 1999.

Bedbugs, illustrated by Paul Brett Johnson, Orchard (New York, NY), 1999.

Lucky Star, illustrated by Andrea Wallace, Golden Books (New York, NY), 2000.

Reptiles Are My Life, illustrated by Paul Brett Johnson, Orchard (New York, NY), 2001.

Ant and Honey Bee, illustrated by Tom Payne, Candlewick Press (Cambridge, MA), 2001.

Shining Star, illustrated by Andrea Wallace, Random House (New York, NY), 2003.

Penguin and Little Blue, illustrated by Katherine Tillotson, Atheneum (New York, NY), 2003.

Baya, Baya, Lulla-by-a, illustrated by Vera Rosenberry, Atheneum (New York, NY), 2003.

Beetle McGrady Eats Bugs!, illustrated by Jane Manning, Greenwillow (New York, NY), 2004.

When the Library Lights Go Out, illustrated by Katherine Tillotson, Atheneum (New York, NY), 2005.

Ant and Honey Bee: What a Pair!, illustrated by G. Brian Karas, Candlewick Press (Cambridge, MA), 2005.

Beetle McGrady Eats Bugs!, illustrated by Jane Manning, Greenwillow (New York, NY), 2005.

Saving the Liberty Bell, illustrated by Marsha Gray Carrington, Atheneum Books for Young Readers (New York, NY), 2005.

Daisy Jane, Best-Ever Flower Girl, illustrated by Claudine Gevry, Random House (New York, NY), 2007.

Hen Hears Gossip, illustrated by Joung un Kim, Greenwillow (New York, NY), 2008.

(Reteller) *The Hinky-Pink: An Old Tale,* illustrated by Brian Floca, Atheneum (New York, NY), 2008.

It's Picture Day Today!, illustrated by Katherine Tillotson, Atheneum (New York, NY), 2009.

Ant and Honey Bee: A Pair of Friends at Halloween, illustrated by G. Brian Karas, Candlewick Press (Somerville, MA), 2010.

Contributor to *I Fooled You: Ten Stories of Tricks, Jokes, and Switcheroos,* edited by Johanna Hurwitz, Candlewick Press (Somerville, MA), 2010.

FOR CHILDREN; "BEEZY" CHAPTER-BOOK SERIES; ILLUSTRATED BY NANCY POYDAR

Beezy, Orchard (New York, NY), 1997.

Beezy at Bat, Orchard (New York, NY), 1998.

Beezy Magic, illustrated by Nancy Poydar (New York, NY), Orchard, 1998.

Beezy and Funnybone, Orchard (New York, NY), 2000.

FOR CHILDREN; "JUDY MOODY" NOVEL SERIES

Judy Moody, illustrated by Peter H. Reynolds, Candlewick Press (Cambridge, MA), 2000.

Judy Moody Gets Famous!, illustrated by Peter H. Reynolds, Candlewick Press (Cambridge, MA), 2001.

Judy Moody Saves the World!, illustrated by Peter H. Reynolds, Candlewick Press (Cambridge, MA), 2002.

Judy Moody Predicts the Future, illustrated by Peter H. Reynolds, Candlewick Press (Cambridge, MA), 2003.

Judy Moody, M.D.: The Doctor Is In!, illustrated by Peter H. Reynolds, Candlewick Press (Cambridge, MA), 2004.

Judy Moody Declares Independence, illustrated by Peter H. Reynolds, Candlewick Press (Cambridge, MA), 2005.

Judy Moody's Double-Rare Way-Not-Boring Book of Fun Stuff to Do, illustrated by Peter H. Reynolds, Candlewick Press (Cambridge, MA), 2005.

Judy Moody: Around the World in Eight and a Half Days, illustrated by Peter H. Reynolds, Candlewick Press (Cambridge, MA), 2006.

Judy Moody and Stink: The Holiday Joliday, illustrated by Peter H. Reynolds, Candlewick Press (Cambridge, MA), 2007.

Judy Moody Goes to College, illustrated by Peter H. Reynolds, Candlewick Press (Cambridge, MA), 2008.

Judy Moody and Stink: The Mad, Mad, Mad Treasure Hunt, illustrated by Peter H. Reynolds, Candlewick Press (Cambridge, MA), 2009.

Judy Moody's Way Wacky Über-Awesome Book of More Fun Stuff to Do, illustrated by Peter H. Reynolds, Candlewick Press (Somerville, MA), 2010.

Judy Moody, Girl Detective, illustrated by Peter H. Reynolds, Candlewick Press (Somerville, MA), 2010.

Judy Moody Star-Studded Collection (contains *Judy Moody, Judy Moody Gets Famous!,* and *Judy Moody Saves the World!*), Candlewick Press (Somerville, MA), 2010.

Judy Moody Goes to Hollywood: Behind the Scenes with Judy Moody and Friends, photographs by Suzanne Tenner, Candlewick Press (Somerville, MA), 2011.

Judy Moody and the NOT Bummer Summer (based on the screenplay by McDonald and Kathy Waugh), Candlewick Press (Somerville, MA), 2011, new edition illustrated by Peter H. Reynolds, Candlewick Press (Somerville, MA), 2012.

Judy Moody: Twice as Moody, illustrated by Peter H. Reynolds, Candlewick Press (Somerville, MA), 2011.

The Judy Moody Double-Rare Collection (contains *Judy Moody Predicts the Future, Judy Moody, M.D.,* and *Judy Moody Declares Independence*), Candlewick Press (Somerville, MA), 2011.

The Judy Moody Über-Awesome Collection , nine volumes, Candlewick Press (Somerville, MA), 2011.

Judy Moody's Mini-Mysteries, and Other Sneaky Stuff for Super-Sleuths, illustrated by Peter H. Reynolds, Candlewick Press (Somerville, MA), 2012.

Judy Moody: The Mad Rad Collection (contains *Judy Moody: Around the World in Eight and a Half Days, Judy Moody Goes to College,* and *Judy Moody, Girl Detective*), Candlewick Press (Somerville, MA), 2012.

FOR CHILDREN; "STINK" NOVEL SERIES; ILLUSTRATED BY PETER H. REYNOLDS

Stink: The Incredible Shrinking Kid, Candlewick Press (Cambridge, MA) 2005.

Stink and the Incredible Super-Galactic Jawbreaker, Candlewick Press (Cambridge, MA), 2006.

Stink and the World's Worst Super-Stinky Sneakers, Candlewick Press (Cambridge, MA), 2007.

Stink and the Great Guinea Pig, Candlewick Press (Cambridge, MA) 2008.

Stink: The Super-incredible Collection (contains *Stink: The Incredible Shrinking Kid, Stink and the Incredible Super-Galactic Jawbreaker,* and *Stink and the World's Worst Super-Stinky Sneakers*), Candlewick Press (Somerville, MA), 2008.

Stink-o-pedia: Super Stink-y Stuff from A to ZZZZ, Candlewick Press (Cambridge, MA) 2009.

Stink-o-pedia, Volume Two: More Stink-y Stuff from A to Z, Candlewick Press (Somerville, MA), 2010.

Stink: Solar System Superhero, Candlewick Press (Somerville, MA), 2010.

Stink and the Ultimate Thumb-Wrestling Smackdown, Candlewick Press (Somerville, MA), 2011.

Stink and the Midnight Zombie Walk, Candlewick Press (Somerville, MA), 2012.

Stink: The Absolutely Astronomical Collection (contains *Stink and the Great Guinea Pig, Stink: Solar System Superhero,* and *Stink and the Ultimate Thumb-wrestling Smackdown*), Candlewick Press (Somerville, MA), 2012.

FOR CHILDREN; "JULIE" SERIES; ILLUSTRATED BY ROBERT HUNT

Meet Julie, American Girl Publishing (Middleton, WI), 2007.

Julie Tells Her Story, American Girl Publishing (Middleton, WI), 2007.

Happy New Year, Julie, American Girl Publishing (Middleton, WI), 2007.

Julie and the Eagles, American Girl Publishing (Middleton, WI), 2007.

Julie's Journey, American Girl Publishing (Middleton, WI), 2007.

Changes for Julie, American Girl Publishing (Middleton, WI), 2007.

FOR YOUNG ADULTS

The Bridge to Nowhere (novel), Orchard (New York, NY), 1993.

Shadows in the Glasshouse, Pleasant Company (Middleton, WI), 2000.

The Sisters Club, American Girl (Middleton, WI), 2003, illustrated by Pamela A. Consolazio, Candlewick Press (Somerville, MA), 2008.

All the Stars in the Sky: The Santa Fe Trail Diary of Florrie Mack Ryder, Scholastic (New York, NY), 2003.

The Rule of Three (sequel to *The Sisters Club*), illustrated by Pamela A. Consolazio, Candlewick Press (Somerville, MA), 2009.

Cloudy with a Chance of Boys (sequel to *The Rule of Three*), illustrated by Pamela A. Consolazio, Candlewick Press (Somerville, MA), 2011.

SCREENPLAYS

(With Kathy Waugh) *Judy Moody and the NOT Bummer Summer,* Relativity Media, 2011.

Adaptations

Several of McDonald's books have been adapted as audiobooks by Listening Library, Brilliance Audio, and Recorded Books. *Judy Moody and the NOT Bummer Summer: The Poop Picnic* and *Judy Moody and the NOT Bummer Summer: The Thrill Points Race,* both written by Jamie Michalak, were based on the motion picture screenplay by McDonald and Kathy Waugh.

Sidelights

Inspired by her fond memories of growing up with four older sisters, Megan McDonald is the author of the "Judy Moody" chapter books, a series that has proved popular with audiences and critics alike. McDonald also draws on her diverse experiences as a park ranger, bookseller, museum guide, and librarian in crafting picture books and beginning readers, among them award-winning works such as *The Hinky-Pink: An Old Tale.* "I am lucky to be a writer, because I get to live in my imagination," the author stated on her home page. "I spend my days looking at things upside down, inside-out, sideways, wondering, imagining, questioning everything, always wanting to see the inside."

McDonald's chapter-book series are designed for readers in training. Her "Beezy" books feature a young girl and the stray dog she adopts and names Funnybone. Growing up in Florida, Beezy's life incorporates that region's characteristics—like hurricanes—as well as universal day-to-day experiences of childhood in short vignettes designed for easy reading. In *Beezy* the girl joins friends in a neighborhood baseball game, spends time with her grandmother, and begins her friendship with Funnybone, while in *Beezy and Funnybone* new friends and new adventures—like jumping out of a hot-air balloon—enter the mix. *School Library Journal* reviewer Maura Bresnahan praised "the warm and friendly tone" of *Beezy and Funnybone* and considered it a good choice for readers who want "to practice their new skills."

In the "Judy Moody" series McDonald introduces a spunky, somewhat chameleon-like heroine. Of her character, McDonald once explained that "Judy is one part me, three parts imagination. The original spark for Judy Moody came to me because I wanted to write about a girl with moods. An 'everykid' sort of character, who felt real to me. A kid with ups and downs, highs and lows, joys AND disappointments."

Third-grader Judy approaches life with some trepidation but also with resilience and creativity, whether vying for membership in the exclusive Toad Pee club or attempting to create the winning entry in her school's adhesive-bandage contest. In *Judy Moody* readers follow the spunky third grader on her first day back at school, which begins badly when there is no suitable T-shirt to wear, but begins to perk up due to the resourcefulness of McDonald's "entertainingly mercurial" protagonist, according to a *Publishers Weekly* contributor. The book's large, easy-to-read type was a hit with reviewers, among them *Booklist* critic Shelle Rosenfeld, who noted that McDonald's ability to tell her story from Judy's third-grade perspective enhances the "simple, expressive prose" and offers a healthy dose of "child-appealing humor."

Rosenfeld also offered praise for *Judy Moody Saves the World!*, citing that installment's "characteristically snappy, humorous prose" and the "expressive, witty" line drawings by illustrator Peter H. Reynolds. Reviewing *Judy Moody, M.D.: The Doctor Is In!*, *Booklist* critic Linda Perkins observed that McDonald "finds ample comedy in the way children mishear words and mangle information." *School Library Journal* contributor Tracey Karbel wrote of the same series installment that McDonald's "feisty" heroine wins over readers due to her "active imagination, keen wit, and . . . strong desire to explore the word around her."

Other volumes featuring the feisty and funny heroine include *Judy Moody Goes to College* and *Judy Moody, Girl Detective*. The former book centers on the young-

McDonald's entertaining "Judy Moody" books, such as **Judy Moody Predicts the Future,** *feature humorous ink drawings by Peter H. Reynolds.* (Illustration copyright © 2003 by Peter H. Reynolds. Reproduced by permission of Candlewick Press Inc., Somerville, MA.)

ster's relationship with her college-age math tutor. Judy's fascination with the "Nancy Drew" mystery series inspires her to investigate a variety of cases, including that of a missing police dog, in *Judy Moody, Girl Detective*. "Judy is an endearing mix of precocious and familiar," Amelia Jenkins wrote in *School Library Journal*. McDonald has also turned her talents to the silver screen, coauthoring the screenplay for *Judy Moody and the NOT Bummer Summer*, a "rambunctiously exuberant film," according to Andy Webster in the *New York Times*.

Judy's little brother "Stink" stars in several stories of his own, among them *Stink and the Great Guinea Pig Express* and *Stink and the Incredible Super-Galactic Jawbreaker*. Citing McDonald's "charismatic narrative" and Reynolds' engaging drawings, Jennifer Mattson concluded her *Booklist* review of *Judy Moody Declares Independence* that the story's "characterization of a dauntless, endearingly emotional third-grader is as spot-on as ever." In a review of *Stink and the World's Worst Super-Stinky Sneakers* for *School Library Journal*, Elaine Lesh Morgan called Judy's pesky little brother "a delightful protagonist, comical and bright." "The characters ring true," Morgan added, and the story's "vocabulary . . . stretches but doesn't strain young readers."

In *Stink: Solar System Superhero* the youngster stands up for Pluto when he learns that the celestial body has been demoted to dwarf planet status. Writing in *School Library Journal,* Elizabeth Swistock called Stink "an entertaining character" and predicted that young readers "will appreciate his jokes." A book release party sets the stage for spooky fun in *Stink and the Midnight Zombie Walk,* a "playful salute to those who (kind of—well, not really) like things that go bump in the night," observed a writer in *Kirkus Reviews.* The Moody siblings join forces on a pirate-themed scavenger hunt during a family vacation in *Judy Moody and Stink: The Mad, Mad, Mad Treasure Hunt,* a book Madigan McGillicuddy in *School Library Journal* called "a humorous summer read."

Illustrated by S.D. Schindler, McDonald's picture book *Is This a House for Hermit Crab?* has its roots in a puppet show the author performed at a public library where she served as a children's librarian. In the story, a hermit crab searches a rocky shoreline for a new home, finding the perfect abode in time to avoid becoming an afternoon snack for a crab-eating prickle-pine fish. Praising the book's rhythmic text and pastel illustrations, *Five Owls* contributor Margaret Mary Kimmel described *Is This a House for Hermit Crab?* as "a beautiful book to look at again and again, to repeat over

McDonald's chapter book Stink and the World's Worst Super-Stinky Sneakers *gains a double dose of humor due to Reynolds' fun-filled artwork.* (Illustration copyright © 2007 by Peter H. Reynolds. Reproduced by permission of Candlewick Press Inc., Somerville, MA.)

and over." "Best of all . . .," Carolyn Phelan pointed out in *Booklist,* McDonald "knows when to ask questions to involve the children and when to stop."

Another McDonald-Schindler collaboration, *Whoo-oo Is It?,* revolves around a mother barn owl's attempt to hatch her eggs in peace while all of nature seems to be intent on making noise. One particular sound—a strange noise that gradually gets louder—persists and is discovered to be the first young owlet pecking its way out of its shell. While the source of the noise, which begins at nightfall, is at first a mystery to listeners, "the final tender family scene will relieve any lingering concerns," according to *Horn Book* reviewer Elizabeth S. Watson. Praising McDonald's story, *Five Owls* critic Anne Lundin called *Whoo-oo Is It?* "a spirited book to read aloud, in a kind of celebration of life."

The Potato Man and its sequel, *The Great Pumpkin Switch,* are based on stories McDonald's father told about what it was like growing up in Pittsburgh before the Great Depression of the 1930s. In the book, a young boy tries to play tricks on Mr. Angelo, the Potato Man, but gets caught each time. When his hijinks cause him to be assigned extra chores at home, the boy decides to make peace with the old peddler. Praising *The Potato Man* for its evocation of the past, *Horn Book* critic Mary M. Burns noted that McDonald's "text . . . sets forth conflict and solution without moralizing."

Featuring watercolor illustrations by Ted Lewin, *The Great Pumpkin Switch* finds the same mischievous boy and friend Otto smashing his sister's prize pumpkin, by accident of course. Mr. Angelo comes to their rescue, replacing the smashed pumpkin with another squash just as good, in a story that *School Library Journal* contributor Susan Scheps maintained "will not seem the least old-fashioned to today's readers." Describing the author's "warm, beautifully cadenced storytelling," a *Kirkus Reviews* critic also commented favorably on the book's "engaging period details."

In the intriguingly titled *Insects Are My Life,* first-grader Amanda Frankenstein has a passion for bugs, much to the dismay of her friends and family. Not content merely to catch and collect dead bugs like most insect aficionados, Amanda thinks of her home as a bug sanctuary and invites her flying and crawling friends *inside* the house rather than shooing them out. She remains terribly misunderstood until the arrival of Maggie, the new girl in school, who happens to feel equally as passionate about reptiles. "McDonald's single-minded, sometimes naughty heroine evokes chuckles with her feisty independence," according to Margaret A. Bush in a review for *Horn Book,* while in *School Library Journal,* Virginia Opocensky dubbed "refreshing" McDonald's creation of "nonsqueamish female characters . . . willing to take on all adversaries in defense of their causes."

McDonald focuses on Maggie's plight in a companion volume, *Reptiles Are My Life,* as the young reptile lover finds a kindred spirit in Emily, leaving bug-loving

Amanda feeling left out. Finally, the three girls find a new camaraderie when Amanda saves the "Snake Sisters" from being called to the office for sticking out their tongues in a book a *Kirkus Reviews* critic noted for its "sprightly writing" and focus on girls with unusual interests. *Childhood Education* contributor Jill Quisenberry praised McDonald's humorous text as "full of great insect and reptile references," while *School Library Journal* contributor Linda M. Kenton concluded that *Reptiles Are My Life* "accurately portrays the rollercoaster ride that some friendships take."

Other picture books by McDonald include *The Bone Keeper, Penguin and Little Blue, Saving the Liberty Bell,* and *The Hinky-Pink.* In *The Bone Keeper* an ancient creature of the desert wanders in search of sunbaked bones, then returns to her cave to magically fashion these bones into a living creature. Told in verse, McDonald's "lyrical" and "evocative" tale was praised as "an original creation story of power and force" by *Bulletin of the Center for Children's Books* contributor Janice M. Del Negro, while in *School Library Journal* Rosalyn Pierini dubbed *The Bone Keeper* "an eerie tale with mythical qualities."

Like *The Bone Keeper, The Hinky-Pink* also features a mysterious creature with an unusual mission. Based on the traditional folk tale "The Bed Just So," *The Hinky-Pink* finds hard-working seamstress Anabel hired to create a beautiful dress for a princess to wear to an upcoming ball. She works diligently each day, but at night Anabel is unable to rest because her sleep is broken by a sprightly creature that steals her blankets and leaves her shivering. Finally, the pesky spirit is identified as a hinky-pink and the talented but sleepy seamstress uses her sewing skills to solve the dilemma and complete her dress in time for the ball. "A fine storyteller," McDonald "embroiders her tale with colorful language and playful usage," wrote *Horn Book* contributor Joanna Rudge Long, and in *Publishers Weekly* a critic dubbed *The Hinky-Pink* "a happy hybrid of traditional tale and quirky cartoon."

Animals on the move are also the subject of *Penguin and Little Blue,* which finds two water-park performers taking their show on the road and trying to make their hotel room in Kansas a little more Antarctic-like. Praising McDonald's pun-filled text, a *Publishers Weekly* reviewer cited the picture book for featuring a story that "touts the importance of home and friends," while a *Kirkus Reviews* critic was caught up enough in the spirit of the story to claim that "young readers will flap their flippers at this tongue-in-cheek jaunt." McDonald's award-winning *It's Picture Day Today!* focuses on an unusual school where the student body is composed of buttons, feathers, popsicle sticks, and other art materials. "The spare, rhyming text lightly moves the action along," Mary Jean Smith commented in reviewing this story for *School Library Journal.*

Based on an actual story from the American Revolution, *Saving the Liberty Bell* returns readers to 1777, as British troops moved toward Philadelphia, desperate to locate and confiscate any metal that could be used to make cannons or musket balls. The British knew that a giant bell was housed somewhere in the city, and through the narrative of McDonald's eleven-year-old observer readers learn how the bell was hidden in a farmer's cart and wheeled away. Noting that the story features "imminent danger, . . . courage, [and] close calls," *Booklist* critic Connie Fletcher praised *Saving the Liberty Bell* as "an entertaining way to introduce kids to" the story of their nation's dramatic early history. In *School Library Journal* Bethany A. Lafferty cited the "humorous, cartoon-like" illustrations by Marsha Gray Carrington and the story's presentation, which is "reminiscent of tall tales."

In addition to picture books and beginning readers, McDonald has penned several novels for older readers. *The Bridge to Nowhere,* a semi-autobiographical novel for young adults, finds seventh-grader Hallie O'Shea frustrated over her now-out-of-work father's inability to cope with the loss of his job. Depressed and withdrawn from the rest of the family, Mr. O'Shea spends his time in the basement building metal sculptures or driving to his former job site, a still-unfinished bridge over the Allegheny River that he calls the "bridge to nowhere." With Hallie's mother absorbed with worry about her husband and older sister Shelley escaping to college, the young teen is left to fend for herself. Things improve after Hallie meets Crane Henderson, a ninth grader for whom she soon develops a crush, but when Mr. O'Shea attempts suicide by driving off the unfinished bridge the young couple's relationship is tested. Praising the book as a fine first effort for former picture-book writer McDonald, a *Kirkus Reviews* critic called *The Bridge to Nowhere* "unusually well crafted: accessible, lyrical, with wonderful natural dialogue" between parent and teen. Deborah Abbott pointed out in *Booklist* that the novel provides "realistic characters, an attention-holding plot . . . and an upbeat ending."

Other novels by McDonald include the history mystery *Shadows in the Glasshouse,* which follows twelve-year-old Merry Shipman after she is forced to sail from London to the newly colonized Jamestown settlement to work for a glassblower. Taking place in 1621, the novel weaves together drama, mystery, and interesting information about life during that period of U.S. history. Also in the genre of historical fiction is *All the Stars in the Sky: The Santa Fe Trail Diary of Florrie Mack Ryder,* which is based on an actual Santa Fe trail diary of the mid-1800s. Here McDonald presents a fictionalized account of what life was like for a young teen traveling with her family from Independence, Missouri, to points southwest. Praising the book as a "solid entry" in Scholastic's "Dear America" series of fictional journals, a *Kirkus Reviews* contributor described the story's young narrator as "a heroine readers will enjoy joining on her travels."

McDonald mines more-recent history in her novels for the "American Girl" book series. Set in the 1970s, her

"Julie" books focus on a girl growing up in a single-parent family now that her mom and dad are divorced. Readers first meet Julie in the appropriately titled *Meet Julie,* as she and her mom move to a San Francisco apartment and Julie starts fourth grade at a new school. *Julie Tells Her Story* follows Julie's efforts to complete a school assignment that requires her to interview family members and create a family history, while in *Changes for Julie* the now-fifth grader befriends a deaf girl and decides to run for class president. "McDonald does an excellent job of developing characters who reflect the 1970s, and keeping the action moving," noted *School Library Journal* critic Sharon R. Pearce in a review of *Changes for Julie,* and Krista Tokarz wrote in the same periodical that the "Julie" books "are easy to read, have likeable characters, and feature situations many kids will relate to."

McDonald introduces a trio of loving siblings with distinct personalities in *The Sisters Club,* a middle-grade novel. Hailing from a theatrical family, Alex, Stevie, and Joey describe their often humorous antics through a series of dramatic scripts and illustrated diary entries. *Booklist* critic Ellen Mandel applauded "McDonald's flair for quick repartee and her skill at transforming pre-adolescent high jinks into hilarious episodes." In *The Rule of Three,* a sequel, Alex and Stevie vie for the same role in a play, while a third installment, *Cloudy with a Chance of Boys,* centers on teen crushes and first kisses. "McDonald manages to squeeze a lot of action into one story," a *Kirkus Reviews* writer stated in appraising *The Rule of Three.* According to another *Kirkus Reviews* critic, *Cloudy with a Chance of Boys* "balances middle-school co-ed hilarity with values and pre-adolescent angst."

Discussing the inspiration for her works with *Kidsreads.com* interviewer Terry Miller Shannon, McDonald stated, "I follow my instincts and my own interests. A plot has to be one that compels and excites me, something I'm willing to spend a LOT of time thinking about, since I'll imaginatively be living with it for months. A good plot is one I find funny and holds great potential for humor."

Biographical and Critical Sources

PERIODICALS

Booklist, March 1, 1990, Carolyn Phelan, review of *Is This a House for a Hermit Crab?,* p. 1347; April 1, 1993, Deborah Abbott, review of *The Bridge to Nowhere,* pp. 1424-1425; April 15, 1999, Susan Dove Lempke, review of *The Bone Keeper,* p. 1531; November 1, 1999, John Peters, review of *The Night Iguana Left Home,* p. 540; July, 2000, Shelle Rosenfeld, review of *Judy Moody,* p. 2028, and Carolyn Phelan, review of *Beezy and Funnybone,* p. 2045; September 1, 2002, Shelle Rosenfeld, review of *Judy Moody Saves the World!,* p. 125; July, 2003, Gillian Engberg, review of *Shining Star,* p. 1899; August, 2003, Hazel Rochman, review of *Baya, Baya, Lulla-by-a,* p. 1990; September 15, 2003, Kay Weisman, review of *Judy Moody Predicts the Future,* p. 240; November 1, 2003, Lauren Peterson, review of *Penguin and Little Blue,* p. 502; December 1, 2003, Ellen Mandel, review of *The Sisters Club,* p. 677; October 15, 2004, Linda Perkins, review of *Judy Moody, M.D.: The Doctor Is In!,* p. 406; March 1, 2005, Hazel Rochman, review of *Stink: The Incredible Shrinking Kid,* p. 1198; June 1, 2005, Jennifer Mattson, review of *Judy Moody Declares Independence,* p. 1813; July, 2005, Connie Fletcher, review of *Saving the Liberty Bell,* p. 1928; November 1, 2005, Karen Hutt, review of *When the Library Lights Go Out,* p. 53; April 15, 2006, Carolyn Phelan, review of *Stink and the Incredible Super-Galactic Jawbreaker,* p. 53; April 15, 2007, Carolyn Phelan, review of *Stink and the World's Worst Super-Stinky Sneakers,* p. 49; August 1, 2006, Carolyn Phelan, review of *Judy Moody: Around the World in Eight and a Half Days,* p. 70; November 15, 2007, Hazel Rochman, review of *Judy Moody and Stink: The Holiday Joliday,* p. 38; March 1, 2008, Carolyn Phelan, review of *Stink and the Great Guinea Pig Express,* p. 70; July 1, 2008, Shelle Rosenfeld, review of *Hen Hears Gossip,* p. 72; September 15, 2008, Gillian Engberg, review of *The Hinky-Pink: An Old Tale,* p. 57; May 1, 2009, Daniel Kraus, review of *It's Picture Day Today!,* p. 86; July 1, 2009, Carolyn Phelan, review of *The Mad, Mad, Mad, Mad Treasure Hunt,* p. 58; January 1, 2010, Hazel Rochman, review of *Stink: Solar System Superhero,* p. 86; September 1, 2010, Ilene Cooper, review of *Judy Moody, Girl Detective,* p. 101; January 1, 2011, Hazel Rochman, review of *Stink and the Ultimate Thumb-Wrestling Smackdown,* p. 107; March 15, 2011, Shelle Rosenfeld, review of *Cloudy with a Chance of Boys,* p. 56.

Bulletin of the Center for Children's Books, April, 1995, Deborah Stevenson, review of *Insects Are My Life,* p. 280; March, 1999, Janice M. Del Negro, review of *The Bone Keeper,* pp. 245-246.

Childhood Education, mid-summer, 2002, Jill Quisenberry, review of *Reptiles Are My Life,* p. 307.

Five Owls, July-August, 1990, Margaret Mary Kimmel, review of *Is This a House for a Hermit Crab?,* p. 105; May-June, 1992, Anne Lundin, review of *Whoo-oo Is It?,* p. 58.

Horn Book, May, 1991, Mary M. Burns, review of *The Potato Man,* p. 318; May-June, 1992, Elizabeth S. Watson, review of *Whoo-oo Is It?,* p. 332; March-April, 1995, Margaret A. Bush, review of *Insects Are My Life,* p. 185; September, 1999, review of *The Night Iguana Left Home,* p. 596; September, 2001, review of *Judy Moody Gets Famous!,* p. 589; November-December, 2008, Joanna Rudge Long, review of *The Hinky-Pink,* p. 692; July-August, 2009, Susan Dove Lempke, review of *It's Picture Day!,* p. 411.

Kirkus Reviews, July 1, 1992, review of *The Great Pumpkin Switch,* p. 851; March 15, 1993, review of *The Bridge to Nowhere,* p. 374; July 15, 1999, review of *Bedbugs,* p. 1141; July 1, 2001, review of *Reptiles*

Are My Life, p. 943; July 1, 2002, review of *Judy Moody Saves the World!,* p. 958; June 15, 2003, review of *Baya, Baya, Lulla-by-a,* p. 861; August 15, 2003, reviews of *The Sisters Club* and *All the Stars in the Sky,* both p. 1076; September 1, 2003, review of *Penguin and Little Blue,* p. 1128; January 1, 2005, review of *Ant and Honey Bee,* p. 55; April 1, 2005, review of *Beetle Grady Eats Bugs!,* p. 421; April 15, 2006, review of *Stink and the Incredible Super-Galactic Jawbreaker,* p. 410; July 15, 2008, review of *The Hinky-Pink;* April 15, 2009, review of *Hen Hears Gossip;* June 15, 2009, review of *It's Picture Day Today!;* July 1, 2009, review of *The Rule of Three;* February 1, 2011, review of *Cloudy with a Chance of Boys;* January 1, 2012, review of *Stink and the Midnight Zombie Walk.*

New York Times Book Review, February 13, 2000, Jane O'Reilly, review of *The Night Iguana Left Home,* p. 27.

New York Times, June 10, 2011, Andy Webster, movie review of *Judy Moody and the NOT Bummer Summer,* p. C8.

Publishers Weekly, October 6, 1997, review of *Tundra Mouse,* p. 55; February 1, 1999, review of *The Bone Keeper,* p. 84; October 4, 1999, review of *The Night Iguana Left Home,* p. 74; April 17, 2000, review of *Judy Moody,* p. 81; July 30, 2001, review of *Judy Moody Gets Famous!,* p. 85; June 30, 2003, review of *Baya, Baya, Lulla-by-a,* p. 77; August 25, 2003, reviews of *Penguin and Little Blue,* p. 63, and *The Sisters Club,* p. 65; January 31, 2005, review of *Ant and Honey Bee: What a Pair!,* p. 68; August 11, 2008, review of *The Hinky-Pink,* p. 45.

School Librarian, summer, 2002, Andrea Rayner, review of *Judy Moody,* p. 89.

School Library Journal, August, 1992, Susan Scheps, review of *The Great Pumpkin Switch,* pp. 143-144; March, 1995, Virginia Opocensky, review of *Insects Are My Life,* pp. 183-184; October, 1996, Sally R. Dow, review of *My House Has Stars,* pp. 102-103; May, 1999, Rosalyn Pierini, review of *The Bone Keeper,* p. 93; September, 1999, Heide Piehler, review of *Bedbugs,* p. 194, Gay Lynn van Vleck, review of *The Night Iguana Left Home,* p. 195; July, 2000, Janie Schomberg, review of *Judy Moody,* p. 83; September, 2000, Maura Bresnahan, review of *Beezy and Funnybone,* p. 204; February, 2001, Kristen Oravec, review of *Shadows in the Glasshouse,* p. 118; August, 2001, Linda M. Kenton, review of *Reptiles Are My Life,* p. 156; October, 2001, Sharon R. Pearce, review of *Judy Moody Gets Famous!,* p. 124; March, 2002, Maura Bresnahan, review of *Lucky Star,* p. 194; November, 2003, Alison Grant, review of *Judy Moody Predicts the Future,* p. 106, Catherine Threadgill, review of *Penguin and Little Blue,* p. 107, and Lee Bock, review of *All the Stars in the Sky,* and Laurie von Mehren, review of *The Sisters Club,* both p. 142; September, 2004, Tracy Karbel, review of *Judy Moody, M.D.,* p. 172; April, 2005, Deanna Romriell, review of *Stink: The Incredible Shrinking Kid,* p. 106; May, 2005, Suzanne Myers Harold, review of *Beetle McGrady Eats Bugs!,* p. 90; July, 2005, Roxanne Burg, review of *Saving the Liberty Bell,* p. 91; August, 2005, Sharon R. Pearce, review of *Judy Moody Declares Independence,* p. 100; November, 2005, Kathie Meizner, review of *When the Library Lights Go Out,* p. 98; May, 2007, Elaine Lesh Morgan, review of *Stink and the World's Worst Super-Stinky Sneakers,* p. 102; January, 2008, Sharon R. Pearce, review of *Julie and the Eagles,* p. 90, and Krista Tokarz, review of *Happy New Year, Julie,* p. 92; March, 2008, Bethany A. Lafferty, review of *Stink and the Guinea Pig Express,* p. 172; August, 2008, Mary Jean Smith, review of *The Hinky-Pink,* p. 98; June, 2009, Mary Jean Smith, review of *It's Picture Day!,* p. 95; August, 2009, Madigan McGillicuddy, review of *Judy Moody and Stink: The Mad, Mad, Mad, Mad Treasure Hunt,* p. 80; September, 2009, Laura Stanfield, review of *The Rule of Three,* p. 166; February, 2010, Elizabeth Swistock, review of *Stink: Solar System Superhero,* p. 90; March, 2010, Carol A. Edwards, review of *I Fooled You: Ten Stories of Tricks, Jokes, and Switcheroos,* p. 160; August, 2010, Amelia Jenkins, review of *Judy Moody, Girl Detective,* p. 80; March, 2011, Colleen S. Banick, review of *Cloudy with a Chance of Boys,* p. 166.

ONLINE

Candlewick Press Web site, http://www.candlewick.com/ (August 1, 2012), "Megan McDonald."

Judy Moody Web site, http://www.judymoody.com/ (August 1, 2012).

Kidsreads.com, http://www.kidsreads.com/ (August, 2008), Terry Miller Shannon, interview with McDonald.

Megan McDonald Home Page, http://www.megan mcdonald.net (August 1, 2012).*

* * *

McENTIRE, Myra

Personal

Born in TN; married; husband's name Ethan (a baseball player); children: Andrew, Charlie. *Education:* Carson Newman College, B.A. (English and sociology).

Addresses

Home—Nashville, TN. *Agent*—Holly Root, Waxman Leavell Literary Agency Literary, 80 5th Ave., Ste. 1101, New York, NY 10011. *E-mail*—myramcentire@ gmail.com.

Career

Novelist.

Member

Romance Writers of America.

Awards, Honors

RITA Best First Book finalist and Best Young-Adult Romance finalist, both 2012, both for *Hourglass.*

Writings

YOUNG-ADULT NOVELS

Hourglass, Egmont USA (New York, NY), 2011.
Timepiece (sequel to *Hourglass*), Egmont USA (New York, NY), 2012.

Adaptations

Film rights to *Hourglass* were optioned by Twentieth Century-Fox.

Sidelights

Myra McEntire captures the magic, mystery, and dusky romance of her native Tennessee in her young-adult novels *Hourglass* and *Timepiece*. Described by *School Library Journal* critic Elizabeth C. Johnson as "a compelling story that is difficult to put down," *Hourglass* transports readers to a small southern town, where seventeen-year-old Emerson "Em" Cole has grown up, acutely aware that residents from the distant past still

exist as shadows among the living. Em has seen these ghosts ever since her parents were killed four years ago, and she now confides her problem to older brother Thomas and his wife Dru, as well as to best friend Lily. Enter Michael Weaver, from the Hourglass Institute, who tells Em that she actually may have the ability to change the past, including the accident that killed her mom and dad.

"Em is an entertainingly cheeky narrator and appealingly resilient heroine," noted a *Kirkus Reviews* writer in appraising *Hourglass,* and McEntire's "portrait of [the teenager's] grief is particularly poignant." Calling *Hourglass* "all about romance," Debbie Carton predicted in her *Booklist* review that the novelist will appeal to teens looking for "a little vacation from reality," and *Voice of Youth Advocates* contributor Judy Brink-Drescher recommended McEntire's fiction debut for its "humor, pace, and endlessly appealing paranormal theme."

The aftereffects of Em's efforts to avert the tragedies of the past play out in *Timepiece,* which is narrated by Kaleb Ballard. A teen whose father, Liam, was brought back from the dead with Em's help, Kaleb is experiencing unusual abilities of his own, abilities that he has attempted to block out with drugs and alcohol and out-of-control behavior. Now he focuses his empathic talent in an effort to help his comatose mom and also win the confidence of romantic interest Lily Garcia. Together with Em and several other teens recruited by the Hourglass Institute, Kaleb must also channel his powers in a collective goal: to stop a man named Jack Landers from causing chaos throughout time. Over the course of *Timepiece* McEntire's teen narrator "reveals a sensitive side," noted a *Kirkus Reviews* writer, and the combination of a high-action plot and building romance "makes time fly by."

Biographical and Critical Sources

PERIODICALS

Booklist, March 1, 2011, Debbie Carton, review of *Hourglass,* p. 57.
Bulletin of the Center for Children's Books, May, 2011, April Spisak, review of *Hourglass,* p. 431.
Kirkus Reviews, April 15, 2011, review of *Hourglass;* May 1, 2012, review of *Timepiece.*
Publishers Weekly, March 14, 2011, review of *Hourglass,* p. 74.
School Library Journal, September, 2011, Elizabeth C. Johnson, review of *Hourglass,* p. 162.
Voice of Youth Advocates, June, 2011, Judy Brink-Drescher, review of *Hourglass,* p. 169.

ONLINE

Myra McEntire Web log, http://myramcentier.blogspot.com (August 1, 2012).
Voice of Youth Advocates Online, http://www.voya.com/ (July 15, 2012), Stacey Hayman, interview with McEntire.*

Cover of Myra McEntire's paranormal romance Hourglass, *which focuses on a Tennessee teen who discovers her ability to see the spirits walking, hidden, among the living.* (Jacket illustration photograph © 2011 by Lissy Laricchia. Reproduced by permission of Egmont USA.)

McGEE, Holly

Personal

Born in NY. *Education:* Florida State University, B.F.A. (film and visual art), 1994.

Addresses

Home—Asheville, NC. *E-mail*—hollymcgee71@ hotmail.com.

Career

Illustrator. Westville Pub, Asheville, NC, member of staff. *Exhibitions:* Paintings exhibited at galleries in North Carolina.

Member

Society of Children's Book Writers and Illustrators.

Illustrator

Dianne Moritz, *Hush, Little Beachcomber,* Kane/Miller (La Jolla, CA), 2011.

Contributor to periodicals, including *Carolina Home & Garden* and *Pen & Palette.*

Sidelights

Holly McGee studied art at Florida State University and earned a B.F.A. in film and visual art, but she had more to learn when she decided to focus her creative talents on book illustration. A longtime resident of North Carolina, McGee spent several years studying the craft of picture-book creation and finally received her first illustration project: creating the artwork for Dianne Moritz's story in *Hush, Little Beachcomber.*

In *Hush, Little Beachcomber* Moritz presents readers with an unique update on the traditional song "Hush,

Holly McGee started her illustration career by creating the colorful artwork featured in Dianne Moritz's nursery-rhyme retelling **Hush Little Beachcomber.** (Illustration copyright © 2011 by Holly McGee. Reproduced by permission of Kane Miller, a division of EDC Publishing.)

Little Baby" in her story about several families who join together for a fun day at the seaside. After McGee received the text for the story, she was given two weeks to create rough pencil sketches of the thirty-two pages required for the standard picture-book format. With so little notice, she did many of these during breaks from her full-time job as a member of the staff at a popular local restaurant where many of the patrons now learned of her artistic talents. Fortunately, the publisher's schedule was more generous once McGee's sketches were approved; the illustrations that appear in Moritz's story are detailed pencil-and-acrylic was images in an array of brilliant colors and required hours of studio time to complete.

Noting the naïf style of McGee's illustrations in *Hush, Little Beachcomber,* Ilene Cooper wrote in *Booklist* that "there is no doubt that [they were] . . . done by a practiced hand" and their multiethnic elements will help give the picture book "wide appeal." The picture book gives the song that inspired it "a brilliant makeover," a *Kirkus Reviews* writer asserted while also praising McGhee's contribution by commenting that her use of "thick strokes convey the water's intensity" and "clean white edges maintain the focus on the energetic pictures."

Biographical and Critical Sources

PERIODICALS

Booklist, May 1, 2011, Ilene Cooper, review of *Hush, Little Beachcomber,* p. 93.
Kirkus Reviews, February 15, 2011, review of *Hush, Little Beachcomber.*

ONLINE

Holly McGee Home Page, http://www.hollymcgee.com (August 1, 2012).
Verve Online (Asheville, NC), http://www.vervemag.com/ (January 30, 2011), Jonathan Rich, "Fetch and Sketch."*

*   *   *

McKINNON, Tanya
See SIMON, T.R.

*   *   *

MITCHELL, Hazel

Personal

Born in Scarborough, Yorkshire, England; immigrated to United States, 2000; married. *Education:* Attended York College of Art & Design; Sunderland University, B.A. (art).

Addresses

Home—Detroit, ME. *E-mail*—hazel-mitchell@hotmail.com.

Career

Illustrator. Graphic designer for British Royal Navy for four years; operator of print business; freelance illustrator and graphic designer.

Member

Society of Children's Book Writers and Illustrators.

Illustrator

Maura Lane, *Sabu and Me,* Alton Road (Chicago, IL), 2009.
Matthew Kelly, *Why Am I Here?,* Beacon Publishing, 2009.
Daniel Stefanski, *How to Talk to an Autistic Kid,* Free Spirit Pub. (Minneapolis, MN), 2011.
The Ugly Duckling (ebook), UTales, 2011.
Linda J. Barth, *Hidden New Jersey,* Charlesbridge Publishing (Watertown, MA), 2012.

"ALL-STAR CHEERLEADERS" READER SERIES BY ANASTASIA SUEN

Tick Tock, Taylor!, Kane Miller (La Jolla, CA), 2012.
Save the Best for Last, Abby, Kane Miller (La Jolla, CA), 2012.
Just So, Brianna,, Kane Miller (La Jolla, CA), 2012.
Fly, Emma, Fly, Kane Miller (La Jolla, CA), 2012.

Biographical and Critical Sources

PERIODICALS

Booklist, April 15, 2011, Angela Leeper, review of *How to Talk to an Autistic Kid,* p. 44.
Kirkus Reviews, March 1, 2011, review of *How to Talk to an Autistic Kid.*
School Library Journal, June, 2011, Wendy Smith D'Arezzo, review of *How to Talk to an Autistic Kid,* p. 147.

ONLINE

Hazel Mitchell Home Page, http://hazelmitchell.com (August 1, 2012).*

*   *   *

MONIR, Alexandra 1986(?)-

Personal

Born c. 1986.

Addresses

Home—Los Angeles, CA. *Agent*—William Morris Endeavor, 9601 Wilshire Blvd., Beverly Hills, CA 90210.

Career

Vocalist and novelist.

Writings

Timeless, Delacorte Press (New York, NY), 2011.

Sidelights

Singer-songwriter Alexandra Monir comes from an artistically gifted family of Persian heritage: Her grandmother, Monir Vakili, was one of Iran's most famous opera singers prior to her death. Monir's first book, the young-adult novel *Timeless,* was launched with a distinctive twist: two songs she wrote to accompany the time-travel romance were released simultaneously on iTunes. "I think music and literature are both powerful ways of telling a story," Monir explained in an interview for *Cosmogirl* online. "I love the narrative form of storytelling in literature, and the way music can take you on this emotional high and express feelings that are just too overwhelming for words."

In *Timeless* Monir's heroine is Michele Windsor, a teen who lives in California's oceanfront enclave of Venice Beach with her free-spirited single mom. Michele's idyllic life comes to an abrupt end when her mother dies in a car accident and she is forced to move to the East Coast and into the palatial Manhattan home of her much-older and ultra-conservative grandparents. The relationship is a new one for all involved because Michele's mother had been estranged from her parents since they voiced disapproval over her relationship with Michele's father, a man who confirmed their low opinion of him by disappearing.

Ensconced in her mother's former bedroom, Michele uncovers a diary written a century before by a distant ancestor and is transported back into the teenaged writer's life in New York City. Even more remarkably, Michele meets Philip, a boy who has periodically appeared in her dreams. In her visits back to 1910, the modern teen learns that Philip's family once lived in the Fifth Avenue mansion next door to her grandparents and that he was once engaged to one of her relatives.

"Like all good historical fiction, this novel effectively compares courtship, the constraints of society living, and differences in language," remarked Ann Reddy Damon in a *Voice of Youth Advocates* review of *Timeless.* Critiquing Monir's debut for *School Library Journal,* Nancy Menaldi-Scanlan asserted that "there are enough twists and turns to make the story interesting" and readers "intrigued by time travel will revel in Michele's adventures into the past."

Alexandra Monir takes time out from her musical career to write young-adult novels such as **Timeless.** *(Jacket illustration illustration © 2011 by Delacorte Books for Young Readers. Reproduced by permission of Delacorte Press, an imprint of Random House Children's Books, a division of Random House, Inc.)*

Monir explained the genesis of *Timeless* in her *Cosmogirl* interview. "What if everyone's soul mate isn't necessarily found in your own time?" she wondered. "What if someone's true soul mate exists in the past, or the future?" Two songs she wrote, "Chasing Time" and "Bring the Colors Back," express the longings described in the pages of *Timeless.*

Biographical and Critical Sources

PERIODICALS

Kirkus Reviews, December 15, 2010, review of *Timeless.*
School Library Journal, May, 2011, Nancy Menaldi-Scanlan, review of *Timeless,* p. 118.
Voice of Youth Advocates, April, 2011, Ann Reddy Damon, review of *Timeless,* p. 64.

ONLINE

Alexandra Monir Home Page, http://www.alexandramonir. com (August 1, 2012).

Cosmogirl Online, http://www.seventeen.com/cosmogirl/ (January 31, 2011), interview with Monir.

Huffington Post Online, http://www.huffingtonpost.com/ (July 6, 2011), Kia Makarechi, "For Alexandra Monir, Book Is Just the Beginning."*

* * *

MOORE, Jodi

Personal

Married; husband's name Larry; children: two sons.

Addresses

Home—Boalsburg, PA.

Career

Writer.

Member

Society of Children's Book Writers and Illustrators.

Writings

When a Dragon Moves In, illustrated by Howard McWilliam, Flashlight Press (Brooklyn, NY), 2011.

Sidelights

Jodi Moore's first book for young readers, *When a Dragon Moves In,* sets up a thrilling premise: a child builds an elaborate, extravagant sandcastle during a day

Jodi Moore captures the storytelling style of an imaginative youngster in her text for When a Dragon Moves In, *a picture book featuring art by Howard McWilliam.* (Illustration copyright © 2011 by Howard McWilliam. Reproduced by permission of Flashlight Press.)

at the beach and a fearsome mythical creature decides to call that sandcastle home. Moore's story comes to life in illustrations by Howard McWilliam, and both text and artwork take readers through the hypothetical pros and cons of the situation.

In *When a Dragon Moves In* Moore's beach-romping youngster is delighted when a dragon takes shelter in his fantastic new sandcastle. The boy quickly appreciates the benefits of having a fire-breathing pal on hand, for the dragon serves as a rapid-response bully repellant as well as a marshmallow-toasting appliance. There are some downsides, however: the boy finds himself in trouble for various infractions incidents of inappropriate combustion when he is unable to manage his dragon friend.

"Moore has a light, sure touch, and she gives McWilliam . . . plenty of room to exercise his considerable gifts," remarked a reviewer appraising *When a Dragon Moves In* for *Publishers Weekly.* A *Kirkus Reviews* contributor predicted that Moore's "deadpan text is sure to illicit giggles as it captures the conundrum of an imaginary friend with a child's eye," and Laura Stanfield asserted in *School Library Journal* that Moore's "story of a runaway imagination will make for an entertaining storytime as well as an enjoyable one-on-one read."

Biographical and Critical Sources

PERIODICALS

Children's Bookwatch, May, 2011, review of *When a Dragon Moves In.*

Kirkus Reviews, April 1, 2011, review of *When a Dragon Moves In.*

Publishers Weekly, March 14, 2011, review of *When a Dragon Moves In,* p. 69.

School Library Journal, September, 2011, Laura Stanfield, review of *When a Dragon Moves In,* p. 126.

ONLINE

Jodi Moore Home Page, http://www.writerjodimoore.com (August 1, 2012).*

* * *

MOULTON, Courtney Allison 1986-

Personal

Born August 18, 1986, in Austin, TX. *Hobbies and other interests:* Riding and showing horses.

Addresses

Home—Haslett, MI. *Agent*—Rosemary Stimola, Stimola Literary Studio; info@stimolaliterarystudio.com. *E-mail*—Courtney@courtneyallisonmoulton.com.

Career

Novelist and photographer.

Writings

"ANGELFIRE" NOVEL SERIES

Angelfire, Katherine Tegen Books (New York, NY), 2011.
Wings of the Wicked, Katherine Tegen Books (New York, NY), 2012.
Shadows in the Silence, Katherine Tegen Books (New York, NY), 2012.

Author's work has been translated into French, German, Portuguese, Polish, Taiwanese, and Turkish.

Sidelights

Courtney Allison Moulton decided to become a writer when she discovered R.L. Stine novels as a third grader. While her twin passions of photography and riding show horses have occupied much of Moulton's free time ever since, she has also continued to write. Her novel *Angelfire* was a product of her decision to participate in NaNoWriMo—National Novel Writing Month—in the fall of 2008. The first part of a trilogy that continues in *Wings of the Wicked, Angelfire* draws readers into "a dark and compelling world of action and intrigue," according to *Voice of Youth Advocates* contributor Julie Watkins.

On the eve of her seventeenth birthday, Michigan teen Ellie Monroe is busy worrying about grades, boys, and the odds of her quarreling parents calling a truce long enough to team up and surprise her with a new car when readers meet her in *Angelfire.* Ellie has been troubled by unpleasant dreams about dark-cloaked demons and when she meets a young man named Will on her birthday she learns that those dreams may be something more. Ellie is actually a Preliator, a person fated to be repeatedly reincarnated in order to fight these demon Reapers and thwart their effort to drag human souls into Hell. Together with the handsome and immortal Will, the teen must now learn how to manage her powers, the most important of which is mastery over the angelfire that can destroy her demonic foe. Meanwhile, Ellie's current life is threatened by Bastian, a reaper who has hunted her before and sometimes won.

"Reworking traditional Judeo-Christian beliefs to suit one's plot . . . takes chutzpah," noted a *Publishers Weekly* critic, and in *Angelfire* Moulton introduces a feisty heroine whose effort to save humanity "is unimpeachable." Watkins enjoyed the mix of "fascinating characters and storylines" in the novel, and *School Library Journal* critic Angela J. Reynolds recommended *Angelfire* to paranormal-fiction fans who enjoy "action, clothes, shopping, drama, and romance."

Cover of Courtney Alison Moulton's young-adult novel Angelfire, *part of her "Angelfire" fantasy series.* (Jacket illustration photograph © 2011 by Amber Gray; cover illustration by Joel Tippie based on image by Amber Abram. Reproduced by permission of HarperCollins Children's Books, a division of HarperCollins Publishers.)

Moulton continues her "Angelfire" trilogy in *Wings of the Wicked,* which finds Ellie—actually the reincarnation of the archangel Gabriel—still dedicated to fighting the evil reapers while her heart feels torn between her guardian will and the sexy demon Cadan. As the battle with Bastian escalates, both she and Will realize that they may have abilities that have not yet been tapped in a novel that *Voice of Youth Advocates* critic Karen Sykeny predicted "will engage readers easily" due to its mix of "angst-filled, romantic tension . . . and fast-paced action."

Biographical and Critical Sources

PERIODICALS

Bulletin of the Center for Children's Books, March, 2011, Kate Quealy-Gainer, review of *Angelfire,* p. 339.
Kirkus Reviews, February 15, 2011, review of *Angelfire;* January 1, 2012, review of *Wings of the Wicked.*

Publishers Weekly, January 17, 2011, review of *Angelfire,* p. 50.

School Library Journal, August, 2011, Angela J. Reynolds, review of *Angelfire,* p. 113.

Voice of Youth Advocates, April, 2011, Julie Watkins, review of *Angelfire,* p. 85; February, 2012, Karen Sykeny, review of *Wings of the Wicked,* p. 613.

ONLINE

Courtney Allison Moulton Home Page, http://www.court neyallisonmoulton.com (August 1, 2012).

Courtney Allison Moulton Web log, http://courtney-allison. blogspot.com (August 1, 2012).*

*   *   *

MULDER, Michelle 1976-

Personal

Born 1976, in British Columbia, Canada; married; children: one. *Education:* B.A. (religion and literature); M.A. (comparative literature). *Hobbies and other interests:* Reading, yoga, baking, bicycling, hiking.

Addresses

Home—Victoria, British Columbia, Canada. *E-mail*—michelle@michellemulder.com.

Career

Novelist and writing mentor. Former travel writer; teacher of creative writing.

Member

Writers Union of Canada, Canadian Children's Book Centre, Canadian Society of Children's Authors, Illustrators, and Performers, Canadian Writers and Illustrators League of British Columbia Society, International Board on Books for Young People (Canada chapter).

Awards, Honors

Canadian Children's Book Centre (CCBC) Best Books for Kids and Teens selection, and Canada IODE recommended title, both 2009, both for *Yeny and the Children for Peace;* Bolen Book Children's Book Prize shortlist, 2010, and CCBC Best Books for Kids and Teens selection, Chocolate Lily Award shortlist, and Rocky Mountain Book Award shortlist, all 2011, all for *After Peaches;* CCBC Best Books for Kids and Teens selection, 2012, for *Out of the Box.*

Writings

Maggie and the Chocolate War, Second Story Press (Toronto, Ontario, Canada), 2007.

Yeny and the Children for Peace, Second Story Press (Toronto, Ontario, Canada), 2008.

After Peaches, Orca Book Publishers (Custer, WA), 2009.

Out of the Box, Orca Book Publishers (Custer, WA), 2011.

Pedal It! How Bicycles Are Changing the World, Orca Book Publishers (Custer, WA), 2013.

Not a Chance, Orca Book Publishers (Custer, WA), 2013.

"THEODORE TOO" PICTURE-BOOK SERIES; ILLUSTRATED BY YOLANDA POPLAWSKA

Theodore Too and the Too-Long Nap, Nimbus Publishing (Halifax, Nova Scotia, Canada), 2006.

Theodore Too and the Shipwreck School, Nimbus Publishing (Halifax, Nova Scotia, Canada), 2007.

Theodore Too and the Mystery Guest, Nimbus Publishing (Halifax, Nova Scotia, Canada), 2008.

Theodore Too and the Excuse-Me Monster (board book), Nimbus Publishing (Halifax, Nova Scotia, Canada), 2011.

Sidelights

Michelle Mulder grew up in British Columbia, Canada, where she divided her time between reading and enjoying the local forest. A degree in literature and time spent exploring the world followed, along with making a bicycle trek across Canada. Mulder first channeled her talent for writing into work as a travel journalist, and refocused on children's literature. Her books for young readers include the "Theodore Too" picture books about a tenacious little tug boat as well as novels such as *Maggie and the Chocolate War, Yeny and the Children for Peace, After Peaches,* and *Out of the Box.* "I began writing for kids because kids' books have always been the ones I most enjoyed reading," she noted on her home page.

Mulder transports readers to 1947 British Columbia in *Maggie and the Chocolate War,* which finds Maggie hoping that wartime rationing is over and she can surprise her friend Jo with a chocolate bar on her birthday. However, shortages still exist and the price of chocolate has climbed so high that Maggie's saving are not enough; this economic catastrophe prompts her to team up with other children in protest. Noting the story's easy-reading text, a *Children's Bookwatch* critic recommended *Maggie and the Chocolate War* as a story about a young girl who"has more impact than one might think," and Lori Giles-Smith noted in *Canadian Review of Materials* that Mulder's mix of text, news reports, and photographs of real-life post-World War II children's protest helps to "teach young readers that everyone—regardless of age or gender—can participate in public debate."

Rosario Ramirez is ten years old when her family flees Mexico and moves to Canada in *After Peaches.* Rosario is still trying to process her older brother's death for defying the Mexican government when she enters her

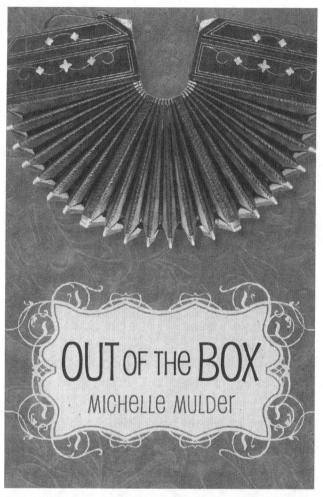

Cover of Canadian writer's Michelle Mulder's Out of the Box, *which focuses on a teen learning to cope with an unstable parent.* (Jacket photograph © Getty Images. Reproduced by permission of Orca Book Publishers.)

new fifth-grade class, and now she is teased by a bully for her unusual accent. She decides not to say another word until she can speak like a born Canadian, and when her family's rent goes up the girl convinces her farmworker parents to save rent money altogether and spend the summer traveling from crop to crop rather than working for local tulip growers; When a family friend becomes ill, however, the Ramirez clan returns home and voluntarily mute Rosario is depended upon to translate communications between doctor and patient.

Citing *After Peaches* for countering the perception "that coming to Canada will magically solve everyone's problems," Roseanne Gauthier added in her *Resource Links* review that Mulder's story focuses on a heroine who has a "desire to be Canadian and still maintain pride in her Mexican heritage." Emily Blobaum cited the novel as "a good book about facing your fears even if you don't want to," in her *Faces* review, and *Canadian Review of Materials* critic Kimberly Siwak and Gregory Bryan praised *After Peaches* as "an interesting and engaging read" that will be useful "for introducing and discussing the experiences of new Canadians."

Ellie, Mulder's thirteen-year-old heroine in *Out of the Box*, is enjoying a summer visiting her mom's sister Jeanette, who is recovering from the death of her longtime partner. In addition to gaining a reprieve from her parents' bickering, Ellie also realizes that while living away from home she does not have to be on guard against her mother's unpredictable outbreaks of temper. Learning to assess her family dynamic with some objectivity, Ellie also discovers a *bandoneón* (an Argentinian instrument similar to an accordion) in Jeanette's basement that inspires her musical interest. The instrument also carries clues to an interesting story and information about a country's modern-day battle against political upheaval and unpredictable violence.

Praising the interesting cast of characters in *Out of the Box, Canadian Review of Materials* critic Keith McPherson described Mulder's novel as "very rich and engaging," adding that it "not only contains a believable, dense, and complex plot, but . . . also captures many of the struggles faced by middle-school children." "Ellie's struggle to show her mother love while creating healthy boundaries resonates," according to *Booklist* contributor Suzanne Harold, and Maria B. Salvadore concluded in her *School Library Journal* appraisal of *Out of the Box* that Mulder's inclusion of "a bit of Argentine history rounds out the believable plot."

Biographical and Critical Sources

PERIODICALS

Booklist, March 15, 2011, Suzanne Harold, review of *Out of the Box,* p. 57.

Canadian Review of Materials, December 7, 2007, Lori Giles-Smith, review of *Magie and the ChocolateWar;* February 5, 2010, Kimberly Siwak and Gregory Bryan, review of *After Peaches;* February 18, 2011, Keith McPherson, review of *Out of the Box.*

Childhood Education, spring, 2008, Caleb Graham and Luke Graham, review of *Maggie and the ChocolateWar,* p. 173.

Children's Bookwatch, May, 2008, review of *Maggie and the Chocolate War;* December, 2008, review of *Yeny and the Children for Peace.*

Faces: People, Places & Cultures, September, 2010, Emily Blobaum, review of *After Peaches,* p. 47.

Kirkus Reviews, March 15, 2011, review of *Out of the Box.*

Resource Links, October, 2006, Suzanne Finkelstein, review of *Theodore Too and the Too-longNap,* p. 6; October, 2007, Michelle Gowans, review of *Theodore Too and the Shipwreck School,* p. 8; February, 2010, Roseanne Gauthier, review of *After Peaches,* p. 11.

School Library Journal, March, 2009, Kathleen Isaacs, review of *Yeny and the Children forPeace,* p. 124; June, 2011, Maria B. Salvadore, review of *Out of the Box,* p. 128.

ONLINE

Michelle Mulder Home Page, http://www.michellemulder. com (August 1, 2012).

* * *

MURGUIA, Bethanie Deeney

Personal

Surname pronounced "mer-GEE-ya; born in NY; married; children: two daughters. *Education:* University of Rochester, B.A. (psychology and fine art; summa cum laude); School of Visual Arts, M.F.A. (illustration). *Hobbies and other interests:* Nature, bicycling.

Addresses

Home—Los Angeles, CA. *Agent*—Mary Kole, Andrea Brown Literary Agency; mary@andreabrownlit.com. *E-mail*—bethanie@aquapup.com.

Career

Author and illustrator of picture books. Hearst Magazines, New York, NY, former art director; freelance art director for design and marketing companies, with clients including National Wildlife Federation.

Awards, Honors

Oppenheim Toy Portfolio Best Book Award, 2011, for *Buglette the Messy Sleeper.*

Writings

Buglette the Messy Sleeper, Tricycle Press (Berkeley, CA), 2011.
Zoe Gets Ready, Arthur A. Levine Books (New York, NY), 2012.
Snippet the Early Riser, Tricycle Press (Berkeley, CA), 2013.

Sidelights

Bethanie Deeney Murguia has wanted to write and illustrate children's stories since she was a child, but it was only after had children of her own that she found her voice and focus. Drawn to quirky characters and wild imaginations, Murguia strives to write books that both parents and children will find humorous and truthful. Her self-illustrated stories for young children include *Buglette the Messy Sleeper, Zoe Gets Ready,* and *Snippet the Early Riser.*

Any one who spends time with a little girl of a certain age will enjoy Bethanie Deeney Murguia's story in *Zoe Gets Ready.* In her ink-and-watercolor art, Murguia shares the story of a little girl who approaches every minute of every day as a special event that demands a special costume. From dancing to doing cartwheels to hiking, Zoe's worries over the correct wardrobe concern her parents until a special routine saves the day. "With layers of meaning, [and] a spunky, fun-loving heroine, . . . this one is a keeper," asserted Patricia Austin in her *Booklist* review of *Zoe Gets Ready,* and a *Publishers Weekly* contributor praised the picture-book star as a "spirited, creative heroine."

In *Buglette the Messy Sleeper* and *Snippet the Early Riser* Murguia pairs her spare yet evocative line-and-watercolor illustrations with whimsical stories that capture the everyday quirks of childhood. *Snippet the Early Riser* introduces a snail who likes to start the day far earlier than anyone else in his snoozy snail family. In *Buglette the Messy Sleeper* a young bug is proud of being neat and tidy, so she cannot understand why she wakes up with her sheets and blankets all a-twist and a-tangle. Worried that Buglette's active dreaming may attract the attention of predatory Mr. Crow, her brothers attempt to calm her sometimes scary dreams in a story that a *Kirkus Reviews* writer praised as "charmingly depicted." In *Booklist* Hazel Rochman predicted that *Buglette the Messy Sleeper* captures nighttime issues that "many children will recognize."

Bethanie Deeney Murguia mixes her whimsical drawings with a humorous story that captures a child's point of view in **Buglette the Messy Sleeper.** (Copyright © 2011 by Bethanie Deeney Murguia. Reproduced by permission of Tricycle Press, an imprint of Random House Children's Books, a division of Random House, Inc.)

Biographical and Critical Sources

PERIODICALS

Booklist, April 15, 2011, Hazel Rochman, review of *Buglette the Messy Sleeper,* p. 58; May 1, 2012, Patricia Austin, review of *Zoe Gets Ready,* p. 110
Kirkus Reviews, April 15, 2011, review of *Buglette the Messy Sleeper.*
Publishers Weekly, March 12, 2012, review of *Zoe Gets Ready,* p. 56.

ONLINE

Bethanie Deeney Murguia Home Page http://www.aquapup.com (August 1, 2012).
California Readers Web site, http://www.californiareaders.org/ (February, 2011), Bonnie O'Brian, interview with Murguia.

*   *   *

MURRAY, Peter
See HAUTMAN, Pete

*   *   *

MYERS, Matthew

Personal

Born in Portland, OR; father a commercial artist. *Education:* Museum Art School (now Pacific Northwest College of Art), B.F.A. (graphic art).

Addresses

Home—Brooklyn, NY. *Agent*—Steven Malk, Writers House, 21 W. 26th St., New York, NY 10010. *E-mail*—myerspaints@mac.com.

Career

Illustrator. Worked as an advertising art director for eighteen years.

Illustrator

Kelly DiPucchio, *Clink,* Balzer & Bray (New York, NY), 2011.
Liz Rosenberg, *Tyrannosaurus Dad,* Neal Porter Books (New York, NY), 2011.
Mac Barnett, *Danger Goes Berserk,* Simon & Schuster Books for Young Readers (New York, NY), 2012.
Erin Cabatingan, *A Is for Musk Ox,* Roaring Brook Press (New York, NY), 2012.
Garry Ross, *Bartholomew Biddle and the Very Big Wind,* Candlewick Press (New York, NY), 2012.

Sidelights

Raised in Oregon, where he spent his formative years hanging around in his parents' advertising agency, Matthew Myers moved to New York City and built his own career as an ad man. Eventually he decided to make the shift to book illustration by creating artwork for stories by Liz Rosenberg, Mac Barnett, Kelly DiPucchio, and others. "Advertising is sort of like somebody throwing a puzzle into your room and saying, 'Put it together!,'" Myers told *Publishers Weekly* interviewer Antonia Saxon. "Illustrating for adults just builds the illustrator's imagination," he added. "Illustrating for children builds the child's imagination."

Reviewing Rosenberg's *Tyrannosaurus Dad,* a story about the differences that can help bind a family together, Myers' digital illustrations "offer inventive perspectives, dynamic action, . . . and cool details," according to *Booklist* critic Andrew Medlar, and a *Publishers Weekly* critic asserted that the tale's "premise shines through, thanks to Myers's saturated, sculptural" art. In *School Library Journal,* Marge Loch-Wouters also praised the family-centered story, predicting that the combination of text and art in *Tyrannosaurus Dad* "will have dinosaur lovers and dads going back for more."

Clink features illustrations that "burst with loud colors," according to *Horn Book* contributor Katrina Hedeen, and here the artist's work injects "an energy that's perfect" for DiPucchio's robot-centered tale. Praising *Clink* as "a fresh take on the unwanted-puppy story," Ian

Supersized prehistoric creatures stand in for a typical American family in Liz Rosenberg's **Tyrannosaurus Dad,** *a picture book featuring Matthew Myers' art.* (Illustration copyright © 2011 by Matthew Myers. Reproduced by permission of Henry Holt & Company, LLC.)

Chipman added in *Booklist* that Myers' "feisty artwork" helps to accentuate the "humor and pathos" of the saga of an out-of-fashion robot looking for a special home.

Biographical and Critical Sources

PERIODICALS

Booklist, April 1, 2011, Ian Chipman, review of *Clink,* p. 73; April 15, 2011, Andrew Medlar, review of *Tyrannosaurus Dad,* p. 61.
Horn Book, May-June, 2011, Katrina Hedeen, review of *Clink,* p. 73.

Publishers Weekly, February 14, 2011, review of *Clink,* p. 54; March 28, 2011, review of *Tyrannosaurus Dad,* p. 54; June 20, 2011, Antonia Saxon, "Flying Starts," p. 22.
School Library Journal, March, 2011, Martha Simpson, review of *Clink,* p. 120; May, 2011, Marge Loch-Wouters, review of *Tyrannosaurus Dad,* p. 88.

ONLINE

Matthew Myers Home Page, http://www.myerspaints.com (August 1, 2012).*

N-P

NELSON, Blake 1960-

Personal

Born 1960, in Portland, OR. *Education:* Wesleyan University, B.A.; attended New York University.

Addresses

Home—Portland, OR. *Agent*—Jodi Reamer, Writers House, W. 26th St., New York, NY 10010. *E-mail*—theblaker@gmail.com.

Career

Fiction writer and columnist. Humor columnist for *Details* magazine.

Awards, Honors

Grinzane literary award (Italy), 2007, for *Paranoid Park;* Editor's Choice selection, *Kliatt* magazine, 2007, for *They Came from Below.*

Writings

YOUNG-ADULT NOVELS

The New Rules of High School, Viking (New York, NY), 2003.
Rock Star Superstar, Viking (New York, NY), 2004.
Gender Blender, Delacorte (New York, NY), 2006.
Paranoid Park, Viking (New York, NY), 2006.
Prom Anonymous, Viking (New York, NY), 2006.
They Came from Below, Tor (New York, NY), 2007.
Destroy All Cars, Scholastic Press (New York, NY), 2009.
Recovery Road, Scholastic Press (New York, NY), 2011.

ADULT NOVELS

Girl (originally serialized in *Sassy* magazine), Simon & Schuster (New York, NY), 1994.
Exile, Scribner (New York, NY), 1997.

User, Versus Press (San Francisco, CA), 2001.
Dream School (sequel to *Girl*), Figment, 2012.

Adaptations

Girl was adapted as a motion picture, 1998. *Paranoid Park* was adapted as a motion picture, directed by Gus Van Sant, 2006. *Gender Blender* was optioned for film by Nickelodeon.

Sidelights

Blake Nelson is the author of several thought-provoking novels for young adults, including *The New Rules of High School, Paranoid Park,* and *Recovery Road.* "I guess in some part of my brain I have always been younger than I really am," Nelson admitted to an interviewer for *Teenreads.com.* "I love high school. I think it is a great time in a person's life, an epic time, when love seems absolute and infinite and there's still room for heroism and bravery and romance. After that, everyone just gets jobs and watches TV."

Born in Portland, Oregon, Nelson developed an early interest in literature and music and played in several alternative bands before landing a job writing humor pieces for *Details* magazine. His fiction attracted the interest of a publisher after excerpts from his first novel, *Girl,* appeared in the popular teen magazine *Sassy.* Published in book form and marketed to adults, *Girl* focuses on Andrea Marr, a high-school student living in Portland who is struggling to find her identity.

Although Nelson wrote two more works for adult readers following *Girl,* he soon hit hit his stride writing for teens, and *The New Rules of High School* marked this transition. In *The New Rules of High School* readers meet Max Caldwell, an overachieving high school senior. At first glance, Max appears to have it all: he serves as editor-in-chief of the school newspaper and captain of the debate team, earns straight A's in class, and dates a beautiful girl. When the pressure to live up to his own high standards becomes too much for him,

Cover of Blake Nelson's young-adult novel The New Rules of High School, *featuring an illustration by Hadley Hooper.* (Cover illustration copyright © 2003 by Hadley Hooper. Reproduced by permission of Speak, a division of Penguin Putnam Books for Young Readers.)

Max begins to self-destruct, slacking off on his studies, dumping his girlfriend, and also jeopardizing his other close relationships.

The New Rules of High School shares "an intense journey of self-discovery, told in an achingly honest narrative," observed a critic in *Publishers Weekly*. "Nelson skillfully reveals Max's character and problems in 'show-don't-tell' style," a *Kirkus Reviews* contributor wrote, and Gillian Engberg noted of Max in her *Booklist* review that "there's a refreshing honesty in his 'averageness" and in his bewildered disconnection." "Whether Max is grieving over his breakup or testing the waters of singledom," asserted *School Library Journal* critic Vicki Reutter, "readers are empathetic to his emotional vulnerability."

A teenager takes aim at fame and fortune in *Rock Star Superstar,* "a brilliant, tender, funny, and utterly believable novel about music and relationships," according to *School Library Journal* contributor Miranda Doyle. In Nelson's story, Pete, a talented bass player whose par-

ents were also musicians, is asked to join the Tiny Masters of Today, a rock band on the verge of hitting it big. Despite reservations about his bandmates' devotion to their craft, Pete agrees to tour with the group, learning some hard lessons about the music industry along the way. He also enters an intense, complicated relationship with Margaret, his first true love. "Nelson paints Pete as endearingly clueless," remarked a critic in *Publishers Weekly,* "yet the teen proves his loyalty throughout the book—to his girlfriend, to his dad and ultimately to his music."

Two sixth graders learn first hand what it is like to be a member of the opposite sex in Nelson's humorous novel *Gender Blender.* Colliding mid-air during a jump on a trampoline, Tom Witherspoon and Emma Baker magically swap bodies. While forced to impersonate each other, Tom must learn the intricacies of fastening a bra while Emma copes with her counterpart's goofy male friends and their childish pranks. "Speaking in alternating chapters, the shell-shocked pre-teens hilariously navigate (and gain insights from) their differing hobbies, social situations, [and] academic reputations," noted *Booklist* reviewer Jennifer Mattson in a review of

Cover of Nelson's humorous middle-grade novel Gender Blender, *featuring artwork by Molly Zakrajsek.* (Jacket illustration copyright © 2006 by Delacorte Books for Young Readers. Reproduced by permission of Dell Children's Books, and imprint of Random House Children's Books, a division of Random House, Inc.)

the novel, while a *Publishers Weekly* critic remarked that in *Gender Blender* "Nelson demonstrates his keen understanding of peer pressure and gender stereotyping."

A skateboarder's journey to a rough-and-tumble neighborhood goes terribly wrong in *Paranoid Park,* a "deeply disturbing cautionary tale," in the words of a *Kirkus Reviews* critic. When the unnamed sixteen-year-old narrator decides one night to visit Paranoid Park, an area of town with a reputation as a sketchy, dangerous place, he meets Scratch, a street kid who convinces him to hop a train. Confronted by a vicious security guard, the narrator lashes out with his skateboard and watches in horror as the guard falls beneath a moving box car. "Written in the form of a confessional letter . . . ," a *Publishers Weekly* contributor noted, *Paranoid Park* "details the narrator's moral dilemma after the incident." "Gritty and aching, the narrative will have readers pondering what they might do under the circumstances," concluded *Kliatt* reviewer Paula Rohrlick in her appraisal of Nelson's tale.

In *Prom Anonymous* a high-school junior hopes to reunite with two old friends for the night of the big dance. Although Laura has drifted apart from former friends Chloe and Jace, she is determined to play matchmaker for them, although she begins to ignore her own boyfriend in the process. "As might be expected, prom night is filled with crises, but creative resolutions make for a gratifying all's-well-that-ends-well conclusion," noted a critic in *Publishers Weekly.*

Framed as a young-adult novel, *They Came from Below* draws on contemporary fears of environmental collapse in its story of seventeen-year-old best friends Emily and Reese. Vacationing on Cape Cod, the girls' prayers seem to be answered when they meet two cute guys. Tagged by the girls as respectable love interests, Steve and Dave turn out to be not what they seem, not by a long shot. In addition to being exponentially older than they appear, they are also not even human: in fact, their home base is deep beneath the sea. Although their dreams of summer romance are crushed, Emily and Reese decide to help these two visitors, joining a group of other seaside residents as well as Emily's biologist dad in contributing to the aliens' goal of saving the earth's environment. Reviewing *They Came from Below* in *Kliatt,* Claire Rossner praised Nelson's quirky novel as "smart, witty, and suspenseful," while a *Publishers Weekly* critic concluded of the work that the author "reaches a new level of depth and creativity with this intriguing depiction of one very weird summer."

Nelson again weaves a novel around an environmental theme in *Destroy All Cars,* which is framed as the diary of high-school junior James Hoff. Frustrated by the consumerism of a U.S. culture hooked on designer labels and reality TV, James finds a home in the environmentalist movement and he takes every opportunity—including classroom writing assignments—to promote

A teen's walk on the wild side is the focus of Nelson's novel **Paranoid Park,** *featuring artwork by Emilian Gregory.* (Jacket illustration copyright © 2006 by Emilian Gregory. Reproduced by permission of Viking Children's Books, a division of Penguin Young Readers Group, a member of Penguin Group (USA) Inc.)

the Earth-first mantra. Increasingly reactionary since breaking up with fellow activist Sadie, he hopes that his enthusiasm for saving the planet might help win her back.

In *Destroy All Cars* "Nelson capably conveys" teens' tendency to view "the entire world through a defining prism," asserted *Booklist* contributor Ian Chipman, and in the *New York Times Book Review* Regina Marler dubbed the work "smart and entertaining." For a *Publishers Weekly* critic the novel serves up an "elegant and bittersweet story of a teenager who is . . . trying to make meaning in a world he often finds hopeless," while Jonathan Hunt noted in *Horn Book* that the character of James is a refreshing and "thoroughly amusing combination of angst, idealism, narcissism, and nihilism."

Praised by a *Publishers Weekly* contributor as a "sharply focused portrait of a teen in crisis," *Recovery Road* was also "a book I had to write," as Nelson admitted on his home page. In the story high-school junior Madeline Graham must return to her old school after spending several weeks at the Spring Meadows rehab center. A former party girl who abused alcohol and exhibited an erratic temper, Maddie has established a well-earned notoriety at school, where everyone knows her as "Mad Dog Maddie." Lonely and hopeful of fitting in with her former friends, as well as attempting to maintain a tenuous romance with another recovering addict, the teen begins to rationalize the down-side of being sober in trying times.

In *Recovery Road* "Nelson gives a hard, honest appraisal of addiction," and this "important story . . . pulls no punches," wrote a *Publishers Weekly* critic. In *Voice of Youth Advocated* contributor Walter Hogan praised the author for his ability to "resist . . . numerous young adult problem novel clichés in this well-told story." Maddie, as well as her friends and family, are "sharply drawn," asserted a *Kirkus Reviews* writer, and Hunt concluded in *Horn Book* that the balance in *Recovery Road* between one character's "triumphant victory" and another's "backsliding . . . gives readers a realistic ending."

Discussing his motivation for becoming a writer, Nelson once remarked on his home page: "You have one life. What are you gonna do with it? If you go into the arts, that's a big risk. There's no certain reward. You are really sort of throwing yourself at the mercy of the fates. But if that's really what you feel called to do, then you do it."

Biographical and Critical Sources

PERIODICALS

Booklist, August, 2003, Gillian Engberg, review of *The New Rules of High School,* p. 1972; November 1, 2004, Todd Morning, review of *Rock Star, Superstar,* p. 476; March 1, 2006, Jennifer Mattson, review of *Gender Blender,* p. 88; April 1, 2006, Anne O'Malley, review of *Prom Anonymous,* p. 37; September 1, 2006, Ilene Cooper, review of *Paranoid Park,* p. 115.

Horn Book, July-August, 2009, Jonathan Hunt, review of *Destroy All Cars,* p. 428; March-April, 2011, Jonathan Hunt, review of *Recovery Road,* p. 121.

Journal of Adolescent & Adult Literacy, May, 2010, Donna L. Miller, review of *Destroy All Cars,* p. 700.

Kirkus Reviews, June 1, 2003, review of *The New Rules of High School,* p. 809; August 1, 2004, review of *Rock Star, Superstar,* p. 746; February 15, 2006, review of *Gender Blender,* p. 188, and review of *Prom Anonymous,* p. 189; August 1, 2006, review of *Paranoid Park,* p. 793; June 1, 2009, Ian Chipman, review of *Destroy All Cars,* p. 50; February 1, 2011, review of *Recovery Road.*

Kliatt, September, 2006, Paula Rohrlick, review of *Paranoid Park,* p. 16; July, 2007, Claire Rosser, review of *They Came from Below,* p. 19.

New York Times Book Review, September 13, 2009, Regina Marler, review of *Destroy All Cars,* p. 16.

Publishers Weekly, June 23, 2003, review of *The New Rules of High School,* p. 68; September 20, 2004, review of *Rock Star, Superstar,* p. 63; February 6, 2006, reviews of *Gender Blender* and *Prom Anonymous,* both p. 70; August 21, 2006, review of *Paranoid Park,* p. 69; July 9, 2007, review of *They Came from Below,* p. 55; May 25, 2009, review of *Destroy All Cars,* p. 59; January 10, 2011, review of *Recovery Road,* p. 51.

School Library Journal, June, 2003, Vicki Reutter, review of *The New Rules of High School,* p. 148; October, 2004, Miranda Doyle, review of *Rock Star, Superstar,* p. 173; March, 2006, Morgan Johnson-Doyle, review of *Prom Anonymous,* p. 228; April, 2006, Laurie Slagenwhite, review of *Gender Blender,* p. 145; May, 2011, Kimberly Castle, review of *Recovery Road,* p. 119.

Voice of Youth Advocates, October, 2004, Patrick Jones, review of *Rock Star, Superstar,* p. 306; April, 2011, Walter Hogan, review of *Recovery Road,* p. 52.

ONLINE

Blake Nelson Web log, http://blakenelsonteennovelist. blogspot.com (August 1, 2012).

Teenreads.com, http://www.teenreads.com/ (February 26, 2002), "Blake Nelson."

* * *

PÉREZ, Ashley Hope 1984-

Personal

Born March 5, 1984; married; husband's name Arnulfo; children: Liam Miguel. *Education:* University of Texas—Austin, B.A., 2004; Indiana University, Ph.D. (comparative literature).

Addresses

Home—IN. *Agent*—The Chudney Agency, 72 N. State Rd., Ste. 501, Briarcliff Manor, NY 10510. *E-mail*—novels@ashleyperez.com.

Career

Novelist. High school teacher in Houston, TX, c. 2004-07.

Writings

YOUNG-ADULT NOVELS

What Can't Wait, Carolrhoda Lab (Minneapolis, MN), 2011.

The Knife and the Butterfly, Carolrhoda Lab (Minneapolis, MN), 2012.

Sidelights

Ashley Hope Pérez mines her previous career as an educator in writing her young-adult novels. Her debut work, *What Can't Wait,* was shaped by her experiences at a high school in Houston, Texas, and introduces Marisa Moreno. A math-minded teen with promising grades, Marisa hopes to enter the University of Texas on a scholarship to study engineering. Unfortunately, her Mexican-immigrant family places demands on her time that limit her study hours. Her older sister, who is raising a child, is forced to work long hours when her husband is injured and it falls to Marisa to baby-sit her little niece. Marisa's mother is dubious about her daughter's plan to leave home for college and her illiterate father scoffs at her prowess in advanced math, a subject he deems unsuitable for women. Supportive of the girl's dreams, a teacher helps Marisa prioritize these competing pressures while also recognizing the fact that the Morenos believe that family comes first.

In *What Can't Wait* "Perez breathes credible and engaging life into her calculus-loving protagonist," asserted Francesca Goldsmith in a *Voice of Youth Advocates* review, the critic going on to recommended Pérez's novel as "an excellent story for . . . teens anywhere." Courtney Jones commented in *Booklist* that the author "deftly explores the daily struggle of some students to perse-

In Ashley Hope Pérez's touching young-adult novel **What Can't Wait,** *a young woman is forced to chose between her academic aspirations and the needs of her close-knit Mexican-American family.* (Jacket photographs by Juan Estey/iStockphoto.com (girl); Amy Nicolai/Dreamstime.com (butterfly); Raúl Touzon/National Geographic/Getty Images (concrete). Reproduced by permission of Carolrhoda LAB, an imprint of Lerner Publishing Group. All rights reserved. No part of may be used or reproduced in any manner whatsoever without the prior written permission of Lerner Publishing Group, Inc.)

vere in the face of long odds," and in *Kirkus Reviews* a critic commended Pérez for "giving Marisa an authentic voice that . . . captures the pressures of both Latina life and being caught between two cultures."

The Knife and the Butterfly is a story with a paranormal twist that is told in flashbacks. Fifteen-year-old Houston, Texas, teen Martin "Azael" Arevalo is incarcerated in a curious holding facility where his only contact with the outside world is through a one-way window. Looking out, he can sees Alexis "Lexi" Allen in her own detention cell. As the story plays out, readers learn that Azael is somehow involved with the notorious multinational MS-13, a gang founded by immigrants from El Salvador and other Central American nations. His mother has died and his father has been deported, leaving the teen and his brother Eddie with a substitute family affiliated with the powerful MS-13. Azael yearns to break free of a life of graffiti tagging, petty crime, and violent clashes with rival gangs and hopes to start a different life with Betta, his girlfriend.

In *The Knife and the Butterfly* Pérez "demonstrates why gangs appeal to many teens with family problems without glorifying the violence that often accompanies their activities," remarked a *Kirkus Reviews* contributor. Sam Bloom, writing for *School Library Journal,* commended the author's skill in creating "a dynamic and sympathetic main character with an authentic voice," and *Voice of Youth Advocates* critic Laura Woodruff described Azael and his gangbangers as "children trapped in desperate circumstances." "Based on a true incident, [*The Knife and the Butterfly*] . . . is gritty, sad, and not for the faint-hearted," Woodruff added.

Biographical and Critical Sources

PERIODICALS

Booklist, March 15, 2011, Courtney Jones, review of *What Can't Wait,* p. 60; February 1, 2012, Daniel Kraus, review of *The Knife and the Butterfly,* p. 89.
Bulletin of the Center for Children's Books, April, 2011, Karen Coats, review of *Wait,* p. 388.
Kirkus Reviews, February 1, 2011, review of *What Can't Wait;* January 1, 2012, review of *The Knife and the Butterfly.*
School Library Journal, May, 2011, Georgia Christgau, review of *What Can't Wait,* p. 120; February, 2012, Sam Bloom, review of *The Knife and the Butterfly,* p. 130.
Voice of Youth Advocates, April, 2011, Francesca Goldsmith, review of *What Can't Wait,* p. 66; April, 2012, Laura Woodruff, review of *The Knife and the Butterfly,* p. 62.

ONLINE

Ashley Hope Pérez Home Page, http://www.ashleyperez.com (August 1, 2012).*

PLUM, Amy 1967-
[A pseudonym]

Personal

Born 1967, in AL; married; two children. *Education:* M.A. (art history).

Addresses

Home—France. *Agent*—Stacey Glick, Dystel & Goderich Literary Management, 1 Union Square W., Ste. 904, New York, NY 10003. *E-mail*—amy@amyplumbooks. com.

Career

Educator and author. Worked in art and antiques industry; Tours University, Tours, France, professor of English until 2010.

Member

Authors Guild, Society of Children's Book Writers and Illustrators.

Writings

"REVENANTS" YOUNG-ADULT NOVEL SERIES

Die for Me, HarperTeen (New York, NY), 2011.
Until I Die, HarperTeen (New York, NY), 2012.

Sidelights

Amy Plum is the pen name of an American writer living in France, and her first novel for teens, *Die for Me,* introduces her "Revenants" trilogy. Revenants are a type of ghost or zombie common to the medieval folklore of Western Europe, particularly that of France. These walking corpses are generally nefarious in intent, but in her trilogy Plum creates a benign class of revenant that serves as protectors of the living.

Die for Me centers on sixteen-year-old Kate Mercier, a Brooklyn native whose parents have recently died in an accident. Kate and her sister Georgia now move in with their grandparents in Paris, where they have previously spent long family vacations. The more-outgoing Georgia readily adapts to this new life, but Kate is depressed and mopes around the cafés and museums of the city with a book in hand. On one outing she encounters a handsome young Frenchman named Vincent and she learns of his curious status as a revenant after she sees what appears to be a fatal accident in a Paris Metro station. Vincent's revenant family serves as protectors of others, dying in their stead when innocent mortal lives are at risk. Although romance soon blooms, Kate realizes the doomed nature of loving an immortal. Further complicating their love are the undead Numa, which are at war with Vincent's clan.

"Action and drama abound," wrote Genevieve Gallagher in her *School Library Journal* assessment of *Die for Me.* "Plum has done an excellent job of setting up the roles for her creations and following them closely," the critic added. A contributor to *Publishers Weekly* also praised the author's first novel, remarking that the "lush Parisian setting and gorgeous characters" in *Die for Me* "make this an immersing, franchise-ready story."

The second installment in Plum's "Revenants" trilogy is *Until I Die,* which finds Kate now a part of Vincent's group and undergoing intensive training in the martial arts. "Street battles with ancient weapons and treachery from within complicate this fast-moving tale of star-crossed lovers," wrote Judith A. Hayn in a *Voice of Youth Advocates* review of the sequel, while a *Kirkus Reviews* critic concluded that "Plum handles the intrigue and builds tension, ending with a major cliffhanger."

Biographical and Critical Sources

PERIODICALS

Booklist, March 1, 2011, Frances Bradburn, review of *Die for Me,* p. 56.
Kirkus Reviews, April 15, 2011, review of *Die for Me;* April 1, review of *Until I Die.*
Publishers Weekly, March 28, 2011, review of *Die for Me,* p. 59.
School Library Journal, May, 2011, Genevieve Gallagher, review of *Die for Me,* p. 121.
Voice of Youth Advocates, June, 2011, Lisa Martincik, review of *Die for Me,* p. 190; Judith A. Hayn, April, 2012, review of *Until I Die,* p. 79.

ONLINE

Amy Plum Home Page, http://www.amyplumbooks.com (August 1, 2012).*

*   *   *

POLISNER, Gae 1964-

Personal

Born 1964, in NY; married David Miller (an attorney), June 27, 1993; children: Sam, Holden. *Education:* Boston University, B.S.; Brooklyn Law School, J.D., 1991. *Hobbies and other interests:* Swimming.

Addresses

Home—Long Island, NY. *Agent*—Jim McCarthy, Dystel & Goderich Literary Management, 1 Union Square W., Ste. 904, New York, NY 10003. *E-mail*—g.polisner@ gmail.com.

Gae Polisner (Photograph by Rick Kopstein. Reproduced by permission.)

Career

Family law attorney and author.

Member

Society of Children's Book Writers and Illustrators.

Writings

The Pull of Gravity, Frances Foster Books (New York, NY), 2011.

Sidelights

Gae Polisner wrote her first young-adult novel, *The Pull of Gravity,* after surveying the genre and recognizing that there was a distinct lack of male teen protagonists in contemporary teen fiction. Writing was not Polisner's first career, however; she spent several years as a practicing attorney following her graduation from Brooklyn Law School in 1991. "My first law school paper came back with a big red X on it and a note, 'This is not a creative writing class,'" the author confessed to *New York Times* contributor Aileen Jacobson. In addi-

tion to young-adult fiction, Polisner contributes to several Web logs, one of which—Trying to Stay Afloat in a Sea of Words—references her swims in Long Island Sound. "I realized that when I was blocked in my writing, it would all come to me in the water," she told Jacobson in the *New York Times* profile, "so it became a creative outlet."

The hero of Polisner's debut novel is fourteen-year-old Nick, whose life in his fictional home town just outside of Albany, New York, fills him with stress. His morbidly obese father is unemployed and seems content to spend his life on the couch while Nick's mom works long hours to maintain their household. Not surprisingly, the couple fights often. After one particularly grim war of words, Nick's dad leaves and decides to walk from Albany to New York City, his hometown. The man's story piques the interest of local news outlets, which begin covering his trek. Nick has a more-pressing dilemma, however: His best friend Scooter is afflicted with Hutchinson-Gilford progeria syndrome and will soon die of old age. Recently suffering a stroke and with his vital signs worsening, Scooter wants the chance to return a valuable, signed first-edition copy of John Steinbeck's *Of Mice and Men* to his estranged father. To help his dying friend, Nick teams up with potential girlfriend Jaycee to make the bus trip across New York State to return the book to Scooter's dad. On the way, he learns some uncomfortable truths about his own family.

The Pull of Gravity "begins with a bang and ends with another," declared Michael Cart in his *Booklist* review of Polisner's fiction debut. The author won plaudits for introducing two believable teen males in the pages of her story, several critics enjoying Scooter's habit of quoting the wise Yoda from the "Star Wars" movie trilogy. "Scooter, with his love of life, is a character people will enjoy," predicted Ed Goldberg in a *Voice of Youth Advocates* review. "He is a bundle of hope in a hopeless situation."

Biographical and Critical Sources

PERIODICALS

Booklist, June 1, 2011, Michael Cart, review of *The Pull of Gravity,* p. 82.
Bulletin of the Center for Children's Books, Karen Coats, review of *The Pull of Gravity,* p. 535.
Kirkus Reviews, March 15, 2011, review of *The Pull of Gravity.*
New York Times, May 1, 2011, Aileen Jacobson, "To Sell First Novel, Putting That Marketing Degree to Use," p. 9.
School Library Journal, June, 2011, Suzanne Gordon, review of *The Pull of Gravity,* p. 130.
Voice of Youth Advocates, June, 2011, Ed Goldberg, review of *The Pull of Gravity,* p. 171.

ONLINE

Gae Polisner Home Page, http://gaepolisner.com (August 1, 2012).
Gae Polisner Web log, http://gpolisner.blogspot.com/ (August 1, 2012).
Gae Polisner Young-Adult Web log, http://ghpolisner. blogspot.com/ (August 1, 2012).

* * *

PULVER, Robin 1945-

Personal

Born August 14, 1945, in Geneva, NY; daughter of Willard B. (a biochemist) and Alice Robinson; married Donald Pulver (a physician), June 12, 1971; children: Nina, David. *Education:* William Smith College, B.A., 1967; attended Syracuse University. *Hobbies and other interests:* Hiking, swimming, bird-watching, reading.

Addresses

Home—Pittsford, NY.

Career

Writer. Has worked in public relations.

Member

Society of Children's Book Writers and Illustrators, Authors Guild, National Coalition against Censorship, Association for Retarded Citizens, Sierra Club, Rochester Area Children's Writers and Illustrators.

Awards, Honors

Pick of the Lists selection, American Booksellers Association, 1990, for *Mrs. Toggle's Zipper,* and 1994, for *Homer and the House Next Door;* Children's Choice designation, International Reading Association/Children's Book Council, 1992, for *The Holiday Handwriting School; Smithsonian* magazine Notable Children's Book designation, Nest Literary Classic selection, and nominations for six state reading awards, all 1999, all for *Axle Annie;* Best Books designation, Bank Street College of Education, and Chapman Award, PlanetEsme. com, both 2003, both for *Punctuation Takes a Vacation.*

Writings

Mrs. Toggle's Zipper, illustrated by R.W. Alley, Four Winds Press (New York, NY), 1990.
The Holiday Handwriting School, illustrated by G. Brian Karas, Four Winds Press (New York, NY), 1991.
Mrs. Toggle and the Dinosaur, illustrated by R.W. Alley, Four Winds Press (New York, NY), 1991.

Nobody's Mother Is in Second Grade, illustrated by G. Brian Karas, Dial Books for Young Readers (New York, NY), 1992.
Homer and the House Next Door, illustrated by Arnie Levin, Four Winds Press (New York, NY), 1994.
Mrs. Toggle's Beautiful Blue Shoe, illustrated by R.W. Alley, Four Winds Press (New York, NY), 1994.
Alicia's Tutu, illustrated by Mark Graham, Dial Books for Young Readers (New York, NY), 1997.
Way to Go, Alex!, illustrated by Elizabeth Wolf, Albert Whitman (Morton Grove, IL), 1999.
Axle Annie, illustrated by Tedd Arnold, Dial Books for Young Readers (New York, NY), 1999.
Mrs. Toggle's Class Picture Day, illustrated by R.W. Alley, Scholastic (New York, NY), 2000.
Christmas for a Kitten, illustrated by Layne Johnson, Albert Whitman (Morton Grove, IL), 2003.
Punctuation Takes a Vacation, illustrated by Lynn Rowe Reed, Holiday House (New York, NY), 2003.
Author Day for Room 3T, illustrated by Chuck Richards, Clarion Books (New York, NY), 2005.
Axle Annie and the Speed Grump, illustrated by Tedd Arnold, Dial Books for Young Readers (New York, NY), 2005.
Nouns and Verbs Have a Field Day, illustrated by Lynn Rowe Reed, Holiday House (New York, NY), 2006.
Silent Letters Loud and Clear, illustrated by Lynn Rowe Reed, Holiday House (New York, NY), 2008.
Never Say Boo!, illustrated by Deb Lucke, Holiday House (New York, NY), 2009.
Christmas Kitten, Home at Last, paintings by Layne Johnson, Albert Whitman (Chicago, IL), 2010.
Thank You, Miss Doover!, illustrated by Stephanie Roth Sisson, Holiday House (New York, NY), 2010.
Happy Endings: A Story about Suffixes, illustrated by Lynn Rowe Reed, Holiday House (New York, NY), 2011.
The Case of the Incapacitated Capitals, illustrated by Lynn Rowe Reed, Holiday House (New York, NY), 2012.

Contributor of articles and stories to periodicals, including *Highlights for Children, Jack and Jill, Pockets, Cricket, Spider,* and *Ranger Rick.*

Adaptations

Punctuation Takes a Vacation was adapted for audiobook, narrated by John Beach, Live Oak Media, 2009.

Sidelights

As a child growing up in upstate New York, Robin Pulver loved writing and reading and she began publishing magazine articles in her twenties, after graduating from college. Pulver's decision to write for young people came after her own two children reached read-to-me age and resulted in her first published picture books, *Mrs. Toggle's Zipper.* Illustrated by R.W. Alley and featuring several stories about a lovable, frumpy schoolteacher, Pulver's "Mrs. Toggle" tales have been followed by numerous other picture books, among them *Axle Annie, Punctuation Takes a Vacation* and its sequels, *Author Day for Room 3T,* the new-ghost-in-school story *Never Say Boo!,* and *Thank You, Miss Doover!,* the last featuring artwork by Stephanie Roth Sisson.

Pulver's well-received "Mrs. Toggle" picture books focus on a group of students that often comes to the rescue of befuddled teacher Mrs. Toggle. In *Mrs. Toggle's Zipper* the accident-prone teacher cannot remove her winter jacket after its zipper jams, and no amount of tugging will free her. After asking the school nurse for help, the children turn to their clueless principal, who in turn sends for the custodian, Mr. Abel. Using the right tool, Mr. Abel is able to un-stick the jacket zipper, much to the relief of the children and the overheated Mrs. Toggle. A *Publishers Weekly* critic called *Mrs. Toggle's Zipper* "a funny, slightly subversive story," adding that Alley's illustrations "complement the witty tale perfectly."

A new student proves to be a problem in *Mrs. Toggle and the Dinosaur,* when Mrs. Toggle is led to believe that her new pupil is actually a dinosaur. More strange events transpire in *Mrs. Toggle's Beautiful Blue Shoe* as the accident-prone teacher loses her shoe after joining her students in a game of kickball. Landing high up in a tree, the shoe stays stubbornly put, resisting all attempts by the children and their not-very-helpful principal, Mr. Stickler, to retrieve it. A different sort of emergency arises in *Mrs. Toggle's Class Picture Day* when the teacher arrives at school with a less-than-perfect coiffure. After scaring the children with her disheveled locks, Mrs. Toggle turns to the school nurse, then the custodian, principal, librarian, and art teacher for help before the photographer arrives.

Mrs. Toggle and the Dinosaur is "a fine sequel to the equally delightful *Mrs. Toggle's Zipper,*" asserted a contributor to *Kirkus Reviews.* Calling *Mrs. Toggle's Beautiful Blue Shoe* "another winner," *School Library Journal* critic Joyce Richards predicted that "older [children] will enjoy the [story's] problem-solving aspect." In *Booklist* Julie Corsaro wrote of the same book that Pulver's "simple text has appealing repetition," and her story's ending "serves up the right dose of schoolyard justice."

Tedd Arnold's collaborations with Robin Pulver include his illustrations for **Axel Annie**. (Illustration copyright © 1999 by Tedd Arnold. Reproduced by permission of Dial Books for Young readers, a division of Penguin Group (USA) Inc.)

Schooltime is also a key element in *Axle Annie* and *Axle Annie and the Speed Grump,* both of which focus on a good-hearted school-bus driver. Much to the disappointment of her bus-driving colleague Shifty Rhodes, Axle Annie never lets a snowstorm prevent her riders from getting to school on time and her students have no chance to enjoy a snowday every once in awhile. Hoping for a day off from work, Shifty conspires with the owner of a local ski resort to cover a particularly dangerous stretch of road with a heavy coat of slippery ice using a snow-making machine. The scheming duo does not count on the generosity of the other Burskyville residents who help push Axle Annie's bus up the slippery incline as repayment for the many times she gave them a ride in inclement weather. "With hilarious, over the top characters, this satisfyingly outrageous tale will tickle readers' funny bones," suggested a *Kirkus Reviews* critic. Other reviewers cited Pulver's well-drawn characters, a *Publishers Weekly* contributor remarking that the author "creates a memorable character in Annie."

Readers return to Burskyville in *Axle Annie and the Speed Grump* as the helpful bus driver goes head to head with local leadfoot Rush Hotfoot. When Rush breaks the speed limit and several safety rules besides, his driving puts Annie's young passengers at risk. The man's good luck does not last forever, however, and when Rush escapes a tragic accident with the help of Annie and the students, he turns in his car keys for a three-wheeled bike. Pulver's story will "keep kids laughing out loud," observed Julie Cummins in her review of *Axle Annie and the Speed Grump* for *Booklist,* and Tedd Arnold's colored pencil-and-watercolor illustrations for the story are "as over the edge as Rush's car." *School Library Journal* critic Susan Weitz also praised Arnold's colorful art, noting that his "enormously appealing" cartoons combine with Pulver's "bouncy language" to "present a lesson in road safety that's both goofy and memorable."

Homer and the House Next Door features a dog that grows upset when it learns its owner intends to sell the family home, while *Way to Go, Alex!* finds Carly ashamed that she feels jealous of her mentally handicapped younger brother, Alex after he wins a place in the upcoming Special Olympics, where he hopes to race in the fifty-yard dash. Although Alex stops short of the finish line on race day, Carly's experience as a coach helps her realize that her brother is still a success because he had the courage to try. Remarking on Pulver's ability to capture Carly's conflicting emotions in *Way to Go, Alex!, Booklist* contributor Susan Dove Lempke claimed that the book "will fill a need for materials on disabilities and is a solid story in its own right."

Pulver returns to school for an inspiring visit in *Author Day for Room 3T,* while in *Thank You, Miss Doover!* she focuses on a little boy whose teacher encourages her students to acknowledge their appreciation for gifts and other kind gestures with words. "A wacky

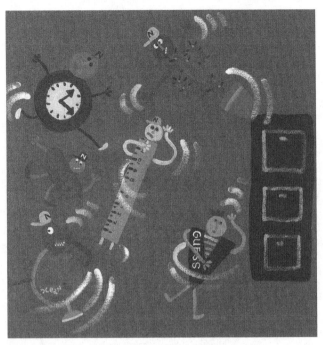

Pulver gives words an interesting twist in **Nouns and Verbs Have a Field Day,** *featuring illustrations by Lynne Rowe Reed.* (Illustration copyright © 2006 by Lynn Rowe Reed. Reproduced by permission of Holiday House, Inc.)

take on an Author's Day that goes awry," according to *Booklist* critic Ilene Cooper, *Author Day for Room 3T* captures what happens to a class full of normal third graders when a chimpanzee takes the place of a visiting teacher and all manner of antics result. Capturing the humor of Pulver's silly story in "goofy caricatures" and "topsy-turvy settings," illustrator Chuck Richards contributes to making *Author Day for Room 3T* "sublimely silly" and "a surefire hit," according to *School Library Journal* critic Marian Creamer. "Pulver's cheerful and often funny instructions . . . take the edge off learning," asserted Michael Cart in his *Booklist* appraisal of *Thank You, Miss Doover!,* while a *Kirkus Reviews* critic suggested that the "characterization of the elementary schoolers' thought processes and lack of tact" in the story "is spot on."

A collaboration between Pulver and artist Lynn Rowe Reed has produced several entertaining picture books set in a third-grade classroom that take grammar as their subject. In *Punctuation Takes a Vacation* Mr. Wright's students play fast and loose with commas, periods, apostrophes, colons, and hyphens, and their actions worry each of the symbols in question. A casual remark from the teacher convinces the punctuation marks to depart the classroom for a holiday, and they leave behind a room full of incomprehensible textbooks, reports, and signs.

While Mr. Wright's students are away on a field trip, the classroom's nouns and verbs are left to their own devices in *Nouns and Verbs Have a Field Day* and the students return to find some entertaining messages spelled out on the room's bulletin boards. When Mr. Wright's students decide to ban silent letters in *Silent*

Letters Loud and Clear, they are taught yet another lesson after Silent e and his associates depart. *Happy Endings: A Story about Suffixes* returns readers to Mr. Wright's class, this time as students are insulting the suffixes and prompting them to build up their muscle at the school gym in preparation for a kid-versus-suffix showdown.

Reed's naïve-styled art adds a playful element to Pulver's text, creating books that are "brightly colored, boldly labeled, and packed with personality," asserted Gloria Koster in her *School Library Journal* review of *Nouns and Verbs Have a Field Day.* "Although the emphasis is on silliness," wrote *Booklist* critic Kay Weisman, the same book "makes [its] . . . point about the parts of speech," and a *Kirkus Reviews* writer called *Silent Letters Loud and Clear* "so clever and fun that both teachers and students alike will be enthralled." *Happy Endings* "tells a classroom story with wit, attitude, and pizzazz," according to *Booklist* reviewer Carolyn Phelan, and a second *Kirkus Reviews* writer deemed Reed's colorful illustrations "as quirky and colorful as ever." "Pulver has outdone herself in this ingenious take on learning," concluded yet another *Kirkus Reviewer* critic commenting on *Punctuation Takes a Vacation,* and in *Publishers Weekly* a contributor maintained that the volume "manages to teach a good deal about punctuation. . . . between the verbal shenanigans and the eye-popping illustrations."

Created for holiday-season story hours, *Christmas for a Kitten* and *Christmas Kitten, Home at Last* pair Pulver's quiet stories about a stray kitten's meeting with Santa Claus with what a *Kirkus Reviews* writer described as "glowing" paintings by artist Layne Johnson. In the latter book, after Santa is discovered to be allergic to cats, he and Mrs. Claus attempt to find a new home for Cookie, a tiny kitten. Characterizing Pulver's text as "chatty in tone," a *Kirkus Reviews* writer praised *Christmas Kitten, Home at Last* for featuring "dramatic oil paintings [which] have a striking impact." In *School Library Journal* Linda Israelson dubbed the same picture book as "a sweet . . . read-aloud for the cat-loving crowd."

Pulver once told *SATA:* "I have always enjoyed writing and reading. As a child, I was shy about speaking and relied on writing to express what I knew and felt. I think I unwittingly served an apprenticeship in writing for children when I studied journalism in graduate school, then short story writing. Both forms require economy of language and respect for every word.

"My appreciation of children's books deepened when my own children were born. I remember carrying my newborn infant daughter into a children's bookstore in 1978 and being swept off my feet by the beautiful language and extraordinary art. Reading to my two children from their earliest days gave me a profound appreciation of the impact of literature on children and families. Sharing books with my bright, language-loving daughter has been a joy. Reading to my son, who is handicapped but also bright and language-loving in his own way, has been a salvation. It has brought us precious moments of calm and touchstones for moments of recognition and laughter.

"It came as a happy surprise when I found that I could write and sometimes publish stories for children. . . . My goal is to write well enough to move people and offer them a good story to share. I would like to give back to children's literature the kind of gifts I have received from it."

Biographical and Critical Sources

PERIODICALS

Booklist, June 15, 1992, Stephanie Zvirin, review of *Nobody's Mother Is in Second Grade,* p. 1851; March 1, 1994, Julie Cosaro, review of *Mrs. Toggle's Beautiful Blue Shoe,* p. 1270; January 1, 1995, Ilene Cooper, review of *Homer and the House Next Door,* p. 826; September 1, 1997, Helen Rosenberg, review of *Alicia's Tutu,* p. 134; January 1, 2000, Susan Dove Lempke, review of *Way to Go, Alex!,* p. 936; February 15, 2000, Ilene Cooper, review of *Axle Annie,* p. 1120; September 15, 2003, Ilene Cooper, review of *Christmas for a Kitten,* p. 248; May 1, 2005, Ilene Cooper, review of *Author Day for Room 3T,* p. 1592; Novem-

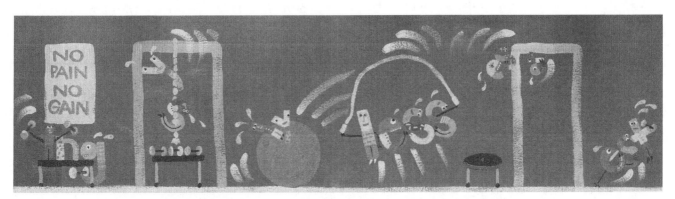

Grammar continues to serve as fodder for the collaborative Pulver and Reed in **Happy Endings: A Story about Suffixes.** (Illustration copyright © 2011 by Lynn Rowe Reed. Reproduced by permission of Holiday House.)

ber 1, 2005, Julie Cummins, review of *Axle Annie and the Speed Grump,* p. 54; April 1, 2006, Kay Weisman, review of *Nouns and Verbs Have a Field Day,* p. 49; September 1, 2009, Shelle Rosenfeld, review of *Never Say Boo!,* p. 100; October 15, 2010, Randall Enos, review of *Christmas Kitten, Home at Last,* p. 56; November 15, 2010, Michael Cart, review of *Thank You, Miss Doover,* p. 51; April 15, 2011, Carolyn Phelan, review of *Happy Endings: A Story about Suffixes,* p. 60.

Horn Book, May-June, 2003, Peter D. Sieruta, review of *Punctuation Takes a Vacation,* p. 335; May-June, 2006, Vicky Smith, review of *Nouns and Verbs Have a Field Day,* p. 299; May-June, 2008, Kitty Flynn, review of *Silent Letters Loud and Clear,* p. 298; March-April, 2011, L. Robin Smith, review of *Happy Endings,* p. 105.

Kirkus Reviews, August 15, 1991, review of *Mrs. Toggle and the Dinosaur;* July 15, 1992, review of *Nobody's Mother Is in Second Grade;* March 15, 1994, review of *Mrs. Toggle's Beautiful Blue Shoe,* p. 402; August 1, 1999, review of *Axle Annie,* p. 1230; February 15, 2003, review of *Punctuation Takes a Vacation,* p. 315; November 1, 2003, review of *Christmas for a Kitten,* p. 1319; May 1, 2005, review of *Author Day for Room 3T,* p. 544; August 15, 2005, review of *Axle Annie and the Speed Grump,* p. 920; April 15, 2008, review of *Silent Letters Loud and Clear;* July 15, 2009, review of *Never Say Boo!;* September 1, 2010, reviews of *Thank You, Miss Doover* and *Christmas Kitten, Home at Last;* February 15, 2011, review of *Happy Endings.*

Publishers Weekly, March 30, 1990, review of *Mrs. Toggle's Zipper,* p. 60; August 24, 1992, review of *Nobody's Mother Is in Second Grade,* p. 79; September 19, 1994, review of *Homer and the House Next Door,* p. 69; August 23, 1999, review of *Axle Annie,* p. 58; January 20, 2003, review of *Punctuation Takes a Vacation,* p. 82.

School Library Journal, May, 1990, Patricia Pearl, review of *Mrs. Toggle's Zipper,* p. 90; June, 1991, Lisa Dennis, review of *The Holiday Handwriting School,* p. 88; November, 1991, Marie Orlando, review of *Mrs. Toggle and the Dinosaur,* p. 106; January, 1993, Virginia E. Jeschelnig, review of *Nobody's Mother Is in Second Grade,* p. 84; May, 1994, Joyce Richards, review of *Mrs. Toggle's Beautiful Blue Shoe,* p. 103; February, 1995, Margaret C. Howell, review of *Homer and the House Next Door,* p. 79; October, 1997, Amy Kellman, review of *Alicia's Tutu,* p. 108; October, 1999, Kathy Piehl, review of *Axle Annie,* p. 123; November, 1999, Christine A. Moesch, review of *Way to Go, Alex!,* p. 128; October, 2003, Eva Mitnick, review of *Christmas for a Kitten,* p. 67; April, 2005, Marian Creamer, review of *Author Day for Room 3T,* p. 110; December, 2005, Susan Weitz, review of *Axle Annie and the Speed Grump,* p. 120; March, 2006, Gloria Koster, review of *Nouns and Verbs Have a Field Day,* p. 200; June, 2008, Lynne Mattern, review of *Silent Letters Loud and Clear,* p. 113; August, 2009, Kristine M. Casper, review of *Never Say Boo!,* p. 83; October, 2010, Linda Israelson, reviews of *Christmas Kitten, Home at Last,* p. 75, and *Thank You, Miss Doover,* p. 92; March, 2011, Mary Hazelton, review of *Happy Endings,* p. 132.

ONLINE

Robin Pulver Home Page, http://www.robinpulver.com (August 1, 2012).*

*　　*　　*

PYRON, Bobbie

Personal

Born in Hollywood, FL; married Todd Blackley; children: three stepchildren. *Education:* College degrees (psychology and anthropology); M.L.S. *Hobbies and other interests:* Dogs, travel, biking, hiking, cross-country skiing.

Addresses

Home—Park City, UT. *Agent*—Alyssa Eisner Henkin, Trident Media, 41 Madison Ave., 36th Fl., New York, NY 10010. *E-mail*—bobbiepyron@gmail.com.

Career

Author and librarian. Worked variously as a dog trainer, gladiola harvester, and wilderness education instructor; Park City Library, Park City, UT, librarian for twenty-five years.

Member

Dog Writers Association of America.

Writings

The Ring, WestSide Books (Lodi, NJ), 2009.
A Dog's Way Home, Katherine Tegen Books (New York, NY), 2011.
The Dogs of Winter, Arthur A. Levine (New York, NY), 2012.

Sidelights

Utah-based writer Bobbie Pyron has always loved books and reading, and she has translated this love into a long and rewarding career as a children's librarian. Over the years, Pyron had ample opportunity to read books and gauge the response of young readers, and she draws on this experience in crafting her own novels, which included *The Ring, A Dog's Way Home,* and *The Dogs of Winter.* Based on a true story, *The Dogs of Winter* reflects its author's love of dogs in a story of a Russian orphan who survives a harsh winter on the streets of Moscow with the help of a pack of wild dogs.

Capturing the close relationship between a dog and its human companion, *A Dog's Way Home* introduces a Sheltland sheepdog named Tam and Abby Whistler, who cares for Tam. When girl and dog are separated following an automobile accident in which Tam is left behind in the mountains of North Carolina, eleven-year-old Abby is broken-hearted, not knowing that her beloved dog is alive and valiantly attempting the 400-mile journey back to the place he knows as home.

"A heartwarming story filled with suspense," *A Dog's Way Home* "will keep animal lovers turning pages," according to *Voice of Youth Advocates* critic Lona Trulove. Narrated in turn by Abby and the determined Tam, Pyron's novel "offers a fresh and inspired tale," according to Erin Anderson in *Booklist,* and a *Publishers Weekly* critic praised *A Dog's Way Home* as "an inspiring portrayal of devotion and survival against all odds." "Fans of the 'Lassie' stories and *The Incredible Journey* by Sheila Burnford . . . will lose themselves in this harrowing adventure," predicted a *Kirkus Reviews* writer, and in *School Library Journal* Tina Martin wrote that Pyron's "subject matter and page-turning intensity will hood animal animal lovers, including reluctant readers."

A fifteen year old is caught in an escalating cycle of violence in *The Ring,* Pyron's first novel for young adults. To self-medicate her feelings of insecurity and sorrow, Mardie turns to alcohol, drugs, and stealing and eventually lands up in the hands of the police. Fortunately her stepmother encourages the teen to find an outlet in physical activity, and the members of a female boxing group may provide Mardie with the lifeline she needs while the challenges of athletic competition fuel her self-confidence.

Featuring "training details" that "feel authentic," according to *Booklist* contributor Daniel Kraus, *The Ring* is a good choice for "reluctant readers in search of a longer page count." "Mardie's character development . . . will hook readers," wrote a *Publishers Weekly,* adding that the author "does an admirable job of conveying teenage troubles," while in *School Library Journal* Richard Luzer praised the "smart, sassy narration" that propels Pyron's story in *The Ring.*

"I was a painfully shy child growing up," Pyron recalled to *SATA,* "and books and dogs became my best friends. Although I (mostly) outgrew my shyness, dogs and books are still the great passions in my life. I'm very lucky to have found two professions—librarianship and being an author—that allow me to translate those loves into something I can share with other people. I write because I love to read, and I read because I want to experience the world in all its many wonderments as much as I can. I may not always write books about dogs, but I hope I will always write books that readers hold to their hearts when they've finished the last page and say, 'Oh, I loved that book!'"

Biographical and Critical Sources

PERIODICALS

Booklist, October 15, 2009, Daniel Kraus, review of *The Ring,* p. 63; February 15, 2011, Erin Anderson, review of *A Dog's Way Home,* p. 73.

Kirkus Reviews, January 15, 2011, review of *A Dog's Way Home.*

Publishers Weekly, October 5, 2009, review of *The Ring,* p. 52; January 31, 2011, review of *A Dog's Way Home,* p. 50.

School Library Journal, January, 2010, Richard Luzer, review of *The Ring,* p. 112; April, 2011, Tina Martin, review of *A Dog's Way Home,* p. 182.

Voice of Youth Advocates, April, 2011, Lona Trulove, review of *A Dog's Way Home,* p. 67.

ONLINE

Bobbie Pyron Home Page, http://www.bobbiepyron.com (August 1, 2012).

Bobbie Pyron Web log, http://bobbiepyron.blogspot.com (August 1, 2012).

Cover of Bobbie Pyron's A Dog's Way Home, *featuring cover art by* **Wayne McLoughlin.** (Jacket illustration © 2011 by Wayne McLoughlin. Reproduced by permission of HarperCollins Children's Books, a division of HarperCollins Publishers.)

Q-R

QUATTLEBAUM, Mary 1958-

Personal

Born May 2, 1958, in Bryan, TX; daughter of Con (an operations analyst) and Helen (a school nurse) Quattlebaum; married Christopher David (a chief technical officer and director of information systems), September 24, 1988; children: Christy. *Education:* College of William and Mary, B.A. (high honors), 1980; Georgetown University, M.A., 1986. *Politics:* "Independent." *Religion:* Roman Catholic. *Hobbies and other interests:* Travel, juggling, playing harmonica, Greyhound buses, local history, wildlife gardening.

Addresses

Home—Washington, DC. *E-mail*—mary@maryquattlebaum.com.

Career

Writer, editor, and teacher. Children's National Medical Center, Washington, DC, medical writer/editor, 1986-88; Arts Project Renaissance, Washington, DC, part-time director of creative-writing program for older adults, 1986-98; Georgetown University School for Summer and Continuing Education, Washington, DC, writing instructor, 1986-2002; freelance writer and editor, 1989—. Teacher at Writer's Center, Bethesda, MD; Maryland Writer's Center; and Vermont College M.F.A. program in writing for children and young adults.

Member

Society of Children's Book Writers and Illustrators, Women's National Book Association, Authors Guild, Children's Book Guild of Washington.

Awards, Honors

Marguerite de Angeli Prize, and Best Book selection, *Parenting* magazine, both 1994, both for *Jackson Jones and the Puddle of Thorns;* Judy Blume novel-in-

Mary Quattlebaum (Photograph by Mark Darling. Reproduced by permission.)

progress grant, Society of Children's Book Writers and Illustrators, 1991; creative-writing fellowships, District of Columbia Commission on the Arts and Humanities, 1994, 1999, 2001; Sugarman Award for Children's Literature, 1998, for *The Magic Squad and the Dog of Great Potential;* American Bookseller Association Kids' Pick of the List choice, 1999, for *Aunt CeeCee, Aunt Belle, and Mama's Surprise;* Best Picture Book Award finalist, Texas Institute of Letters, 2004, for *Family Reunion* illustrated by Andrea Shine; Notable Social Studies Trade Book designation, Children's Book Council/ National Council for the Social Studies, 2004, for *Jackson Jones and Mission Greentop;* Bank Street School of Education Best Book selection, 2006, for *Sparks Fly High;* gold and bronze medals for children's book reviews, Parenting Publications of America; NAPPA Gold Award and Mom's Choice Gold Award, both 2011, and SIBA Best Children's Book selection, 2012, all for *Jo MacDonald Saw a Pond* illustrated by Laura J. Bryant; books included on many state children's choice lists.

Writings

MIDDLE-GRADE NOVELS

Jackson Jones and the Puddle of Thorns, illustrated by Melodye Rosales, Delacorte (New York, NY), 1994.

Jazz, Pizzazz, and the Silver Threads, illustrated by Robin Oz, Delacorte (New York, NY), 1996.

The Magic Squad and the Dog of Great Potential, illustrated by Frank Remkiewicz, Delacorte (New York, NY), 1997.

Grover G. Graham and Me, Delacorte (New York, NY), 2001.

Jackson Jones and Mission Greentop, Delacorte (New York, NY), 2004.

Jackson Jones and the Curse of the Outlaw Rose, Delacorte (New York, NY), 2006.

PICTURE BOOKS

In the Beginning, illustrated by Bryn Barnard, Time-Life Books (New York, NY), 1995.

Jesus and the Children, illustrated by Bill Farnsworth, Time-Life Books (New York, NY), 1995.

A Year on My Street, illustrated by Cat Bowman Smith, Delacorte (New York, NY), 1996.

Underground Train, illustrated by Cat Bowman Smith, Doubleday (New York, NY), 1997.

Aunt CeeCee, Aunt Belle, and Mama's Surprise, illustrated by Michael Chesworth, Doubleday (New York, NY), 1999.

The Shine Man, illustrated by Tim Ladwig, Eerdmans Books for Young Readers (Grand Rapids, MI), 2001.

Family Reunion, illustrated by Andrea Shine, Eerdmans Books for Young Readers (Grand Rapids, MI), 2004.

Winter Friends, illustrated by Hiroe Nakata, Doubleday (New York, NY), 2005.

(Reteller) *Sparks Fly High: The Legend of Dancing Point,* illustrated by Leonid Gore, Farrar, Straus & Giroux (New York, NY), 2006.

Jo MacDonald Saw a Pond, illustrated by Laura J. Bryant, Dawn Publications (Nevada City, CA), 2011.

Pirate vs. Pirate: The Terrific Tale of a Big, Blustery Maritime Match, illustrated by Alexandra Boiger, Disney Hyperion Books (New York, NY), 2011.

The Hungry Ghost of Rue Orleans, illustrated by Patricia Castelao, Random House (New York, NY), 2011.

Jo MacDonald Had a Garden, illustrated by Laura J. Bryant, Dawn Publications (Nevada City, CA), 2012.

OTHER

Contributor of numerous stories and poems to children's magazines, including *Babybug, Boys' Life, Children's Digest, Cricket, Ladybug,* and *Spider,* and to literary magazines for adults, including *Formalist, Gettysburg Review,* and *Poet Lore.* Contributor of articles and reviews to *Washington Post,* 1995—. Reviewer of children's books, 1986—, and columnist, 1997—, for *Washington Parent.*

Sidelights

Mary Quattlebaum is the author of picture books for children as well as novels for middle-grade readers. A frequent contributor to the *Washington Post* and *Washington Parent,* Quattlebaum also teaches courses in writing books for children at Vermont College of Fine Arts' M.F.A. program in Writing for Children and Young Adults. She writes children's books on a wide variety of topics, from a young girl's experience on riding the subway in Washington, DC, in *Underground Train* to a story about a long-time foster child who becomes attached to a foster baby living with the same family in *Grover Graham and Me.* "Ideas are all around," commented Quattlebaum on her home page. "For me, they come from a hodge-podge of experiences."

"My first memory is of my dad reciting nursery rhymes right before bedtime," Quattlebaum recalled on the Children's Book Guild Web site. Since childhood, she added, "I've been fascinated with sounds and try to bring a sense of different rhythms and voices to my poems and books for children." The oldest child in a family of seven children, she often read aloud to her younger siblings and would make up stories and plays for them to perform. It was not until she began working as a medical writer for Children's National Medical Center, however, that Quattlebaum seriously considered writing her stories down. "While there," she recalled in an interview on the Eerdmans Books for Young Readers Web site, "my husband (who had been a professional magician as a kid) and I started a volunteer project called Magic Words. Once a week we would visit one or two of the hospitalized kids and, through magic and poetry, encourage them to write their own stories and poems. What a range of emotions their work expressed—courage, curiosity, anger, fear, boredom, tenderness, love! Their example was truly inspiring and encouraged me to try writing for an audience of children."

"I grew up with three brothers, three sisters, and lots of pets, and often draw upon my childhood adventures (and misadventures) in my writing," the author once recalled. "For example, the warm and wacky family in

Aunt CeeCee, Aunt Belle, and Mama's Surprise is a lot like my own family. The hamster in *Jazz, Pizzazz, and the Silver Threads* and the big, goofy dog in *The Magic Squad and the Dog of Great Potential* are based on real-life pets."

"A strong sense of place is also very important to my work," Quattlebaum noted. "The poems in *A Year on My Street* focus on images and sounds from my neighborhood in Washington, DC. There's a sax-playing man, a jump-roping girl, and an old cat who likes to be scratched. The setting for my first book, *Jackson Jones and the Puddle of Thorns,* is a plot in a city community garden, similar to my own, which started fifty years ago as a Victory Garden to grow food during World War II. Like my main character Jackson, I often feel my most abundant crop is weeds! And the country setting and sweet gum trees of *Grover G. Graham and Me* were inspired by my childhood in rural Virginia, whereas *Sparks Fly High: The Legend of Dancing Point* drew upon my college years and time spent working in Colonial Williamsburg, Virginia." My "Jo MacDonald"

Cover of Quattlebaum's middle-grade novel Jazz, Pizzazz, and the Silver Threads, *featuring an illustration by Robin Oz.* (Jacket illustration © 1996 by Delacorte Books for Young Readers. Reproduced by permission of Random House Children's Books, a division of Random House, Inc.)

books draw upon my love of the natural world, nurtured by my father, who is the model for the title character's grandfather."

Jackson Jones and the Puddle of Thorns is a humorous story about a ten-year-old boy who wants a basketball for his birthday but gets instead a plot in the community garden. The resourceful lad decides to grow flowers in his garden, sell them, and in this way raise the money he will need to buy himself a basketball. Unfortunately, Jackson does not find flower-growing as easy as it appears, and the teasing he gets from "Blood" Green, the neighborhood bully, a fight with best friend Reuben over a rosebush, and the unexpected pleasure he gets from gardening further complicate Jackson's money-making scheme. "A host of colorful characters and their lively banter keep the bloom on these pages," remarked a *Publishers Weekly* contributor in a favorable review of *Jackson Jones and the Puddle of Thorns.*

Several reviewers of *Jackson Jones and the Puddle of Thorns* singled out Quattlebaum's array of secondary characters, noting her realistic rendering of personal speech patterns. The novel's cast was described as one comprised of "distinctive and dignified individuals" by a reviewer for *Bulletin of the Center for Children's Books.* The young narrator's "humorous, street-smart style" draws in readers immediately, according to a *Publishers Weekly* critic, and "the cozy, apparently multi-ethnic apartment building makes for a lively urban milieu," according to a reviewer for the *Bulletin of the Center for Children's Books.*

In a sequel, *Jackson Jones and Mission Greentop,* the enthusiastic ten year old learns that a land developer plans to build an apartment complex at the community garden where he grows roses and zucchini amid the weeds. Undaunted, Jackson uses his wits to prevent a corporate takeover and meet another challenge from nemesis "Blood" Green along the way. "Jackson's way of looking at life is original and appealing," observed *School Library Journal* contributor Edith Ching. According to *Horn Book* reviewer Susan Dove Lempke, "Quattlebaum's talent for depicting a lively, diverse neighborhood and funny interchanges between kids remains strong," and a *Kirkus Reviews* critic wrote that the author "has created a warm neighborhood with a good-hearted boy at its center."

Bad luck follows Jackson and Reuben after they steal a rose clipping from an abandoned cemetery in *Jackson Jones and the Curse of the Outlaw Rose,* "a well-written, fast-paced adventure," according to Jennifer Cogan in *School Library Journal.* "With *Outlaw Rose,* I wanted to play with the conventions of the ghost story," Quattlebaum explained on her home page. "Rather than an old house, this ghost haunts an antique rosebush. Because this ghost doesn't moan and rattle chains in stereotypical fashion, Jackson is slow to realize that he is, indeed, dealing with a ghost, which hopefully makes for some funny moments in the book."

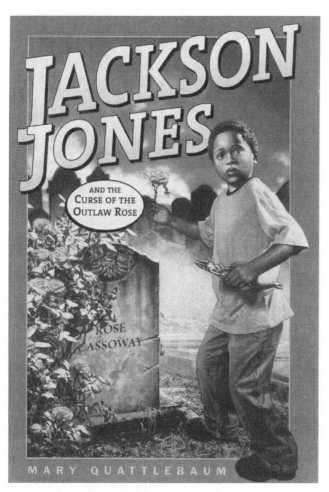

Cover of Quattlebaum's middle-grade mystery Jackson Jones and the Curse of the Outlaw Rose, *featuring artwork by Patrick Faricy.* (Jacket illustration copyright © 2006 by Delacorte Books for Young Readers. Reproduced by permission of Random House Children's Books, a division of Random House, Inc.)

The Shine Man: A Christmas Story is based on Quattlebaum family lore and takes place in 1932, just three years after the start of the Great Depression. Times are hard, but a poor shoeshine man still finds it in his heart to give a child his cap, gloves, and a toy angel made from empty wooden spools. In the process of shining the child's shoes, the man discovers the youngster's true identity and becomes an angel himself. "With a light touch, Quattlebaum leaves the deeper meaning of the story to the reader's imagination," wrote a contributor to *School Library Journal,* and a *Publishers Weekly* reviewer deemed *The Shine Man* a "lyrical, mystical tale."

A novel for middle graders, *Grover G. Graham and Me* centers on Ben Watson, a young boy who has lived in several foster homes. Over the years, Ben has hardened himself to leaving his various foster parents behind. At age eleven, he lands in a foster home where he cannot help but become attached to the family, especially to Grover G. Graham, an infant whose birth mother is trying to regain custody of him. Fearing for Grover's well being and convinced that he can care for the infant better than his teenaged mom can, Ben makes a rash decision and takes Grover along for the ride. Reviewing

Grover G. Graham and Me in *Horn Book,* Kitty Flynn remarked that "Quattlebaum pulls off this unlikely pairing with restraint and without resorting to sentimentality" in a story that "build[s] . . . naturally to a heartbreaking climax." A *Kirkus Reviews* contributor commented that, "as the tension skillfully builds, Quattlebaum ratchets up the stakes, thrusting her sympathetic but wrongheaded protagonist in a position where he could lose everything, finally delivering a credible, emotionally satisfying ending that will have readers reaching for their hankies."

In *Why Sparks Fly High* Quattlebaum retells a Virginia folktale about Colonel Lightfoot, a skillful but vain dancer, and the devil who challenges him to a contest for his stretch of land along the James River. "I discovered the tale . . . in a book of Williamsburg ghost stories and loved the idea of opponents fighting not with fists but with fancy footwork," Quattlebaum recalled in an interview on the Farrar, Straus & Giroux Web site. *Horn Book* reviewer Joanna Rudge Long called *Why Sparks Fly High* "witty and nimbly paced," and in *Booklist* Gillian Engberg praised the author's "folksy words, which have all the infectious rhythm of a country dance."

Quattlebaum updates a traditional nursery song with an eye toward nature in *Jo MacDonald Saw a Pond* and *Jo MacDonald Had a Garden,* companion picture books that are illustrated by Laura J. Bryant. In *Jo MacDonald Saw a Pond* a girl named Jo is the granddaughter of the original "Old MacDonald" of the perennial favorite. During a visit to Old MacDonald's farm, Jo discovers a serene pond and describes this tiny ecosystem in terms of the frogs, fish, dragonflies, and ducks that call it home, many of which are hiding in Bryant's watercolor illustrations. "Young children will chime in" and "enjoy the onomatopoeia," predicted Patricia Austin in her *Booklist* review of *Jo MacDonald Saw a Pond,* and a *Kirkus Reviews* writer noted that the artist's depiction of "softly colored . . . creatures echo Jo's rosy-cheeked childhood innocence."

Jo joins her cousin Mike at her grandfather's idyllic country home in *Jo MacDonald Had a Garden,* and here the children point out such garden helpers as earthworms, bumblebees, birds, and even toads while also illustrating the steps of building a garden by tilling, planting, watering, and harvesting. Predicting that Quattlebaum's story will be "a popular spring and garden story-time choice," a *Kirkus Reviews* writer added that *Jo MacDonald Had a Garden* allows young children to join Jo and Mike and "tend their own imaginary gardens."

Quattlebaum moves from the quiet of the country to the splash and roar of the high seas in *Pirate vs. Pirate: The Terrific Tale of a Big, Blustery Maritime Match.* Illustrated by Alexandra Boiger, this animated picture book focuses on two pirates who are engaged in a test of strength: which pirate is the baddest of the bad? Bad Bart and Mean Mo decide to tussle for that title by competing to see who can throw cannonballs the farthest, win at arm-wrestling, chew through the toughest sea biscuits, and swim alongside a shark and live to tell about it. The final contest—seeing who has amassed the most treasure—proves to be the key to the winner in a story that contains "adventure aplenty, with a little romance to boot," according to *Booklist* critic Thom Barthelmess. A *Publishers Weekly* contributor praised *Pirate vs. Pirate,* calling it "an all-around winner" that is enlivened by Boiger's "extravagant" illustrations full of "billowy curves."

An historic Louisiana city is the setting for Quattlebaum's story in *The Hungry Ghost of Rue Orleans,* and the tale is given additional atmosphere by the animation-style illustrations of Spanish-based artist Patricia Castelao. In the story, a ghost named Fred has the run of a spacious mansion in New Orleans until the building is purchased by new owners. Pierre, a talented restauranteur, and his daughter Marie quickly renovate the manse into an upscale restaurant, and when Fred attempts to frighten the diners away his antics are misinterpreted as the evening's entertainment. Fortunately, all ends well in a story Judith Constantinides recommended in *School Library Journal* "for both storytime and a one-on-one read." The "pacing and patterns" in Quattlebaum's jaunty narrative make *The Hungry Ghost of Rue Orleans* "ideal for letting the reading aloud roll," quipped *Booklist* critic Andrew Medlar, and in *Kirkus Reviews* a contributor cited Castelao's artwork for injecting the story with "an ethereal, quirky quality."

Quattlebaum's books for young readers allow the author to create a rhyming text that will gain in meaning when accompanied by engaging artwork. "Poems are these amazing little word packages," she told *Washington Post Book World* contributor Ron Charles. "In just a few lines you can play around with form, rhythm, rhyme, image and sound." In *Family Reunion,* a collection of fifteen poems, she looks at a family gathering through the eyes of ten-year-old Jodie. "The rhythms and rhymes in many of the selections lend an easy tone to the text," remarked *School Library Journal* contributor Shawn Brommer. Another book comprised of verse, *Winter Friends,* focuses on a young girl as she spends a snowy day playing outdoors. Here Quattlebaum "uses a variety of forms to good effect, including haiku and concrete poems," noted a *Kirkus Reviews* contributor of the book.

"Writing for young readers continues to be a wonderful challenge," Quattlebaum noted on her home page. "I try to listen carefully to the world (to others this might look like daydreaming) and bring a sense of different voices and rhythms to the page."

Biographical and Critical Sources

PERIODICALS

Booklist, February 1, 1997, Kay Weisman, review of *The Magic Squad and the Dog of Great Potential,* p. 942;

December 1, 1997, review of *Underground Train,* p. 643; September 1, 2001, Ilene Cooper, review of *The Shine Man: A Christmas Story,* p. 121; April 1, 2004, Ilene Cooper, review of *Family Reunion,* p. 1367; November 1, 2005, Ilene Cooper, review of *Winter Friends,* p. 41; October 15, 2006, Gillian Engberg, review of *Sparks Fly High: The Legend of Dancing Point,* p. 52; January 1, 2007, Hazel Rochman, review of *Jackson Jones and the Curse of the Outlaw Rose,* p. 81; March 1, 2011, Thom Barthelmess, review of *Pirate vs. Pirate: The Terrific Tale of a Big Blustery Maritime Match,* p. 66; September 15, 2011, Andrew Medlar, review of *The Hungry Ghost of Rue Orleans,* p. 70; November 1, 2011, Patricia Austin, review of *Jo MacDonald Saw a Pond,* p. 77.

Bulletin of the Center for Children's Books, March, 1994, review of *Jackson Jones and the Puddle of Thorns,* pp. 230-231; February, 1997, review of *The Magic Squad and the Dog of Great Potential,* p. 220; December, 1997, review of *Underground Train,* p. 137.

Children's Book Review Service, March, 1998, review of *Underground Train,* p. 87; August, 1999, review of *Aunt Ceecee, Aunt Belle, and Mama's Surprise,* p. 165.

Horn Book, May-June, 1997, Elizabeth S. Watson, review of *The Magic Squad and the Dog of Great Potential,* p. 327; fall, 1999, review of *Aunt Ceecee, Aunt Belle, and Mama's Surprise,* p. 624; January-February, 2002, Kitty Flynn, review of *Grover G. Graham and Me,* p. 83; September-October, 2004, Susan Dove Lempke, review of *Jackson Jones and Mission Greentop,* p. 595; September-October, 2006, Joanna Rudge Long, review of *Sparks Fly High,* p. 601.

Kirkus Reviews, November 1, 1997, review of *Underground Train,* p. 1648; May 1, 1999, review of *Aunt Ceecee, Aunt Belle, and Mama's Surprise,* p. 726; October 15, 2001, review of *Grover G. Graham and Me,* p. 1490; July 1, 2004, review of *Jackson Jones and Mission Greentop,* p. 636; September 15, 2005, review of *Winter Friends,* p. 1032; September 15, 2006, review of *Sparks Fly High,* p. 964; February 1, 2011, review of *Pirate vs. Pirate;* August 1, 2011, reviews of *The Hungry Ghost of Rue Orleans* and *Jo MacDonald Saw a Pond;* January 15, 2012, review of *Jo MacDonald Had a Garden.*

Publishers Weekly, November 29, 1993, review of *Jackson Jones and the Puddle of Thorns,* p. 66; November 24, 1997, review of *Underground Train,* p. 73; June 7, 1999, review of *Aunt Ceecee, Aunt Belle, and Mama's Surprise,* p. 82; September 24, 2001, review of *The Shine Man,* p. 53; February 23, 2004, review of *Family Reunion,* p. 74; November 28, 2005, review of *Winter Friends,* p. 50; January 17, 2011, review of *Pirate vs. Pirate,* p. 47.

School Library Journal, May, 1997, review of *The Magic Squad and the Dog of Great Potential,* p. 111; November, 1997, review of *Underground Train,* p. 97; July, 1999, review of *Aunt Ceecee, Aunt Belle, and Mama's Surprise,* p. 78; October, 2001, review of *The Shine Man,* p. 68; June, 2004, Shawn Brommer, review of *Family Reunion,* p. 132; November, 2004, Edith Ching, review of *Jackson Jones and Mission Greentop,* p. 116; October, 2005, Kara Schaff Dean, review of *Winter Friends,* p. 144; November, 2006,

Jennifer Cogan, review of *Jackson Jones and the Curse of the Outlaw Rose,* p. 108; December, 2006, Lucinda Snyder Whitehurst, review of *Sparks Fly High,* p. 127; March, 2011, Susan Weitz, review of *Pirate vs. Pirate,* p. 132; September, 2011, Judith Constantinides, review of *The Hungry Ghost of Rue Orleans,* p. 127; December, 2011, Anne Beier, review of *Jo MacDonald Saw a Pond,* p. 104.

Washington Post Book World, April 29, 2007, Ron Charles, interview with Quattlebaum, p. 9.

ONLINE

Childrens Book Guild Web site, http://www.childrensbook guild.org/ (December 1, 2007), "Mary Quattlebaum."

Eerdmans Books for Young Readers Web site, http://www. eerdmans.com/ (June 1, 2004), interview with Quattlebaum.

Farrar, Straus & Giroux Web site, http://www.fsgkidsbooks .com/ (December 1, 2007), "Q&A with Mary Quattlebaum."

Mary Quattlebaum Home Page, http://www.maryquattle baum.com (September 1, 2012).

*   *   *

RUIZ-FLORES, Lupe 1942-

Personal

Born 1942. *Education:* Master's degree (computer information management).

Addresses

Home—TX. *E-mail*—lrflores@luperuiz-flores.com

Career

Author. U.S. Department of Defense, aerospace engineering technician until late 1990s.

Member

Society of Children's Book Writers and Illustrators, Society of Latino & Hispanic Writers, Writers League of Texas.

Writings

Lupita's Papalote/El papalote de Lupita, illustrated by Pauline Rodriguez Howard, Spanish translation by Gabriela Baeza Ventura, Piñata Books (Houston, TX), 2002.

The Woodcutter's Gift/El regalo del lenador, illustrated by Elaine Jerome, Spanish translation by Gabriela Baeza, Piñata Books (Houston, TX), 2007.

The Battle of the Snow Cones/La guerra de las raspas, illustrated by Alisha Gambino, Spanish translation by Amira Plascencia, Piñata Books (Houston, TX), 2010.

Alicia's Fruity Drinks/Alicia's aguas frescas, illustrated by Laura Lacámara, Spanish translation by Gabriela Baeza Ventura, Piñata Books (Houston, TX), 2012.

Sidelights

Lupe Ruiz-Flores writes bilingual picture books for children who speak Spanish as a first language or are learning it as their second. Raised in Texas in a close-knit family of Mexican immigrants, Ruiz-Flores drew upon her own childhood when writing her first book, *Lupita's Papalote.* The story, illustrated by Pauline Rodriguez Howard, introduces a little girl who loves to watch the kites flying in her neighborhood and wishes that her family could afford to buy one for her. One day, her father shows her how to make a kite out of re-purposed materials, as he had done in his own youth, using the colored comics pages of a newspaper, some string, and lightweight bamboo sticks as the *papalote's* skeleton. Papa stays close by as little Lupita, initially a little nervous, feels the homemade kite soar up into the air for the first time. "The pictures [in *Lupita's Papalote*] show a warm father-daughter relationship and an engagingly stocky heroine with whom youngsters can identify," wrote Ann Welton in a *School Library Journal* review of Ruiz-Flores's debut.

Ruiz-Flores has also authored *The Woodcutter's Gift/El regalo del lenador* and *The Battle of the Snow Cones/La guerra de las raspas,* the latter which describes how the friendship between Elena and Alma dissolves in favor of a competition to see which girl can attract the most customers to her *raspa* (snow cone) stand. Both girls devise unique ways to lure customers, such as unusual flavors, colorful garlands of traditional Mexican paper flowers, and even live entertainment. The rush of orders intensifies to the point where both snow-cone machines break down at the same time and the cascading multi-colored slush becomes a giant ice sled in an unplanned party for all. "Learning that true friendship can be more important than success is an elemental concept," noted Rhonda Jeffers in her *School Library Journal* review of *The Battle of the Snow Cones..*

Delicious frozen treats also appear in Ruiz-Flores's bilingual picture book *Alicia's Fruity Drinks/Alicia's aguas frescas.* Here young Alicia attends a fair and tastes the delectable "fresh waters" flavored with fruit that are a culinary staple in the tropical regions of Latin America. Her mother shows her how aguas frescas can be made in their kitchen at home, and the fruity drinks are a hit when mother and daughter bring several pitchers of raspa to her soccer practice. "The dual English/ Spanish text is augmented by summery scenes in opaque, rich colors," wrote a *Kirkus Reviews* contributor in a positive appraisal of *Alicia's Fruity Drinks.*

Ruiz-Flores spent much of her adult life working in the defense industry as an aerospace engineering technician. She began writing in earnest after she retired and learned that the publishing industry was keen on acquir-

Lupe Ruiz-Flores describes a fanciful summertime world in her bilingual picture book The Battle of the Snow Cones/La guerra de las raspas, *featuring artwork by Alisha Gambino.* (Illustration copyright © 2010 by Alisha Gambino. Reproduced by permission of Arte Público Press-University of Houston.)

ing bilingual Spanish-English stories for young readers. In an interview with Cynthia Leitich Smith for *Cynsations* online, Ruiz-Flores said that the publication of *Lupita's Papalote* was a milestone. "Bringing the book to life gave me a real sense of accomplishment," she recalled, and at her first major bookstore event "my entire family of 10 brothers and sisters, plus nephews, nieces, aunts, uncles, my son, daughters, grandchildren . . . close to 100 friends and relatives" gathered to celebrate her achievement. "The characters . . . were named after my real brothers and sisters," Ruiz-Flores also told Smith. "My sisters cried when they heard the inspiration for the story because they remembered."

Biographical and Critical Sources

PERIODICALS

Kirkus Reviews, October 15, 2010, review of *The Battle of the Snow Cones/La guerra de las raspas,* May 1, 2012, review of *Alicia's Fruity Drinks/Las aguas frescas de Alicia.*

School Library Journal, November, 2002, Ann Welton, review of *Lupita's Papalote/El papalote de Lupita,* p. 153; March, 2011, Rhonda Jeffers, review of *The Battle of the Snow Cones,* p. 152.

ONLINE

Cynsations Web log, http://cynthialeitichsmith.blogspot. com/ (September 21, 2005), Cynthia Leitich Smith, interview with Ruiz-Flores.
Lupe Ruiz-Flores Home Page, http://www.luperuiz-flores. com (August 1, 2012).*

*   *   *

RYAN, Pam Muñoz 1951-

Personal

Born December 25, 1951, in Bakersfield, CA; married; children: two boys, two girls. *Education:* Bakersfield Junior College, associate's degree; San Diego State

University, B.A. (child development), M.Ed. (post-secondary education). *Hobbies and other interests:* Reading, traveling, walking on the beach.

Addresses

Home—San Diego County, CA. *Agent*—Kendra Marcus, BookStop Literary Agency, 67 Meadow View Rd., Orinda, CA 94563. *E-mail*—PMunozRyan@aol.com.

Career

Writer and educator. U.S. Naval Base, Camp Pendleton, CA, former Red Cross coordinator; former bilingual Head Start teacher in Escondido, CA; former director of early-childhood program.

Awards, Honors

Notable Book selection, American Library Association (ALA), 1999, and Notable Social Studies Trade Books for Young People selection, National Council for the Social Studies/Children's Book Council (NCSS/CBC), and Notable Book for a Global Society designation, International Reading Association (IRA), all for *Amelia and Eleanor Go for a Ride;* Jane Addams Children's Book Award, 2001, Pura Belpré Award for Narrative, Association for Library Service to Children/National Association to Promote Library and Information Services to Latinos and the Spanish-Speaking, 2002, ALA Top-Ten Best Books for Young Adults selection, and Américas Award Honor Book designation, Consortium of Latin American Studies Program, all for *Esperanza Rising;* California Young Reader Medal, and Willa Cather Award, both 1997, both for *Riding Freedom;* ALA Notable Book selection, 2001, for *Mice and Beans;* Robert Siebert Honor Book designation, ALA Notable Book designation, Parents Choice Gold Award, and Orbis Pictus Award, all 2002, and Jefferson Cup Honor selection, Virginia Library Association, and Notable Children's Book in the Language Arts, National Council of Teachers of English (NCTE) both 2003, all for *When Marian Sang;* Pura Belpré Honor Book designation, Tomás Rivera Mexican-American Children's Book Award, Notable Book for a Global Society designation, ALA Notable Book designation, Schneider Family Book Award, NCTE Notable Children's Book in the Language Arts selection, and New York Public Library Top-Ten Titles for Reading and Sharing selection, all 2006, all for *Becoming Naomi León;* Human and Civil Rights Award, National Education Association, 2007; Willa Cather Award finalist, 2007, for *Paint the Wind;* National Parenting Publications Gold Award, PEN USA Award, *Boston Globe/Horn Book* Honor Book selection, Notable Book for a Global Society designation, White Raven Outstanding International Book selection, Carla Cohen Free Speech Award, NCTE Notable Children's Book in the Language Arts selection, NCSS/CBC Notable Social Studies Trade Books for Young People selection, Pura Belpré Award, and Américas Award, all 2011, all for *The Dreamer.*

Pam Muñoz Ryan (Reproduced by permission of Scholastic, Inc.)

Writings

FOR CHILDREN

One Hundred Is a Family, illustrated by Benrei Huang, Hyperion (New York, NY), 1994.

The Flag We Love, illustrated by Ralph Masiello, Charlesbridge (Watertown, MA), 1996, tenth anniversary edition, 2006.

A Pinky Is a Baby Mouse, and Other Baby Animal Names, illustrated by Diane de Groat, Hyperion (New York, NY), 1997.

Armadillos Sleep in Dugouts, and Other Places Animals Live, illustrated by Diane de Groat, Hyperion (New York, NY), 1997.

California, Here We Come!, illustrated by Kay Salem, Charlesbridge (Watertown, MA), 1997.

Riding Freedom, illustrated by Brian Selznick, Scholastic (New York, NY), 1998.

Doug Counts Down, illustrated by Matthew C. Peters, Disney Press (New York, NY), 1998.

Disney's Doug's Treasure Hunt, created by Jim Jenkins, illustrated by Jumbo Pictures, Mouse Works (New York, NY), 1998.

Funnie Family Vacation, illustrated by William Presing and Tony Curanaj, Disney Press (New York, NY), 1999.

Amelia and Eleanor Go for a Ride, illustrated by Brian Selznick, Scholastic (New York, NY), 1999.

Hello, Ocean!, illustrated by Mark Astrella, Charlesbridge/Talewinds (Watertown, MA), 2001.

Mice and Beans, illustrated by Joe Cepeda, Scholastic (New York, NY), 2001.

When Marian Sang: The True Recital of Marian Anderson, illustrated by Brian Selznick, Scholastic (New York, NY), 2002.

Mud Is Cake, illustrated by David McPhail, Hyperion (New York, NY), 2002.

How Do You Raise a Raisin?, illustrated by Craig Brown, Charlesbridge (Watertown, MA), 2003.

A Box of Friends, illustrated by Mary Whyte, McGraw-Hill (New York, NY), 2003.

Nacho and Lolita, illustrated by Claudia Rueda, Scholastic (New York, NY), 2005.

There Was No Snow on Christmas Eve, illustrated by Dennis Nolan, Hyperion Books (New York, NY), 2005.

Our California, illustrated by Rafael López, Charlesbridge (Watertown, MA), 2008.

Cornelia and the Show-and-Tell Showdown, illustrated by Julia Denos, Scholastic (New York, NY), 2010.

The Dreamer, illustrated by Peter Sís, Scholastic (New York, NY), 2010.

Tony Baloney, illustrated by Edwin Fotheringham, Scholastic (New York, NY), 2011.

Also author of children's books *Netty, Netty Goes to School,* and *Netty Goes around the World,* all published in Japan. Contributor to anthologies *A Joyful Christmas: A Treasury of New and Classic Songs, Poems, and Stories for the Holiday,* edited by James Ransome, Holt (New York, NY), 2010, and *Because of Shoe and Other Dog Stories,* edited by Ann M. Martin, Holt, 2012.

Author's works have been translated into Spanish.

YOUNG-ADULT NOVELS

Esperanza Rising, Scholastic (New York, NY), 2000.
Becoming Naomi León, Scholastic (New York, NY), 2004.
Paint the Wind, Scholastic (New York, NY), 2007.

Adaptations

Several of Ryan's works have been adapted for audiobook. *Esperanza Rising* was adapted as a play by Lynne Alvarez and produced by Children's Theatre Company, Minneapolis, MN, 2006.

Sidelights

Pam Muñoz Ryan is the author of award-winning books for children and teens that include *Amelia and Eleanor Go for a Ride, Becoming Naomi León,* and *The Dreamer.* A number of Ryan's works draw upon her Hispanic heritage, among them the young-adult novel *Esperanza Rising* and the picture books *Our California* and *Nacho and Lolita.*

A native of California's San Joaquin Valley, Ryan was an avid reader and a frequent visitor to her local library by the time she moved to a new neighborhood the summer before fifth grade. "It was through books that I coped and fit in," she recalled on her home page. "I became what most people would consider an obsessive reader." Ryan did not try her hand at writing until she was working on her master's degree and a colleague wondered if she would coauthor a book for adults. "After I started I couldn't stop thinking about the possibility of writing my own stories," Ryan explained on her home page, "and one thing led to another."

Ryan's first book for a younger audience was published in 1994. *One Hundred Is a Family,* a counting book for children aged four to eight, depicts groups of one through ten and then continues on by stages of ten up to one hundred. The author's aim was to show the human family in all its permutations and illustrated how people are related by kinship, community, and heritage. According to *Booklist* contributor Annie Ayres, Ryan's text for *One Hundred Is a Family* is "comforting in that it presents and embraces a world in which every form of family is welcome."

Based on the stories of Ryan's Mexican-American family, *Mice and Beans* focuses on a warm-hearted grandmother's excited preparations for the birthday feast of her little granddaughter, Catalina. Rosa Maria is obsessed with ridding her casita of mice and tries to keep them away from the party food. The woman is also a bit absentminded and she forgets to fill Catalina's birthday piñata, the showpiece of the celebration. The colorful tissue-paper sculpture proves to be laden with candy and treats anyway when it is broken on feast day, and Rosa Maria ultimately discovers that the mice she tried to chase away were actually busy helping her. In *Booklist* reviewer Kelly Milner Halls wrote of *Mice and Beans* that "what makes it special is the quiet authenticity of the Hispanic characterizations."

Ryan embellishes an actual historical event in *Amelia and Eleanor Go for a Ride!,* a picture book featuring artwork by Brian Selznick. After a White House dinner in April of 1933, famed aviatrix Amelia Earhart piloted First Lady Eleanor Roosevelt, wife of newly elected President Franklin D. Roosevelt, up in her plane at a time when few aircraft could be seen in the sky. Roosevelt had taken some flying lessons but never earned a pilot's license, and Ryan's story concludes as the first lady chauffeurs Earhart—who would disappear somewhere over the Pacific Ocean a few years later—for a reciprocal drive in her new automobile. A reviewer for *Publishers Weekly* called *Amelia and Eleanor Go for a Ride!* "a brief but compelling slice from the lives of two determined, outspoken and passionate women," and *School Library Journal* critic Steven Engelfried noted that Ryan's "fictionalized tale is lively and compelling, and the courage and sense of adventure that these individuals shared will be evident." *Booklist* critic Ilene Cooper predicted of the same book that "children will get a sense of the importance of Earhart and Roosevelt to America's history in general, and women's history in particular."

Ryan and Selznick team up again for *When Marian Sang: The True Recital of Marian Anderson.* Here author and illustrator profile one of the most dramatic incidents of the U.S. civil-rights era: the day in 1939 when noted African-American vocalist Marian Anderson was prohibited from performing at Washington, DC's Constitution Hall and instead gave a free concert on the steps of the Lincoln Memorial. Hazel Rochman described the picture book as "lush," adding in *Booklist* that Ryan's "passionate words and [Selznick's] beautifully detailed sepia-tone pictures . . . present a true story that seems like a theatrical Cinderella tale." While noting that author and illustrator "indulge in a . . . mythification" of their subject, *Horn Book* reviewer Roger Sutton concluded that *When Marian Sang* features "an intimacy of tone that gives life to the legend" upon which it is based.

A host of honors, including the Pura Belpré Award and the Américas Award, were awarded to Ryan's *The Dreamer,* a fictional biography of celebrated Chilean poet Pablo Neruda. Born Neftalì Reyes in 1904, the sensitive and inventive Neruda often drew the ire of his autocratic father. With support from his loving stepmother and uncle, however, the young man learned to channel his concerns about indigenous peoples and the environment concerns into his writings. Illustrated by Peter Sís, *The Dreamer* "has all the feel of a classic, elegant and measured, but deeply rewarding and eminently readable," as Ian Chipman remarked in *Booklist.* Renee Steinberg noted in *School Library Journal* that "Ryan artfully meshes factual details with an absorbing story of a shy Chilean boy whose spirit develops and thrives despite his father's relentless negativity," while Joanna Rudge Long, writing in *Horn Book,* applauded "Ryan's perceptive reconstruction of the poet's early

*Our California **teams Ryan with illustrator Rafael López in a colorful ode to the popular and westernmost contiguous U.S. state.*** (Illustration copyright © 2008 by Rafael López. Reproduced by permission by Charlesbridge Publishing, Inc. Watertown, MA. All rights reserved.)

Ryan introduces a penguin with a difference in her picture book Tony Baloney, *featuring artwork by Edwin Fotheringham.* (Illustration copyright © 2011 by Edwin Fotheringham. Reproduced by permission of Scholastic, Inc.)

years" in *The Dreamer.* A contributor to *Kirkus Reviews* dubbed the award-winning picture-book biography "rich, resonant and enchanting."

Ryan presents a colorful tribute to her home state in *Our California,* featuring illustrations by Rafael López. Beginning in the coastal city of San Diego, the book takes readers on a tour of sites both well known (such as the metropolises of Los Angeles and San Francisco) and unfamiliar (such as the Channel Islands, a National Park that is home to unique flora and fauna, and the historic town of Coloma, the center of the California Gold Rush of 1849). "The text . . . gives a feel for the locale," Cooper noted in *Booklist,* and a writer in *Kirkus Reviews* described *Our California* as a "brilliant tickler for budding historians and travel bugs."

An energetic and imaginative penguin is the focus of *Tony Baloney,* a story illustrated by Edwin Fotheringham. Caught between a bossy older sister and irksome twin baby penguins, Tony grows frustrated with his older sibling when she forces him to be her pet kitty whenever they play house. Seeking respite in his special hiding spot, the young penguin takes solace in his relationship with his understanding stuffed toy, Dandelion. "The trials and tribulations of middle children get zesty, energetic treatment in this story," remarked Christine M. Heppermann in *Horn Book,* and a *Kirkus Reviews* contributor observed that *Tony Baloney* offers "scenes of realistically uneasy sibling détente." "Totally goofy, but totally fun," is how Daniel Kraus described Ryan's amusing story in *Booklist.*

Ryan turns to older readers in her historical novel *Riding Freedom,* which focuses on the African-American woman who came to be known as "One-Eyed Charley."

Charlotte Darkey Parkhurst is believed to be the first woman ever to cast a ballot in a federal election, although she did so by deception. Orphaned as a child in the mid-nineteenth century, Charlotte endured some bleak years at a New Hampshire orphanage where her only solace was helping out in the stables. She was forbidden to ride a horse because she was a girl and the orphanage authorities also prevented her from being adopted into a family in order that she remain on the grounds as a servant. In Ryan's story Parkhurst listens to another stable worker describe his flight from slavery to freedom. Inspired, she escapes by donning boys' clothing and uses her skill with horses to find a well-paying job as a stagecoach driver. As Ryan noted, the real-life Parkhurst retained her disguise as a man and was able to own property and even vote in an 1868 election in California. A *Publishers Weekly* critic praised *Riding Freedom* as "ebullient and tautly structured," adding that, "with a pacing that moves along at a gallop, this is a skillful execution of a fascinating historical tale." In *School Library Journal* Carol A. Edwards described *Riding Freedom* as "a compact and exciting story about real people who exemplify traits that readers admire."

Ryan's multi-award-winning young-adult novel *Esperanza Rising* is based on the life story of her own grandmother, who came to California from Mexico during

Cover of Ryan's award-winning young-adult novel Esperanza Rising, *featuring artwork by Joe Cepeda.* (Jacket illustration copyright © 2000 by Joe Cepeda. Reproduced by permission of Scholastic, Inc.)

the 1930s. Thirteen-year-old Esperanza Ortega enjoys a privileged life in Aguascalientes, Mexico, where her beloved father, a landowner, instills in her a deep appreciation for the land as part of their family heritage. Tragedy strikes when Señor Ortega is slain by robbers and the girl's step-uncles then try to force her mother into marrying one of them. After their home is destroyed by arson, mother and daughter flee north to California. Now refugees and with few of their possessions remaining, Esperanza and her mother must fend for themselves in a harsh and racist environment. Working as migrant laborers, they pick fruit for mere pennies and live in dire poverty in a rustic farmworker camp. When some workers attempt to form a union, the increasing tensions lead to violence and foster worries that they will be deported to Mexico as troublemakers. When Esperanza's mother becomes ill, the girl supports the family and ultimately earns enough money to pay for the trip to bring her beloved abuelita north.

Reviewing *Esperanza Rising*, *Reading Today* contributor Lynne T. Burke termed it a "passionate novel" that is "written with an uncommon understanding of the plight of Mexican farm workers," while *School Library Journal* critic Francisca Goldsmith described Ryan's novel as a "compelling story of immigration and assimilation, not only to a new country but also into a different social class." A reviewer for *Publishers Weekly* praised the "lyrical, fairy tale-like style" and commended the author for interweaving "subtle metaphors via Abuelita's pearls of wisdom." In *Booklist* Gillian Engberg asserted that "Ryan's lyrical novel manages the contradictory: [it tells] a story of migration and movement deeply rooted in the earth."

Becoming Naomi León introduces another resilient young heroine in Naomi Soledad León Outlaw. Living in a trailer park in Lemon Tree, California, with her great-grandmother and her disabled younger brother Owen, eleven-year-old Naomi feels burdened by both her name and her family's poverty. When her alcoholic mother, Skyla, resurfaces after seven years and wants to take her daughter to live with her and her boyfriend in Las Vegas, Naomi is confused. Ultimately, guardian Gran and the two children drive the trailer across the border into Mexico, hoping to find a way to stop Skyla's plan with the help of the children's father. "In true mythic tradition, Ryan . . . makes Naomi's search for her dad a search for identity, and both are exciting," wrote *Booklist* critic Hazel Rochman in a review of *Becoming Naomi León,* and a *Kirkus Reviews* writer praised the "potent, economic prose" that brings to life Ryan's "tender tale about family love and loyalty." In *Horn Book* Christine M. Heppermann noted that, "with its quirky characterizations and folksy atmosphere," *Becoming Naomi León* is an "engrossing family drama" with an "uniquely affecting emotional core."

Narrated in alternating third-person accounts of eleven-year-old Maya and a wild mare named Artemesia, *Paint the Wind* focuses on how a girl changes when she leaves her pampered life for time on a working ranch. Orphaned at age six, Maya has been catered to by her wealthy grandmother. When the woman has a stroke, the girl is sent to live with Great-Aunt Vi on Vi's Wyoming ranch. There, as Maya learns to know and love the herd of wild horses roaming near her new home, she also reconnects with the mother she scarcely knew. "Details surrounding the care and riding of horses are both authentic and copious," asserted a *Publishers Weekly* reviewer, the critic adding that the combination of girls and horses is a perennial favorite among preteens. According to *Booklist* critic Francesca Goldsmith, *Paint the Wind* features "lots of adventure . . . (both human and equine), and the pace never lags for an instant."

A versatile writer, Ryan notes that her inspiration comes from a variety of sources. "An idea for a book is like a confluence of rivers coming together in my mind," she stated in an interview on the Scholastic Web site. "I am inspired by what I read, events in my life, and subjects that intrigue me." Ryan also takes a practical approach to her craft, writing on her home page: "People frequently ask me, 'What is your motivation to write?' The answer is simple. I want the reader to turn the page."

Biographical and Critical Sources

PERIODICALS

Booklist, November 1, 1994, Annie Ayres, review of *One Hundred Is a Family,* p. 509; January 1, 1996, Carolyn Phelan, review of *The Flag We Love,* p. 841; January 1, 1998, Hazel Rochman, review of *Riding Freedom,* p. 814; October 15, 1999, Ilene Cooper, review of *Amelia and Eleanor Go for a Ride,* p. 447; December 1, 2000, Gillian Engberg, review of *Esperanza Rising,* p. 708; September 15, 2001, Kelly Milner Halls, review of *Mice and Beans,* p. 233; June 1, 2002, Lauren Peterson, review of *Mud Is Cake,* p. 1743; November 15, 2002, review of *When Marian Sang: The True Recital of Marian Anderson,* p. 799; July, 2003, GraceAnne A. DeCandido, review of *A Box of Friends,* p. 1898; August, 2003, Ellen Mandel, review of *How Do You Raise a Raisin?,* p. 1986; September 15, 2004, Hazel Rochman, review of *Becoming Naomi León,* p. 245; October 1, 2005, Jennifer Mattson, review of *Nacho and Lolita,* p. 66; October 15, 2005, Julie Cummins, review of *There Was No Snow on Christmas,* p. 60; November 15, 2007, Francisca Goldsmith, review of *Paint the Wind,* p. 44; December 15, 2007, Ilene Cooper, review of *Our California,* p. 48; February 1, 2010, Ian Chipman, review of *The Dreamer,* p. 44; February 1, 2011, Daniel Kraus, review of *Tony Baloney,* p. 83.

Horn Book, January, 2001, review of *Esperanza Rising,* p. 96; November-December, 2002, Roger Sutton, review of *When Marian Sang,* p. 780; September-October,

2004, Christine M. Heppermann, review of *Becoming Naomi León,* p. 598; March-April, 2010, Joanna Rudge Long, review of *The Dreamer,* p. 70; March-April, 2011, Christine M. Heppermann, review of *Tony Baloney,* p. 106.

Instructor, October, 2001, Alice Quiocho, review of *Esperanza Rising,* p. 18.

Journal of Adolescent & Adult Literacy, December, 2001, Tasha Tropp, review of *Esperanza Rising,* p. 334.

Kirkus Reviews, December 1, 1997, review of *Riding Freedom,* pp. 1778-1779; August 1, 2001, review of *Mice and Beans,* p. 1131; September 1, 2002, review of *When Marian Sang,* p. 1319; September 1, 2004, review of *Becoming Naomi León,* p. 873; October 1, 2005, review of *Nacho and Lolita,* p. 1088; August 1, 2007, review of *Paint the Wind;* December 15, 2007, review of *Our California;* March 15, 2010, review of *The Dreamer;* December 1, 2010, review of *Tony Baloney.*

Publishers Weekly, November 7, 1994, review of *One Hundred Is a Family,* p. 78; February 5, 1996, review of *The Flag We Love,* p. 88; February 2, 1998, review of *Riding Freedom,* p. 91; September 27, 1999, review of *Amelia and Eleanor Go for a Ride!,* p. 105; October 9, 2000, review of *Esperanza Rising,* p. 88; January 8, 2001, review of *Hello, Ocean!,* p. 65; September 13, 2004, review of *Becoming Naomi León,* p. 79; August 22, 2005, review of *Nacho and Lolita,* p. 63; August 20, 2007, review of *Paint the Wind,* p. 68; December 17, 2007, review of *Our California,* p. 50.

Reading Today, October, 2000, Lynne T. Burke, review of *Esperanza Rising,* p. 32.

School Library Journal, October, 1994, Christine A. Moesch, review of *One Hundred Is a Family,* p. 97; May,

1996, Eunice Weech, review of *The Flag We Love,* p. 108; July, 1997, Lisa Wu Stowe, review of *A Pinky Is a Baby Mouse, and Other Baby Animal Names,* p. 87; December, 1997, Patricia Manning, review of *Armadillos Sleep in Dugouts, and Other Places Animals Live,* p. 114; March, 1998, Carol A. Edwards, review of *Riding Freedom,* p. 218; September, 1999, Steven Engelfried, review of *Amelia and Eleanor Go for a Ride!,* p. 202; October, 2000, Francisca Goldsmith, review of *Esperanza Rising,* p. 171; May, 2001, Sally R. Dow, review of *Hello, Ocean!,* p. 133; October, 2001, Mary Elam, review of *Mice and Beans,* p. 130; May, 2002, Sheilah Kosco, review of *Mud Is Cake,* p. 126; November, 2002, Wendy Lukehart, review of *When Marian Sang,* p. 147; August, 2003, Dona Ratterree, review of *How Do You Raise a Raisin?,* p. 151; September, 2003, Kathleen Kelly MacMillan, review of *A Box of Friends,* p. 189; September, 2004, Sharon Morrison, review of *Becoming Naomi León,* p. 216; October, 2005, Rosalyn Pierini, review of *Nacho and Lolita,* p. 144; November, 2007, Ann Robinson, review of *Paint the Wind,* p. 136; June, 2008, Marian Drabkin, review of *Our California,* p. 130; April, 2010, Renee Steinberg, review of *The Dreamer,* p. 168; February, 2011, Julie R. Ranelli, review of *Tony Baloney,* p. 90.

ONLINE

Pam Muñoz Ryan Home Page, http://www.pammunozryan. com (July 15, 2012).

PaperTigers.org, http://www.papertigers.org/interviews/ (September, 2008), Aline Pereira, interview with Ryan.

Scholastic Web site, http://www.scholastic.com/ (March 15, 2006), interview with Ryan.*

S

SANDSTROM, Karen

Personal
Married; children: two daughters. *Education:* B.A.; Cleveland Institute of Art, (B.A.), illustration.

Addresses
Home—Cleveland, OH. *E-mail*—Karen.sandstrom@gmail.com.

Career
Illustrator. Worked as a writer, editor, and journalist for Northeast OH daily papers for twenty-five years; freelance illustrator. Volunteer at Medina Raptor Center.

Member
Northern Ohio Illustrators Society.

Illustrator
Sara Holbrook, *Weird? (Me, Too!): Let's Be Friends,* Wordsong (Honesdale, PA), 2010.
Sara Holbrook, *Zombies! Evacuate the School!,* Wordsong (Honesdale, PA), 2010.

Contributor to periodicals, including Cleveland, OH, *Plain Dealer* and *Pittsburgh Post-Gazette.*

Biographical and Critical Sources

PERIODICALS

Kirkus Reviews, July 1, 2010, review of *Zombies! Evacuate the School!*; March 1, 2011, review of *Weird? (Me, Too!): Let's Be Friends.*
Publishers Weekly, August 9, 2010, review of *Zombies!,* p. 50; February 14, 2011, review of *Weird? (Me, Too!),* p. 55.

School Library Journal, November, 2010, Shawn Brommer, review of *Zombies!,* p. 139; April, 2011, Lauralyn Persson, review of *Weird? (Me, Too!),* p. 192.

ONLINE

Karen Sandstrom Home Page, http://www.karensandstrom.com (August 1, 2012).
Karen Sandstrom Web log, http://www.karensantstrom.blogspot.com (August 1, 2012).*

*   *   *

SCHUTZ, Samantha 1978-

Personal
Born 1978, in New York, NY. *Education:* Skidmore College, B.A. (English).

Addresses
Home—Brooklyn, NY. *E-mail*—samanthaschutz@hotmail.com.

Career
Children's book editor and poet. Simon & Schuster Children's Books, New York, NY, editorial assistant; Penguin, New York, NY, currently senior editor.

Awards, Honors
Quick Pick for Reluctant Readers nomination, American Library Association, 2010, for *You Are Not Here.*

Writings

I Don't Want to Be Crazy, Scholastic (New York, NY), 2006.
You Are Not Here, Push (New York, NY), 2010.

Sidelights

Samantha Schutz became a published writer while working as an editor for a New York City publisher. In her first book, the memoir, *I Don't Want to Be Crazy*, Schutz uses the verse-novel format to capture her experience with anxiety disorder, while *You Are Not Here* uses the same creative format to describe the concerns of a teen dealing with the death of a beloved friend.

Schutz begins *I Don't Want to Be Crazy* at the point where she was heading off for her freshman year at college and new friends, new passions, and new experiences awaited, such a spending a semester in France. She recognized that she was leaving a lot behind, including the expectations of her parents and an unhealthy romantic relationship. Amid all these life changes, Schutz began to experience panic attacks, which hit unexpectedly and added to her growing insecurity in an ever-widening world. Noting that the author's memoir "ends without absolute closure," Jill Heritage Maza added in her *School Library Journal* review that *I Don't Want to Be Crazy* will give teens moving forward into adulthood an eye into one young woman's "overwhelming, seemingly never-ending, search for identity."

Schutz's teen years were touched by death and although that touch was relatively light—a friend of her friend

Cover of Samantha Schutz' young-adult novel **You Are Not Here**, *which was inspired by the author's memories of a friend's death during her teen years.* (Jacket illustration photograph copyright © 2009 by OGPhoto/ iStockphoto.com. Reproduced by permission of iStockphoto.com.)

died—it resonated with her and became and element in *You Are Not Here*. For Annaleah, the book's sixteen-year-old narrator, handsome basketball-playing boyfriend Brian is her entire world although their relationship has been a secret one. When Brian dies unexpectedly, Annaleah is left to reflect on what their relationship was and was not. Cycling down into self-imposed emotional isolation and depression, the young woman indulges in "endless self-examination and occasional self-pity," noted Michael Cart in his *Booklist* review. *You Are Not Here* "is skillfully written and successfully captures and enhances" Annaleah's inner world, Cart added, while *School Library Journal* critic Jill Heritage Maza suggested that Schutz creates a reader reaction that "echoes the feelings of [Annaleah's] . . . patiently skeptical friends." "Well-written," according to *Voice of Youth Advocates* contributor Paula Brehm-Heeger, *You Are Not Here* presents "a genuine tale of self-discovery," and a *Kirkus Reviews* writer asserted that, in "refreshingly spare lines," the novel addresses "tough relational issues . . . with aplomb."

Biographical and Critical Sources

PERIODICALS

Booklist, October 15, 2010, Michael Cart, review of *You Are Not Here,* p. 62.
Kirkus Reviews, October 1, 2010, review of *You Are Not Here.*
School Library Journal, January, 2007, Jill Heritage Maza, review of *I Don't Want to Be Crazy,* p. 155; February, 2011, Jill Heritage Maza, review of *You Are Not Here,* p. 118.
Voice of Youth Advocates, December, 2006, Amanda MacGregor, review of *I Don't Want to Be Crazy,* p. 460; December, 2010, Paula Brehm-Heeger, review of *You Are Not Here,* p. 460.

ONLINE

Samantha Schutz Home Page, http://samanthaschutz.net (August 1, 2012).
YA Review Network, http://yareview.net/ (April 6, 2011), Kerri Smith Majors, interview with Schutz.

* * *

SENISI, Ellen B. 1951-

Personal

Born May 18, 1951, in Little Falls, NY; daughter of William Martin (an electrical troubleshooter) and Elizabeth Anne (a teacher) Babinec; married John P. Senisi (an architect) August 25, 1973; children: Kate, Will, Steven. *Education:* State University of New York at Oswego, B.S. (education), 1974; State University of New York at Cortland, M.S. (curriculum and instruction), 1979; Boston University, C.A.G.S. (educational media and technology), 1987. *Hobbies and other interests:* Music, reading, travel.

Addresses

Home—Schenectady, NY; New York, NY. *E-mail*—ellen@ellensenisi.com.

Career

Author, photographer, and multimedia producer. Senisi Multimedia, New York, NY, and Schenectady, NY, cofounder with son Steven Senisi, 2010—; EdTEchLens, cofounder, 2012. Teacher in public and private elementary schools, 1974-79; curriculum editor, 1980-82.

Member

Society of Children's Book Writers and Illustrators, National Association of Photoshop Professionals, American Society of Picture Professionals, Picture Archive Council of America.

Awards, Honors

Educational Press Association Distinguished Achievement Award, 1993, for photo essay "Fall Came"; American Booksellers Pick of the Lists selection, 1993, for *Brothers and Sisters;* Best Children's Books of the Year selection, Bank Street College of Education, and Notable Children's Trade Book in the Field of Social Studies designation, National Council of Social Studies/ Children's Book Council, both 1998, both for *Just Kids; Skipping Stones* Honor Book selection in multicultural and international category, 2003, for *All Kinds of Friends, Even Green;* Charlotte Award nomination, New York State Reading Association, 2007, for *Steel Drumming at the Apollo* by Trish Marx.

Writings

AND PHOTOGRAPHER

Brothers and Sisters, Scholastic (New York, NY), 1993.
Kindergarten Kids, Scholastic (New York, NY), 1994.
Secrets, Dutton (New York, NY), 1995.
For My Family, Love, Allie, Albert Whitman (Morton Grove, IL), 1998.
Just Kids: Visiting a Class for Children with Special Needs, Dutton (New York, NY), 1998.
Reading Grows, Albert Whitman (Morton Grove, IL), 1999.
Hurray for Pre-K!, HarperCollins (New York, NY), 2000.
Berry Smudges and Leaf Prints: Finding and Making Colors from Nature, Dutton (New York, NY), 2001.
Fall Changes, Scholastic (New York, NY), 2001.

All Kinds of Friends, Even Green!, Woodbine House (Bethesda, MD), 2002.
Spring Changes, Scholastic (New York, NY), 2002.
A 3-D Birthday Party, Children's Press (New York, NY), 2007.
Shapes on the Playground, Lee & Low (New York, NY), 2007.
Counting Pumpkins, Lee & Low (New York, NY), 2011.

Author's work has been translated into Spanish.

PHOTOGRAPHER

Trish Marx, *Steel Drumming at the Apollo: The Road to Super Top Dog,* Lee & Low Books (New York, NY), 2007.
Trish Marx, *Elephants and Golden Thrones: Inside China's Forbidden City,* foreword by Mr. Li Ji, Abrams Books for Young Readers (New York, NY), 2008.
Trish Marx, *Kindergarten Day USA and China: A Flip-Me-Over Book,* Charlesbridge (Watertown, MA), 2010.

Adaptations

Several of Senisi's books were adapted as e-books or mobile apps by Auryn, Inc., beginning 2011.

Sidelights

Photographer and writer Ellen B. Senisi has combined her talents to create a number of works of both fiction and nonfiction for young readers, including *Hurray for Pre-K!* and *All Kinds of Friends, Even Green!* In several of her stories, which feature photographs rather than drawn illustrations, readers meet boys and girls whose experiences allow them to grow as people. In *Just Kids: Visiting a Class for Children with Special Needs,* for example, a second grader named Cindy spends part of each school day in her school's special-needs classroom and learns that each student, although struggling with a unique disability, has much in common with her.

Senisi was born in Little Falls, New York, a small town on the Mohawk River. "I lived in that town until I was eighteen," she once told *SATA,* "and by then was sufficiently restless to be on the move for the next fourteen years. By the time I ended up at my current home in Schenectady, New York, I had attended seven colleges, earned three degrees, and lived in thirty places, including upstate New York, rural Virginia, Boston, New York, and Oxford, England. (My husband, who lived in twenty-six of them with me, kept a list of them all.) I arrived in Schenectady with two children and one soon to come. Shortly after the third one arrived, in 1987, I began work on my first children's book.

"I had gotten involved in photography about ten years before that, when my husband bought a camera and insisted, after all we'd paid for it, that I learn how to use it, too. I felt intimidated by the technicalities but eventually learned and became absolutely hooked. I now own a number of cameras, all of which intimidate him."

Even in elementary school, Senisi loved to write and she accumulated a vast number of stories, poems, plays, letters, and journals throughout her school years. Once she reached college she "decided writing would be pretty impractical work. She changed her major from English to teaching. "I quit teaching after five years when I realized how susceptible I was to photography disease," she added, "and then went to graduate school for educational media and technology, which is where I got my only formal training in photography."

Senisi's first published book, *Brothers and Sisters,* captures the relationship between siblings from a variety of families and reflects the "ethnic, gender, and generational diversity" of modern families," according to *School Library Journal* contributor Jody McCoy. Presenting both the playful and conflict-riddled sides of sibling relationships, Senisi's "handsomely done" photoessay was deemed suitable for "a parent to use with a child one-on-one, or for a story hour with a family theme," in the opinion of *Booklist* contributor Janice Del Negro.

In *Secrets* Senisi examines the many secrets that young people encounter in their day-to-day activities. The author/photographer "adds a new layer of understanding by exploring different kinds of secrets . . . and the emotions associated with them," noted *Booklist* reviewer Stephanie Zvirin. Senisi "gleaned most of her information from interviews with a second-grade class," explained *School Library Journal* contributor Marianne Saccardi, "and young readers will easily identify with the various situations presented" in the author's "satisfying presentation."

In *Reading Grows* Senisi introduces parents and caregivers to the stages a child goes through during the learning-to-read process. Highlighted with what *School Library Journal* contributor Lucinda Snyder Whitehurst described as "bright, cheerful photographs" of children and grown-ups reading together, *Reading Grows* captures the joy to be found in books. Senisi's minimalist text augments her photographs, showing youngsters progressing from a knowledge of basic shapes and colors, through the alphabet, to vocabulary-building and the realization that, as the text exclaims, "I can read anywhere!"

Senisi follows one day in the life of a group of active preschool students in *Hurray for Pre-K!* Featuring an easy-to-read narrative and illustrated with colorful photographs, *Hurray for Pre-K!* finds the photographer's young subjects engaged in a variety of activities, including a puppet show, the construction of a fort, and a group painting project. "The pictures lend themselves to discussion," remarked *School Library Journal* critic

Blair Christolon, and Kathy Broderick predicted in *Booklist* that "new preschoolers will feel both comforted and enticed by these school scenes."

In *Berry Smudges and Leaf Prints: Finding and Making Colors from Nature* Senisi demonstrates more than a dozen ways in which children can create artwork using fruits, vegetables, and other plants. Each spread focuses on a specific color, discussing its role in nature and its effect on people's moods and feelings. Senisi also presents a host of craft ideas, from printing with potatoes and creating dyes from berries to pressing wild flowers. "The step-by-step, illustrated crafts encourage children to try many different types of media and techniques," observed Lynda Ritterman in her *School Library Journal* review of *Berry Smudges and Leaf Prints.*

In addition to melding text and art in her own books, Senisi has also enjoyed a successful collaboration with author Trish Marx, providing the photographs for *Steel Drumming at the Apollo: The Road to Super Top Dog* and *Elephants and Golden Thrones: Inside China's Forbidden City,* among other works. In the former, Marx focuses on seven high-school musicians who perform at the legendary Apollo Theater in Harlem, New York. "Senisi's color photographs enliven every page with shots of the teens . . . and the theater, capturing the thrill of the experience," Joyce Adams Burner commented in her review of the work for *School Library Journal.*

Marx takes readers inside the Forbidden City, an incredible palace complex in Beijing, China, in *Elephants and Golden Thrones.* A writer in *Kirkus Reviews* described Senisi's photographs for this book as "striking," and *Booklist* contributor Jennifer Mattson also praised the images, stating that "their evocatively vacant courtyards and pavilions will encourage contemplative musings about the structures' long endurance" through the ages. "Of particular note are the photos of the interiors of buildings, a number of which are not regularly open to the public," commented Barbara Scotto in *School Library Journal.* Marx and Senisi explore the similarities between American and Chinese schools in *Kindergarten Day USA and China: A Flip-Me-Over Book.* Carolyn Phelan in *Booklist* applauded the "clear, colorful photos" in this volume.

In addition to her works of nonfiction, Senisi has also written several fictional works, illustrating each with photographs of real-life children in situations reflecting those in her texts. In *Just Kids* an unfeeling remark about the "retard class" that is uttered by a second grader named Cindy results in time in the local elementary school's special-needs classroom where both Cindy and the reader come to learn that autism, Down's syndrome, and epilepsy do not make kids essentially different. Praising the work—which was photographed in a New York State elementary school—*Booklist* reviewer Helen Rosenberg called *Just Kids* a "sensitive, informative book that immerses us in a world that many of us know little about." Praising Senisi's "bright, vibrant, and upbeat" color photographs, *School Library Journal* contributor Whitehurst commented that they "project the powerful message that these children are not to be pitied; rather readers . . . are encouraged to . . . see that there are many different ways to learn."

In *For My Family, Love, Allie* Senisi follows a young girl from a mixed-race family as she does her share to prepare for an upcoming family gathering. Linda Greengrass commented in *School Library Journal* on the naturalism of the photographs in *For My Family, Love, Alice,* as well as on their success in "convey[ing] the powerful image of a comfortable interracial mix." A wheelchair-bound first grader writes about an iguana with missing toes for a class assignment in *All Kinds of Friends, Even Green!* "The message of acceptance, coupled with a matter-of-fact portrayal of a disabled youngster, makes this a good choice," Susan McCaffrey concluded of this illustrated story in *School Library Journal.*

Senisi takes a different approach to her art than many professional photographers, viewing her work as photodocumentary in nature. "When I set up my equipment on a site," she explained to *SATA,* "I strive to become invisible so I can catch faces coming alive with natural expressions in a natural environment. I also listen to what goes on while I'm photographing so I can blend natural-sounding language with the images in my books."

"I love creating books, I love exploring the relationships between words and images, and the best part is moving on to whatever stage is next," Senisi once commented. "Welding words and images with music may be next for me, or perhaps montages of photographs blended on the computer. I'll go with whatever methods work to show that illumination of expression I look for as I photograph children experiencing the world."

True to her words, Senisi and son Steven Senisi cofounded Senisi Multimedia, which uses still images, video, and audio—including original music—to create conceptual videos. In 2012 she also collaborated with Steven Senisi and Monica Maxwell Paegle to create EdTechLens, which produces nonfiction education-related Web sites utilizing both text and multimedia. "It's exciting to be working right as the definition of author is changing!," Senisi stated on her home page. "This is not just about writing books anymore, it's about authoring a variety of media, including print books, to increase engagement and involvement through interactivity."

Biographical and Critical Sources

PERIODICALS

Booklist, October 1, 1993, Janice Del Negro, review of *Brothers and Sisters,* p. 348; August, 1995, Stephanie Zvirin, review of *Secrets,* p. 1953; May 1, 1998, Helen Rosenberg, review of *Just Kids: Visiting a Classroom with Special Needs,* p. 1517; September 15, 2000, Kathy Broderick, review of *Hurray for Pre-K!,* p. 250; June 1, 2001, Gillian Engberg, review of *Berry Smudges and Leaf Prints: Finding and Making Colors from Nature,* p. 1872; June 1, 2008, Jennifer Mattson, review of *Elephants and Golden Thrones: Inside China's Forbidden City,* p. 69; July 1, 2010, Carolyn Phelan, review of *Kindergarten Day USA and China: A Flip-Me-Over-Book,* p. 64.

Kirkus Reviews, November 1, 2002, review of *All Kinds of Friends, Even Green!,* p. 1613; April 15, 2008, review of *Elephants and Golden Thrones* ; June 1, 2010, review of *Kindergarten Day USA and China.*

School Library Journal, December, 1993, Jody McCoy, review of *Brothers and Sisters,* p. 108; January, 1996, Marianne Saccardi, review of *Secrets,* p. 106; April, 1998, Lucinda Snyder Whitehurst, review of *Just Kids,* p. 110; December, 1998, Linda Greengrass, review of *For My Family, Love, Allie,* p. 92; August, 1999, Lucinda Snyder Whitehurst, review of *Reading Grows,* p. 150; September, 2000, Blair Christolon, review of *Hurray for Pre-K!,* p. 209; May, 2001, Lynda Ritterman, review of *Berry Smudges and Leaf Prints,* p. 146; November, 2002, Susan McCaffrey, review of *All Kinds of Friends, Even Green!,* p. 138; April, 2008, Joyce Adams Burner, review of *Steel Drumming at the Apollo: The Road to Super Top Dog,* p. 167; July, 2008, Barbara Scotto, review of *Elephants and Golden Thrones,* p. 115; August, 2010, Jennifer Rothschild, review of *Kindergarten Day USA and China,* p. 91.

ONLINE

EdTechLens Web site, http://edtechlens.com/ (September 15, 2012).
Ellen B. Senisi Education Photographs Web site, http://ellensenisi-educationphotographs.com (July 15, 2012).
Ellen B. Senisi Home Page, http://www.ellensenisi.com (July 15, 2012).
New York State Reading Association Youth Book Web log, http://charlotteaward.wordpress.com/ (October 22, 2009), Liz Yanoff, interview with Senisi.
Senisi Multimedia Web site, http://senisimultimedia.com/ (July 15, 2012).

*   *   *

SIMON, T.R. 1966(?)-
(Tanya McKinnon)

Personal

Born c. 1966; children: one daughter. *Education:* Bachelor's degree; M.A. (cultural anthropology).

Addresses

Home—Dobbs Ferry, NY. *Agent*—Victoria Sanders & Associates, 241 Avenue of the Americas, Ste. 11H, New York, NY 10014.

Career

Literary agent and author. South End Press, New York, NY, former editor; foreign scout for film clients and publishers; Victoria Sanders & Associates, New York, NY, literary agent. City University of New York, instructor in publishing certificate program at City College.

Awards, Honors

(With Victoria Bond) Notable Books for a Global Society selection, International Reading Association, One Hundred Titles for Reading and Sharing listee, New York Public Library, Notable Children's Book citation, National Council of Teachers of English, Edgar Award nomination, Mystery Writers of America, Notable Children's Book in the Language Arts selection, Children's Literature Assembly, and John Steptoe New Talent Award, American Library Association, all 2011, all for *Zora and Me*.

Writings

(With Victoria Bond) *Zora and Me*, Candlewick Press (Somerville, MA), 2010.

Adaptations

Zora and Me was adapted for audiobook, Brilliance Audio, 2011.

Sidelights

T.R. Simon was inspired with the idea for her first children's book when she was pregnant and reflected upon the books that had inspired her as a child. As a young African American, *Caddie Woodlawn*—a novel by Carolyn Ryrie Brink that won the Newbery Medal in 1935—had filled Simon with a desire for adventures similar to that of its young heroine. In *Zora and Me,* which she coauthored with friend and fellow writer Victoria Bond, Simon creates an equally inspiring young heroine by re-envisioning the childhood of Zora Neale Hurston, a celebrated African-American folklorist, novelist, and anthropologist. Winner of the 2011 John Steptoe New Talent Award and endorsed by the Zora Neale Hurston Trust, *Zora and Me* also earned an Edgar Allan Poe Award nomination from the Mystery Writers of America.

After Simon approached Bond and asked her to collaborate on the project, the two women reviewed Simon's roughed-out storyline and began to expand the novel's plot, developing characters, and weaving serious yet relevant themes such as racism into a child-friendly story. During the writing process they passed drafts of their manuscript back and forth, taking over a year to ready it for publication. They also studied Hurston's writings, which included an autobiography as well as novels and short stories, taking special note of

any references to her experiences as a child. For Simon, such research was more of a review: "Zora had been my inspiration throughout my two years of graduate school in cultural anthropology," she explained to Carol H. Rasco on the Reading Is Fundamental Web log. "I loved her irrepressible brilliance, her defiance of all limitations, her restless nature, her pitch-perfect quill, but most of all I love her connection to the natural world—no matter how far across the world her branches stretched, her roots were always anchored in the rich soil of Eatonville." Hurston's home town, Eatonville was also one of the first all-African-American communities to be established in the United States.

An entertaining novel for upper-elementary-grade readers, *Zora and Me* takes place at the turn of the twentieth century and introduces young Zora and her fourth-grade friends as they investigate a gruesome mystery in their small Florida town. Eleven-year-old Carrie Brown, the story's narrator, lets readers know early on that her best friend Zora has earned a reputation for creating outrageous tall tales. When the decapitated body of an itinerant worker is discovered near the railroad tracks of their home town of Eatonville, Zora deduces the man's death to be a run in with an alligator-human hybrid. As she digs deeper into the mystery, however, the spunky fourth grader learns some unpleasant truths about the people in her community.

"A spirit of gentleness" combines with "an air of mystery and natural magic," wrote Maggie Knapp in her *School Library Journal* review of Simon and Roth's fiction debut. In *Booklist* Hazel Rochman described *Zora and Me* as "both thrilling and heartbreaking," while a *Publishers Weekly* reviewer asserted that the coauthors "do their subject proud" by introducing a young character full of "imagination and [a] love of storytelling." The *Publishers Weekly* critic also cited the novel's ability to "adeptly evoke a racially fraught era," and a *Kirkus Reviews* contributor ranked *Zora and Me* as "absolutely outstanding" on the strength of its "rendering of African-American child life during the Jim Crow era as [partly] a time of wonder and imagination."

Biographical and Critical Sources

PERIODICALS

Booklist, October 15, 2010, Hazel Rochman, review of *Zora and Me,* p. 64.
Kirkus Reviews, October 1, 2010, review of *Zora and Me.*
New York Times, November 1, 2010, Felicia R. Lee, review of *Zora and Me.*
Publishers Weekly, September 27, 2010, review of *Zora and Me,* p. 61.
School Library Journal, November, 2010, Maggie Knapp, review of *Zora and Me,* p. 104.
USA Today, November 8, 2010, Bob Minzesheimer, "*Zora and Me* Reimagines Neale Hurston as a Girl," p. 3D.

ONLINE

Zora and Me Web site, http://zoraandme.com (June 15, 2012).

Carol H. Rasco/Reading Is Fundamental Web site, http://www.rascofromrif.org/ (October 10, 2010), Carol H. Rasco, "Sisterhood Is Powerful."*

* * *

SLOAN, Holly Goldberg 1958-

Personal

Born 1958, in Ann Arbor, MI; father a professor, mother an architect; married Chuck Sloan, 1982 (divorced, 1992); married Gary Rosen (a writer); children: (first marriage) two sons. *Education:* Wellesley College, B.A. (English and political science). *Hobbies and other interests:* Walks by the ocean, reading, cooking, dogs, sports.

Addresses

Home—Los Angeles, CA. *Agent*—Kenneth Wright, Writers House, 21 W. 26th St., New York, NY 10010.

Career

Writer and film producer and director. Grey Advertising, New York, NY, receptionist for three months; producer of television commercials. Film work includes: (associate producer) *Maid to Order,* 1987; (co-producer) *Indecency* (television movie), 1992; (associate producer) *Angels in the Outfield,* 1994; (director) *The Big Green,* 1995; (director) *The Secret Life of Girls,* 1999; (co-producer and author of story) *Angels in the Infield* (television movie), 2000; (director) *Tangled up in Blue* (television movie), 2004; (director with others) *Merry F#%$in' Christmas* (television movie), 2005; (executive producer) *Three Moons over Milford* (television pilot), 2006; and (director) *Heidi 4 Paws,* 2008.

Writings

I'll Be There, Little, Brown (New York, NY), 2011.

Author of screenplays, including *Indecency* (teleplay), 1992, *Made in America,* 1993, *Angels in the Outfield,* 1994, *The Big Green,* 1995, *The Secret Life of Girls,* 1999, *Whispers: An Elephant's Tale,* 2000, *The Crocodile Hunter: Collision Course,* 2002, *Tangled up in Blue* (teleplay), 2004, *Heidi 4 Paws,* 2008, and *All Riled Up,* 2009.

Author's work has been translated into several languages, including Chinese, Danish, Finnish, French, German, Hebrew, Portuguese, Spanish, and Swedish.

Sidelights

Holly Goldberg Sloan had a peripatetic childhood: her parents' careers and life choices caused her family to relocate with frequency from the Midwest to the West Coast, and from there to Washington, DC, the Netherlands, a camping excursion throughout Europe, and then to Turkey, where Sloan completed her junior year of high school. Taking a break from her career as a successful film producer and scriptwriter, Sloan draws on her childhood experiences in her first young-adult novel, *I'll Be There.*

In *I'll Be There* seventeen-year-old Sam Border and his twelve-year-old brother Riddle have been living on the run with Clarence, their mentally unstable father—and a burglar—for ten years, and the constant moves mean that Sam has not been enrolled in public school since grade two. While Sam does his best to scavenge for food and act as parent to Riddle, the younger boy withdraws into a world without verbal sound and instead communicates via drawings. While living in one of their many temporary hometowns, Sam attends a church service, drawn by the chance to listen to music. There he meets Emily Bell, a young vocalist, and the two develop a friendship. As Sam and Riddle are welcomed into Emily's loving and stable family, Sam gains a new perspective on his own life, but he also realizes that the bond he and Riddle are developing with the Bells—as well as his growing love for Emily—will be viewed as a threat by the violent Clarence.

The love story that propels the plot of *I'll Be There* is "rich with emotion and enhanced by the powerful forces of destiny," noted Susan Redman Parodi in reviewing Sloan's debut novel for *Voice of Youth Advocates.* In *Publishers Weekly* a critic deemed the book a "cinematic, psychologically nuanced" story "of star-crossed love and the power of human empathy and connection," while for *Booklist* reviewer Michael Cart Sam and Riddle serve as "wonderfully appealing characters." Praising *I'll Be There* in *Horn Book,* Karen Alexander concluded of the work that "a heartwarming ending" culminates Sloan's "life-affirming exploration of the subtleties of love, compassion, and relationships."

Biographical and Critical Sources

PERIODICALS

Booklist, April 1, 2011, Michael Cart, review of *I'll Be There,* p. 65.

Horn Book, July-August, 2011, Rachel L. Smith, review of *I'll Be There,* p. 162.

Kirkus Reviews, April 1, 2011, review of *I'll Be There.*

Publishers Weekly, April 11, 2011, review of *I'll Be There,* p. 54.

Register-Guard (Eugene, OR), July 24, 2011, Randi Bjornstad, "Writer Comes Back to Eugene, Where Her Novel Is Set," p. E31.

School Library Journal, October, 2003, Nancy P. Reeder, review of *Keeper,* p. 178; May, 2011, Karen Alexander, review of *I'll Be There,* p. 124.

Voice of Youth Advocates, April, 2003, review of *Keeper,* p. 59; June, 2011, Etienne Vallee, review of *I'll Be There,* p. 174; August, 2011, Susan Redman Parodi, review of *I'll Be There,* p. 279.

ONLINE

Holly Goldberg Sloan Home Page, http://www.hollygoldbergsloan.com (August 1, 2012).*

* * *

SMIBERT, Angie 1963-

Personal

Born 1963, in Blacksburg, VA. *Education:* Multiple degrees.

Addresses

Office—P.O. Box 4601, Roanoke, VA 24015. *Agent*—Tina Wexler, ICM, 825 8th Ave., New York, NY 10019. *E-mail*—asmibert@gmail.com.

Career

Novelist. U.S. Department of Energy, former writer; National Aeronautics & Space Administration, Cape Canaveral, FL, member of staff at John F. Kennedy Space Center.

Writings

Memento Nora, Marshall Cavendish (New York, NY), 2011.
The Forgetting Curve, Marshall Cavendish (New York, NY), 2012.

Sidelights

Angie Smibert collected a slew of positive accolades for her young-adult dystopian novel *Memento Nora.* Set in a near-distant future, Smibert's story centers on Nora, who leads a contented, middle-class teenage life in which Homeland Inc. is the dominant government. Nora's country is rocked by frequent terrorist acts while her family lives insulated from this violence in their secure, gated community; then she intersects with reality at the local mall when she survives a bomb blast and witnesses its gruesome fallout. Nora's mother takes the teen to a government-run Therapeutic Forgetting Clinic (TFC) where those who have experienced such ghastly terrorist incidents can take a pill called Ameliorol and have their memory erased. Nora intends to take the

medication until Micah, a teen she meets in the clinic's waiting room, encourages her to reconsider. Soon the young woman is leading a double life, aware of the violent reality outside her gated bubble but pretending to her parents that she has successfully completed the memory-erasing course of therapy. Joining the underground rebellion, Nora, Micah, and friend Winter soon begin to suspect that the ominous black vans of Homeland Inc. may be related to a series of bomb attacks like the one Nora witnessed. Once their activities are uncovered, the teens run the risk of having to undergo involuntary treatment.

"The rebellion of Nora, Micah, and Winter may seem small, but their actions have tremendous results," wrote Jennifer McConnel in her *Voice of Youth Advocates* review of *Memento Nora,* the critic citing Smibert's debut novel for its "good mix of romance, intrigue, and a chillingly powerful antagonist." Necia Blundy, writing in *School Library Journal,* commended Nora as a captivating heroine, noting that the teen "has a truly defined voice and her transformation from perfect and 'glossy' into strong and thoughtful is well done." *Horn Book* contributor Deirdre F. Baker lauded *Memento Nora* as a "subtle commentary on art, memory, and historical evidence" that is "taut and lean; Smibert's prose is quick and fluid."

Cover of Angie Smiberg's futuristic young-adult novel Memento Nora, *which focuses on a near future where technology has forced humans into relative isolation from one another.* (Jacket illustration by Alex Ferrari; cover photograph by Tyler Stalman/iStockphoto.com. Reproduced by permission of Marshall Cavendish.)

Biographical and Critical Sources

PERIODICALS

Booklist, June 1, 2011, Cindy Welch, review of *Memento Nora,* p. 82.

Horn Book, July-August, 2011, Deirdre F. Baker, review of *Memento Nora,* p. 163.

Kirkus Reviews, March 1, 2011, review of *Memento Nora.*

School Library Journal, April, 2011, Necia Blundy, review of *Memento Nora,* p. 184.

Voice of Youth Advocates, June, 2011, Jennifer McConnel and Rachel McGrath, review of *Memento Nora,* p. 192.

ONLINE

Angie Smibert Home Page, http://www.angiesmibert.com (August 1, 2012).

Cynsations Web log, http://cynthialeitichsmith.blogspot.com/ (May 9, 2011), Cynthia Leitich Smith, interview with Smibert.

School Library Journal Web log, http://blog.schoollibraryjournal.com/ (May 19, 2011), Elizabeth Bird, review of *Memento Nora.**

*   *   *

SOETORO-NG, Maya 1970-

Personal

Born August 15, 1970, in Jakarta, Jakarta Territory, Indonesia; daughter of Lolo Soetoro (a company executive) and Stanley Ann Dunham (an anthropologist); married Konrad Ng (a professor), 2003; children: Suhaila, Savita. *Education:* Barnard College, B.A., 1993; New York University, M.A. (secondary education); University of Hawaii, Ph.D., 2006.

Addresses

Home—HI. *Office*—East-West Center, 1601 East-West Rd., Honolulu, HI 96848.

Career

Novelist and educator. High-school history teacher and curriculum-development specialist; University of Hawaii, Honolulu, assistant professor of education, 2000-06; East-West Center, Honolulu, education specialist.

Writings

Ladder to the Moon, illustrated by Yuyi Morales, Candlewick Press (Somerville, MA), 2011.

Sidelights

Maya Soetoro-Ng is the half-sister of U.S. president Barack Obama and author of a children's book about their mother. Soetoro-Ng wrote *Ladder to the Moon* to help her own young daughters appreciate a grandmother she never met, for the siblings' late mother, Stanley "Ann" Dunham, had died before the girls were born.

Born in Jakarta, Indonesia, in 1970, Soetoro-Ng is nine years younger than her famous half-brother. Her father, Lolo Soetoro, was Ann Dunham's second husband; the couple met while attending the University of Hawaii. In 1973, Obama joined Soetoro-Ng and Dunham while the older woman attended graduate school. Mother and daughter later returned to Indonesia, where Soetoro-Ng's parents divorced in 1980. At that point, they once again returned to Honolulu, where the now-college-aged Obama became Soetoro-Ng's bossy older guardian, as she revealed to Wintle in the *Times* of London interview. "His point was that I shouldn't be engaged in frivolous pursuits. I should be more studious. And he took it upon himself to give me guidance, which I needed."

Ladder to the Moon takes its title from a painting by American artist Georgia O'Keeffe, who Dunham admired. Soetoro-Ng was inspired to write the book in 2008, while working on behalf of the campaign leading to Obama's historic election. Married and the mother of toddler daughter Suhaila by that time, she lived in Hawaii with her husband, a Canadian professor of Chinese heritage. "Just before Suhaila was born, I discovered a box buried in a storage locker, labeled 'for Maya's children,'" she told London *Times* contributor Angela Wintle. "Inside were my childhood books and toys, many of which had been gathered by my mother on her travels."

With illustrations by Yuyi Morales, *Ladder to the Moon* features a little girl who asks her mother what "Grandma

Yuyi Morales creates the gentle, soft-edged art that brings to life Maya Soetoro-Ng's multigenerational story in **Ladder to the Moon.** (Illustration copyright © 2011 by Yuyi Morales. Reproduced by permission of Candlewick Press, Somerville, MA.)

Annie" was like. Mother explains that she was like the moon, glowing and always present, before she puts the girl to bed. That night, a grandmotherly fairy-tale figure visits the little girl and invites her to spend some time on the moon with her. They listen to moon songs, but also hear calls of distress from Earth. From her lunar vantage point, the little girl can also see how many people are suffering and how many are praying for peace. The grandmother explains that it is important to reach out to others and lend support when needed.

Booklist writer Ilene Cooper called *Ladder to the Moon* "a lush, haunting story," and Marianne Saccardi suggested in *School Library Journal* that a lap-sit reading would allow children "to grasp the story's full import and discover . . . their own responsibilities as citizens of the world." A reviewer for *Publishers Weekly* remarked that "nontraditional spiritual literature for children often falters in the execution; this work fulfills its promise."

Biographical and Critical Sources

PERIODICALS

Booklist, March 1, 2011, Ilene Cooper, review of *Ladder to the Moon,* p. 48.
Kirkus Reviews, March 1, 2011, review of *Ladder to the Moon.*
New York Times, April 13, 2011, Sheryl Gay Stolberg, "First Family of Writers Grows by One," p. C1.
Publishers Weekly, February 21, 2011, review of *Ladder to the Moon,* p. 130.
School Library Journal, April, 2011, Marianne Saccardi, review of *Ladder to the Moon,* p. 154.
Times (London, England), April 12, 2011, Angela Wintle, profile of Soetoro-Ng, p. 42.*

* * *

SUY, Sandra

Personal

Born in Spain; married; children: two. *Education:* La Llotja (Barcelona, Spain), degree (fashion design).

Addresses

Home—Barcelona, Spain. *Agent*—Jelly Motion Illustration, 9-10 Charlotte Mews, London W1T 4EF, England. *E-mail*—hola@sandrasuy.com.

Career

Fashion illustrator.

Illustrator

Bianca Turetsky, *The Time-Traveling Fashionista,* Little, Brown (New York, NY), 2011.

Contributor to periodicals internationally, including *Allure, Economist, Glamour,* and *So Chic.*

Biographical and Critical Sources

PERIODICALS

Booklist, April 1, 2011, Cindy Welch, review of *The Time-Traveling Fashionista,* p. 66.
Bulletin of the Center for Children's Books, April, 2011, Kate Quealy-Gainer, review of *The Time-Traveling Fashionista,* p. 394.
Kirkus Reviews, March 15, 2011, review of *The Time-Traveling Fashionista.*
Publishers Weekly, February 7, 2011, review of *The Time-Traveling Fashionista,* p. 58.
School Library Journal, April, 2011, Tina Zubak, review of *The Time-Traveling Fashionista,* p. 186.
Voice of Youth Advocates, June, 2011, Michelle Young, review of *The Time-Traveling Fashionista,* p. 193.

ONLINE

Live Citizen Web log, http://blog.livecitizen.com/ (October 30, 2009), Patricio Maya, interview with Suy.
Sandra Suy Home Page, http://sandrasuy.com (August 1, 2012).*

T-W

TOWNLEY, Rod
See TOWNLEY, Roderick

*   *   *

TOWNLEY, Roderick 1942-
(Rod Townley)

Personal

Born June 7, 1942, in Orange, NJ; son of William Richard (a businessman) and Elise Townley; married Libby Blackman, April 4, 1970 (divorced, 1980); married Wyatt Baker (a poet and yoga instructor), February 15, 1986; children: (first marriage) Jesse Blackman; (second marriage) Grace Whitman. *Education:* Attended Hamilton College, 1960-61, and University of Chicago, 1961-62; Bard College, A.B., 1965; Rutgers University, M.A., 1970, Ph.D., 1972.

Addresses

Home—Leawood, KS. *Agent*—Jodi Reamer, Writers House, 21 W. 26th St., New York, NY 10010. *E-mail*—roderick@rodericktownley.com.

Career

Writer. Passaic County Community College, Paterson, NJ, associate professor of world literature, 1972-73; *Philadelphia Enquirer,* Philadelphia, PA, journalist on retainer, 1974-77; *TV Guide,* New York, NY, staff writer, 1980-89; *US* (magazine), New York, NY, senior editor, 1989-90; freelance journalist, beginning 1990. Fulbright visiting professor, University of Concepcion, Chile, 1978-79. Writers Place, Kansas City, MO, executive director, 1994-95.

Awards, Honors

First prize, Academy of American Poets contest; Fulbright fellowship, 1978-79; master artist fellowship for fiction, Kansas Arts Commission; Peregrine Prize for Short Fiction; Thorpe Menn Award, and Kansas Governor's Arts Award, both 2002, both for *Into the Labyrinth;* Books for the Teen Age selection, New York Public Library, and Best Books for Young Adults designation, American Library Association, both 2004, both for *Sky;* Books for the Teen Age selection, 2007, for *The Red Thread;* Kansas Notable Book selection, 2010, for *The Blue Shoe,* 2012, for *The Door in the Forest;* Best Books selection, Bank Street College of Education, 2012, for *The Door in the Forest.*

Writings

JUVENILE FICTION

(Translator) Rene Escudie, *Paul and Sebastian,* Kane Miller (La Jolla, CA), 1988.
Sky: A Novel in Three Sets and an Encore, Atheneum Books for Young Readers (New York, NY), 2004.
The Red Thread: A Novel in Three Incarnations, Atheneum Books for Young Readers (New York, NY), 2007.
The Blue Shoe: A Tale of Thievery, Villainy, Sorcery, and Shoes, illustrated by Mary GrandPré, Alfred A. Knopf (New York, NY), 2009.
The Door in the Forest, Bluefire (New York, NY), 2011.

'SYLVIE CYCLE" NOVEL TRILOGY

The Great Good Thing, Atheneum Books for Young Readers (New York, NY), 2001.
Into the Labyrinth, Atheneum Books for Young Readers (New York, NY), 2002.
The Constellation of Sylvie, Atheneum Books for Young Readers (New York, NY), 2005.

POETRY; FOR ADULTS

(Under name Rod Townley) *Blue Angels Black Angels,* privately printed, 1972.

(Under name Rod Townley) *Summer Street* (chapbook), The Smith (New York, NY), 1975.
(Under name Rod Townley) *Three Musicians,* The Smith (New York, NY), 1978.
Final Approach, Countryman Press (Woodstock, VT), 1986.

Contributor to periodicals, including *Paris Review, North American Review,* and *Yale Review.*

OTHER

(Under name Rod Townley) *The Early Poetry of William Carlos Williams* (criticism), Cornell University Press (Ithaca, NY), 1975.
(Under name Rod Townley) *Minor Gods* (novel), St. Martin's Press (New York, NY), 1976.
(Under name Rod Townley) *The Year in Soaps: 1983,* Crown (New York, NY), 1984.
Safe and Sound: A Parent's Guide to Child Protection, Simon & Schuster (New York, NY), 1985.
(Editor) *Night Errands: How Poets Use Dreams,* University of Pittsburgh Press (Pittsburgh, PA), 1998.

Work anthologized in *University and College Poetry Prizes: 1967-1972,* edited by Daniel Hoffman, Academy of American Poets (New York, NY), 1974; *Eleven Young Poets: The Smith Seventeen,* edited by Ray Boxer, The Smith (New York, NY), 1975; *William Carlos Williams: Man and Poet,* edited by Carroll F. Terrell, National Poetry Foundation (Orono, ME), 1983; *Conversations with Ralph Ellison,* edited by Maryemma Graham and Amritjit Singh, University Press of Mississippi (Jackson, MS), 1995; *Mister Rogers' Neighborhood: Children, Television, and Fred Rogers,* edited by Mark Collins and Margaret Mary Kimmel, University of Pittsburgh Press (Pittsburgh, PA), 1996; *Poets at Large,* edited by H.L. Hix, Helicon Nine Editions (Kansas City, MO), 1997; *Spud Songs: An Anthology of Potato Poems,* edited by Gloria Vando and Robert Stewart, Helicon Nine Editions, 1999; *Ravishing Disunities,* edited by Agha Shahid Ali, Wesleyan University Press (Hanover, NH), 2000; *The Color of Absence: 12 Stories about Loss and Hope,* edited by James Howe, Simon & Schuster (New York, NY), 2002; *Poetry, an Introduction,* fourth edition, edited by Michael Meyer, Bedford/ St. Martin's (Boston, MA), 2004; and *The Pittsburgh Reader,* University of Pittsburgh Press (Pittsburgh, PA), 2011. Contributor, sometimes under name Rod Townley, to periodicals, including *Studies in Short Fiction, Philadelphia, New York Times, Washington Post, TV Guide, Village Voice,* and *Detroit Free Press.*

Sidelights

A respected poet and literary critic, Roderick Townley has also made a name for himself as the author of imaginative novels for children and young adults. In addition to *The Great Good Thing* and its sequels *Into the Labyrinth* and *The Constellation of Sylvie,* Townley has also authored stand-alone novels such as *Sky: A*

Novel in Three Sets, The Red Thread: A Novel in Three Incarnations, The Blue Shoe: A Tale of Thievery, Villainy, Sorcery, and Shoes, and *The Door in the Forest.*

In *The Great Good Thing* Townley introduces Princess Sylvie and the many friends who live inside an old, almost forgotten storybook. To perform her role in the story, the twelve-year-old princess yearns to do "one great good thing" before she submits to marriage, and Townley's novel follows her swashbuckling adventures in pursuit of that goal. When young Claire reads the book the characters all scramble to their places, acting out their parts. Disaster strikes when the volume is destroyed by Claire's vile brother. Desperate to survive, the characters, led by Sylvie, cross into Claire's mind where they live on in the young reader's subconscious. Without the printed page to preserve them, the passage of time now threatens Sylvie and her friends, for as Claire grows up she begins to forget the story. To save her world, Sylvie must perform a final "great good thing" that not even she could have foreseen.

In her *School Library Journal* review of *The Great Good Thing,* Debbie Whitbeck deemed Townley's approach "an extremely clever and multilayered concept," but questioned whether younger readers would be able to grasp its multiple levels. A *Publishers Weekly* reviewer called *The Great Good Thing* a "clever, deftly written" novel, and a *Kirkus Reviews* critic deemed the book "utterly winning" and "that most impossible thing: a book beloved from the first page."

Into the Labyrinth follows Princess Sylvie and her cohorts as their story is published on the Internet, a weightless virtual world with unforeseen challenges. Stress proves the least of the characters' problems as strange things start happening—words get changed, scenes disappear, and Sylvie and her friends must launch themselves into the labyrinth of cyberspace to confront a 21st-century evil that threatens to destroy their world.

Sylvie's adventures continue in *The Constellation of Sylvie* as a copy of *The Great Good Thing* finds its way aboard a spaceship bound for Jupiter. During a reading by the ship-bound crew, the princess is confronted by the romantic advances of a blackmailing jester named Pingree. Once again, survival becomes an issue for the fictional cast after the space ship misses its window of reentry to Earth, providing Sylvie and company with yet another challenge.

Reviewing *Into the Labyrinth,* a *Kirkus Reviews* critic dubbed Townley's story a "brilliantly imagined sequel" that continues to explore the concepts of how fiction affects individual readers that were first introduced in *The Great Good Thing. Booklist* contributor John Peters called the first sequel a "grand, tongue-in-cheek adventure" and Beth L. Meister wrote in *School Library Journal* that "Sylvie is an appealing, thoughtful, and involving heroine, pulling the fast-paced plot to its satisfying conclusion." Praising the princess for her "plucky, re-sourceful nature," Krista Hurley added in her *Booklist* appraisal of *The Constellation of Sylvie* that Townley's "metafictional premise is deftly realized," while *Kliatt* reviewer Lesley Farmer predicted that, with its focus on "strong females" and its mix of fantasy and science-fiction, Townley's series "should capture the attention of a special reading niche."

Directed to slightly older readers, Townley's young-adult novel *Sky* centers on fifteen-year-old jazz pianist Alex "Sky" Schuyler. Although his private-school class-mates think little of him, Sky is a driving force in his jazz band, which includes drummer Max, bass player Larry, and manager Suze. Unfortunately for Sky, his conservative, workaday father views jazz as a waste of time and encourages his son to quit the band and de-vote his time to something more practical. As punish-ment for sneaking out to attend a Count Basie concert, Sky's father takes away the teen's piano. Pushed be-yond endurance, Sky runs away to Greenwich Village, where he meets a blind jazz pianist in rapidly declining health. Sky bonds instantly with the weathered musi-cian and ultimately learns important lessons about mu-sic and about life.

Sky "brings the beatnik era to life while expressing timeless, universal themes about the generation gap," observed a *Publishers Weekly* reviewer. Paula Rohrlick, writing in *Kliatt*, praised Townley's novel as an "ap-pealing coming-of-age tale about finding yourself and finding your calling."

Townley profiles another troubled teen in *The Red Thread*. Plagued by horribly realistic nightmares and feelings of claustrophobia, Dana Landgrave hopes therapy can provide her with some relief. However, the belligerent sixteen year old may have misplaced her trust in Dr. Sprague when he uses hypnotic regression to unlock a series of past lives that include those of ten-year-old William, who was murdered in the late 1500s, and Hannah, the niece of an ill-tempered artist who lived in eighteenth-century London. Soon Dana is drawn into an age-old mystery that not only threatens family relationships and her current romance; it also forces her to question the person she has assumed herself to be.

According to a *Publishers Weekly* contributor, in *The Red Thread* Townley "raises an intriguing question about the nature of the soul" and its ability to reincar-nate itself from generation to generation. Viewing the novel as a time-travel mystery, Claire Rosser praised its "highly intelligent" teen protagonist, adding in her *Kli-att* review that Townley "makes the places and people seem real, and he is able to keep the tension high throughout" his imaginative tale. In *Booklist* Stephanie Zvirin found less to like about the petulant Dana, but nonetheless praised *The Red Thread*, citing the book's "deliciously scary premise and the melodramatic out-come" that is guaranteed to captivate teen readers. De-scribing the story as "captivating and shivery," a *Kirkus*

Reviews writer noted that the twin themes of "revenge and devotion" infuse Townley's tale with "first-rate sus-pense and emotion."

A fantasy laced with humor and brought to life in col-orful illustrations by Mary GrandPré, *The Blue Shoe* centers on thirteen-year-old Hap Barlo, a cobbler's ap-prentice living in the mythical town of Aplanap. Al-though Hap is treated well by his kindly mentor, Grel, the youth longs to be reunited with his father, who is imprisoned on nearby Mount Xexnax. While attempting to help a local beggar girl, Hap pilfers a precious stone from Grel's prized blue shoe and is exiled to Mount Xexnax, where he toils in a labor camp. There he con-tinues his search for his dad while befriending the Aukis, a blue-skinned race of elfish creatures that are forced to mine for a valuable diamond.

Kimberly Garnick, writing in *Booklist*, described *The Blue Shoe* as a "fun, whimsical fairy tale" featuring "copious amounts of magic and intrigue." "Themes of racial prejudice, slavery, revolution and environmental-ism swirl through this sometimes dark but ultimately cheerful adventure," observed a writer in *Kirkus Reviews*.

Cover of Townley's middle-grade fantasy **The Door in the Forest,** *fea-turing artwork by Chris Buzelli.* (Jacket illustration by Chris Buzelli © 2011 by Alfred A. Knopf. Reproduced by permission of Alfred A. Knopf, an imprint of Random House Children's Books, a division of Random House, Inc.)

Set in an alternate 1923, Townley's *The Door in the Forest* offers a "suspenseful, thought-provoking fantasy," according to *School Library Journal* critic Eva Mitnick. The work focuses on Daniel Crowley, age fourteen, who lives in the sleepy rural town of Everwood, bordering an unreachable and magically protected island. Daniel is determined to get there, asi s his friend Emily, whose eccentric grandmother reads the future in her bubble bath. Soon Everwood is overrun by a small army led by the brutal Captain Sloper. Suspicious of the captain's interest in the island, Daniel, his brother Wesley, and their new friend Emily embark on a strange and dangerous journey that takes them back in time to an alternate reality.

According to Deirdre F. Baker, writing in *Horn Book*, *The Door in the Forest* "swings like a pendulum from Wild West tall tale to a vague mysticism that is enlivened by colorful imagery." According to a contributor in *Publishers Weekly*, in *The Door in the Forest* Townley serves up a "lovely tale [that] should impress young readers.""The island and its protectors and inhabitants are a lively blend of whimsy and unsettling mystery," Mitnick reported, and in *Booklist* Kay Weisman noted that "a strong sense of quest will keep readers turning the pages of this fast-paced book."

Biographical and Critical Sources

PERIODICALS

Booklist, November 1, 2002, John Peters, review of *Into the Labyrinth*, p. 499; June 1, 2006, Krista Hutley, review of *The Constellation of Sylvie*, p. 76; February 15, 2007, Stephanie Zvirin, review of *The Red Thread: A Novel in Three Incarnations*, p. 73; September 1, 2009, Kimberly Garnick, review of *The Blue Shoe: A Tale of Thievery, Villainy, Sorcery, and the Shoes*, p. 88; March 1, 2011, Kay Weisman, review of *The Door in the Forest*, p. 60.

Bulletin of the Center for Children's Books, September, 2004, Elizabeth Bush, review of *Sky: A Novel in Three Sets and an Encore*, p. 42.

Guardian (London, England), April 26, 2003, Jan Mark, review of *The Great Good Thing*.

Horn Book, March-April, 2011, Deirdre F. Baker, review of *The Door in the Forest*, p. 127.

Kirkus Reviews, September 15, 2002, review of *Into the Labyrinth*, p. 1402; July 1, 2004, review of *Sky*, p. 638; February 1, 2006, review of *The Constellation of Sylvie*, p. 137; January 15, 2007, review of *The Red Thread*, p. 82; September 15, 2009, review of *The Blue Shoe*; February 1, 2011, review of *The Door in the Forest*.

Kliatt, July, 2004, Paula Rohrlick, review of *Sky*, p. 13; March, 2006, Lesley Farmer, review of *The Constellation of Sylvie*, p. 18; March, 2007, Claire Rosser, review of *The Red Thread*, p. 19.

Library Journal, September 1, 1998, Kim Woodbridge, review of *Night Errands: How Poets Use Dreams*, p. 181.

Publishers Weekly, May 21, 2001, review of *The Great Good Thing*, p. 108; August 30, 2004, review of *Sky*, p. 56; March 19, 2007, review of *The Red Thread*, p. 64; October 26, 2009, review of *The Blue Shoe*, p. 58; January 17, 2011, review of *The Door in the Forest*, p. 49.

School Library Journal, July, 2001, Debbie Whitbeck, review of *The Great Good Thing*, p. 114; October, 2001, Louise T. Sherman, review of *The Great Good Thing*, p. 89; October, 2002, Beth L. Meister, review of *Into the Labyrinth*, p. 174; July, 2004, Susan Riley, review of *Sky*, p. 113; August, 2006, Robyn Gioia, review of *The Constellation of Sylvie*, p. 130; April, 2007, Eric Norton, review of *The Red Thread*, p. 150; December, 2009, Nancy D. Tolson, review of *The Blue Shoe*, p. 135; March, 2011, Eva Mitnick, review of *The Door in the Forest*, p. 172.

ONLINE

Kidsreads.com, http://www.kidsreads.com/ (November 5, 2005), Lisa Marx, review of *The Great Good Thing*.

Roderick Townley Home Page, http://www.roderick townley.com (July 15, 2012).

*   *   *

VALIANT, Kristi

Personal

Born in WI; married; children: daughters. *Education:* Columbus College of Art & Design, B.A (illustration; cum laude). *Religion:* Christian. *Hobbies and other interests:* Movies, swing dancing, movie musicals.

Addresses

Home—Evansville, IN. *Agent*—Linda Pratt, Wernick & Pratt Agency; info@wernickpratt.com. *E-mail*—kristi@ kristivaliant.com.

Career

Illustrator. Worked in graphics department of an educational publisher.

Member

Society of Children's Book Writers and Illustrators (regional advisor of Indiana chapter).

Awards, Honors

Asian/Pacific American Award for Literature in picture-book category, 2009, for *Cora Cooks Pancit* by Dorina K. Lazo Gilmore; Best English Language Children's Book selection, Sharjah International Book Fair, 2011, and Choice selection, Cooperative Children's Book Center, 2012, both for *The Goodbye Cancer Garden* by Janna Mathies.

Writings

SELF-ILLUSTRATED

Penguin Cha-Cha, Random House (New York, NY), 2013.

ILLUSTRATOR

Dorina K. Lazo Gilmore, *Cora Cooks Pancit,* Shen's
    Books (Walnut Creek, CA), 2009.
Crystal Bowman and Ava Pennington, *Do You Love Me
    More?,* Standard Pub. (Cincinnati, OH), 2010.
Paula Hannigan, *Oliver's First Christmas,* Accord Pub.
    (Denver, CO), 2010.
Janna Matthies, *The Goodbye Cancer Garden,* Albert
    Whitman (Chicago, IL), 2011.

Contributor to periodicals, including *Highlights for
Children.*

ILLUSTRATOR; "LITTLE WINGS" SERIES

Cecilia Galante, *Be Brave, Willa Bean!,* Random House
    (New York, NY), 2011.
Cecilia Galante, *Willa Bean's Cloud Dreams,* Random
    House (New York, NY), 2011.
Cecilia Galante, *Star-Bubble Trouble,* Random House
    (New York, NY), 2012.

Sidelights

Kristi Valiant's ultimate career path was apparent as
early as the fourth grade, although her teachers' concern
over her drawing during class was not then viewed as
such. As the years went by, Valiant continued to draw,
and by the time she graduated magna cum laude from
Columbus College of Art & Design she was a professional illustrator. Valiant's work creating graphics for an
educational publisher positioned her for a move to
picture-book art and her first illustration project, creating images for Dorina K. Lazo Gilmore's *Cora Cooks
Pancit,* was published in 2009. In the years since she
has illustrated stories by several other authors and in
2013 added "author" to her list of talents when she created the self-illustrated picture book *Penguin Cha-Cha.*

Valiant's artwork for *Cora Cooks Pancit,* a story about
life in a Filipino family, was praised by Mary Landrum,
the critic writing in her *School Library Journal* review
that it "nicely complements the text" and uses "warm
hues . . . [to] highlight the family's loving relationship." Other illustration work includes Cecilia Galante's
"Little Wings" stories for younger children: *Be Brave,
Willa Bean!, Willa Bean's Cloud Dreams,* and *Star-
Bubble Trouble.* Reviewing *Willa Bean's Cloud Dreams,*
in which a curly-haired young cupid heads off to the
Cupid Academy, *Booklist* contributor Suzanne Harold
wrote that Galante's story benefits from Valiant's
"black-and-white illustrations" depicting the "spirited
and quirky" sprite.

*Kristi Valiant's illustration projects include creating the artwork for
Janna Matthies' inspiring story in* **The Goodbye Cancer Garden.** *(Illus-
tration copyright © 2011 by Kristi Valiant. Reproduced by permission of Albert Whitman
& Company.)*

The Goodbye Cancer Garden, a family-centered story
by Janna Matthies, allowed Valiant to once again play
with color, and here her "delicate illustrations" pair effectively with Matthies' "unexpectedly upbeat text," in
the opinion of *Booklist* contributor Kara Dean. A *Publishers Weekly* critic also praised Valiant's work here,
writing that her "wispy" illustrations with their "frenetic sketch outlines," capture the "energy and hopeful-
ness" of children watching a parent win her battle with
cancer, and in *School Library Journal* Heidi Estrin
praised the artwork in *The Goodbye Cancer Garden* as
"tender and sweet."

Biographical and Critical Sources

PERIODICALS

Booklist, February 15, 2011, Kara Dean, review of *The
    Goodbye Cancer Garden,* p. 77; December 15, 2011,
    Suzanne Harold, review of *Willa Bean's Cloud
    Dreams,* p. 57.
Publishers Weekly, January 31, 2011, review of *The Good-
    bye Cancer Garden,* p. 49.
School Library Journal, November, 2009, Mary Landrum,
    review of *Cora Cooks Pancit,* p. 83; February, 2011,
    Heidi Estrin, review of *The Goodbye Cancer Garden,*
    p. 86.

ONLINE

Kristi Valiant Home Page, http://www.kristivaliant.com
    (August 1, 2012).

Kristi Valiant Web log, http://kristivaliant.blogspot.com (August 1, 2012).

Papertigers Web site, http://www.papertigers.org/ (May, 2009), Abigail Sawyer, review of *Cora Cooks Pancit.**

*   *   *

van LIESHOUT, Maria

Personal

Born in the Netherlands; immigrated to United States; married; husband named Peter; children: Max. *Education:* George Washington University, B.F.A. (visual communications).

Addresses

Home—San Francisco, CA. *Agent*—Steven Malk, Writers House; smalk@writershouse.com. *E-mail*—Maria@mariavanlieshout.com.

Career

Author, artist, and illustrator. Coca-Cola Company, former creative director. Designer of cards and art prints.

Awards, Honors

Canadian Children's Book Centre Best Books designation, and Blue Spruce Award finalist, Ontario Library Association, both 2008, and *Storytelling World* Honor designation, all for *The List* by Hazel Hutchins.

Writings

SELF-ILLUSTRATED

Bloom! A Little Book about Finding Love, Feiwel & Friends (New York, NY), 2008.
Splash! A Little Book about Bouncing Back, Feiwel & Friends (New York, NY), 2008.
Peep! A Little Book about Taking a Leap, Feiwel & Friends (New York, NY), 2009.
Tumble! A Little Book about Having It All, Feiwel &Friends (New York, NY), 2010.
Hopper and Wilson, Philomel Books (New York, NY), 2011.
Backseat A-B-See, Chronicle Books (San Francisco, CA), 2012.
Flight 123, Chronicle Books (San Francisco, CA), 2013.

Author's work has been translated into Dutch, German, and Korean.

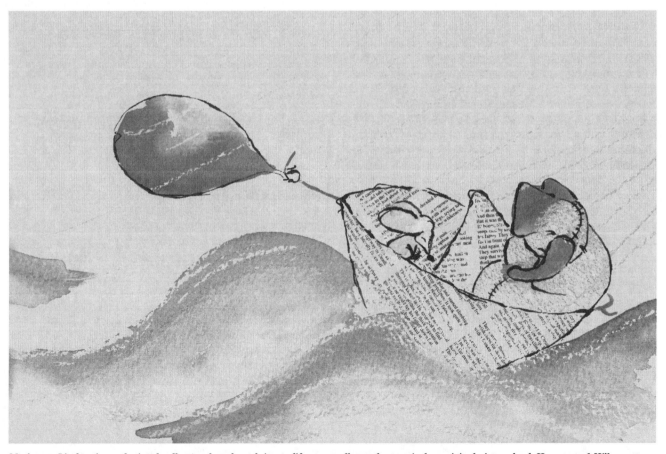

Maria van Lieshout's gently tinted collage-and-wash art bring to life an equally gentle story in her original picture book **Hopper and Wilson.** (Copyright © 2011 by Maria van Lieshout. Reproduced by permission of Philomel Books, a division of Penguin Group (USA), Inc.)

ILLUSTRATOR

Hazel Hutchins, *The List,* Annick Press (Toronto, Ontario, Canada), 2007.

Maryann Cusimano Love, *Sleep, Baby, Sleep,* Philomel Books (New York, NY), 2009.

Sidelights

Now based in San Francisco, artist and author Maria van Lieshout is inspired by the spare, graphic work of well-known illustrators such as Dick Bruna that is popular in the Netherlands, where she grew up. Van Lieshout shares that expressive and colorful art with children in the small-format picture book *Bloom! A Little Book about Finding Love* and its inspiring sequels as well as in toddler-friendly volumes such as *Hopper and Wilson* as well as the companion books *Backseat A-B-See* and *Flight 123,* which use public signage to teach both letters and numbers to tagalong globetrotters.

In *Bloom!* a pink pig with an intense passion for flowers discovers that the best kind of love is the love that is returned, while the blue seal in *Splash! A Little Book about Bouncing Back* learns that caring for others is the best way to raise his own low spirits. A little yellow chick named Peep stars in *Peep! A Little Book about Taking a Leap,* and in van Lieshout's engaging story and sparely tinted art it finally summons up the courage to take a risky leap, with the encouragement of Mother Hen and its siblings. Another dose of encouragement is found in *Tumble! A Little Book about Having It All,* as a polar bear cub learns about sharing after he finds a wonderful red scarf while playing in the snow with two friends.

Reviewing *Bloom!* in *Publishers Weekly,* a contributor predicted that, "as light and sweet as cotton candy," van Lieshout's peppermint-pink-and-blue-tinged story "will win over kids and grownups alike." Tinted in a blue reflecting its hero's own mood, *Splash!* features a "deceptively simple" text that successfully "conveys feelings from a child's point of view," according to *School Library Journal* critic Marian Creamer. Commenting on the "expressive trademark style" of the illustrations in *Tumble!,* Anne Beier added in another *School Library Journal* review that van Lieshout's subtle morality tale makes a "perfect choice for a wintertime storyhour or one-on-one sharing," while Courtney Jones predicted in *Booklist* that readers of *Peep!* "will be heartened by Peep's struggle when facing their own fears." Also praising *Peep* in *School Library Journal,* Kathleen Kelly MacMillan described van Lieshout's "deceptively simple-looking" volume as "a virtual master class in . . . effective picture-book creation."

In her watercolor, ink, and collage art for *Hopper and Wilson* van Lieshout introduces two rumpled stuffed-animal friends: Hopper the blue elephant and Wilson the big-eared yellow mouse. In search of adventure, Hopper and Wilson board their newspaper boat and em-

bark on a voyage to the other side of the world, where Hopper hopes to find a ladder to the moon while Wilson fantasizes about a sea of lemonade. Along their journey, storms threaten to separate them, but the strong bonds of loyal friendship ultimately keep them safe. "Quiet, concise language and poignant watercolor illustrations pull readers into this far-out fable," asserted a *Kirkus Reviews* writer, and in *Publishers Weekly* a contributor remarked on the mix of "adventure, emotion, and imagery" that adds "effervescent warmth" to van Lieshout's illustrated tale.

Biographical and Critical Sources

PERIODICALS

Booklist, May 1, 2009, Courtney Jones, review of *Peep! A Little Book about Taking a Leap,* p. 89.

Kirkus Reviews, December 1, 2007, review of *Bloom! A Little Book about Finding Love;* September 15, 2008, review of *Splash! A Little Book about Bouncing Back;* January 1, 2009, review of *Peep!;* September 15, 2009, review of *Sleep, Baby, Sleep;* September 1, 2010, review of *Tumble! A Little Book about Having It All;* May 15, 2011, review of *Hopper and Wilson.*

New York Times Book Review, April 12, 2009, Julie Just, review of *Peep!,* p. 15.

Publishers Weekly, December 10, 2007, review of *Bloom!,* p. 54; October 6, 2008, review of *Splash! A Little Book about Bouncing Back,* p. 53; May 2, 2011, review of *Hopper and Wilson,* p. 53.

School Library Journal, April, 2008, Julie Roach, review of *Bloom!,* p. 152; November, 2008, Marian Creamer, review of *Splash!,* p. 102; March, 2009, Kathleen Kelly MacMillan, review of *Peep!,* p. 130; December, 2009, Laura Butler, review of *Sleep, Baby, Sleep,* p. 79; November, 2010, Anne Beier, review of *Tumble!,* p. 86; July, 2011, Susan Weitz, review of *Hopper and Wilson,* p. 80.

ONLINE

Maria van Lieshout Home Page, http://www.maria vanlieshout.com (August 1, 2012).

*   *   *

VILLNAVE, Erica Pelton

Personal

Children: one son. *Education:* Maryland Institute College of Art, degree (illustration). *Hobbies and other interests:* Sewing, gardening, road trips, being outdoors.

Addresses

Home—Upstate NY. *Agent*—Lori Nowicki, Painted-Words, Inc., 310 W. 97th St., No. 24, New York, NY 10025; lori@painted-words.com. *E-mail*—epelton@ nycap.rr.com.

Career

Children's author and illustrator.

Writings

SELF-ILLUSTRATED

Sophie's Lovely Locks, Marshall Cavendish Children (Tarrytown, NY), 2011.

ILLUSTRATOR

Laura Gates Galvin, editor, *Oh Where, Oh Where Has My Little Dog Gone?,* Soundprints (Norwalk, CT), 2008.
Ellen Flanagan Burns, *Nobody's Perfect: A Story for Children about Perfectionism,* Magination Press (Washington, DC), 2009.

Sidelights

In her illustrations for young children, Erica Pelton Villnave hopes to inspire the same love of reading and story that she gained during her own childhood. Based in Upstate New York, Villnave has created artwork for stories by several different writers in addition to creating her own original picture book, *Sophie's Lovely*

Erica • Pelton Villnave introduces a spunky young heroine in her self-illustrated picture book Sophie's Long Locks. (Copyright © 2011 by Erica Pelton Villnave. Reproduced by permission of Marshall Cavendish Children.)

Locks. Reviewing Ellen Flanagan Burns' *Nobody's Perfect: A Story for Children about Perfectionism, School Library Journal* critic Laura Butler noted of Villnave's spot and full-page illustrations that her "bright cartoon watercolors will appeal to younger readers."

In *Sophie's Lovely Locks* a little girl has wonderful hair that sometimes gets out of control. Long, blonde, and curly, Sophie's hair is sometimes braided in pigtails and sometimes bound in a pony tale, and sometimes blowing in the breeze. Unfortunately, there is a flip side to having beautiful curly hair: tangles, snarls, and painful bouts of brushing. Sophie eventually decides to take a break from her high-maintenance hairdo by cutting her hair shorter, and her choice is given added meaning when she learns that the beautiful locks can enrich the life of another little girl.

In a *Kirkus Reviews* appraisal of *Sophie's Lovely Locks,* a critic praised the young heroine's "enthusiastic voice" as well as her "bubbly" personality, adding that Sophie's "relationship with her beloved hair is realistically portrayed" in Villnave's rhyming text. Commenting on the artwork in *Sophie's Lovely Locks,* Julie R. Ranelli wrote in *School Library Journal* that the author/illustrator's colorful "watercolor illustrations show [the hair's] . . . movement and her delight in it."

Biographical and Critical Sources

PERIODICALS

Kirkus Reviews, February 15, 2011, review of *Sophie's Lovely Locks.*
School Library Journal, February, 2009, Laura Butler, review of *Nobody's Perfect: A Story for Children about Perfectionism,* p. 73; March, 2011, Julie R. Ranelli, review of *Sophie's Lovely Locks,* p. 138.

ONLINE

Erica Pelton Villnave Home Page, http://www.ericapelton. com (August 1, 2012).
Erica Pelton Villnave Web log, http://peltonvillnave. blogspot.com (August 1, 2012).

*   *   *

WARNER, Sally 1946-

Personal

Born 1946, in New York, NY; daughter of Stuart and Mary Jane Warner; married Reynold Blight, 1968 (divorced, 1978); married Christopher Davis (a writer), 1999; children: (first marriage) Alex, Andrew; (second marriage) four stepdaughters. *Education:* Scripps College, B.A., 1968; Otis Art Institute, B.F.A. and M.F.A. (fine arts), 1971. *Hobbies and other interests:* Gardening, writing to and spending time with friends, reading, travel.

Addresses

Home—Altadena, CA. *Agent*—Ginger Knowlton, Curtis Brown Ltd., 10 Astor Place, New York, NY 10003. *E-mail*—sallywarner@earthlink.net.

Career

Author and artist. Pasadena City College, Pasadena, CA, teacher of art education for ten years. Resident artist at Ragdale Foundation, Villa Montalvo, Virginia Center for the Creative Arts, and Millay Colony. Presenter and workshop teacher at writer's conferences. *Exhibitions:* Work exhibited in solo exhibitions at Adirondack Lakes Center for the Arts; Utah State University, Logan; Ventura College; Alma College, MI; and Carnegie Art Museum, Ventura, CA. Included in group exhibitions at colleges and universities, including Quincy University, IL; Sage College, NY; and Loyola Marymount University, CA. Work included in permanent collection at Bryn Mawr College, Bryn Mawr, PA.

Member

Authors Guild, PEN, Society of Children's Book Writers and Illustrators.

Awards, Honors

Gold Crown Award in Visual Arts, 1996, Pasadena Arts Council.

Writings

FOR CHILDREN

(Self-illustrated) *Dog Years,* Knopf (New York, NY), 1995.
Some Friend (sequel to *Dog Years*), Knopf (New York, NY), 1996.
Ellie and the Bunheads, Knopf (New York, NY), 1997.
Sort of Forever, Knopf (New York, NY), 1998.
Totally Confidential, HarperCollins (New York, NY), 2000.
Bad Girl Blues (sequel to *Totally Confidential*), HarperCollins (New York, NY), 2001.
Finding Hattie, HarperCollins (New York, NY), 2001.
(Self-illustrated) *How to Be a Real Person (in Just One Day),* Knopf (New York, NY), 2001.
Sister Split, American Girl (Middleton, WI), 2001.
This Isn't about the Money, Viking (New York, NY), 2002.
A Long Time Ago Today, Viking (New York, NY), 2003.
(Self-illustrated) *Twilight Child,* Viking (New York, NY), 2006.
(Self-illustrated) *It's Only Temporary,* Viking (New York, NY), 2008.

Author's works have been translated into Danish, Dutch, French, Italian, Japanese, and Norwegian.

"LILY" SERIES; FOR CHILDREN

Sweet and Sour Lily, illustrated by Jacqueline Rogers, Knopf (New York, NY), 1998.
Private Lily, illustrated by Jacqueline Rogers, Knopf (New York, NY), 1998.
Accidental Lily, illustrated by Jacqueline Rogers, Knopf (New York, NY), 1999.
Leftover Lily, illustrated by Jacqueline Rogers, Knopf (New York, NY), 1999.

"EMMA" SERIES; FOR CHILDREN

Only Emma, illustrated by Jamie Harper, Viking (New York, NY), 2005.
Not-So-Weird Emma, illustrated by Jamie Harper, Viking (New York, NY), 2005.
Super Emma, illustrated by Jamie Harper, Viking (New York, NY), 2006.
Best Friend Emma, illustrated by Jamie Harper, Viking Children's Books (New York, NY), 2007.
Excellent Emma, illustrated by Jamie Harper, Viking (New York, NY), 2009.
Happily Ever Emma, illustrated by Jamie Harper, Viking (New York, NY), 2010.

"ELLRAY JAKES" SERIES; FOR CHILDREN

EllRay Jakes Is Not a Chicken, illustrated by Jamie Harper, Viking (New York, NY), 2011.
EllRay Jakes Is Not a Rock Star, illustrated by Jamie Harper, Viking (New York, NY), 2011.
Ellray Jakes Walks the Plank, illustrated by Jamie Harper, Viking (New York, NY), 2012.
Ellray Jakes the Dragon Slayer!, illustrated by Jamie Harper, Viking (New York, NY), 2012.

OTHER

(Self-illustrated) *Encouraging the Artist in Your Child (Even If You Can't Draw),* photographs by Claire Henze, St. Martin's Press (New York, NY), 1989.
(Self-illustrated) *Encouraging the Artist in Yourself: Even If It's Been a Long, Long Time,* photographs by Claire Henze, St. Martin's Press (New York, NY), 1991.
Making Room for Making Art: A Thoughtful and Practical Guide to Bringing the Pleasure of Artistic Expression Back into Your Life, Chicago Review Press (Chicago, IL), 1994.

Contributor of text and art to *Smart about the First Ladies,* Grosset & Dunlap (New York, NY), 2005.

Adaptations

A Long Time Ago Today was adapted for audiobook, read by Julie Dretzin, Recorded Books, 2003.

Sidelights

Since the mid-1990s, Sally Warner has published a steady list of middle-grade novels that most often depict contemporary characters in a host of realistic situations. In *Sister Split* Warner describes two sisters as they each cope with their parents' divorce in different ways, while *It's Only Temporary* finds a preteen turning to art as a way to deal with the move to a new school. In addition to her middle-grade novels, Warner has also produced the "Lily." "Emma," and "EllRay Jakes" chapter-book series, which are geared to younger children, as well as producing several books on creativity for adults. Praising *It's Only Temporary* in *School Library Journal,* Amanda Raklovitz described Warner's tale as a "solid" story that interweaves "themes of creative expression, friendship, and self-discovery."

Warner first made her name as a novelist for children with *Dog Years* and its sequel, *Some Friend.* In these works readers get to know sixth-grader Case, who has major challenges to contend with: his father is in prison for armed robbery, he lives with his mother and little sister in a tiny apartment with no privacy, and he has made only one friend, Ned, at his new school. Things

Cover of Sally Warner's middle-grade novel **It's Only Temporary,** *featuring artwork by the author.* (Jacket illustration copyright © Sally Warner, 2008. Reproduced by permission of Viking Children's Books, a division of Penguin Young Readers Group, a member of Penguin Group (USA) Inc.)

take a turn for the better when Case's English class starts a newspaper and he contributes a cartoon about a dog named Spotty. In the sequel, Case tries to help Ned, who has run away from the foster home in which he was placed after his grandmother/guardian became hospitalized.

Discussing *Dog Years* in the *Bulletin of the Center for Children's Books,* Susan Dove Lempke praised the author's "light touch," "vivid characters," and "remarkable economy of words," while *Booklist* contributor Mary Harris Veeder also praised Warner's willingness to tackle the consequences of lying and the tension among school cliques. As she does in *Dog Years,* in *Some Friend* the author balances the "hard-hitting, realistic edge" with "witty, lighthearted moments," according to a *Publishers Weekly* critic.

Warner reprises Lily, Case's little sister from *Dog Years* and *Some Friend,* for a four-volume chapter-book series. Lily has her own take on many of the same problems as her brother. In *Sweet and Sour Lily* she tries to make friends at a new school, while in *Private Lily,* she attempts to create a private space for herself within her family's crowded apartment. *Accidental Lily* focuses on Lily's bed-wetting problem and *Leftover Lily* depicts what happens when she fights with her two best friends. In *Booklist* Lauren Peterson called *Sweet and Sour Lily* a "charming chapter book" and Hazel Rochman described *Private Lily* as a "tender, very funny" story.

In her "Emma" readers, which are illustrated by Jamie Harper and include *Only Emma, Not-So-Weird Emma, Super Emma, Best Friend Emma, Excellent Emma,* and *Happily Ever Emma,* Warner follows the everyday adventures of another elementary schooler. Readers meet eight-year-old Emma McGraw in *Only Emma,* and she is not happy. In addition to moving to a new apartment because of her mother's loss of a job, Emma has to deal with an annoying young house guest and the moodiness of best friend Cynthia. Fortunately, she rises above the drama and finds the positive in a chapter book that will appeal to "fans of the Amber Brown and Judy Moody books," according to *Booklist* critic Jennifer Locke.

In *Super Emma* Emma helps classmate EllRay Jakes deal with an older bully, while a competition with archnemesis Cynthia for the friendship of a new girl in school takes center stage in *Best Friend Emma.* Hopeful of impressing her now-distant dad, the third grader decides to go for the gold at her school's upcoming winter games in *Excellent Emma,* while Emma's divorced mom has a surprise in store in *Happily Ever Emma.*

"Harper's whimsical drawings add humor and warmth" to Emma's realistic narrative in *Best Friend Emma,* according to *School Library Journal* contributor Debbie Whitbeck, and in *Super Emma* readers can share the adventures of what a *Kirkus Reviews* writer described as a "plucky young heroine struggling with . . . the social issues that many children face." The author "is a

Warner's elementary-grade story in **Best Friend Emma** *is brought to life in illustrations by Jamie Harper.* (Puffin Books, 2007. Illustration copyright © 2007 by Jamie Harper. Reproduced by permission of Viking Children's Books, a division of Penguin Young Readers Group, a member of Penguin Group (USA) Inc.)

dead-on observer of playground politics," maintained Lucinda Whitehurst in her review of *Excellent Emma* for *School Library Journal*. "Warner realistically depicts a child's confusing feelings" when dealing with dating parents, noted *Booklist* reviewer Abby Nolan in appraising *Happily Ever Emma*, and Terry Ann Lawler cited the mix of "fetching" illustrations and an "appealing" story in her *School Library Journal* review of the sixth installment in Warner's "Emma" series.

Emma's short-of-stature classmate EllRay steals the limelight in his own chapter-book series, which includes *EllRay Jakes Is Not a Chicken!*, *EllRay Jakes Is Not a Rock Star!*, and *Ellray Jakes Walks the Plank!*, all which feature artwork by Harper. When readers meet the upbeat eight year old in *EllRay Jakes Is Not a Chicken!* he hopes to avoid a run-in with school bully Jared Matthews long enough to take advantage of his dad's offer of a family trip to Disneyland. The innocent appropriation of someone else's valuable rock collection causes problems for EllRay in *EllRay Jakes Is a Rock Star!*, and in *EllRay Jakes Walks the Plank* the lad must come up with a Zippy-the-goldfish substitute after his sister overfeeds the class pet while it is in his care.

Praising *EllRay Jakes Is Not a Chicken!* in *Publishers Weekly*, a reviewer noted that "Warner's clever plotting brings an unexpected . . . ending" to her "lively series launch." "Dialogue, setting and plot" in the second "EllRay Jakes" chapter book "are accessible and realistic," in the opinion of a *Kirkus Reviews* writer, while another contributor to the same periodical praised EllRay as "a likeable everykid with a sense of humor." "Harper's illustrations bring even more life to the already spunky characters," asserted *School Library Journal* critic Kari Allen, and Allen's colleague Sarah Polace suggested that the humor in *EllRay Jakes Is a Rock Star!* makes the story a good choice "for reluctant readers."

Warner's middle-grade novel *Ellie and the Bunheads* tells the story of almost-thirteen-year-old Ellie, a dance student who is pressured by her parents to pursue a ballet career. The story was inspired by the author's son Andrew, whose own interest in dance eventually led him to a career as a professional dancer and choreographer. While *Booklist* reviewer Lauren Peterson found the book's ending "anticlimactic and unconvincing," she judged Warner's depiction of "preteen angst" to be "authentic." A *Publishers Weekly* reviewer wrote of *Ellie and the Bunheads* that "dialogue . . . gives this narrative its fleet pace," while in *Kirkus Reviews* a critic applauded the work, writing that "Ellie's experiences and observations ring true, and the ways she solves her problems make for an admirable character."

Warner introduces a pair of memorable characters—Cady and Nana—in *Sort of Forever*, which focuses on the girls' relationship as Nana suffers from a fatal illness. Calling the work a "piercing novel," a *Publishers Weekly* critic commented that "Warner is honest and convincing, writing without sentimentality." In the *Bulletin of the Center for Children's Books*, Deborah Stevenson described *Sort of Forever* as "sometimes talky and awkward," but especially good at portraying the effect of Nana's illness on those around her, and *Booklist* critic Chris Sherman asserted that Warner "skillfully adds flashes of humor" to balance her "heartbreaking but satisfying story." *Sort of Forever* has continued to find readers through the Scholastic Book Club, where it remains a popular selection.

Totally Confidential and sequel *Bad Girl Blues* focus on middle-schooler Quinney. In the first novel Quinney decides that her summer job is to become a professional listener . . . that is, until she finds out that she needs some advice herself. In the latter book she is forced to deal with a friend who has taken a different path than she has chosen. Writing about *Totally Confidential* in *Publishers Weekly*, a reviewer found the maturity of the main character to be implausible but praised Warner for a "tight and well-told story, full of empathy for kids' anxieties and concerns." *Booklist* contributor Shelle Rosenfeld also enjoyed *Totally Confidential*, calling it a "lively, engaging novel [that] sympathetically portrays some familiar themes."

Warner's engaging young heroine returns in Happily Ever Emma, *a story featuring artwork by Jamie Harper.* (Illustration copyright © 2010 by Jamie Harper. Reproduced by permission of Viking Children's Books, a division of Penguin Young Readers Group, a member of Penguin Group (USA) Inc.)

Other novels by Warner include *How to Be a Real Person (in Just One Day),* about a girl whose mother is mentally ill; *Sister Split,* about the effects of their parents' divorce on two sisters; and *Bad Girl Blues.* In *How to Be a Real Person (in Just One Day)* sixth-grader Kara has been hiding the truth from others: her father is gone and her mother is slipping into mental illness. By the end of this particular day, Kara realizes that she cannot hold her life together any longer and must seek help. Lauding Warner in *Booklist* for her accurate depiction of mental illness, Kelly Milner called *How to Be a Real Person (in Just One Day)* a "brave, troubling novel" that features a "riveting, well-crafted story." Terrie Dorio, writing in *School Library Journal,* noted that the author's "descriptions of living with a manic-depressive hit the mark," and a *Publishers Weekly* contributor concluded that "Warner has shaped a haunting, ultimately hopeful story, whose heroine is indisputably real."

Another story that introduces a memorable heroine, *A Long Time Ago Today* focuses on twelve-year-old Dilly Howell as she travels with her father from their home in California to a family cottage in upper New York State. Dilly is angry about being motherless and the cottage reminds her of the mom who died six years before. A family friend now shows the preteen a letter written by her late mother that helps Dilly understand who she is and leave her anger behind as she moves into adolescence. Writing that *A Long Time Ago Today* is "peopled with complex, sympathetic characters," *Booklist* critic Carolyn Phelan described the novel as "both entertaining and involving." Barbara Auerbach, reviewing the same book in *School Library Journal,* praised Warner's middle-grade novel as "a painful but realistic treatment of grief and healing."

Warner turns to historical fiction in *Finding Hattie,* a middle-grade novel that is set in the early 1880s. After the deaths of her great-aunt and brother, Hattie is taken in by an aunt who lives in New York City and is sent with her cousin to a boarding school. There Hattie must choose between friendship with the popular group or with a lonely girl who, like Hattie, is of a different background. Because Warner modeled Hattie after her own great-grandmother and even used part of the relative's journal entries in the text, it is not surprising that reviewers remarked on the author's "scrupulous attention to period detail," to quote a *Horn Book* critic. Kathryn Kosiorek called it a "well-written, carefully researched novel" in her *School Library Journal* review, and a *Publishers Weekly* contributor wrote that Warner "seamlessly details Hattie's domestic and academic life" in *Finding Hattie* and keeps Hattie's "observations historically accurate."

Warner weaves an element of fantasy into her middle-grade novel *Twilight Child,* which takes place in the late 1790s. Young Eleni is able to speak to the fairies that live on her family's rural farm in Finland, but her talent is lost on her hard-working father when he becomes enmeshed in the region's volatile politics. After a series of tragedies, the girl finds herself on a remote Scottish island and gains work in a laundry. Ultimately, she makes her way to Nova Scotia, where life holds more promise. In all her travels, Eleni gains a unique sense of her sometimes austere surroundings through her communications with local sprites in a story that *School Library Journal* contributor Caitlin Augusta described as "intriguing" and featuring both a "likable heroine" and "vivid settings." In *Booklist* Anne O'Malley also praised Eleni's courage and resourcefulness, adding that in *Twilight Child* Warner "deftly interweaves fantastical elements with the "rich cultural" backdrop of the late eighteenth century.

"I started writing only after earlier careers as a teacher and exhibiting artist," Warner told *SATA*, "but I believe that with writing, I have truly found my most important calling. I especially relish the direct contact with young readers that today's technology makes possible."

Biographical and Critical Sources

BOOKS

Beckett, Sister Wendy, *The Mystical Now: Art and the Sacred,* Universe (New York, NY), 1993.

Warner passes the torch from Emma to one of the girl's young classmates in Ellray Jakes Is a Rock Star!, *a chapter book featuring Jamie Harper's engaging line art.* (Illustration copyright © 2011 by Jamie Harper. Reproduced by permission of Viking Children's Books, a division of Penguin Young Readers Group, a member of Penguin Group (USA), Inc.)

Sally Warner: Contemplative Landscape (monograph), Grady Harp, 1986.

PERIODICALS

Booklist, April 15, 1995, Mary Harris Veeder, review of *Dog Years,* p. 1501; June 1, 1996, Susan Dove Lempke, review of *Some Friend,* p. 1724; June 1, 1997, Lauren Peterson, review of *Ellie and the Bunheads,* p. 1707; June 1, 1998, Chris Sherman, review of *Sort of Forever,* p. 1769; August, 1998, Lauren Peterson, review of *Sweet and Sour Lily,* p. 2009; September 15, 1998, Hazel Rochman, review of *Private Lily,* p. 232; March 15, 1999, Stephanie Zvirin, review of *Accidental Lily,* p. 1330; July, 1999, Lauren Peterson, review of *Leftover Lily,* p. 1947; June 1, 2000, review of *Totally Confidential,* p. 1898; February 1, 2001, GraceAnne A. DeCandido, review of *Finding Hattie,* p. 1054; February 15, 2001, Kelly Milner, review of *How to Be a Real Person (in Just One Day),* p. 1138; July, 2001, Kay Weisman, review of *Bad Girl Blues,* p. 2007; January 1, 2002, Julie Cummins, review of *Sister Split,* p. 860; November 1, 2003, Carolyn Phelan, review of *A Long Time Ago Today,* p. 497; March 1, 2005, Jennifer Locke, review of *Only Emma,* p. 1199; May 15, 2006, Anne O'Malley, review of *Twilight Child,* p. 59; June 1, 2008, Jennifer Hubert, review of *It's Only Temporary,* p. 76; December 15, 2010, Abby Nolan, review of *Happily Ever Emma,* p. 54; June 1, 2011, Erin Anderson, review of *EllRay Jakes Is Not a Chicken!,* p. 85.

Book Report, November-December, 1997, Allison Trent Bernstein, review of *Ellie and the Bunheads,* p. 43.

Bulletin of the Center for Children's Books, May 9, 1995, Susan Dove Lempke, review of *Dog Years,* pp. 325-326; May, 1998, Deborah Stevenson, review of *Sort of Forever,* pp. 342-343; September, 1998, Deborah Stevenson, review of *Private Lily,* p. 38; September, 2006, April Spisak, review of *Twilight Child,* p. 41; July-August, 2011, Hope Morrison, review of *EllRay Jakes Is Not a Chicken!,* p. 545.

Horn Book, May, 2001, review of *Finding Hattie,* p. 338.

Kirkus Reviews, April 15, 1997, review of *Ellie and the Bunheads,* pp. 651-652; September 1, 2002, review of *This Isn't about the Money,* p. 1322; August 1, 2005, review of *Not-so-Weird Emma,* p. 860; August 1, 2006, review of *Super Emma,* p. 797; May 1, 2008, review of *It's Only Temporary;* April 15, 2011, review of *EllRay Jakes Not a Chicken!;* August 15, 2011, review of *Ellray Jakes Is a Rock Star!*

Kliatt, May, 2004, Jacqueline Edwards, review of *A Long Time Ago Today,* p. 53.

Publishers Weekly, March 6, 1995, review of *Dog Years,* p. 70; June 10, 1996, review of *Some Friend,* p. 100; April 14, 1997, review of *Ellie and the Bunheads,* p. 76; March 30, 1998, review of *Sort of Forever,* p. 83; June 7, 1999, review of *Leftover Lily,* p. 85; June 26, 2000, review of *Totally Confidential,* p. 75; January 1, 2001, review of *How to Be a Real Person (in Just One Day),* p. 93; January 1, 2001, review of *Finding Hattie,* p. 93; March 14, 2011, review of *EllRay Jakes Is Not a Chicken!,* p. 73.

School Library Journal, April, 1995, Connie Tyrrell Burns, review of *Dog Years,* p. 138; May, 1996, Carrie A. Guarria, review of *Some Friend,* p. 118; September, 1997, Amy Kellman, review of *Ellie and the Bunheads,* pp. 226-227; July, 1998, Carrie A. Guarria, review of *Sort of Forever,* p. 100; October, 1998, Mary M. Hopf, review of *Private Lily,* p. 117, and Susan Helper, review of *Sweet and Sour Lily,* pp. 117-118; July, 1999, Faith Brautigam, review of *Accidental Lily,* pp. 82-83; July, 1999, Susan Helper, review of *Leftover Lily,* p. 83; June, 2000, Victoria Kidd, review of *Totally Confidential,* p. 155; February, 2001, Kathryn Kosiorek, review of *Finding Hattie,* p. 122; February, 2001, Terrie Dorio, review of *How to Be a Real Person (in Just One Day),* p. 123; July, 2001, Laura Glaser, review of *Bad Girl Blues,* p. 116; September, 2002, Lee Bock, review of *This Isn't Really about the Money,* p. 236; December, 2003, Barbara Auerbach, review of *A Long Time Ago Today,* p. 161; April, 2005, Linda Zeilstra Sawyer, review of *Only Emma,* p. 114; November, 2005, Carol L. MacKay, review of *Not-so-Weird Emma,* p. 110; July, 2006, Caitlin Augusta, review of *Twilight Child,* p. 114; October, 2006, Debbie Lewis O'Donnell, review of *Super Emma,* p. 129; July, 2007, Debbie Whitbeck, review of *Best Friend Emma,* p. 87; August, 2008, Amanda Raklovits, review of *It's Only Temporary,* p. 137; March, 2009, Lucinda Snyder Whitehurst, review of *Excellent Emma,* p. 130; January, 2011, Terry Ann Lawler, review of *Happily Ever Emma,* p. 86; August, 2011, Kari Allen, review of *EllRay Jakes Is Not a Chicken!,* p. 87; September, 2011, Sarah Polace, review of *EllRay Jakes Is a Rock Star!,* p. 132.

ONLINE

Sally Warner Home Page, http://www.sallywarner.com (August 1, 2012).

*   *   *

WILLIAMS, Sophy 1965-

Personal

Born October 23, 1965, in Surrey, England; married Mark Robertson (an illustrator), June, 1990; children: Oscar, Leo. *Education:* Central School of Art (London, England), B.A. (graphic design; with honors); attended Kingston Polytechnic.

Addresses

Home—Bradford-on-Avon, Wiltshire, England. *E-mail*—sophy.williams@o2.co.uk.

Career

Illustrator and author.

Awards, Honors

Young Illustrators Award, *Readers Digest,* 1988; Mother Goose Award, 1990, for *When Grandma Came.*

Writings

SELF-ILLUSTRATED

Nana's Garden, Hutchinson (London, England), 1993, Viking (New York, NY), 1994.

The First Christmas: A Changing-Picture Story, Templar Books (Somerville, MA), 2010.

ILLUSTRATOR

Jill Paton-Walsh, *When Grandma Came,* Viking (New York, NY), 1992.

Michael Rosen, *Moving,* Viking (New York, NY), 1993.

Robert Westall, *The Witness,* Dutton (New York, NY), 1994.

Peter Elbling, *Aria,* Viking (New York, NY), 1994.

Belinda Hollyer, *Stories from the Classical Ballet,* Viking (New York, NY), 1995.

Richard Edwards, *You're Safe Now, Waterdog,* Viking (New York, NY), 1996.

Paul and Emma Rogers, *Cat's Kittens,* Viking (New York, NY), 1996.

Aneve Turnball, *The Sleeping Beauty,* MacDonald (London, England), 1997.

Robert Nye, *Lord Fox and Other Spine-Chilling Tales,* Orion (London, England), 1997.

Geraldine McCaughrean, *The Orchard Book of Starry Tales,* Orchard (London, England), 1998, published as *Starry Tales,* Margaret K. McElderry Books (New York, NY), 2001.

Adrian Mitchell, *My Cat Mrs Christmas,* Orion (London, England), 1998.

Fiona Waters, *Cat in the Dark: A Flurry of Feline Verse,* Francis Lincoln (London, England), 1999.

Martin Waddell, *The Orchard Book of Ghostly Stories,* Orchard (London, England), 2000.

Toby Forward, *Once upon an Everyday,* Transworld, 2000.

Wendy McCormick, *The Night You Were Born,* Peachtree (Atlanta, GA), 2000.

Richard Hamilton, *Polly's Picnic,* Bloomsbury Children's Book (New York, NY), 2003.

Dyan Sheldon, *The Last Angel,* Macmillan Children's (London, England), 2003.

Geraldine McCaughrean, *The Oxford Treasury of Fairy Tales,* Oxford University Press (Oxford, England), 2003.

Kate Tym, reteller, *Princess Stories from around the World,* Chrysalis Children's (London, England), 2004.

Caroline Pitcher, *The Winter Dragon,* Frances Lincoln (London, England), 2004.

Philip Pullman, reteller, *Aladdin and the Enchanted Lamp,* Scholastic (London, England), 2004, Arthur A. Levine Books (New York, NY), 2005.

Giles Andreae, *Princess Pearl,* Orchard (London, England), 2005.

Holly Webb, *Lost in the Snow,* Stripes (London, England), 2006.

Julia Hubery, *A Christmas Wish,* Good Books (Intercourse, PA), 2007.

Geraldine McCaughrean, *The Nativity Story,* Lion Children's (Oxford, England), 2007.

Holly Webb, *Alfie All Alone,* Stripes (London, England), 2007.

Holly Webb, *Sam the Stolen Puppy,* Stripes (London, England), 2008.

Holly Webb, *Timmy in Trouble,* Stripes (London, England), 2008.

Holly Webb, *Sky the Unwanted Kitten,* Stripes (London, England), 2008.

Holly Webb, *Max the Missing Puppy,* Stripes (London, England), 2008.

Michael Catchpool, *Grandpa's Boat,* Anderson Press (London, England), 2008.

Holly Webb, *Harry the Homeless Puppy,* Stripes (London, England), 2009.

Holly Webb, *Buttons the Runaway Puppy,* Stripes (London, England), 2009.

Holly Webb, *Ginger the Stray Kitten,* Stripes (London, England), 2009.

Holly Webb, *All Alone in the Night,* Stripes (London, England), 2009.

Bob Hartman, *The Easter Angels,* Lion Children's (Oxford, England), 2009.

Holly Webb, *Ellie the Homesick Puppy,* Stripes (London, England), 2010.

Holly Webb, *Misty the Abandoned Kitten,* Stripes (London, England), 2010.

Holly Webb, *Oscar's Lonely Christmas,* Stripes (London, England), 2010.

Holly Webb, *The Rescued Puppy,* Stripes (London, England), 2011.

Holly Webb, *Lucy the Poorly Puppy,* Stripes (London, England), 2011.

Ruth Martin, *Santa's on His Way,* Templar Books (Somerville, MA), 2011.

Andrea Skevington, reteller, *The Lion Classic Bible,* Lion Children's (Oxford, England), 2011.

Work included in anthology *A Kiss Goodnight,* written by Claire Freedman, Good Books, 2007.

Sidelights

Sophy Williams is an author and illustrator whose artwork has enhanced stories by several other authors of

Sophy Williams' illustrations are featured in a number of picture books, among them Santa's on His Way *written by Ruth Martin.* (Text copyright © 2011 by Ruth Martin. Illustration copyright © 2011 by Sophy Williams. Reproduced by permission of Candlewick Press, Somerville, MA.)

children's picture books, among them Robert Westall, Jill Paton Walsh, Philip Pullman, Holly Webb, and Robert Nye. Praised for her softly colored pastel renderings, Williams has also created the original, self-illustrated *Nana's Garden* and *The First Christmas: A Changing-Picture Story,* the latter which recounts the birth of the baby Jesus in an interactive lift-the-flap format. Praising *The First Christmas* in *Kirkus Reviews,* a contributor cited both its "smoothly retold" story and "soft-focus" images, which are alight with "shimmering light from the special star" of Bethlehem. In *School Library Journal* contributor Mara Alpert dubbed the same work a "lovely presentation of the Nativity story."

Called a "quiet, understated story, beautifully told" by a *Junior Bookshelf* reviewer, *Nana's Garden* quickly made its way across the Atlantic, much to the excitement of picture-book aficionados in the United States. Williams' story focuses on a young boy named Thomas who is left alone in a deserted garden, saddened that his Nana is too elderly to play with him. A newfound if somewhat mysterious friend named Rose, the discovery of a toy bunny, and the exploration of many out-of-the-way places keep Thomas amused within his grandmother's fragrant, much-loved garden. Praising the work for its depiction of a child engaging in imaginative play outside the home, Mary Harris Veeder added in *Booklist* that the story of *Nana's Garden* is "nicely evoked in the pictures."

Born in Surrey, England, in 1965, Williams recalled her childhood as a happy one. Most of her time was spent in Berkshire, but, as she told *SATA,* there were "with periods living in Singapore, the United Arab Emirates, where we had no television, and Hong Kong. I was always reading stories (Joan Aiken being one of my favorite children's authors), and drawing or painting, and when I wasn't training for gymnastic competitions, I used to make scrapbooks and illustrate the (awful) poems that I had written. My bedroom carpet was ruined by glue and paint."

Williams met her husband, fellow children's book author and illustrator Mark Robertson, in 1986, while both were attending Kingston Polytechnic. Her first illustration project, creating the art for Joan Paton Walsh's *When Grandma Came,* was published in 1992. Praising Williams' artistic contribution as this story's "greatest strength," *School Library Journal* contributor Jody McCoy added that Walsh's tale of a young girl and her granddaughter is successfully "captured in rich, warm colors."

Other works illustrated by Williams include Michael Rosen's *Moving,* wherein her "soft, striking pastel drawings capture the mysterious quality . . . of Rosen's evocative poem," according to *Booklist* contributor Julie Corsaro. The artist's "softly colored" renderings for Richard Edwards's *You're Safe Now, Waterdog* "complement the story perfectly," in the opinion of *Booklist* reviewer Shelley Townsend-Hudson, the critic going on

to note the "rich texture" and "tactile quality" of Williams' art. Remarking on her illustrations for Wendy McCormick's *The Night You Were Born,* a *Publishers Weekly* critic wrote that pastel images "glow[ing] with soothing tones" enhances McCormick's sensitive portrayal of a boy awaiting the arrival of a new member of the family, and *School Library Journal* contributor Shirley Wilton asserted that Williams' illustrations for Peter Elbling's *Aria* are "worth a leisurely inspection and lingering appreciation."

One of Williams' most highly regarded illustration projects, Pullman's *Aladdin and the Enchanted Lamp,* prompted Michael Rosen to note in the London *Guardian* that the collaboration results in a "lustrous" retelling of the story of Aladdin that is "full of purple and maroon mystery" and perfect for "family reading." Echoing Rosen's praise, *Booklist* contributor Jennifer Mattson characterized the story's visual element as "a bazaar of burnished colors and dramatic, imagination-tickling scenes," while Lemony Snicket (pen name of author Daniel Handler) declared the illustrations "splendid to behold" in his review of *Aladdin and the Enchanted Lamp* for the *New York Times.*

Another popular picture book, Caroline Pitcher's *The Winter Dragon,* features "realistic pastel illustrations" by Williams that capture the growing confidence of a young lad faced with nighttime terrors, "amplifying his fears as well as his emerging courage," according to a *Kirkus Reviews* writer. Also citing these "richly textured" images, GraceAnne A. DeCandido added in her *Booklist* review that Williams' contributions transport readers "from the quiet of a hushed bedroom to a wild dragon rumpus."

Williams works in chalk pastel and pastel pencil. "I love layering colours (a trick I borrowed from Degas)," she once told *SATA,* "and inventing colour combinations—soft subtle ones and vibrant bright ones. I'm happiest drawing animals, especially groups of animals. I'm sure that spending some of my childhood in Asia has influenced the sort of landscapes that appeal to me—empty deserts for example—but the frosty breath and hazy horizons of the English countryside have provided lots of inspiration."

Biographical and Critical Sources

PERIODICALS

Booklist, November 1, 1992, Stephanie Zvirin, review of *When Grandma Came,* p. 523; December 15, 1993, Julie Corsaro, review of *Moving,* p. 766; June 1, 1994, Mary Harris Veeder, review of *Nana's Garden,* p. 1846; November 15, 1994, Hazel Rochman, review of *Aria,* p. 611; February 15, 1997, Shelley Townsend-Hudson, review of *Cat's Kittens,* p. 1029; July, 1997, Shelley Townsend-Hudson, review of *You're Safe Now, Waterdog,* p. 1821.

Horn Book, November-December, 1994, Ann A. Flowers, review of *The Witness,* p. 715; March-April, 1996, Mary M. Burns, review of *Stories from the Classical Ballet,* p. 225; January 1, 2001, Lauren Peterson, review of *The Night You Were Born,* p. 968; February 15, 2001, Karen Hutt, review of *Starry Tales,* p. 1136; October 15, 2004, GraceAnne A. DeCandido, review of *The Winter Dragon,* p. 411; May 1, 2005, Jennifer Mattson, review of *Aladdin and the Enchanted Lamp,* p. 1582.

Guardian (London, England), November 27, 2004, Michael Rosen, review of *The Scarecrow and His Servant,* p. A&E 33.

Junior Bookshelf, April, 1994, review of *Nana's Garden,* pp. 51-52.

Kirkus Reviews, November 15, 2004, review of *The Winter Dragon,* p. 1092; September 1, 2010, review of *The First Christmas: A Changing Picture Story;* September 1, 2011, review of *Santa's on His Way.*

New York Times Book Review, June 5, 2005, Lemony Snicket, review of *Aladdin and the Enchanted Lamp,* p. A&E 39.

Publishers Weekly, September 19, 1994, review of *The Witness,* p. 27; September 26, 1994, review of *Aria,* p. 69; October 9, 2000, review of *The Night You Were Born,* p. 86; June 16, 2003, review of *Polly's Picnic,* p. 68; April 4, 2005, review of *Aladdin and the Enchanted Lamp,* p. 60; June 30, 2008, review of *Princess Stories from around the World,* p. 184.

School Librarian, autumn, 2011, Nick Hunt, review of *The Lion Classic Bible,* p. 172.

School Library Journal, March, 1993, Jody McCoy, review of *When Grandma Came,* p. 187; March, 1994, Carolyn Noah, review of *Moving,* p. 208; October, 1994, Jane Marino, review of *The Witness,* p. 45; January, 1995, Shirley Wilton, review of *Aria,* pp. 84-85; July, 1997, Susan M. Moore, review of *You're Safe Now, Waterdog,* p. 67; December, 2000, Martha Topol, review of *The Night You Were Born,* p. 114; August, 2003, Mary Elam, review of *Polly's Picnic,* p. 129; January, 2005, Roxanne Burg, review of *The Winter Dragon,* p. 96; September, 2005, Heide Piehler, review of *Aladdin and the Enchanted Lamp,* p. 185; October, 2007, Eva Mitnick, review of *A Christmas Wish,* p. 99; December, 2008, Meg Smith, review of *Princess Stories from around the World,* p. 117; October, 2010, Mara Alpert, review of *The First Christmas,* p. 71; September, 2011, Linda L. Walkins, review of *The Lion Classic Bible,* p. 138; October, 2011, Mara Albert, review of *Santa's on His Way,* p. 96.

ONLINE

Sophy Williams Portfolio Home Page, http://www.sophywilliams.co.uk (August 1, 2012).*